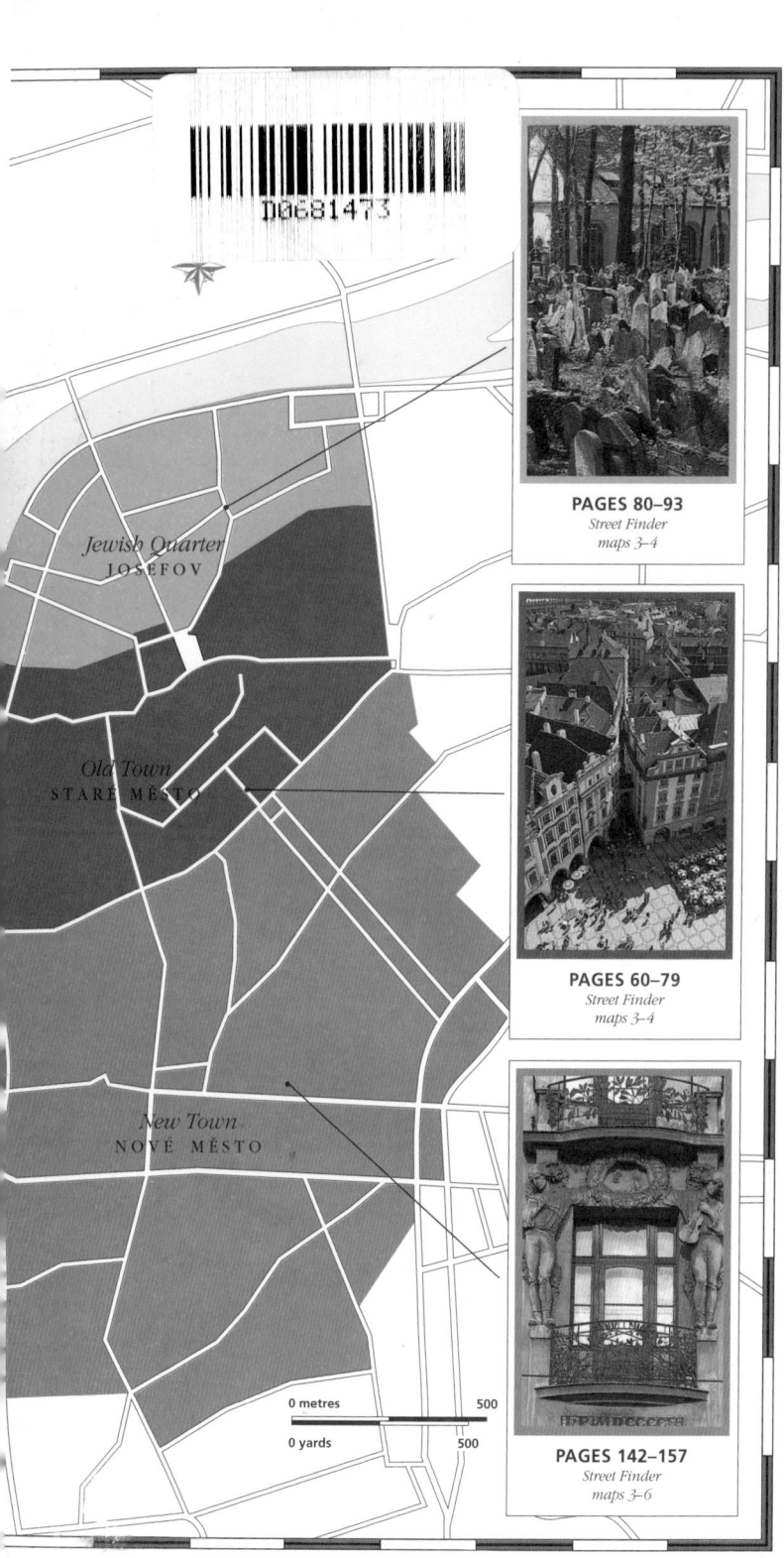
D0681473
Jewish Quarter
JOSEFOV
Old Town
STARÉ MĚSTO
New Town
NOVÉ MĚSTO
0 metres
500
0 yards
500
PAGES 80–93
Street Finder
maps 3–4
PAGES 60–79
Street Finder
maps 3–4
PAGES 142–157
Street Finder
maps 3–6

EYEWITNESS TRAVEL GUIDES

PRAGUE

EYEWITNESS TRAVEL GUIDES

PRAGUE

Main contributor: VLADIMÍR SOUKUP

DK

LONDON, NEW YORK,
MELBOURNE, MUNICH AND DELHI
www.dk.com

PROJECT EDITOR Heather Jones
ART EDITOR Lisa Kosky
EDITORS Ferdie McDonald, Carey Combe
US EDITOR Mary Ann Bruchac Lynch
DESIGNERS Louise Parsons, Nicki Rawson

CONTRIBUTORS
Petr David, Vladimír Dobrovodský, Nicholas Lowry,
Polly Phillimore, Joy Turner-Kaděcková, Craig Turp

PHOTOGRAPHERS
Jiří Doležal, Jiří Kopřiva, Vladimír Kozlík, František Přeučil,
Milan Posselt, Stanislav Tereba, Peter Wilson

ILLUSTRATORS
Gillie Newman, Chris Orr, Otakar Pok, Jaroslav Staněk

This book was produced with the assistance of
Olympia Publishing House, Prague.

Reproduced by Colourscan, Singapore
Printed and bound in China by Toppan Printing Co., (Shenzhen Ltd)

First American Edition, 1994
06 07 08 09 10 9 8 7 6 5 4 3 2

Published in the United States by DK Publishing, Inc.,
375 Hudson Street, New York, New York 10014

Reprinted with revisions 1996, 1997, 2001, 2002, 2003, 2004, 2005, 2006

Copyright © 1994, 2006 Dorling Kindersley Limited, London

ALL RIGHTS RESERVED UNDER INTERNATIONAL AND PAN-AMERICAN COPYRIGHT CONVENTIONS. NO PART OF THIS PUBLICATION MAY BE REPRODUCED, STORED IN A RETRIEVAL SYSTEM, OR TRANSMITTED IN ANY FORM OR BY ANY MEANS, ELECTRONIC, MECHANICAL, PHOTOCOPYING, RECORDING, OR OTHERWISE, WITHOUT THE PRIOR WRITTEN PERMISSION OF THE COPYRIGHT OWNER.

Published in Great Britain by Dorling Kindersley Limited.

ISSN 1542-1554
ISBN-13: 978-0-7566-1548-2
ISBN-10: 0-7566-1548-8

FLOORS ARE REFERRED TO THROUGHOUT IN ACCORDANCE WITH EUROPEAN USAGE; IE THE "FIRST FLOOR" IS THE FLOOR ABOVE GROUND LEVEL.

The information in this Dorling Kindersley Travel Guide is checked annually.
Every effort has been made to ensure that this book is as up-to-date as possible at the time of going to press. Some details, however, such as telephone numbers, opening hours, prices, gallery hanging arrangements and travel information are liable to change. The publishers cannot accept responsibility for any consequences arising from the use of this book, nor for any material on third party websites, and cannot guarantee that any website address in this book will be a suitable source of travel information. We value the views and suggestions of our readers very highly. Please write to: Publisher, DK Eyewitness Travel Guides,
Dorling Kindersley, 80 Strand, London WC2R 0RL, Great Britain.

CONTENTS

HOW TO USE THIS GUIDE **6**

Rudolph II (1576–1612)

INTRODUCING PRAGUE

FOUR GREAT DAYS IN PRAGUE **10**

PUTTING PRAGUE ON THE MAP **12**

THE HISTORY OF PRAGUE **16**

PRAGUE AT A GLANCE **36**

PRAGUE THROUGH THE YEAR **50**

A RIVER VIEW OF PRAGUE **54**

Outdoor café tables

PRAGUE AREA BY AREA

OLD TOWN **60**

JEWISH QUARTER **80**

PRAGUE CASTLE AND HRADČANY **94**

Church of Our Lady before Tťn

LITTLE QUARTER **122**

NEW TOWN **142**

FURTHER AFIELD **158**

DAY TRIPS **168**

FOUR GUIDED WALKS **172**

Wallenstein Palace and Garden in the Little Quarter

TRAVELLERS' NEEDS

WHERE TO STAY **184**

RESTAURANTS, CAFÉS AND PUBS **196**

SHOPPING IN PRAGUE **212**

ENTERTAINMENT IN PRAGUE **218**

SURVIVAL GUIDE

PRACTICAL INFORMATION **226**

GETTING TO PRAGUE **236**

Czech beer bottle cap

GETTING AROUND PRAGUE **240**

STREET FINDER **246**

Fiacre, Old Town Square

GENERAL INDEX **258**

ACKNOWLEDGMENTS **270**

PHRASE BOOK **272**

TRANSPORT MAP *INSIDE BACK COVER*

Baroque façades of houses at the southern end of Old Town Square

HOW TO USE THIS GUIDE

This Eyewitness Travel Guide helps you get the most from your stay in Prague with the minimum of difficulty. The opening section, *Introducing Prague*, locates the city geographically, sets modern Prague in its historical context and describes events through the entire year. *Prague at a Glance* is an overview of the city's main attractions, including a feature on the River Vltava. Section two, *Prague Area by Area*, starts on page 58. This is the main sightseeing section, which covers all the important sights, with photographs, maps and drawings. It also includes day trips from Prague and four guided walks around the city. Carefully researched tips for hotels, restaurants, shops and markets, cafés and bars, enter- tainment and sports are found in *Travellers' Needs*. The last section, the *Survival Guide*, contains useful practical advice on all you need to know, from making a telephone call to using the public transport system.

Planning the day's itinerary in Prague

FINDING YOUR WAY AROUND THE SIGHTSEEING SECTION

Each of the five sightseeing areas in the city is colour-coded for easy reference. Every chapter opens with an introduction to the part of Prague it covers, describing its history and character, followed by a Street-by-Street map illustrating the heart of the area. Finding your way around each chapter is made simple by the numbering system used throughout. The most important sights are covered in detail in two or more full pages.

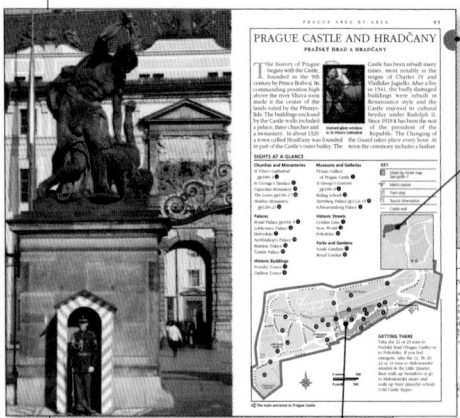

Each area has colour-coded thumb tabs.

A locator map shows where you are in relation to other areas in the city centre.

A suggested route takes in the most interesting and attractive streets in the city area.

Locator map

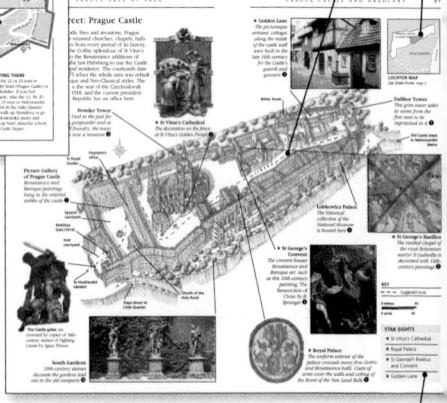

1 Introduction to the area
For easy reference, the sights in each area are numbered and plotted on an area map. To help the visitor, this map also shows metro stations, tram stops, river boat boarding points and parking areas. The area's key sights are listed by category: Churches; Museums and Galleries; Historic Streets and Squares; Palaces; and Parks and Gardens.

2 Street-by-Street map
This gives a bird's eye view of the most important parts of each sightseeing area. The numbering of the sights ties in with the area map and the fuller descriptions on the pages that follow.

The area shaded pink is shown in greater detail on the Street-by-Street map on the following pages.

The list of star sights recommends the places that no visitor should miss.

PRAGUE AREA MAP

The coloured areas shown on this map *(see inside front cover)* are the five main sightseeing areas of Prague – each covered in a full chapter in *Prague Area by Area (pp58–157)*. They are highlighted on other maps throughout the book. In *Prague at a Glance (pp36–57)*, for example, they help locate the top sights. They are also used plot the routes of the river trip *(pp56–7)* and the four guided walks *(p172)*.

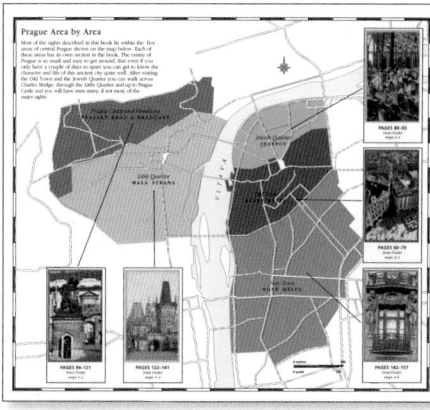

Numbers refer to each sight's position on the area map and its place in the chapter.

Practical information lists all the information you need to visit every sight, including a map reference to the *Street Finder (pp252–7)*.

Façades of important buildings are often shown to help you recognize them quickly.

The visitors' checklist provides all the practical information needed to plan your visit.

3 Detailed information on each sight

All the important sights in Prague are described individually. They are listed in order, following the numbering on the area map. Practical information on opening hours, telephone numbers, admission charges and facilities available is given for each sight. The key to the symbols used can be found on the back flap.

4 Prague's major sights

Historic buildings are dissected to reveal their interiors; and museums and galleries have colour-coded floorplans to help you find important exhibits.

A timeline charts the key events in the history of the building.

Stars indicate the features no visitor should miss.

INTRODUCING PRAGUE

FOUR GREAT DAYS IN PRAGUE 10–11
PUTTING PRAGUE ON THE MAP 12–15
THE HISTORY OF PRAGUE 16–35
PRAGUE AT A GLANCE 36–49
PRAGUE THROUGH THE YEAR 50–53
A RIVER VIEW OF PRAGUE 54–57

FOUR GREAT DAYS IN PRAGUE

Few cities have as much to offer as Prague, so it can be difficult to decide how best to spend your time. The Old Town is a joy in itself, and you could amble around here admiring its old houses for days. Yet, with some planning you can see much more of what makes this historic city special. Here are four distinct days packed with the best that Prague has to offer. Feel free to mix and match: leaving out a museum or sight will not alter the overall effect. The price guides include cost of travel, food and admission fees.

Astronomical clock

NATIONAL TREASURES

- **Hradčany Square guards**
- **Lunch in the Little Quarter**
- **Cross the Charles Bridge**
- **Watch the Town Hall clock**
- **Majestic art or church**

TWO ADULTS allow at least Kč2,400

Morning

Starting at **Hradčany Square**, admire the guards in their elaborate costumes then walk through Prvni Nadrovi to **St Vitus's Cathedral** *(see pp100–3)*, the soul of the Castle. Take a short tour around here before moving on to look at the Baroque art collection in **St George's Convent** *(see pp106–7)*. If you fancy some souvenir shopping, go for the artisans' cottages on **Golden Lane** *(see p99)*. Alternatively, head to **Lobkowicz Palace**, and tour the **National Museum** inside *(see p99)*. Take the easy route along Nerudova to **Little Quarter Square**. Here, enjoy a late lunch and admire the architectural gems of the **Little Quarter** *(see pp124–5)*.

The sumptuous interior of the Spanish synagogue

Afternoon

It is a short walk from here to **Charles Bridge** *(see pp136–9)*, and on to Old Town Square. Time your arrival on the hour to see the **Old Town Square's Astronomical Clock** *(see pp72–4)* in action. The **Old Town Hall Tower** *(see p73)* is well worth a visit for amazing views of Prague Castle and the Little Quarter. Next, choose between seeing the art in the Rococo **Kinský Palace** *(see p70)* or the bare majesty of **St Nicholas' Church** *(see pp70–1)*. The narrow streets and shops of the Tyn courtyard now await exploration. Enjoy dinner at the **Kinski Palace** restaurant, which serves traditional Czech food in elegant surroundings *(see p203)*.

A little respite for visitors at an outdoor café in Old Town Square

LITERARY, ART AND RELIGIOUS LANDMARKS

- **Kafka's home**
- **The Jewish Quarter**
- **Decorative and Medieval Art collections**
- **Quality shopping**

TWO ADULTS allow at least Kč4,560

Morning

Jewish Prague and Franz Kafka are inseparable, so you may want to start the day with a coffee at **Café Grand Praha** *(see p209)* in Old Town Square. Kafka lived above here and the café was once named after his journalist girlfriend, Milena. Refreshed, head along Pařížska into the **Jewish Quarter** *(see pp80–9)*. Stop at the **Maisel Synagogue** *(see p90)*, then cross the road to the historic **Old Jewish Cemetery** *(see pp86–7)*. A good walk around here, as well as a look inside the **Klausen Synagogue** *(see p85)* will set you up for lunch. Try one of the local Jewish restaurants or the non-Jewish **Les Moules** *(see p204)*.

Afternoon

Admire the Gobelin tapestries at the **Museum of Decorative Arts** *(see p84)*. Stroll along to the **Jewish Town Hall** *(see p85)*, and the **Old-New Synagogue** *(see pp88–9)*. The eastern side of the Jewish Quarter is home to two must-see sights: the glorious **Spanish Synagogue** *(see p90)* and the medieval art in **St Agnes of Bohemia Convent** *(see pp92–3)*. After a day of high cultural input, it's time for a little quality shopping on Pařížska – a large thoroughfare in the Jewish Quarter. Eat at **King Solomon,** one of Prague's best Jewish restaurants *(see p204)*.

FAMILY DAY

- **Funicular ride and tower**
- **Mirror Maze**
- **Peacocks and caves**
- **Church of St James**

FAMILY OF 4 allow at least Kč2,900

Morning

Take the funicular railway up **Petřin Hill** *(see p141)*, to see Prague's mini-Eiffel Tower – the **Observation Tower** *(see p140)* which has it has a spiral staircase to the top. The Mirror Maze *(see p140)*, a short walk away, will keep youngsters happy for hours, as will the nearby **Observatory** *(see p140)*. Take the funicular halfway back down the hill for lunch at the **Nebozízek** *(see p205)* with its outdoor patio and panoramic views.

The Mirror Maze, great fun for young and old alike

Wenceslas Square and monument in front of the National Museum

Afternoon

Take a stroll on Střelecký Ostrov, where the swans await the remnants of your lunchtime bread. There's more wildlife to be seen at the **Wallenstein Palace** *(see p126)*, home to peacocks and a bizarre replica of a limestone cave. Walk or take the metro over the river to catch the Old Town Square's **Astronomical Clock** *(see pp72–4)* in action. Eat at one of the cafés on the square. Then on to the **Church of St. James** *(see p65)*. Children will be intrigued by the mummified arm, which has been hanging above the church entrance for 400 years.

HISTORY AND HEROES

- **Wenceslas Square – the rise and fall of Communism**
- **Lunch in splendid style**
- **Wartime history**
- **Shopping for antiques**

TWO ADULTS allow at least Kč3,060

Morning

Start the day with a walk along **Wenceslas Square** *(see pp144–5)* to see where the communist regime was toppled. Walk the length of the square and imagine it lined with people as it was for weeks in 1989. Pay your respects at the **Monument to the Victims of Communism** *(see p145)*, and to Jan Palach, who set himself alight here in 1969 in protest at the Soviet invasion. Just off the Square is the former Gestapo HQ on Politickych věznů (now the national trade office) where thousands of Czechs were imprisoned during WWII. Stop for lunch at the Art Nouveau **Evropa Hotel** *(see p206)* on Wenceslas Square.

Afternoon

Walk to the Baroque **Church of St Cyril and St Methodius** *(see p152)*, where Czech resistance fighters took their own lives in 1942. Bullet holes can still be seen on the wall of the crypt, where a fascinating museum chronicles the events. End the day with a bit of antique browsing. **Military Antiques** in Charvatova *(see p214)*, is a treasure trove of relics from the Nazi and Soviet occupations, as well as military bric-a-brac from all periods.

Putting Prague on the Map

Prague has a population of just over 1 million and covers 500 sq km (200 sq miles) at its outer limits. It is the capital of the recently-formed Czech Republic and head of the region of Bohemia. Prague's geographical position at the centre of Europe makes it a convenient base from which to visit both the Bohemian countryside and many other major cities, such as Nuremberg, Vienna, Bratislava and Budapest.

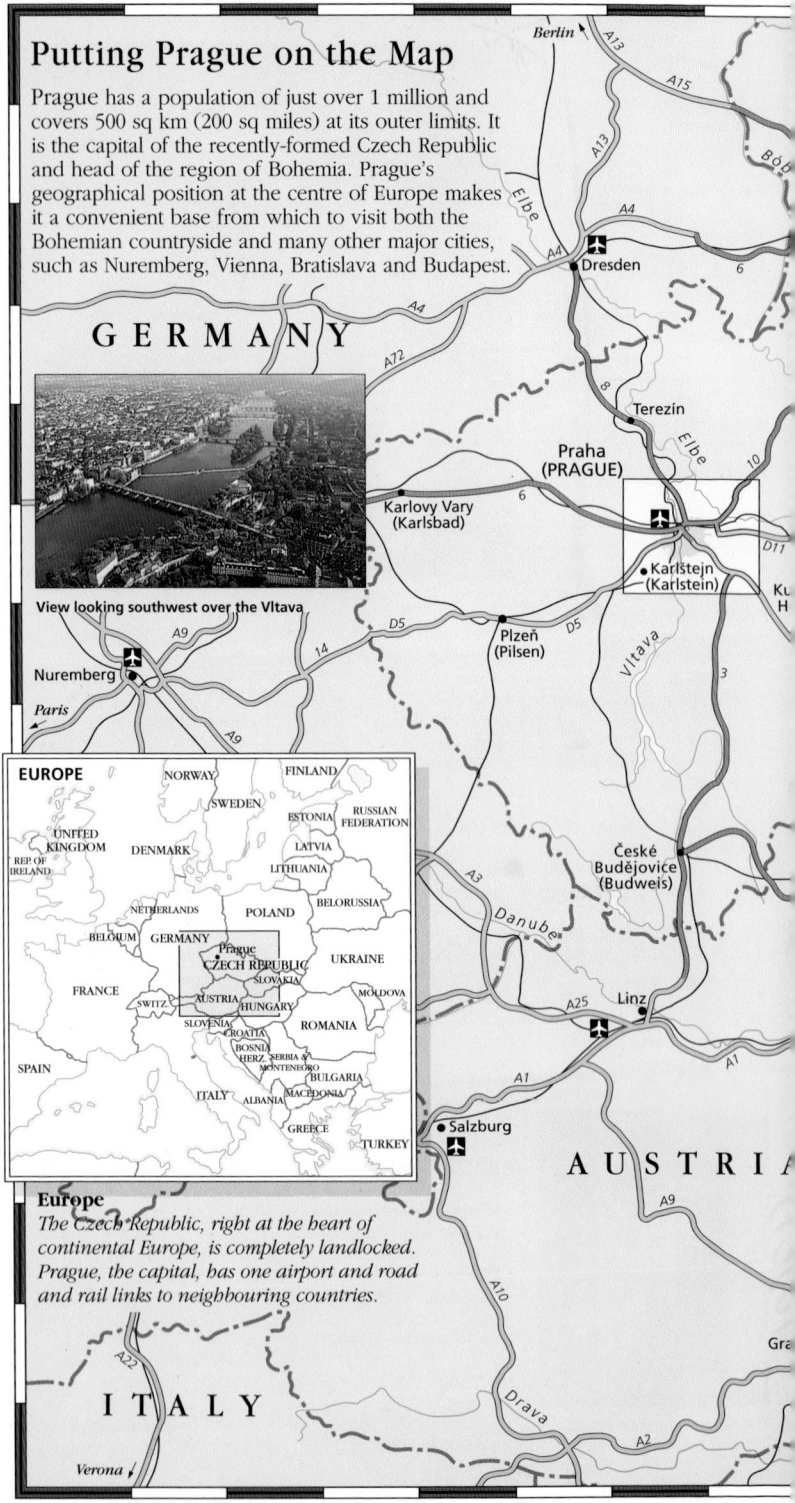

View looking southwest over the Vltava

Europe
The Czech Republic, right at the heart of continental Europe, is completely landlocked. Prague, the capital, has one airport and road and rail links to neighbouring countries.

PRAGUE AND ENVIRONS
Veltrusy
Neratovice
Lysá n. Labem
Slaný
Kralupy n. Vltavou
Vltava
D8
Brandýs n. Labem-Stará Boleslav
Elbe
Čelákovice
D11
Čakovice
Švermov
Roztoky
Kladno
See next page
Horni Počernice
Ruzyně
Unhošt
Úvaly
Český Brod
Říčany
Rudná
Zbraslav
0 km 10
0 miles 5
Beroun
D5
Karlštejn
Berounka
Řevnice
Jílové u Prahy
Sázava
D1
Oder
POLAND
Warsaw
Breslau
A4
Prague and Environs
Most sights are in the central, historic area of Prague. These are covered in detail on pages 58–157. Important sights outside the centre and day trips can be found on pages 160–71. For road and rail networks, see pages 238–9.
Cracow
CZECH REPUBLIC
Ostrava
Brno
Morava
D2
Aerial view of Greater Prague
VIENNA
D61
SLOVAKIA
A21
BRATISLAVA
Váh
M3
M1
BUDAPEST
HUNGARY
A2
Rába
M7
Lake Balaton
Zagreb
0 kilometres 50
0 miles 30
KEY
Greater Prague
Airport
Motorway
Major road
Railway line
Country boundary

Central Prague

PRAŽSKÝ HRAD A HRADČANY
PRAGUE CASTLE AND HRADČANY
MALÁ STRANA
LITTLE QUARTER
Klášter sv. Jiří
St George's Convent
Šternberský palác
Sternberg Palace
Chrám sv. Víta
St Vitus's Cathedral
Královský palác
Royal Palace
Loreta
The Loreto
Kostel sv. Mikuláše
Church of St Nicholas
Strahovský klášter
Strahov Monastery
Malostransk
JELENÍ
MARIÁNSKÉ HRADBY
KRÁLOVSKÁ ZAHRADA
CHOTKOVA
CHOTKOVY SADY
NA OPYŠI
LEDEBURSKÁ ZAHRADA
VALDŠTEJNSKÁ
VALDŠTEJNSKÉ NÁMĚSTÍ
VALDŠTEJNSKÁ ZAHRADA
LETENSKÁ
VOJANOVY SADY
U LUŽICE
NOVÝ SVĚT
ČERNÍNSKÁ
KARLOVSKÁ
KANOVNICKÁ
U KASÁREN
HRADČANSKÉ NÁMĚSTÍ
KEPLEROVA
LORETÁNSKÉ NÁMĚSTÍ
LORETÁNSKÁ
ÚVOZ
KE HRADU
NERUDOVA
VIKÁŘSKÁ
JIŘSKÁ
SNEMOVNÍ
TOMÁŠSKÁ
MALOSTRANSKÉ NÁMĚSTÍ
JOSEFSKÁ
DRAŽICKÉHO NÁMĚSTÍ
MOSTECKÁ
TRŽIŠTĚ
POHOŘELEC
STRAHOVSKÁ
VRTBOVSKÁ ZAHRADA
LOBKOVICKÁ ZAHRADA
SCHÖNBORNSKÁ ZAHRADA
STRAHOVSKÁ ZAHRADA
SEMINÁŘSKÁ ZAHRADA
KARMELITSKÁ
MALTÉZSKÉ NÁMĚSTÍ
VELKOPŘEVORSKÉ NÁMĚSTÍ
KAMPA
Čertovka
MALOSTRANSKÉ NÁBŘEŽÍ
ÚJEZD
ŘÍČNÍ
VÍTĚZNÁ
PETŘÍNSKÉ SADY
KŮZOVÝ SAD
Brusnice

Orb and Cross
An important part of the royal coronation regalia, this orb is now kept at St Vitus's Cathedral (see pp100–3).

KEY

- Major sight
- Metro station
- Coach station
- Tram stop
- Funicular railway
- River boat boarding point
- Parking
- Tourist information
- Hospital
- Police station
- Church
- Synagogue
- City wall

View of the Church of St Lawrence
Petřín Park offers outstanding views of Prague (see p141 and Four Guided Walks, pp176–7).

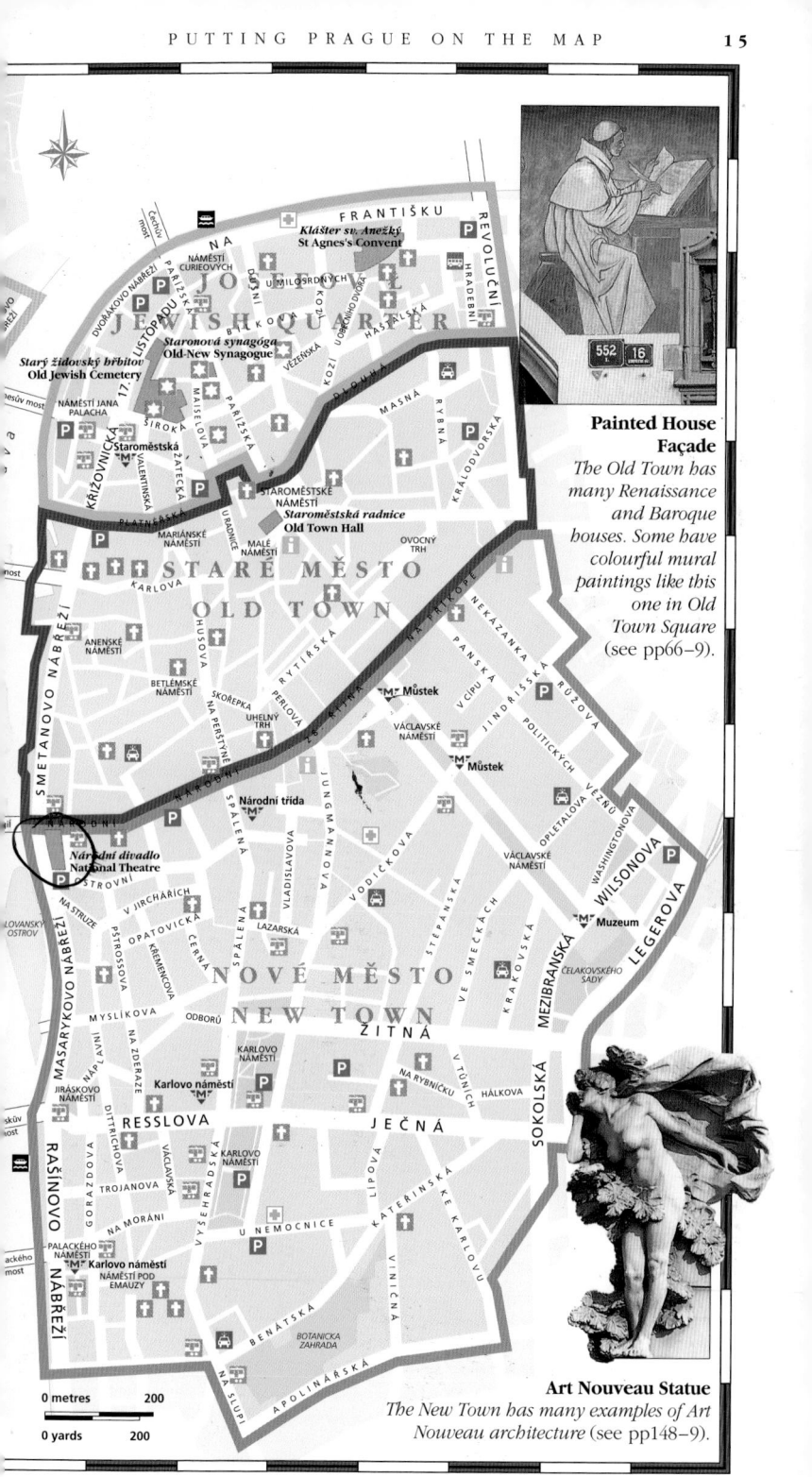

Painted House Façade
The Old Town has many Renaissance and Baroque houses. Some have colourful mural paintings like this one in Old Town Square (see pp66–9).

Art Nouveau Statue
The New Town has many examples of Art Nouveau architecture (see pp148–9).

THE HISTORY OF PRAGUE

Prague's position at the crossroads of Europe has made it a magnet for foreign traders since pre-recorded times. By the early 10th century it had developed into a thriving town with a large market place (the Old Town Square) and two citadels (Prague Castle and Vyšehrad), from where its first rulers, the Přemyslids, conducted their many family feuds. These were often bloody: in 935, Prince Wenceslas was savagely murdered by his brother Boleslav. Wenceslas was later canonized and became Bohemia's best-known patron saint.

Prague coat of arms

During the Middle Ages Prague enjoyed a golden age, especially during the reign of the Holy Roman Emperor, Charles IV. Under the auspices of this wise and cultured king, Prague grew into a magnificent city, larger than Paris or London. Charles instigated the founding and building of many institutions, including the first University of Central Europe in Prague. The University's first Czech rector was Jan Hus, the reforming preacher whose execution for alleged heresy in 1415 led to the Hussite wars. The radical wing of the Hussites, the Taborites, were finally defeated at the Battle of Lipany in 1434. During the 16th century, after a succession of weak kings, the Austrian Habsburgs took over, beginning a rule that would last for almost 400 years. One of the more enlightened of all the Habsburg Emperors was Rudolph II. He brought the spirit of the Renaissance to Prague through his love of the arts and sciences. Soon after his death, in 1618, Prague was the setting for the Protestant revolt which led to the 30 Years' War. Its aftermath brought a serious decline in the fortunes of a city that would revive only in the 18th century. Prague's many fine Baroque churches and palaces date from this time.

The 19th century saw a period of national revival and the burgeoning of civic pride. The great public monuments – the National Museum, the National Theatre and Rudolfinum – were built. But a foreign power still ruled the city, and it was not until 1918 that Prague became the capital of an independent Republic. World War II brought occupation by the German army, followed by four decades of Communism. After the "Velvet Revolution" of 1989, Prague is today on the threshold of a new era.

View of Prague Castle and Little Quarter, 1493

◁ *St Wenceslas and St Vitus*, by Bartholomaeus Spränger, about 1600

Rulers of Prague

The mythical Princess Libuše

Three great dynasties have shaped the history of Prague: the Přemyslids, the Luxemburgs and the Habsburgs. According to Slavonic legend, the Přemyslids were founded by Princess Libuše *(see p21)*. Her line included St Wenceslas and Přemysl Otakar II, whose death on the battlefield at Marchfeld paved the way for the Luxemburgs. This family produced one of Prague's greatest rulers, Charles IV, who was King of Bohemia and Holy Roman Emperor *(see pp24–5)*. In 1526, the city came under the control of the Austrian House of Habsburg whose rule lasted 400 years, until 28 October 1918, when Czechoslovakia gained its independence. Since then there has been a succession of presidents.

1346–78 Charles IV

14
Lad
Posthu

1310–46 John of Luxemburg

1140–72 Vladislav I

935–72 Boleslav I

1305–6 Wenceslas III

1230–53 Wenceslas I

1278–1305 Wenceslas II

1034–55 Břetislav I

900 | **1000** | **1100** | **1200** | **1300** | **140**

PŘEMYSLIDS | LUXEMBURGS

900 | **1000** | **1100** | **1200** | **1300** | **140**

972–99 Boleslav II

1061–92 Vratislav II

921–35 St Wenceslas

1173–9 Soběslav II

1197–1230 Přemysl Otakar I

1378–1419 Wenceslas IV

1253–78 Přemysl Otakar II

1419–37 Sigismund

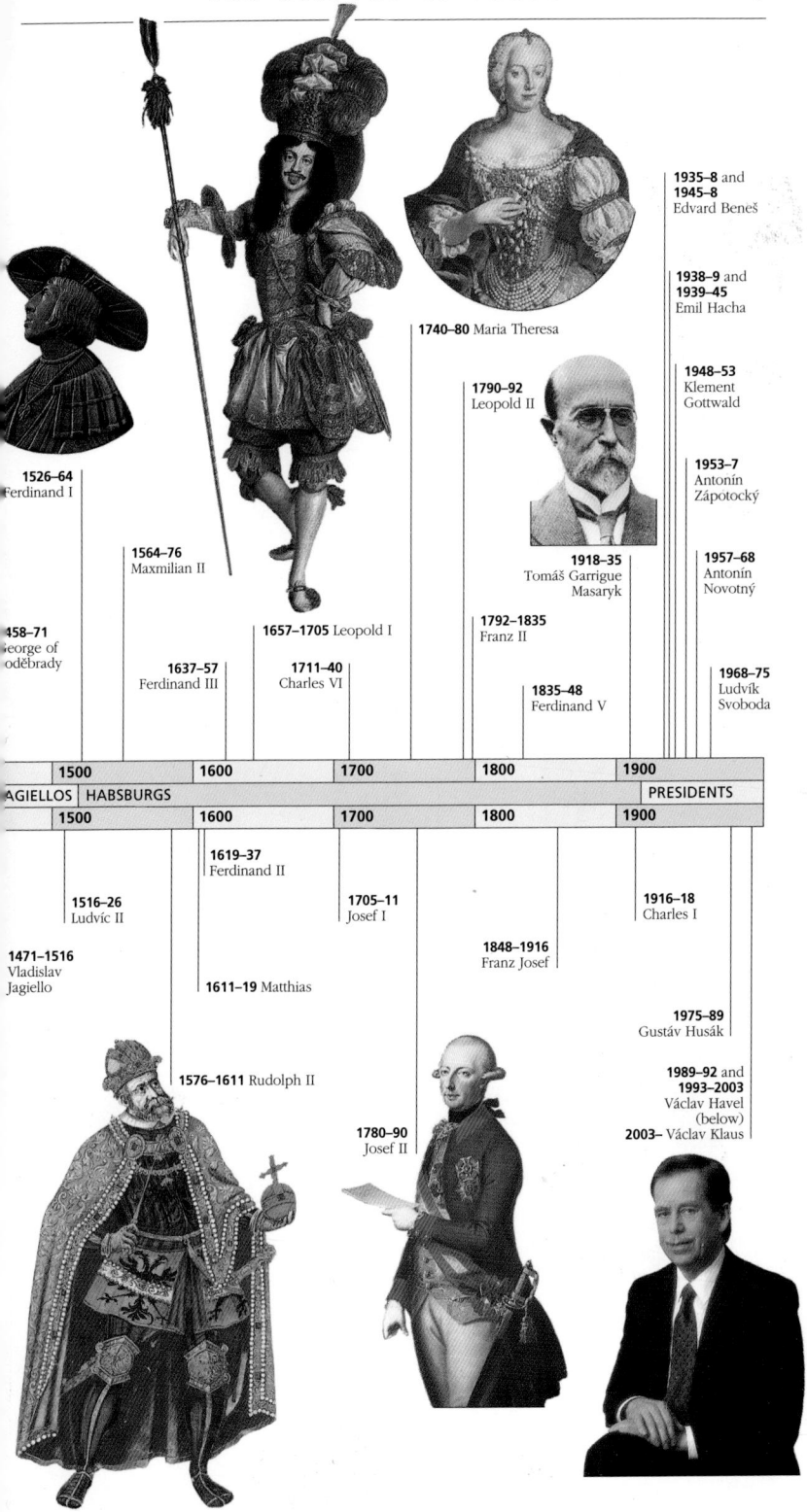
1935–8 and
1945–8
Edvard Beneš
1938–9 and
1939–45
Emil Hacha
1740–80 Maria Theresa
1948–53
Klement
Gottwald
1790–92
Leopold II
1953–7
Antonín
Zápotocký
1526–64
Ferdinand I
1957–68
Antonín
Novotný
1564–76
Maxmilian II
1918–35
Tomáš Garrigue
Masaryk
458–71
George of
oděbrady
1657–1705 Leopold I
1792–1835
Franz II
1637–57
Ferdinand III
1711–40
Charles VI
1968–75
Ludvík
Svoboda
1835–48
Ferdinand V
1500
1600
1700
1800
1900
AGIELLOS
HABSBURGS
PRESIDENTS
1500
1600
1700
1800
1900
1619–37
Ferdinand II
1516–26
Ludvíc II
1705–11
Josef I
1916–18
Charles I
1848–1916
Franz Josef
1471–1516
Vladislav
Jagiello
1611–19 Matthias
1975–89
Gustáv Husák
1576–1611 Rudolph II
1989–92 and
1993–2003
Václav Havel
(below)
1780–90
Josef II
2003– Václav Klaus

Prague under the Přemyslids

9th-century earring

Early Celtic tribes, from 500 BC, were the first inhabitants of the area around the Vltava valley. The Germanic Marcomans arrived in 9–6 BC, and gradually the Celts left. The first Slavic tribes came to Bohemia in about 500 AD. Struggles for supremacy led to the emergence of a ruling dynasty, the Přemyslids, around 800 AD. They built two fortified settlements: the first at Prague Castle *(see pp94–111)*, the second at Vyšehrad, a rocky headland on the right bank of the Vltava *(see pp180–1)*. These remained the seats of Czech princes for hundreds of years. One prince crucial to the emerging Czech State was the pious Wenceslas. He enjoyed only a brief reign but left an important legacy in the founding of St Vitus's rotunda *(see p102)*.

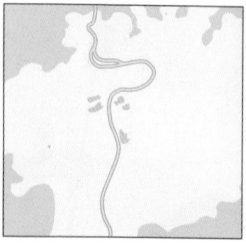

EXTENT OF THE CITY

1000 AD | Today

St Cyril and St Methodius
Originally Greeks from Salonica, these two brothers brought Christianity to Moravia in about 863. They baptized early Přemyslid, Bořivoj, and his wife Ludmilla, grandmother of St Wenceslas.

Boleslav's henchman raises his sword to strike the fatal blow.

Second assassin grapples with the Prince's companion.

Early Coin
Silver coins like this denar were minted in the royal mint of Vyšehrad during Boleslav II's reign from 967–99.

Wild Boar Figurine
Celtic tribes made small talismans of the wild animals that they hunted for food in the forested areas around Prague.

TIMELINE

Bronze head of a Celtic goddess

623–658 Bohemia is part of an empire formed by Frankish merchant, Samo

600 AD

700

500 BC
Celts in Bohemia. Joined by Germanic Marcomans in 1st century AD

6th century
Slavs settle alongside Germanic tribes in Bohemia

8th century
Tribe of Czechs settle in central Bohemia

Vyšehrad acropolis – first Czech settlement on the right bank of the Vltava

Sword and Helmet
St Wenceslas was buried in the southern apse of the rotunda of St Vitus. His sword and helmet were preserved as relics and today form part of the Cathedral's treasure.

Wenceslas seeks sanctuary.

A monk closes the door against Wenceslas.

ASSASSINATION OF PRINCE WENCESLAS

In 929, the young Wenceslas was murdered on the orders of his brother, Boleslav. This manuscript illustration of 1006 shows the moment when the assassins caught up with the prince as he was about to enter the church for the morning mass.

PRINCESS LIBUŠE

The legendary founder of the Přemyslids was Princess Libuše, head of a West Slavic tribe. She took notice of the discord among her clansmen, and succeeded her father to become the first woman ruler. Choosing a humble ploughman (*Přemysl-Oráč*) as consort and ruler, she began a dynasty that was to last 400 years.

Princess Libuše foresaw the glory of Prague in a vision

Rotunda of St Vitus
Founded by Wenceslas in the early 10th century, the rotunda became a place of pilgrimage after the saint's death in 929. It stood where St Wenceslas Chapel is today.

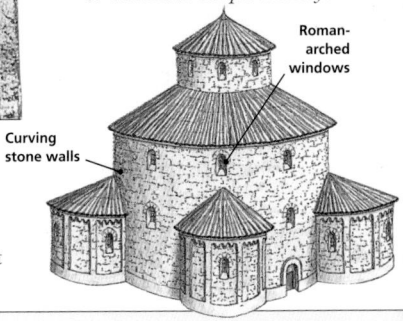

sty of
yslids
ded

Early Christian breast cross

870 Prague Castle founded

921 Wenceslas becomes Prince of Bohemia

993 Bishop Adalbert Vojtěch founds monastery at Břevnov

900

1000

863 St Cyril and St Methodius bring Christianity to Moravia

929 Wenceslas dies

920 Founding of St George's Basilica at Prague Castle

Bishop Adalbert's bejewelled glove

Early Medieval Prague

Prague Castle steadily grew in importance from the beginning of the 9th century onwards. Prone to frequent fires, its wooden buildings were gradually replaced by stone and the area developed into a sturdy Romanesque fortress with a palace and religious buildings. Clustered around the original outer bailey was an area inhabited by skilled craftsmen and German merchants, encouraged to come and stay in Prague by Vladislav II and, later, Přemysl Otakar II. This came to be known as the "Little Quarter" and achieved town status in 1257. It was joined to the Old Town by a bridge, known as the Judith Bridge.

Initial letter D from the Vyšehrad Codex

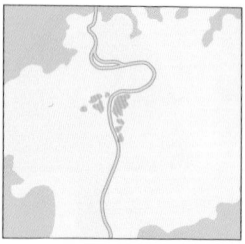

EXTENT OF THE CITY

1230 *Today*

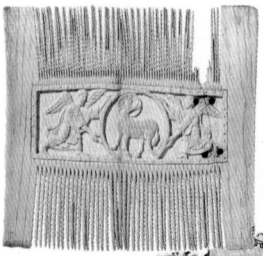

Decorative Comb
This ornate, bone, fine-toothed comb was one of the relics of St Adalbert.

PRAGUE CASTLE IN 1230

Sited on a high ridge, the Romanesque fortress had protective stone walls and easily-guarded gates.

St George's Convent and Basilica ***(see pp106–9 and p98)***

The Prince's Palace grew into the Royal Palace *(see pp104–5).*

Entrance from Old Town

The White Tower gave access from the west.

Site of Hradčany Square

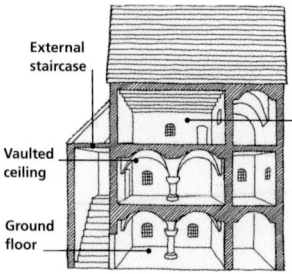

Romanesque Stone House
These three-storeyed houses were based around a very simple floor plan.

St Vitus's Basilica and Chapter House ***(see pp100–3)***

Stone houses were built on what is now Nerudova Street in the Little Quarter *(see p130).*

TIMELINE

St Adalbert with a martyr's palm frond

1040 St Adalbert's remains brought to Prague

1091 Old Town marketplace first mentioned by travellers

1092–1110 Reign of Bretislav II

1110 Small German settlement in Prague

1140 Strahov Monastery founded

1050

1100

1070 Vyšehrad becomes temporary seat of Czech princes

1085 Vratislav I becomes first King of Bohemia

1091 Great fire at Prague Castle

1110–20 Reign of Bořivoj II

1135 Seat of Czech princes moves from Vyšehrad to Prague Castle

Romanesque stone head from Judith Bridge Tower

St Agnes of Bohemia
Sister of Wenceslas I, this devout woman built a convent for the order of the Poor Clares (the female counterparts of the Franciscans) (see pp92–3). *She was not canonized until 1989.*

WHERE TO SEE ROMANESQUE PRAGUE

Remains can be seen in the crypt of St Vitus's *(pp100–3)*, the basements of the Palace of the Lords of Kunštát *(p78)* and the Royal Palace *(pp104–5)*.

St George's Basilica
The vaulting in the crypt dates from the 12th century (p98).

St Martin's Rotunda
This well-preserved building is in Vyšehrad (p180).

Vratislav II
The Vyšehrad Codex, an illuminated selection from the gospels, was made to mark Vratislav's coronation in 1061.

The Black Tower was the exit to Bohemia's second town, Kutná Hora *(see p168)*.

Little Quarter Square

Little Quarter Coat of Arms
Vladislav II's portrait was incorporated into this 16th-century miniature painting.

Přemysl Otakar II
The last great Přemyslid king was killed in battle after trying to carve out a huge empire.

1233 Founding of St Agnes's Convent

1182 Romanesque construction of Prague Castle completed

1257 Little Quarter receives town status

1258–68 Strahov Monastery rebuilt in Gothic style after fire

1200 **1250** **1290**

1212 Přemysl Otakar I receives the Sicilian Golden Bull, confirming the sovereignty of Bohemian kings

1158 Judith Bridge built *(see pp136–9)*

Sicilian Golden Bull

1278 Přemysl Otakar II dies at Marchfeld

Prague's Golden Age

Gift from Pope Urban V in 1368

In the late Middle Ages, Prague attained the height of its glory. The Holy Roman Emperor Charles IV chose Prague as his Imperial residence and set out to make the city the most magnificent in Europe. He founded a university (the Carolinum) and built many fine churches and monasteries in the Gothic style. Of major importance were his town-planning schemes, such as the reconstruction of Prague Castle, the building of a new stone bridge to replace the Judith Bridge, and the foundation of a new quarter, the New Town. A devout Catholic, he owned a large collection of relics which were kept, along with the Crown Jewels, at Karlstein Castle *(see pp168–9)*.

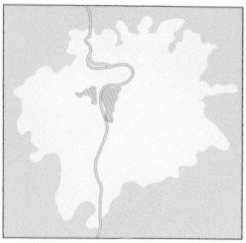

EXTENT OF THE CITY

1350 | Today

Charles IV wears the Imperial crown, set with sapphires, rubies and pearls.

St Wenceslas Chapel
Proud of his direct descent from the Přemyslids, Charles had this shrine to St Wenceslas built in St Vitus's Cathedral (see pp100–3).

St Wenceslas Crown
Worn by Charles at his coronation in 1347, the Bohemian crown was based on early Přemyslid insignia.

The Emperor places the piece of the cross in its reliquary.

TIMELINE

1280 Old-New Synagogue completed in Gothic style

Portal of Old-New Synagogue

Town Hall, Old Town Square

1333 Charles IV makes Prague his home

1344 Elevation of Prague bishopric to archbishopric

1305

1306 Přemyslid dynasty ends

1310 John of Luxemburg occupies Prague

1320

1338 John of Luxemburg gives permission to Old Town to build a town hall

1335

Votive panel showing Charles, Archbishop Jan Očko and Bohemia's patron saints

***St Vitus* by Master Theodoric**
This is one of a series of paintings of saints by the great Bohemian artist for the Holy Rood Chapel at Karlstein Castle (c1365).

University Seal, 1348
The seal depicts the Emperor offering the foundation documents to St Wenceslas.

A jewelled reliquary cross was made to house the new relic.

Building the New Town
This manuscript records Charles IV supervising the building of the New Town during the 14th century.

CHARLES IV AND HIS RELICS

Charles collected holy relics from all over the Empire. In about 1357 he received a part of Christ's cross from the Dauphin. This mural in Karlstein Castle is thought to be the best likeness of the Emperor.

WHERE TO SEE GOTHIC PRAGUE

Prague's rich Gothic legacy includes three of its best-known sights – St Vitus's Cathedral *(pp100–3)*, Charles Bridge *(pp136–9)* and the Old-New Synagogue *(pp88–9)*. Another very important building from Charles IV's reign is the Carolinum *(p65)*. Churches that have retained most of their original Gothic features include the Church of Our Lady before Týn *(p70)*.

Carolinum
This fine oriel window was part of the university (p65).

Old Town Bridge Tower
The sculptural decoration is by Peter Parler (p139).

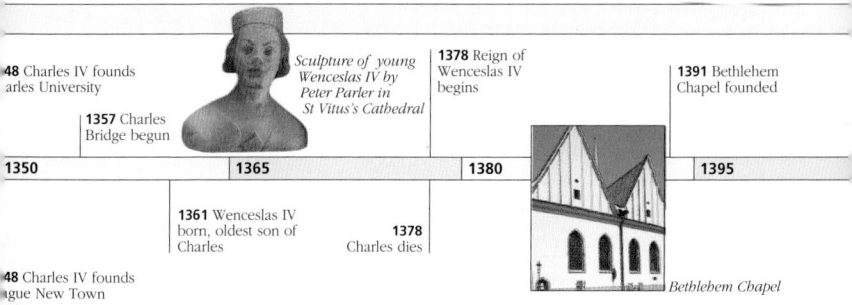

Hussite Prague

George of Poděbrady

In the early 15th century, Europe shook in fear of an incredible fighting force -- the Hussites, followers of the reformist cleric, Jan Hus. Despite simple weapons, they achieved legendary military successes against the Emperor's Catholic crusades, due largely to their religious fervour and to the discipline of their brilliant leader, Jan Žižka, who invented mobile artillery. The Hussites split into two camps, the moderate "Utraquists" *(see p75)* and the radical "Taborites" who were finally defeated at the Battle of Lipany in 1434, paving the way for the moderate Hussite king, George of Poděbrady.

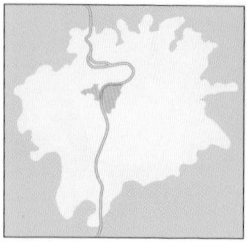

EXTENT OF THE CITY

1500 | Today

Nobles' Letter of Protest

Several hundred seals of the Bohemian nobility were affixed to a letter protesting about the execution of Jan Hus.

GOD'S WARRIORS

The early-16th-century Codex of Jena illustrated the Hussite successes. Here the Hussites, who included artisans and barons, are shown singing their hymn, with their blind leader, Jan Žižka.

The priest held a gilded monstrance.

Jan Žižka

War Machine

For maximum effect, farm waggons were tied together to form a shield. A chilling array of weapons were unleashed including crossbows, flails and an early form of howitzer.

TIMELINE

Jan Hus preaching

1402–13 Jan Hus preaches at Bethlehem Chapel *(see p75)*

1415 Jan Hus burned at the stake at Constance

1419 Defenestration of councillors from New Town Hall

1434 Battle of Lipany

The Taborites made lethal weapons from simple farm tools

1400 | **1420** | **1440**

1410 Jan Hus excommunicated. Building of Old Town Clock

The chalice, symbol of the Utraquists

1420 Hussites victorious under Jan Žižka at Vitkov and Vyšehrad

1424 Jan Žižka dies

1448 Prague conquered by troops of George of Poděbrady

Satan Dressed as the Pope
Lurid images satirizing the corruption of the church were painted on placards and carried through the streets.

The banner was decorated with the Hussite chalice.

A variety of farm implements were used as makeshift weapons by the peasants.

The peasant army marched behind Jan Žižka.

Hussite Shield
Wooden shields like this one that bears the arms of the city of Prague, were used to fill any gaps in the waggon fortress's tight formation.

REFORMER, JAN HUS

Born to poor parents in a small Bohemian town, Jan Hus became one of the most important religious thinkers of his day. His objections to the Catholic Church's corrupt practices, opulent style and wealth were shared by many Czechs – nobles and peasants alike. His reformist preaching in Prague's Bethlehem Chapel earned him a huge following, noticed by the Roman Papacy, and Hus was excommunicated. In 1412 Wenceslas IV, brother of the Emperor Sigismund, asked him to leave Prague. In October 1414, Hus decided to defend his teaching at the Council of Constance. Even though he had the Emperor's safe conduct, he was put in prison. The following year he was declared a heretic and burned at the stake.

Jan Hus at the Stake in 1415
After suffering death at the hands of the Church on 6 July 1415, Jan Hus became a revered martyr of the Czech people.

1458 Coronation of George of Poděbrady *(see p19)*

1485 Hussite uprising in Prague

1492–1502 Vladislav Hall built

1460 | **1480** | **1500**

1487 First book printed in Prague

1485 King Vladislav Jagiello begins to rebuild Royal Palace at Prague Castle

Chalice on the outside of the Týn Church denotes the Hussite cause

Vladislav Jagiello

The Renaissance and Rudolph II

Renaissance tankard

With the accession of the Habsburgs, the Renaissance reached Prague. Art and architecture were dominated by the Italians who enjoyed the patronage of the Imperial court, especially that of Rudolph II. The eccentric Rudolph often neglected politics, preferring to indulge his passions for collecting and science. His court was a haven for artists, astrologers, astronomers and alchemists, but his erratic rule led to revolts and an attempt by his brother Matthias to usurp him. In the course of the Thirty Years' War *(see pp30–31)* many works of art from Rudolph's collection were looted.

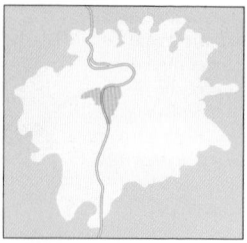

EXTENT OF THE CITY

1550 | Today

Rudolph II
A connoisseur of the bizarre, Rudolph was delighted by this vegetable portrait by Giuseppe Arcimboldo (1590).

Fish pond

Dalibor Tower

Belvedere

Pergola

Orchard

Formal flower beds

Lion House

Mosaic Desk Top
Renaissance table tops with Florentine themes of fountains and gardens were made at Rudolph's court in semi-precious stones.

Rabbi Löw
A revered Jewish sage, he was said to have invented an artificial man (see pp88–9).

TIMELINE

1502 Vladislav Hall built

Vladislav Hall

1520

1526 Habsburg rule begins with Ferdinand I

Ferdinand I

1538–63 Belvedere built

1540

1541 Great fire in Little Quarter, the Castle and Hradčany

1547 Unsuccessful uprising of towns of Prague against Ferdinand I

1556 Ferdinand I invites Jesuits to Prague

1560

Charter for manglers and dyers

Sense of Sight
Jan Brueghel's allegorical painting shows the extent of Rudolph II's huge collection – from globes to paintings, jewels and scientific instruments.

Tycho Brahe
The Danish astronomer spent his last years living in Prague.

ROYAL PALACE GARDENS

No longer a medieval fortress, Prague Castle and its gardens were given over to the pleasure of the King. Here Rudolph enjoyed ball games, exotic plants and his menagerie.

WHERE TO SEE RENAISSANCE PRAGUE

The Royal Garden *(p111)* preserves much of the spirit of Renaissance Prague. Paintings and objects from Rudolph's collections can be seen in the Sternberg Palace *(pp112–15)*, the Picture Gallery of Prague Castle *(p98)* and the Museum of Decorative Arts *(p84)*.

At the Two Golden Bears
Built in 1590, the house is famous for its symmetrical, carved doorway, one of the most graceful in Prague (p71).

Belvedere
The palace is decorated with stone reliefs by Italian architect, Paolo della Stella (p110).

Ball Game Hall
Beautiful Renaissance sgraffito *covers the façade of this building in the Royal Garden, but it has been heavily restored* (p111).

1580

1583 Prague becomes seat of Imperial court of Rudolph II; great art collection begun

1600

1609 Publication of Rudolph's Imperial Charter on religious freedom

1612 Rudolph II dies

1614 Matthias Gate at Prague Castle built

1618 Defenestration of two royal governors from Royal Palace *(see p105)*

1620

A ten-ducat coin (1603)

Baroque Prague

In 1619 the Czech nobles deposed Habsburg Emperor Ferdinand II as King of Bohemia and elected instead Frederick of the Palatinate. The following year they paid for their defiance at the Battle of the White Mountain, the beginning of the Thirty Years' War. There followed a period of persecution of all non-Catholics, accompanied by the Germanization of the country's institutions. The leaders in the fight against Protestantism were the Jesuits and one of their most powerful weapons was the restoration of their churches in Prague in the Baroque style. Many new churches also adopted this style.

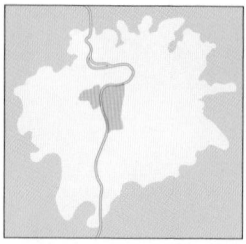

EXTENT OF THE CITY

1750 *Today*

Church of St Nicholas
This outstanding High Baroque church in the Little Quarter was the work of the great Dientzenhofers (see pp128–9).

A sculpture of Atlas (1722) adorns the top of the tower.

Mirror Chapel

Grape Courtyard

Holy Saviour Church

Measuring the World
Some monasteries were seats of learning. Strahov (see pp120–21) *had two libraries built, decorated with Baroque painting. This fresco detail is in the Philosophical Hall.*

TIMELINE

Old Town coat of arms – embellished with the Imperial eagle and 12 flags in recognition of the defence of the city against the Swedes

1620 Battle of the White Mountain

1627 Beginning of Counter-Reformation committee in Prague

1706–14 Decoration of Charles Bridge with statues

1625 | **1645** | **1665** | **1685** | **170**

1621 Execution in Old Town Square of 27 Protestant leaders

1634 Wallenstein killed by Irish mercenaries

1631 Saxon occupation of Prague

1648 Swedes occupy Prague Castle. Treaty of Westphalia and end of Thirty Years' War

1676–8 New bastions built to fortify Vyšehrad

1704–53 Building of Church of St Nicholas in the Little Quarter

Battle of the White Mountain
In 1620 the Czech army was defeated by Habsburg troops at Bílá Hora (White Mountain), a hill northwest of Prague (see p163). *After the battle, Bohemia became a de facto province of Austria.*

Observatory Tower

St Clement's Church gave its name to the whole complex.

Italian Chapel

Monstrance
Baroque monstrances – used to display the communion host – became increasingly elaborate and ornate (see pp116–17).

CLEMENTINUM

The Jesuits exercised enormous power over education. Between 1653 and 1723 they built this College. It was the largest complex of buildings after Prague Castle and included three churches, smaller chapels, libraries, lecture halls and an observatory.

WHERE TO SEE BAROQUE PRAGUE

The Baroque is everywhere in Prague. Almost all the churches were built or remodelled in Baroque style, the finest being St Nicholas *(pp128–9)*. There are also the grand palaces and smaller houses of the Little Quarter *(pp122–41)*, the façades in the Old Town *(pp60–79)*, and statues on churches, street corners and along the parapets of Charles Bridge.

Nerudova Street
At the Golden Cup, No. 16, has preserved its typical Baroque house sign (p130).

Charles Bridge
This statue of St Francis Borgia by Ferdinand Brokof was added in 1710 (pp136–9).

1740 Accession of Empress Maria Theresa

1748 Bohemian Chancellery loses last vestiges of power

1784 Four towns of Prague united to form a single city

1773 Jesuit Order dissolved

Mozart at Bertramka (p160)

Maria Theresa

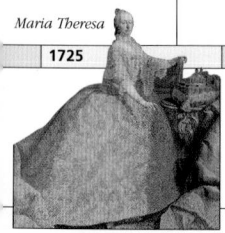

1725 | 1745 | 1765 | 1785

1757 Prague besieged by Prussians

1782 Convents and monasteries closed

1787 Mozart stays at Bertramka preparing for the premiere of *Don Giovanni* at the Estates Theatre *(see p65)*

The National Revival in Prague

Emperor Franz Josef

The 19th century was one of the most glorious periods in the history of Prague. Austrian rule relaxed, allowing the Czech nation to rediscover its own history and culture. Silent for so long, Czech was re-established as an official language. Civic pride was rekindled with the building of the capital's great showpieces, such as the National Theatre, which utilized the talents of Czech architects and artists. The Jewish Quarter and New Town underwent extensive redevelopment and, with the introduction of public transport, Prague grew beyond its ancient limits.

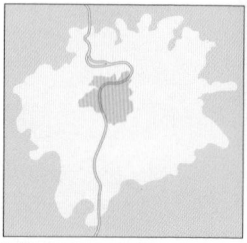

EXTENT OF THE CITY

1890 | Today

Smetana's Libuše
Written for the scheduled opening of the National Theatre in 1881, the opera drew on early Czech legend (see pp20–21).

Rudolfinum
A major concert venue beside the Vltava, the building (see p84) *is richly decorated with symbols of the art of music.*

OLD TOWN CLOCK TOWER CALENDAR

In 1866, the revolving dial on Prague's most enduring landmark was replaced by a new one by celebrated artist, Josef Mánes. His studies of Bohemian peasant life are incorporated into pictures symbolizing the months of the year.

TIMELINE

Restored clock from the east face of the Town Hall Tower

1805 Czechs, Austrians and Russians defeated by Napoleon at Battle of Slavkov (Austerlitz)

1818 National Museum founded

1833 Englishman Edward Thomas begins production of steam engines

1848 Uprising of people of Prague against Austrian troops

1800 | **1820** | **1840**

The battle of Slavkov

1815 First public demonstration of a vehicle driven by a steam engine

1838–45 Old Town Hall undergoes reconstruction

1845 First train arrives in Prague

1 Foundat stone Natic Theatre

Expo 95 Poster
Vojtěch Hynais designed this poster for the ethnographic exhibition of folk culture in 1895. In the Art Nouveau style, it reflected the new appreciation of regional traditions.

Municipal House
Allegories of civic virtues painted by Alfons Mucha adorn this Art Nouveau interior.

Jewish Quarter
From 1897 onwards, the slum housing of the ghetto was replaced with new apartment blocks.

WHERE TO SEE THE NATIONAL REVIVAL

Many of Prague's remarkable monuments, the National Museum for example, were built around this period. One fine example of Art Nouveau architecture is the Municipal House *(p64)*, where the Mayor's Room has murals by Mucha. The Rudolfinum *(p84)* and the National Theatre *(pp156–7)* have gloriously-decorated interiors by great artists of the day. The Prague Museum has many objects from the late 19th and early 20th centuries as well as the original painting for Mánes' Old Town Clock.

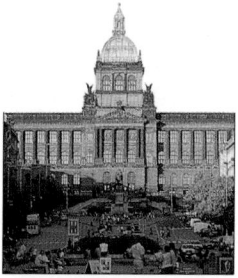

National Museum
The Neo-Renaissance façade dominates the skyline (p147).

National Theatre
The décor has murals by Czech artists, including Aleš (pp156–7).

National Theatre

1881 Newly opened ional Theatre destroyed by fire, then rebuilt

1883 Re-opening of the National Theatre

1891 Jubilee Exhibition

1884–91 Building of the National Museum

1883 First public lighting with electric lamps

1896 Proper city transport of electric trams starts

1912 Municipal House opens

1897–1917 Slums of Jewish Ghetto cleared

Early electric trams

1914 World War I begins

1916 Emperor Franz Josef dies

The satirical novel Good Soldier Švejk (see p154) *explored the futility of war and the inept Austrian military*

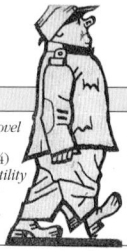

1880 | **1900**

Prague after Independence

Letná Park metronome

Just 20 years after its foundation, the Czechoslovak Republic was helplessly caught up in the political manoeuvring that preceded Nazi domination of Europe. Prague emerged from World War II almost unscathed by bombings, no longer part of a Nazi protectorate but of a Socialist republic. Any resistance was brutally suppressed. Ultimately, the intellectuals spoke out, demanding observance of civil rights. Denial of such rights led these dissidents to unite and prepare for the "Velvet Revolution". In the end, it was a playwright, Václav Havel, who stepped onto the balcony of Prague Castle to lead the country at the start of a long and often difficult return to independence.

1945 Soviet Red Army enter Prague on 9 May to rapturous welcome, following four days of uprisings. In October, provisional National Assembly set up under Beneš

1920 Avant-garde left-wing artists form Devětsil movement in Prague's Union Café

Edvard Beneš

1935 Edvard Beneš succeeds Masaryk as President. Nazi-funded Sudeten German Party, led by Konrad Henlein, makes election gains

1938 Munich Agreement hands over parts of Republic to Hitler. Beneš flees country

1952 Most famous of many show trials under Gottwald, Slánský Trial sends 11 senior politicians to gallows as Trotskyites and traitors

1918	1930	1940	1950

1918 1930 1940 1950

1924 Death of Franz Kafka, author of *The Trial*

1932 Traditional gymnastic rally or *slet* takes place at Strahov stadium

1942 Tyrannical "Protector" for only eight months, Reinhard Heydrich assassinated by Czech resistance

1948 Communist Party assumes power under Klement Gottwald; announces 89% support in May elections

1955 Largest statue of Stalin in the world unveiled in Letná Park, overlooking city

1958 Premiere of innovative animated film, *The Invention of Destruction directed* by Karel Zeman

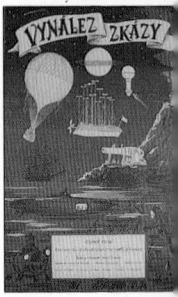

1918 Foundation of Czechoslovak Republic. Tomáš Masaryk first democratically-elected President

1939 German troops march into Prague; city declared capital of Nazi Protectorate of Bohemia and Moravia. Emil Hácha president under the German protectorate

Welcome Home poster, to mark the president's return on 21 December 1918

1966 Jiří Menzel's *Closely Observed Trains* wins Oscar for Best Foreign Film, drawing the world's attention to Czech cinema

1989 The "Velvet Revolution": growing civil discontent prompts demonstrations and strikes. Havel unites opposition groups to form Civic Forum. Temporary Government promises free elections; President Husák resigns and Václav Havel is sworn in by popular demand

1990 First democratic elections for 60 years produce 99% turnout, with 60% of vote going to alliance of Civic Forum and People Against Violence

1968 Alexander Dubček elected to post of First Secretary

1992 The splitting of Czechoslovakia

1962 Statue of Stalin in Letná Park demolished (replaced, in 1991, by a giant metronome)

1999 Czech Republic joins NATO

1979 Playwright Václav Havel founds Committee for the Defence of the Unjustly Persecuted and is sent to prison

2002 Prague suffers its worst flooding in 150 years.

2004 Czech Republic joins the EU

0 | 1970 | 1985 | 2000

0 | 1970 | 1985 | 2000

Czechoslovak alist Republic R) proclaimed

1969 Jan Palach burns to death in protest at Soviet occupation

2001 The biggest street protests since the end of communism force Jiri Hodac to resign as director-general of state television

1967 First Secretary and President, Antonín Novotný, imprisons dissident writers

1977 Human rights manifesto Charter 77 drawn up after arrest of band, Plastic People

1984 Jaroslav Seifert, signatory of Charter 77, wins Nobel Prize for Literature but cannot collect prize in person

The coat of arms of the president of the Czech Republic has the inscription "truth victorious" and the arms for Bohemia (top left, bottom right), *Moravia* (top right) *and Silesia* (bottom left)

1993 Prague is once again declared capital of Czech Republic

1968 Moderate Alexander Dubček adopts the programme of liberal reforms known as "Prague Spring". On 21 August, Warsaw Pact occupies Czechoslovakia and over 100 protesters are killed as troops enter Prague

1989 Canonization of St Agnes of Bohemia *(see pp92–3)* takes place on 4 November. Vatican commissions painting by dissident Prague-born artist Gustav Makarius Tauc for the occasion. Czech legend that miraculous events will accompany her elevation to sainthood prove correct when "Velvet Revolution" begins on 17 November

PRAGUE AT A GLANCE

There are almost 150 places of interest described in the *Area by Area* section of this book. A broad range of sights is covered: from the ancient Royal Palace, which was the site of the Defenestration of 1618 *(see p105)*, to cubist houses built in the Jewish Quarter in the 1920s *(see p91)*; from the peaceful oasis of Petřín Park *(see p141)*, to the bustle of Wenceslas Square *(see pp144–5)*. To help you make the most of your stay, the following 12 pages are a time-saving guide to the best Prague has to offer visitors. Museums and galleries, churches and synagogues, palaces and gardens all have their own sections. Each sight has a cross reference to its own full entry. Below are the attractions that no visitor should miss.

PRAGUE'S TOP TEN SIGHTS

Old Town Square
See pp66–9.

National Theatre
See pp156–7.

Church of St Nicholas
See pp128–9.

Charles Bridge
See pp136–9.

Old Town Hall
See pp72–4.

St Vitus's Cathedral
See pp100–3.

Wallenstein Palace and Garden *See p126.*

Old Jewish Cemetery
See pp86–7.

Prague Castle
See p96–7.

St Agnes's Convent
See pp92–3.

◁ **Mucha's allegory of Vigilance in the Mayor's Room in the Municipal House (*see p64*)**

Prague's Best: Museums and Galleries

With more than 20 museums and almost 100 galleries and exhibition halls, Prague is a city of unexpected and rare delights. Here, religious masterpieces of the Middle Ages vie with the more recent opulence of Art Nouveau and the giants of modern art. New galleries have opened since 1989 with many more temporary exhibitions. There are museums devoted to the history of the state, the city of Prague and its people, many of them housed in buildings that are historical landmarks and works of art in themselves. This map gives some of the highlights, with a detailed overview on pages 40–41.

St George's Conver
Among the fine Bohemia Baroque art on displa is this portrait of Italia gemcutter Dionysi Miseroni and his fami by Karel Škréte

Sternberg Palace
The collection of European art here is outstanding, represented in works such as The Feast of the Rosary by Albrecht Dürer (1506).

The Loreto
The offerings of devout local aristocrats form the basis of this collection of religious decorative art. In 1721 this jewel-encrusted, tree-shaped monstrance was given to the treasury by Countess Wallenstein.

Smetana Museum
The life and work of this 19th-century Czech composer are remembered beside the river that inspired one of his most famous pieces – the Vltava.

Schwarzenberg Palace
The ornate Renaissance palace forms a handsome backdrop to the Museum of Military History's displays of weaponry and memorabilia.

Museum of Decorative Arts
Five centuries of arts and crafts are represented here, with particularly impressive collections of Bohemian glass, graphic art and furniture. This carved and painted chest dates from 1612.

St Agnes of Bohemia Convent
This collection includes the 14th-century Resurrection of Christ *by the Master of the Třeboň Altar.*

Maisel Synagogue
One of the most important collections of Judaica in the world is housed in the Maisel Synagogue and other buildings of the State Jewish Museum. The displays include religious artefacts, furnishings and books. This illuminated page is from the manuscript of the Pesach Haggadah *of 1728.*

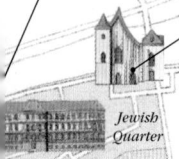

National Museum
The vast skeleton of a whale dominates the other exhibits in one of seven grand halls devoted to zoology. The museum's other displays include fine collections of minerals and meteorites.

Dvořák Museum
This viola, which belonged to the influential 19th-century Czech composer, is among the personal effects and musical scores on display in the charming Michna Summer Palace.

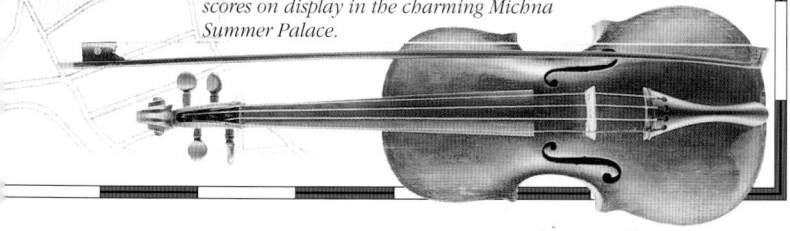

Exploring the Museums and Galleries

Carved figure on façade of the Museum of Decorative Arts

The city's museums give a fascinating insight into the history of the Czechs and of Prague's Jewish population. Also a revelation to visitors unfamiliar with the culture is the art of the Gothic and Baroque periods and of the 19th-century Czech National Revival. The major museums and galleries are cramped for space, but plans are under way to put more of their collections on show in the near future.

CZECH PAINTING AND SCULPTURE

The most important and wide-ranging collection in Prague is that of the National Gallery. Its holdings of Czech art are shown at three venues: medieval art at **St Agnes's Convent**; works dating from the 16th to 18th centuries at **St George's Convent**; and 19th to 20th-century art at the Trades Fair Palace.

The **Picture Gallery of Prague Castle** is a reminder of Emperor Rudolph II's once-great collection. Alongside the paintings are documents and other evidence of just how splendid the original collection must have been.

For the best of the Castle's Bohemian art, you must visit the Renaissance and Baroque works at St George's Convent. These include examples by Baroque masters Karel Škréta and Petr Brandl. Also within the Castle but currently without a permanent display space is the St Vitus Treasure, a collection of religious pieces including a Madonna from the School of Master Theodoric.

Centuries of Czech sculpture are housed in the Lapidarium at the **Exhibition Ground**. Among its exhibits is statuary formerly found on the Charles Bridge, and the Marian pillar that used to stand in the Old Town Square.

The collection at the **St Agnes of Bohemia Convent** includes Bohemian and central European Gothic painting and sculpture, including panels painted for Charles IV by Master Theodoric. Works by 19th- and 20th-century Prague artists can be seen at the Prague Gallery. Its branches include the Baroque **Troja Palace**, where the architecture makes a great backdrop. Exhibitions are drawn from the gallery's collection of 3,000 paintings, 1,000 statues and 4,000 prints.

The superb Centre for Modern and Contemporary Art at **Trades Fair Palace** represents almost every 19th- and 20th-century artistic movement. Romanticism and Art Nouveau are both represented, as are the understandably popular 1920s figures of Otto Gutfreund. The development of such groundbreaking groups as Osma, Devětsil, Skupina 42 and the 12.15 group is also strikingly well documented.

Commerce by Otto Gutfreund (1923), Trades Fair Palace

14th-century *Madonna Aracoeli*, St Vitus Treasure, Prague Castle

EUROPEAN PAINTING AND SCULPTURE

Prague also offers visitors an opportunity to view an exceptional range of masterpieces by Europe's finest artists from antiquity to the 18th century, at **Sternberg Palace**.

The most treasured work in the collection is the *Feast of the Rosary* by Albrecht Dürer, but other equally delightful works include many by 17th-century Dutch masters such as Rubens and Rembrandt.

The Centre for Modern and Contemporary Art at **Trades Fair Palace** has an outstanding collection of Picassos and some fine Rodin bronzes, as well as examples of work from almost every Impressionist, Post-Impressionist and Fauvist. Three notable self-portraits are those of Paul Gauguin (*Bonjour Monsieur Gauguin*, 1889), Henri Rousseau (1890) and Pablo Picasso (1907). Modern German and Austrian painting is also on show, with works by Gustav Klimt and Egon Schiele. The *Dance of Life*, by Norwegian Edvard Munch, is considered greatly influential upon Czech avant-garde art.

The other main venue for European art is the **Picture Gallery of Prague Castle**, which focuses on European painters of the 16th to 18th centuries. As well as Titian's superb *The Toilet of a Young Lady*, there are also works in the collection by Rubens and Tintoretto.

MUSIC

Two Czech composers merit their own museums, as does Prague's much-loved visitor, Mozart. The **Smetana Museum**, **Dvořák Museum** and **Mozart Museum** all contain personal memorabilia, musical scores and correspondence. In the summer, concerts are held on the terrace of the Mozart Museum.

The Museum of Musical Instruments, at Újezd 40, Prague 1 (257 53 34 59), has many rare and historic instruments, and a number of scores by composers such as Josef Haydn.

HISTORY

The historical collections of the **National Museum** are held at the main Wenceslas Square building, and at Prague Castle. The artefacts at Prague Castle are housed in the **Lobkowicz Palace** and focus on Czech life and culture.The **Prague Museum** centres on the history of the city, with period rooms, historical prints and a model of Prague in the 19th century, made of paper and wood by the lithographer Antonín Langweil.

A branch of the museum at Výtoň, on the banks of the Vltava, depicts the way of life of a former settlement. Another at Vyšehrad records the history of this royal seat.

The exquisite Renaissance building of **Schwarzenberg Palace** is a fine setting for the battle charts, weaponry, uniforms and regalia of the Museum of Military History, housed here since 1945.

The Jewish Museum is made up of various sites in the Jewish Quarter, including the **High Synagogue, Maisel Synagogue** and the **Old Jewish Cemetery**. Among its collections are holy artefacts taken from other Jewish communities and brought to Prague by the Nazis as part of a chilling plan for a museum of "an extinct race". Another moving display is of drawings made by children who were imprisoned in the Terezín concentration camp.

DECORATIVE ARTS

With glassware spanning centuries, from medieval to modern, porcelain and pewterware, furniture and textiles, books and posters, the **Museum of Decorative Arts** in the Jewish Quarter is one of Prague's best, but only a small selection of its holdings is on show. Look out for specialized temporary exhibitions mounted either at the museum itself or at other venues in Prague.

Many other museums have examples of the decorative arts, ranging from grandiose monstrances – including one with 6,222 diamonds – in the treasury of **The Loreto** to simple everyday furnishings in the **Prague Museum**. There is also a fascinating collection of pre-Columbian artefacts from Central America in the **Náprstek Museum**.

Bohemian Baroque glass goblet (1730), Museum of Decorative Arts

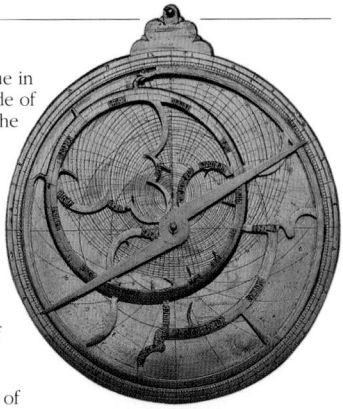

16th-century astrolabe from the National Technical Museum

SCIENCE AND TECHNOLOGY

A vast exhibition hall holds the transport section of the **National Technical Museum**. Ranks of vintage cars, motorcycles and steam engines fill the space, and over them hang examples of early flying machines. Other sections in the museum trace the progress of sciences such as electronics. Visitors even have the opportunity to tour a reconstruction of a coal mine. There is also a fascinating astronomy exhibition.

FINDING THE MUSEUMS AND GALLERIES

Dvořák Museum *p154*
Exhibition Ground *p162*
High Synagogue *p85*
Kampa Museum of Modern Art *p135*
Lobkowicz Palace *p99*
The Loreto *pp116–17*
Maisel Synagogue *p90*
Mozart Museum *p160*
Museum of Decorative Arts *p84*
Museum of Music *p141*
Náprstek Museum *p75*
National Technical Museum *p162*
National Museum *p147*
Old Jewish Cemetery *pp86–7*
Picture Gallery of Prague Castle *p98*
Prague Museum *p161*
St Agnes of Bohemia *pp92–3*
St George's Convent *pp106–9*
Schwarzenberg Palace *p118*
Smetana Museum *p79*
Sternberg Palace *pp112–15*
Trades Fair Palace *pp164–5*
Troja Palace *pp166–7*
Zbraslav Monastery *p163*

Prague's Best: Churches and Synagogues

The religious buildings of Prague vividly record the city's changing architectural styles, and many are treasure houses of religious art. But they also reflect Prague's times of religious and political strife, the lives of its people, its setbacks and growth as a city. This map features highlights of their architecture and art, with a more detailed overview on pages 44–5.

St George's Basilica
St George, sword raised to slay the dragon, is portrayed in this late-Gothic relief, set above the doorway of the magnificent early Renaissance south portal.

St Vitus's Cathedral
The jewel of the cathedral is the Chapel of St Wenceslas. Its walls are decorated with semi-precious stones, gilding and frescoes. Elizabeth of Pomerania, the fourth and last wife of Charles IV, is shown at prayer in the fresco above the Gothic altar.

The Loreto
This shrine to the Virgin Mary has been a place of pilgrimage since 1626. Each hour, its Baroque clock tower chimes a hymn on the carillon of 27 bells.

Church of St Thomas
The skeleton of the martyr St Just rests in a glass coffin below a Crucifixion by Antonín Stevens, one of several superb works of religious art in this church.

Church of St Nicholas
In the heart of the Little Quarter, this is Prague's finest example of High Baroque. The dome over the high altar is so lofty that early worshippers feared it would collapse.

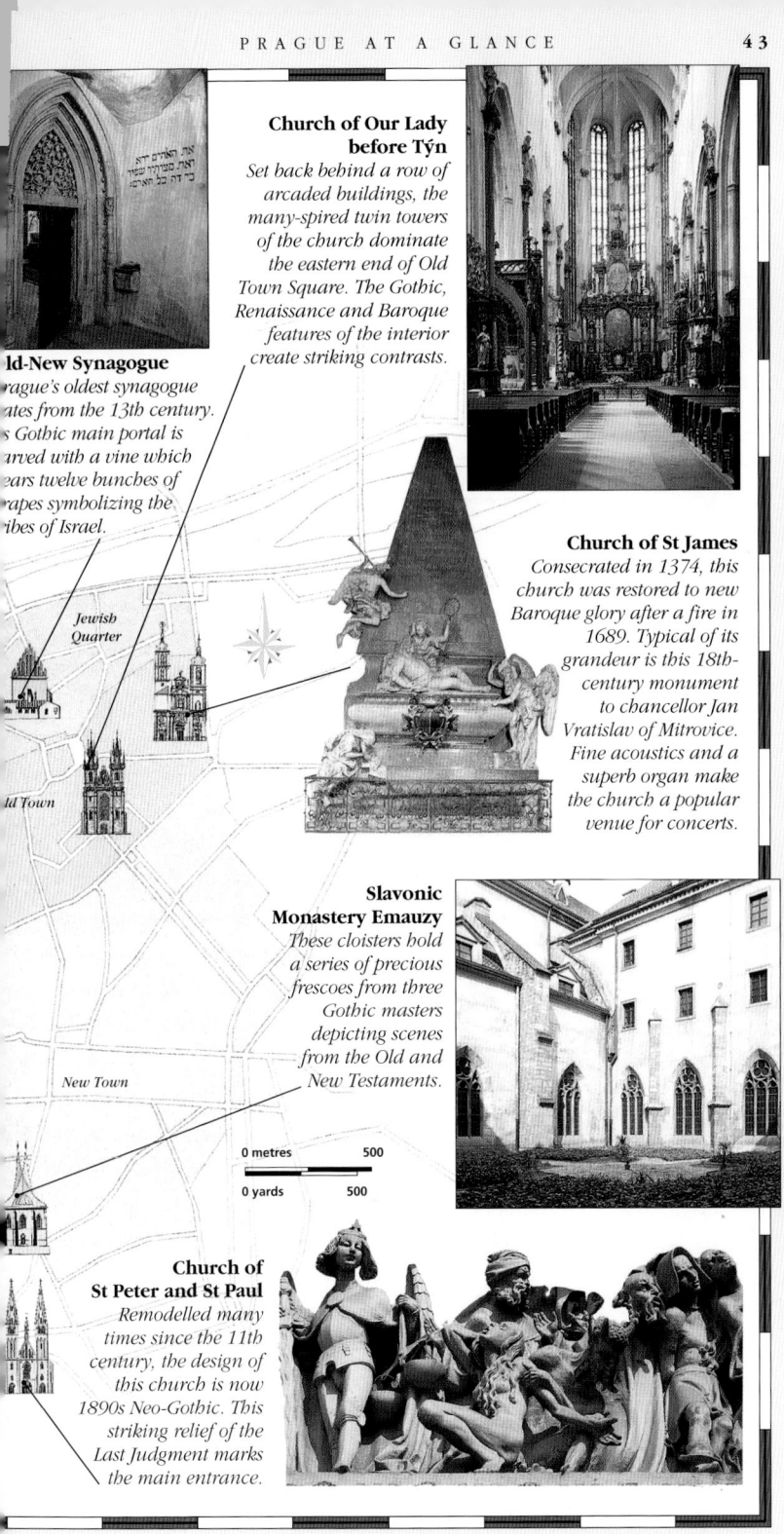

ld-New Synagogue
rague's oldest synagogue ates from the 13th century. s Gothic main portal is arved with a vine which ears twelve bunches of rapes symbolizing the ribes of Israel.

Church of Our Lady before Týn
Set back behind a row of arcaded buildings, the many-spired twin towers of the church dominate the eastern end of Old Town Square. The Gothic, Renaissance and Baroque features of the interior create striking contrasts.

Church of St James
Consecrated in 1374, this church was restored to new Baroque glory after a fire in 1689. Typical of its grandeur is this 18th-century monument to chancellor Jan Vratislav of Mitrovice. Fine acoustics and a superb organ make the church a popular venue for concerts.

Slavonic Monastery Emauzy
These cloisters hold a series of precious frescoes from three Gothic masters depicting scenes from the Old and New Testaments.

Church of St Peter and St Paul
Remodelled many times since the 11th century, the design of this church is now 1890s Neo-Gothic. This striking relief of the Last Judgment marks the main entrance.

Exploring Churches and Synagogues

Religious building began in Prague in the 9th century, reaching its zenith during the reign of Charles IV *(see pp24–5)*. The remains of an 11th-century synagogue have been found, but during the 19th-century clearance of the overcrowded Jewish ghetto three synagogues were lost. Many churches were damaged during the Hussite rebellions *(see pp26–7)*. The political regime of the 20th century also took its toll, but now churches and synagogues have been reclaimed and restored, with many open to visitors.

Altar, Capuchin Monastery

ROMANESQUE

Three reasonably well-preserved Romanesque rotundas, dating from the 11th and 12th centuries, still exist in Prague. The oldest is the **St Martin's Rotunda**; the others are the rotundas of the Holy Rood and of St Longinus. All three are tiny, with naves only 6 m (20 ft) in diameter.

By far the best-preserved and most important Romanesque church is **St George's Basilica**, founded in 920 by Prince Vratislav I. Extensive reconstruction was carried out after a fire in 1142, but its chancel, with some exquisite frescoes on its vaulting, is a Late-Romanesque gem.

The **Strahov Monastery**, founded in 1142 by Prince Vladislav II *(see pp22–3)*, has retained its Romanesque core in spite of fire, wars and extensive renovation.

11th-century Romanesque Rotunda of St Martin in Vyšehrad

GOTHIC

Gothic architecture, with its ribbed vaulting, flying buttresses and pointed arches, reached Bohemia in about 1230 and was soon adopted into religious architecture.

The first religious building in Gothic style was the **St Agnes of Bohemia Convent**, founded in 1233 by Wenceslas I's sister, Agnes. Prague's oldest synagogue, the **Old-New Synagogue**, built in 1270, is rather different in style to the churches but is still a suberb example of Early-Gothic.

The best example of Prague Gothic is **St Vitus's Cathedral**. Its fine tracery and towering nave epitomize the style. Other notable Gothic churches are **Our Lady before Týn** and **Our Lady of the Snows**.

Important for its historical significance is the reconstructed Gothic **Bethlehem Chapel** where Jan Hus *(see p27)* preached for 10 years.

The superb Gothic frescoes found in abundance at the **Slavonic Monastery Emauzy**, were badly damaged in World War II, but have been restored.

High, Gothic windows at the east end of St Vitus's Cathedral

RENAISSANCE

In the 1530s the influence of Italian artists living in Prague sparked the city's Renaissance movement. The style is more clearly seen in secular than religious building. The Late-Renaissance period, under Rudolph II (1576–1611), offers the best remaining examples.

DOMES AND SPIRES

The domes and spires of Prague's churches are the city's main landmarks, as the view from the many vantage points will confirm. You will see a variety of spires, towers and domes: Gothic and Neo-Gothic soar skywards, while Baroque often have rounded cupolas and onion domes. The modern top of the 14th-century Slavonic Monastery, added after the church was struck in a World War II air raid, is a rare example of modernist religious architecture in Prague. Its sweeping, intersecting twin spires are a bold reinterpretation of Gothic themes, and a striking addition to the city's skyline.

Church of Our Lady before Týn (1350–1511)

Church of St Nicholas in Little Quarter (1750)

The **High Synagogue** and the **Pinkas Synagogue** retain strong elements of the style: the former in its 1586 exterior, the latter in the reworking of an original Gothic building.

The Church of St Roch in the **Strahov Monastery** is probably the best example of Late-Renaissance "Mannerism".

Renaissance-influenced vaulting, Pinkas Synagogue (1535)

BAROQUE

The Counter-Reformation *(see pp30–31)* inspired the building of new churches and the revamping of existing ones for a period of 150 years. Prague's first Baroque church was **Our Lady Victorious**, built in 1611–13. **St Nicholas** in the Little Quarter took almost 60 years to build. Its lush interior and frescoed vault make it Prague's most important Baroque building, followed by **The Loreto** (1626–1750), adjoining the **Capuchin Monastery**. The father-and-son team, Christoph and Kilian Ignaz Dientzenhofer designed both buildings, and **St John on the Rock** and **St Nicholas** in the Old Town.

A special place in Prague's history was occupied by the Jesuit **Clementinum**. This influential university's church was the **Holy Saviour**. The Baroque style is closely linked with Jesuit teachings: Kilian Ignaz Dientzenhofer was educated here.

Klausen Synagogue (now the Jewish Museum) was built in 1689 with Baroque stuccoed barrel vaults.

Many early buildings were given Baroque facelifts. The Gothic nave of **St Thomas** has Baroque vaulting, and the once-Gothic **St James** went Baroque after a fire in 1689.

Nave ceiling of the Church of St Nicholas in the Little Quarter

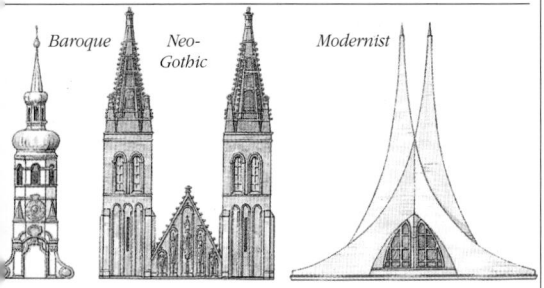

Loreto (1725) **St Peter and St Paul (1903)** **Slavonic Monastery Emauzy (1967)**

19th-century Neo-Gothic portal, Church of St Peter and St Paul

NEO-GOTHIC

During the height of the 19th-century Gothic Revival *(see pp32–3)*, **St Vitus's Cathedral** was completed, in accordance with the original Gothic plan. Work by Josef Mocker, the movement's leader, aroused controversy but his **St Peter and St Paul** at Vyšehrad is a well-loved landmark. The triple-naved basilica of **St Ludmilla** in Náměstí Míru was also designed by Mocker.

FINDING THE CHURCHES AND SYNAGOGUES

St Agnes of Bohemia *pp92–3*
Bethlehem Chapel *p75*
Capuchin Monastery *p118*
Clementinum *p79 (see also History of Prague pp28–9)*
St George's Basilica *p98*
High Synagogue *p85*
Holy Saviour *(see Knights of the Cross Square p79)*
St James *p65*
St John on the Rock *p153*
Klausen Synagogue *p85*
Loreto *pp116–17*
St Ludmilla *(see Náměstí Míru p161)*
St Martin's Rotunda *(see Vyšehrad Walk p180)*
St Nicholas in the Little Quarter *pp128–9*
St Nicholas in the Old Town *p70*
Old-New Synagogue *pp88–9*
Our Lady before Týn *p70*
Our Lady of the Snows *p146*
Our Lady Victorious *p130*
St Peter and St Paul *(see Vyšehrad Walk p181)*
Pinkas Synagogue *p84*
Slavonic Monastery Emauzy *p150*
Strahov Monastery *p120–21*
St Thomas *p127*
St Vitus's Cathedral *pp100–3*

Prague's Best: Palaces and Gardens

Prague's palaces and gardens are among the most important historical and architectural monuments in the city. Many palaces house museums or galleries *(see pp38–41)*, and some are concert venues. The gardens range from formal, walled oases with fountains and grand statuary, to open spaces beyond the city centre. This map features some of the best palaces and gardens, with a detailed overview on pages 48–9.

Royal Garden
Though redesigned in the 19th century, the Renaissance garden preserves much of its original character. Historic statues still in place include a pair of Baroque lions (1730) guarding the entrance.

Belvedere
The Singing Fountain (1568) stan in front of the exquisite Renaissan summer palace.

South Gardens
Starting life as the Castle's defensive bastions, these gardens afford a wonderful view of Prague. First laid out as a park in 1891, their present design was landscaped by Josip Plečnik 40 years later.

Wallenstein Palace
Built in 1624–30 for Duke Albrecht of Wallenstein, this vast Baroque palace was intended to outshine Prague Castle. Over 20 houses and a town gate were demolished to make room for the palace and garden. This Fountain of Venus (1599), stands in front of the arches of the sala terrena.

Wallenstein Garden
The garden statues are copies of 17th-century bronzes. The originals were plundered by the Swedes in 1648.

Prague Castle and Hradčany

0 metres 500

0 yards 500

Little Quarter

Kolowrat-Černín Garden
In the Baroque period, several palace gardens with spectacular terraces were laid out on the hillside below Prague Castle.

Kinský Palace
The Kinský coat of arms adorns the pink and white stuccoed façade designed by Kilian Ignaz Dientzenhofer. The Rococo palace is now part of the National Gallery.

Clam-Gallas Palace
Four giant statues of Hercules (c1715) by Matthias Bernard Braun show the hero straining to support the weight of the massive Baroque front portals of the palace.

Michna Summer Palace
This charming villa was designed by Kilian Ignaz Dientzenhofer in 1712. It now houses the Dvořák Museum. The garden's sculptural decorations are from the workshop of Antonín Braun.

Kampa Island
A tranquil waterside park was created on the island after the destruction of its original gardens in World War II.

Exploring the Palaces and Gardens

Statue on Kampa Island

Prague boasts an amazing number of palaces and gardens, spanning centuries. Comparatively few palaces were lost to the ravages of war. Instead, they tended to evolve in style during restoration or enlargement. Palace gardens became fashionable in the 17th century, but could only be laid out where there was space, such as below Prague Castle. More vulnerable to change, most have been relandscaped several times. In the 19th century, and again after 1989, many of the larger parks and private gardens were opened up to the public.

MEDIEVAL PALACES

The oldest palace in Prague is the **Royal Palace** at Prague Castle. In the basement is the Romanesque ground floor, started in about 1135. It has been rebuilt many times, particularly between the 14th and 16th centuries. The heart of the Palace, Vladislav Hall, dates from the 1490s and is late Gothic in structure. Less well known is the **Palace of the Lords of Kunštát**. Here, the vaulted ground floor of the 13th-century building survives as the basement of a later Gothic structure.

RENAISSANCE PALACES

One of the most beautiful Renaissance buildings in Prague is the 16th-century **Schwarzenberg Palace**. The work of Italian architects, its façade is entirely covered with geometric, two-tone *sgraffito* designs. Italians also worked on the **Belvedere**. Its graceful arcades and columns, all covered with rich reliefs, make this one of the finest Renaissance buildings north of the Alps. The **Martinic Palace**, built in 1563, was the first example of late-Renaissance building in Prague. Soon after came the **Lobkowicz Palace**. Its terracotta relief-decorated windows and plaster *sgraffito* have survived later Baroque modifications. The huge **Archbishop's Palace** was given a later Rococo façade over its Renaissance structure.

Bronze Singing Fountain in the Royal Garden by the Belvedere

Southern façade of Troja Palace and its formal gardens

BAROQUE PALACES

Many palaces were built in the Baroque style, and examples of all its phases still exist in Prague. A handsome, if ostentatious, early Baroque

DECORATIVE PORTALS AND GATES

The elaborate gates and portals of Prague's palaces are among the most beautiful and impressive architectural features in the city. Gothic and Renaissance portals have often survived, even where the buildings themselves have been destroyed or modified by renovations in a later architectural style. The period of most prolific building was the Baroque, and distinctive portals from this time can be seen framing many a grand entrance around the city. Statues of giants, heroes and mythological figures are often depicted holding up the doorways. These were not merely decorative but acted as an integral element of support.

Gateway to Court of Honour of Prague Castle (1768)

example is the **Wallenstein Palace**. Similar ostentation is evident in the **Černín Palace**, one of Prague's most monumental buildings. The mid-Baroque had two strands, one opulent and Italianate, the other formal and French or Viennese in influence. **Troja Palace** and **Michna Summer Palace** are in Italian villa style while the **Sternberg Palace** on Hradčanské náměstí is more Viennese in style. Troja was designed in 1679 by Jean-Baptiste Mathey, who, like the Dientzenhofers *(see p129)*, was a master of the Baroque. The pairs of giants on the portals of the **Clam-Gallas Palace**, and the **Morzin Palace** in Nerudova Street, are a popular Baroque motif. The **Kinský Palace** is a superb Rococo design by Kilian Ignaz Dientzenhofer.

GARDENS

The finest of Prague's palace gardens, such as the **Wallenstein Garden**, are in the Little Quarter. Though the style of Wallenstein Palace is Early Baroque, the garden still displays the geometric formality of the Renaissance, also preserved in the **Royal Garden** behind Prague Castle. The **South Gardens** on the Castle's old ramparts were redesigned in the 1920s.

Many more gardens were laid out in the 17th and 18th centuries, when noble families vied with each other to have fine winter residences in the Little Quarter below the Castle. Many are now the grounds of embassies, but others have been opened to the public. The **Ledebour Garden** has been combined with two neighbouring gardens. Laid out on a steep hillside, the **Kolowrat-Černín Garden**, in particular, makes ingenious use of pavilions, stairs and terraces from which there are wonderful views of the city. The **Vrtba Garden**, landscaped on the site of former vineyards, is a similar Baroque creation with statues and splendid views. Former palace gardens were also used to create a park on **Kampa Island**.

The many old gardens and orchards on Petřín Hill have been transformed into the large public area of **Petřín Park**. Another former orchard is **Vojan Park**, laid out by archbishops in the 13th century. The **Botanical Gardens** are one of the few areas of green open to the public in the New Town.

Generally, the larger parks are situated further out of the city. **Stromovka** was a royal deer park, while **Letná Park** was developed in 1858 on the open space of Letná Plain.

The Royal Garden of Prague Castle, planted with spring flowers

Ancient trees in Stromovka

Troja Palace (c1703)

Clam-Gallas Palace (c1714)

WHERE TO FIND THE PALACES AND GARDENS

Archbishop's Palace *p111*
Belvedere *p110–11*
Botanical Gardens *p153*
Černín Palace *p119*
Clam-Gallas Palace *p78*
Kampa Island *p131*
Kinský Palace *p70*
Kolowrat-Černín Garden
see Ledebour Garden p135
Ledebour Garden *p135*
Letná Park *p161*
Lobkowicz Palace *p99*
Martinic Palace *p118*
Michna Summer Palace
see Dvořák Museum p154
Morzin Palace
see Nerudova Street 130
Palace of the Lords of Kunštát *p78*
Petřín Park *p141*
Royal Garden *p111*
Royal Palace *pp104–5*
Schwarzenberg Palace *p118*
South Gardens *p110*
Sternberg Palace *pp112–13*
Stromovka *p162*
Troja Palace *pp166–7*
Vojan Park *p135*
Vrtba Garden *p130*
Wallenstein Palace and Garden *p126*

PRAGUE THROUGH THE YEAR

Springtime in Prague sees the city burst into colour as its gardens start to bloom. Celebrations begin with the Prague Spring Music Festival. In summer, visitors are entertained by street performers and the city's glorious gardens come into their own. When the weather begins to turn cooler, Prague hosts the International Jazz Festival.

Painted Easter egg

The year often draws to a close with snow on the streets. The ball season starts in December, and in the coldest months, most events are held indoors. At Prague Castle, an all-year-round attraction is the changing of the guard around midday. For details of activities, check the listings magazines *(see p219)* or the Prague Information Service *(see p218)*.

Concert at Wallenstein Palace during the Prague Spring Music Festival

SPRING

As Prague sees its first rays of spring sunshine, the city comes alive. A mass of colours, blooms and cultural events makes this one of the most exciting times of the year to visit. The city's blossoming parks and gardens open their gates again, after the colder months of winter. During April the temperatures rise and an entertainment programme begins – dominated by the Prague Spring Music Festival.

EASTER

Easter Monday *(dates vary)* is a public holiday. Easter is observed as a religious holiday but it is also associated with a bizarre pagan ritual in which Czech men beat their women with willow sticks in order to keep them fertile during the coming year. The women retaliate by throwing water over their male tormentors. Peace is finally restored when the women present the men with a painted egg. Church services are held during the entire Easter period *(see p235)*.

MARCH

The Prague-Prčice March *(third Saturday of March)*. Thousands of people walk to the small town of Prčice in celebration of spring.

APRIL

Boat trips *(1 April)*. A number of boats begin trips up and down the Vltava.
Witch-burning *(30 April)*, at the Exhibition Ground *(see p162)*. Concerts accompany this 500-year-old tradition where old brooms are burnt on bonfires, in a symbolic act to rid nature of evil spirits.

MAY

Labour Day *(1 May)*. Public holiday celebrated with numerous cultural events.
Opening day of Prague's gardens *(1 May)*. Regular summer concerts are held in many parks and gardens.
Anniversary of Prague Uprising *(5 May)*. At noon sirens are sounded for one minute. Flowers are laid at the commemorative plaques of those who died *(see p34)*.
Day of Liberation from Fascism *(8 May)*. Public holiday for VE day. Wreaths are laid on the graves of soldiers at Olšany cemeteries.
Prague International Book Fair *(second week in May)*, Palace of Culture *(see p176)*. The best of Czech and international authors.
Prague International Marathon *(third week in May)*.

THE PRAGUE SPRING MUSIC FESTIVAL

This international festival presents a busy programme of concerts, ballet and opera from 12 May to 3 June. Music lovers can hear a huge selection of music played by some of the best musicians in the world. The main venue is the Rudolfinum *(see p84)* but others include churches and palaces – some of which are only open to the public on these occasions. The festival begins on the anniversary of Bedřich Smetana's death *(see p79)*. A service is held at his grave in Vyšehrad *(see p180)*, and in the evening there is a concert at the Municipal House *(see p64)* where musicians perform his most famous work, *Má Vlast* (My Country). The festival also ends here, with Beethoven's Ninth Symphony.

Bedřich Smetana

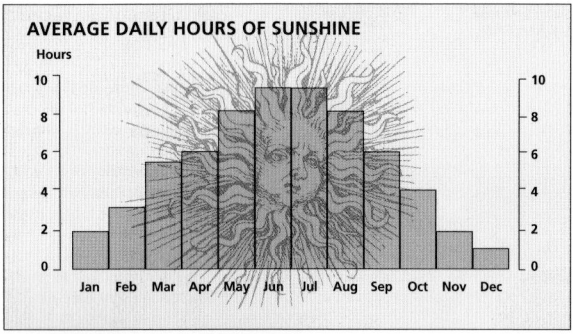

Sunshine Chart
Prague's longest and bottest days fall between May and August. At the height of summer, daylight starts at 5am. The snow-covered city looks stunning on a sunny winter's day. But sunny days can be spoiled by thick smog (see p53).

Czechs and tourists enjoying the beauty of Vyšehrad Park on a sunny afternoon

SUMMER

Summer arrives with high temperatures, frequent, sometimes heavy, showers and thousands of visitors. This is a beautiful, if busy, time to visit. Every weekend, Czechs set out for the country to go hiking in the surrounding hills or stay in country cottages. Those remaining in Prague visit the reservoirs and lakes *(see p213)*, just outside the city to try and escape the heat. There is a wealth of entertainment on offer as culture moves into the open air taking over the squares, streets and gardens. Street performers, buskers and classical orchestras all help to keep visitors entertained. Many cafés have tables outside allowing you to quench your thirst while watching the fun.

JUNE

Mayoral Boat Race *(first weekend in June)*. Rowing races are held on the river Vltava, just below Vyšehrad.

Summer Concerts *(throughout the summer)*. Prague's gardens *(see pp46–9)* are the attractive and popular setting for a large number of free classical and brass-band concerts. One of the most famous, and spectacular, outdoor classical concerts is held by Křižík Fountain at the Exhibition Ground *(see p162)*. Full orchestras play to the stunning backdrop of coloured lights and water, synchronized to the music by computer.
Anniversary of the Murder of Reinhard Heydrich's Assassins *(18 June)*. A mass is held in remembrance at the Church of St Cyril and St Methodius *(see p152)* for those who died there.
Golden Prague *(first week of June)*, Kaiserstein Palace. International TV festival of prize-winning programmes.

Battle Re-enactments *(throughout summer)*, held in Prague's palaces and gardens.
Mozart's Prague *(mid-June to first week in July)*. Celebration of Mozart. International orchestras perform his works at Bertramka *(see p160)* and Lichtenstein Palace.
Dance Prague *(last week in June)*. An international festival of contemporary dance at the National Theatre *(see p156)*.

JULY

Remembrance of the Slavonic Missionaries *(5 July)*. Public holiday in honour of St Cyril and St Methodius *(see p152)*.
Anniversary of Jan Hus's Death *(6 July)*. A public holiday when flowers are laid on his memorial *(see pp26–7)*.

AUGUST

Theatre Island *(all of August)*, Střelecký Island. Czech theatre and puppet festival.

Changing of the Guard at Prague Castle

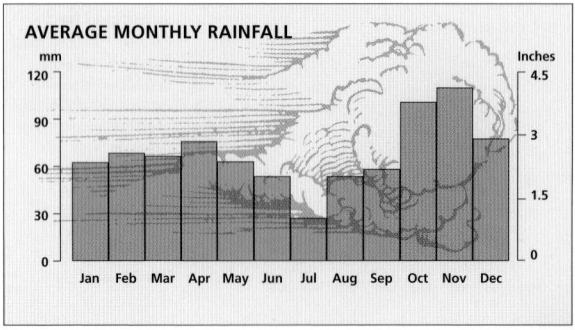

Rainfall Chart
Prague has plenty of rain throughout the year. The wettest months are October and November, but there are frequent light showers in the summer months as well. Winter snowfalls can be quite heavy, but they are rarely severe.

AUTUMN

When the gardens below Prague Castle take on the shades of red and gold, and visitors start to leave, the city gets ready for the cold winter months. This is also the traditional mushroom-gathering season when you encounter people with baskets full of freshly-picked mushrooms. Market places are flooded with fruit and vegetables. The tree-lined slopes above the Vltava take on the beautiful colours of autumn. September and October still have a fair number of warm and sunny days, although November often sees the first snowfalls. Football fans fill the stadiums and the popular steeplechase course at Pardubice reverberates to the cheers of fans.

SEPTEMBER

Prague Autumn *(early September)*, at the Rudolfinum *(see p84)*. An international classical music festival.
The Autumn Fair *(dates vary)*, at the Exhibition Ground *(see p162)*. Fairground, food stalls, puppet shows and theatrical and musical performances.
Kite competitions *(third Sunday in September)*, on Letná Plain in front of Sparta Stadium. Very popular competition for children but open to anyone with a kite.
St Wenceslas *(28 September)*. A sacred music festival is held for the feast of the patron saint.
Bohemia Championship *(last Sunday in September)*. This 10-km (6-mile) road race has been run since 1887. Starts from Běchovice, a suburb of Prague, and ends in Žižkov.

Jazz musicians playing at the International Jazz Festival

OCTOBER

The Great Pardubice Steeplechase *(second Sunday in October)*, held at Pardubice, east of Prague. This horse race has been run since 1874 and is considered to be the most difficult in Europe.
The Locking of the Vltava *(early October)*. Symbolic conclusion of the water sports season, during which the Vltava is locked with a key until the arrival of spring.
International Jazz Festival *(date varies)*, Lucerna Palace. A famous jazz festival, held since 1964, attracts musicians from around the world.
The Day of the Republic *(28 October)*. Despite the splitting up of Czechoslovakia into two separate republics, the founding of the country in 1918 is still a public holiday.

NOVEMBER

Velká Kunratická *(second Sunday in November)*. Popular, but gruelling, cross-country race in Kunratice forest. Anyone can enter.
Celebration of the Velvet Revolution *(17 November)*. Peaceful demonstrations take place around Wenceslas Square *(see pp144–5)*.

A view of St Vitus's Cathedral through autumn trees

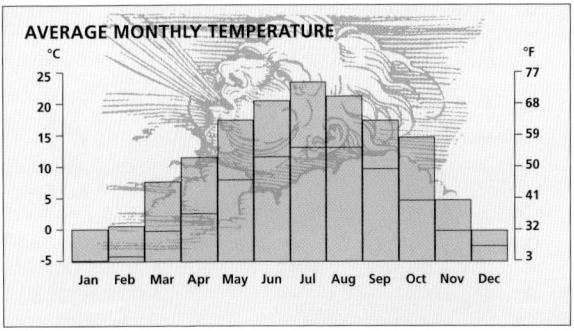

Temperature Chart
The chart shows the average minimum and maximum temperatures for each month in Prague. The summer usually remains comfortably warm, while the winter months can get bitterly cold and temperatures often drop below freezing.

WINTER

If you are lucky enough to catch Prague the morning after a snowfall with the sun shining, the effect is magical. The view over the Little Quarter rooftops with their pristine white covering is a memorable sight. Unfortunately Prague is rarely at its best during the winter months. The weather is changeable. Foggy days with temperatures just above freezing can quickly go down to -5° C (23° F). Pollution and Prague's geographical position in the Vltava basin, lead to smog being trapped just above the city.

As if to try and make up for the winter weather's shortcomings, the theatre season reaches its climax and there are a number of premieres. Balls and dances are held in these cold months. Just before Christmas Eve large barrels containing live carp – which is the traditional Czech Christmas delicacy – appear on the streets. Christmas trees adorn the city, and carol singers can be heard on street corners. Christmas mass is held in most churches and New Year's Eve is celebrated, in time-honoured style, throughout the entire city.

Barrels of the traditional Christmas delicacy, carp, on sale in Prague

View of the Little Quarter rooftops covered in snow

DECEMBER

Christmas markets *(throughout December)*, Můstek metro station, 28. října, Na příkopě, Old Town Square. Stalls sell Christmas decorations, gifts, hot wine, punch and the traditional Czech carp *(see p213)*.
Christmas Eve, Christmas Day and Boxing Day *(24, 25 and 26 December)*. Public holidays. Mass is held in churches throughout the city.
Swimming competitions in the Vltava *(26 December)*. Hundreds of hardened and determined swimmers gather together at the Vltava to swim in temperatures of around 3° C (37° F).
New Year celebrations *(31 December)*. Thousands of people congregate around Wenceslas Square.

JANUARY

New Year's Day *(1 January)*. Public holiday.

FEBRUARY

Dances and Balls *(early February)*.
Matthew Fair *(end of February to beginning of April)*, the Exhibition Ground *(see p176)*. Fairground, stalls and various entertainments.

PUBLIC HOLIDAYS

New Year's Day (1 Jan); **Easter Monday**; **Labour Day** (1 May); **Day of Liberation from Fascism** (8 May); **Remembrance of the Slavonic Missionaries** (5 July); **Anniversary of Jan Hus's death** (6 July); **St Wenceslas** (28 Sep); **Foundation of Czechoslovakia** (28 Oct); **Fall of Communism** (17 Nov); **Christmas Eve, Christmas Day, Boxing Day** (24–26 Dec).

A RIVER VIEW OF PRAGUE

The Vltava river has played a vital part in the city's history (see pp20 –21) and has provided inspiration for artists, poets and musicians throughout the centuries.

Up until the 19th century, parts of the city were exposed to the danger of heavy flooding. To try and alleviate the problem, the river's embankments have been strengthened and raised many times, in order to try to prevent the water penetrating too far (the foundations of today's embankments are made of stone or concrete). During the Middle Ages, year after year of disastrous flooding led to the decision to bury the areas affected under 2 m (6 ft) of earth to try to minimize the damage. Although this strategy was only partially effective, it meant that the ground floors of many Romanesque and Gothic buildings were preserved and can still be seen today *(see pp78–9)*. In 2002 however, a state of emergency was declared as flooding devastated large parts of the city.

Statues on the wrought-iron Čechův Bridge

Despite its destructive side, the Vltava has provided a vital method of transport for the city, as well as a source of income. As technology improved, the river became increasingly important; water mills, weirs and water towers were built. In 1912 a large hydroelectric power plant was built on Štvanice Island, supplying almost a third of Prague's electricity. To make the river navigable, eight dams, a large canal and weirs were constructed along the Slapy-Prague-Mělník stretch, where the Vltava flows into the river Elbe. For the visitor, an excursion on one of the many boats and paddle steamers that travel up and down the river, is well worth it. There are trips to Troja *(see pp166–7)* and as far as Slapy Lake. Catching a boat from one of the piers on the river is one of the best ways of seeing the city.

A view of the steamboat landing stage (přístaviště parníků) on Rašínovo nábřeží

Prague Castle dominates the view along the river. Here it is seen from the boarding point at Čechův most, on the right bank of the Vltava.

Přístaviště lodí Holešovice

Přístaviště lodí Čechův most

See next page

Prague Castle and Hradčany

Jewish Quarter

Old Town

Little Quarter

New Town

V L T A V A

Přístaviště lodí Kampa

Přístaviště parníků (Paroplavební)

0 kilometres 1

0 miles 0.5

KEY

River boat boarding point

Route

Přístaviště lodí Kampa, a jetty in the Little Quarter, is the starting point for some of the organized boat trips along the Vltava.

TOURS

There are frequent trips on the Vltava throughout the summer (April to the end of September). Tours range from trips to Troja Palace in the north of Prague and as far away as Slapy Lake in the south. Dining on board while slowly floating through the city centre is another popular option. These trips can be booked in advance at one of the tour companies. Alternatively, you can go directly to one of the river boat boarding points (see left) and buy tickets for one of the many private ships that land here. (Paroplavební pier is where most trips start.) The cost of each trip varies, depending on the vessel and the length of the excursion, but there are trips to suit almost every budget.

Akasi

Jungmannovo náměstí 9.
Map 3 C5. ***Tel*** *22 22 43 067.*
Fax *22 42 37 235.*
Nápříkopě 3–5. **Map** 3 C4.
Tel & Fax *22 42 36 118.*

Evropská Vodní Doprava

Čechův most, Na Františku.
Map 3 B2. ***Tel*** *22 48 10 030.*
Fax *22 48 10 003.* **www**.evd.cz

Paroplavební (pier)

Rašínovo nábřeží přístaviště.
Map 5 A2. ***Tel*** *22 49 31 013, 22 49 17 640.* ***Fax*** *22 49 13 862.*
www.paroplavba.cz

Prague River Trip

Taking a trip on the Vltava gives you a unique view of many of the city's historic monuments. Although the left bank was the site of the first Slavonic settlement in the 9th century, it was the right bank, heavily populated by merchants and traders, that developed into a thriving and bustling commercial centre, and the tradition continues today. The left bank was never developed as intensively and much of it is still an oasis of parks and gardens. The river's beauty is enhanced by the numbers of swans which have made it their home.

Hanavský Pavilion
This flamboyant cast-iron staircase is part of a pavilion built for the Jubilee Exhibition of 1891.

Little Quarter Bridge Towers
The smaller tower was built in 1158 to guard the entrance to the original Judith Bridge, while the larger one was built on the site of an old Romanesque tower in 1464 (see p136).

Vltava Weir
The thickly-wooded slopes of Petřín Hill tower above one of several weirs on the Vltava. During the 19th century this weir, along with others on this stretch, were built to make the river navigable to ships.

Little Quarter Water Tower
Built in 1560, the tower supplied river water to 57 fountains throughout the Little Quarter.

Kampa

Přístaviště lodi Kampa

Grand Priory Mill

most Legií

Střelecký ostrov

Plavební kanál

The Vltava Statue on the northern tip of Children's Island is where, every year, wreaths are placed in memory of the drowned.

Jiráskův most

Palackého most

Apartment buildings of Art Nouveau design

Železniční most

0 metres 500

0 yards 500

KEY

Tram

River boat boarding point

Boat trip

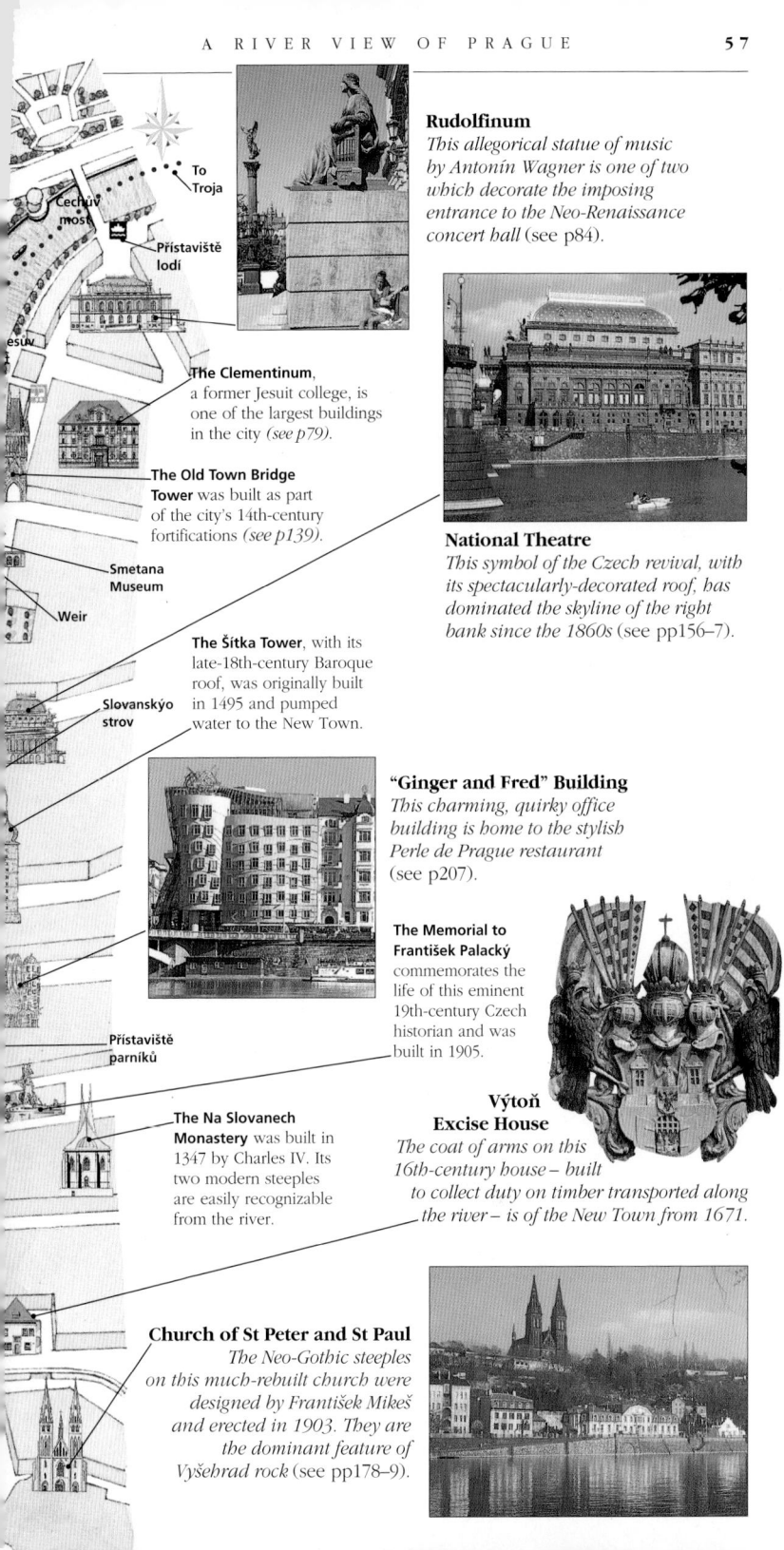

Rudolfinum
This allegorical statue of music by Antonín Wagner is one of two which decorate the imposing entrance to the Neo-Renaissance concert hall (see p84).

The Clementinum, a former Jesuit college, is one of the largest buildings in the city *(see p79)*.

The Old Town Bridge Tower was built as part of the city's 14th-century fortifications *(see p139)*.

National Theatre
This symbol of the Czech revival, with its spectacularly-decorated roof, has dominated the skyline of the right bank since the 1860s (see pp156–7).

The Šítka Tower, with its late-18th-century Baroque roof, was originally built in 1495 and pumped water to the New Town.

"Ginger and Fred" Building
This charming, quirky office building is home to the stylish Perle de Prague restaurant (see p207).

The Memorial to František Palacký commemorates the life of this eminent 19th-century Czech historian and was built in 1905.

Výtoň Excise House
The coat of arms on this 16th-century house – built to collect duty on timber transported along the river – is of the New Town from 1671.

The Na Slovanech Monastery was built in 1347 by Charles IV. Its two modern steeples are easily recognizable from the river.

Church of St Peter and St Paul
The Neo-Gothic steeples on this much-rebuilt church were designed by František Mikeš and erected in 1903. They are the dominant feature of Vyšehrad rock (see pp178–9).

PRAGUE AREA BY AREA

OLD TOWN 60–79

JEWISH QUARTER 80–93

PRAGUE CASTLE AND HRADČANY 94–121

LITTLE QUARTER 122–141

NEW TOWN 142–157

FURTHER AFIELD 158–167

DAY TRIPS 168–171

FOUR GUIDED WALKS 172–181

OLD TOWN

STARÉ MĚSTO

The heart of the city is the Old Town and its central square. In the 11th century the settlements around the Castle spread to the right bank of the Vltava. A market-place in what is now Old Town Square (Staroměstské náměstí) was mentioned for the first time in 1091. Houses and churches sprang up around the square, determining the random network of streets, many of which survive. The area gained the privileges of a town in the 13th century, and, in 1338, a Town Hall. This and other great buildings, such as Clam-Gallas Palace and the Municipal House, reflect the importance of the Old Town.

Physician, Jan Marek (1595–1667)

SIGHTS AT A GLANCE

Churches
- Church of St James 4
- Church of Our Lady before Týn 8
- Church of St Nicholas 11
- Church of St Gall 14
- Church of St Martin in the Wall 15
- Church of St Giles 17
- Bethlehem Chapel 18

Museums and Galleries
- Náprstek Museum 16
- Smetana Museum 24

Historic Streets and Squares
- Celetná Street 3
- *Old Town Square pp66–9* 7
- Mariánské Square 20
- Charles Street 21
- Knights of the Cross Square 25

Historic Monuments and Buildings
- Powder Gate 1
- Municipal House 2
- Carolinum 6
- Jan Hus Monument 10
- *Old Town Hall pp72–4* 12
- House at the Two Golden Bears 13
- Clementinum 23

Theatres
- Estates Theatre 5

Palaces
- Clam-Gallas Palace 19
- Kinský Palace 9
- Palace of the Lords of Kunštát 22

GETTING THERE

Můstek on metro lines A and B and Staroměstská on line A are both handy for the area. Trams do not cross the Old Town, but from Charles Bridge or Náměstí Republiky it is only a short walk to Old Town Square and the other sights.

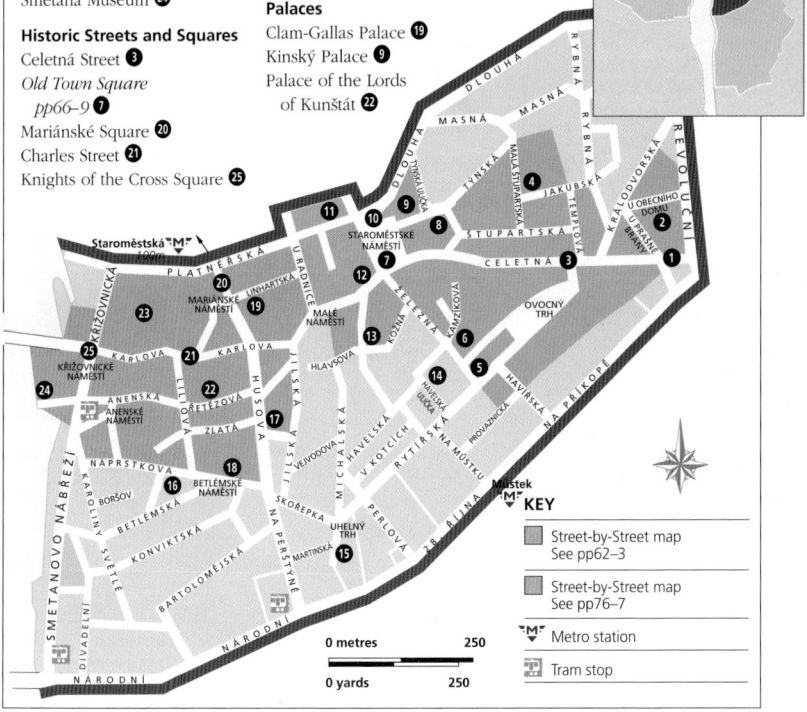

◁ **Café tables and strolling pedestrians in Old Town Square**

Street-by-Street: Old Town (East)

Free of traffic (except for a few horse-drawn carriages) and ringed with historic buildings, Prague's Old Town Square (Staroměstské náměstí) ranks among the finest public spaces in any city. Streets like Celetná and Ovocný trh are also pedestrianized. In summer, café tables spill out onto the cobbles, and though the area draws tourists by the thousands, the unique atmosphere has not yet been destroyed.

Kinský Palace
This stunning Rococo palace now serves as an art gallery ❾

★ Old Town Square
This late-19th-century watercolour by Václav Jansa shows how little the Square has changed in 100 years ❼

Church of St Nicholas
The imposing façade of this Baroque church dominates one corner of Old Town Square ⓫

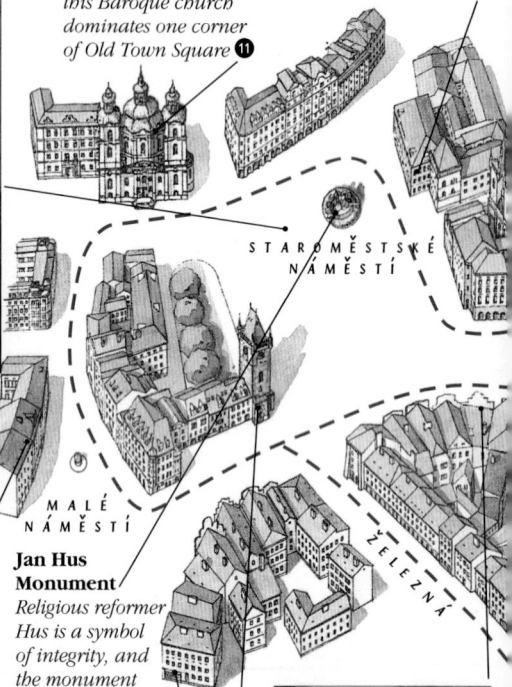

Jan Hus Monument
Religious reformer Hus is a symbol of integrity, and the monument brings together the highest and lowest points in Czech history ❿

U Rotta, now Hotel Rott, is a former ironmonger's shop, decorated with colourful paintings by the 19th-century artist Mikuláš Aleš.

House at the Two Golden Bears
The carved Renaissance portal is the finest of its kind in Prague ⓭

★ Old Town Hall
The famous astronomical clock draws a crowd of visitors every hour ⓬

The Štorch house has painted decoration based on designs by Mikuláš Aleš showing St Wenceslas on horseback.

0 metres 100
0 yards 100

KEY

- - - Suggested route

Church of Our Lady before Týn
The church's Gothic steeples are the Old Town's most distinctive landmark ❽

LOCATOR MAP
See Street Finder, maps 3–4

Church of St James
This wooden Pietà, on the main altar, was made in the 15th century ❹

★ Municipal House
This Art Nouveau building is a popular concert venue ❷

Powder Gate
This much-restored Gothic gate is a relic of when there was a royal palace here at the entrance to the Old Town ❶

Estates Theatre
The theatre featured in director Miloš Forman's film Amadeus ❺

Ovocný trh was Prague's fruit market.

Celetná Street
This ornamental Baroque plaque is the sign of the House at the Black Sun ❸

Carolinum
A magnificently carved Oriel window projects from the oldest surviving part of the Carolinum university – founded by Charles IV in the 14th century ❻

STAR SIGHTS

★ Old Town Square

★ Old Town Hall

★ Municipal House

Powder Gate ❶

PRAŠNÁ BRÁNA

Náměstí Republiky. **Map** 4 D3. *Náměstí Republiky.* *5, 8, 14.* ***Open*** *Apr–Oct: 10am–6pm daily.*

There has been a gate here since the 11th century, when it formed one of the 13 entrances to the Old Town. In 1475, King Vladislav II laid the foundation stone of the New Tower, as it was to be known. A coronation gift from the city council, the gate was modelled on Peter Parler's Old Town bridge tower built a century earlier. The gate had little defensive value; its rich sculptural decoration was intended to add prestige to the adjacent palace of the Royal Court. Building was halted eight years later when the king had to flee because of riots. On his return in 1485 he opted for the safety of the Castle. Kings never again occupied the Royal Court.

The gate acquired its present name when it was used to store gunpowder in the 17th century. The sculptural decoration, badly damaged during the Prussian occupation in 1757 and mostly removed soon afterwards, was replaced in 1876.

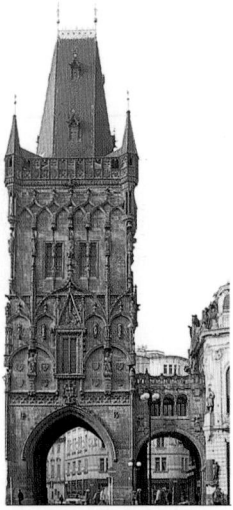

The Powder Gate viewed from outside the Old Town

Karel Špillar's mosaic *Homage to Prague* on Municipal House's façade

Municipal House ❷

OBECNÍ DŮM

Náměstí Republiky 5. **Map** 4 D3. ***Tel*** *22 20 02 111.* *Náměstí Republiky.* *5, 8, 14.* ***Gallery open*** *for exhibitions only, 10am–6pm daily.* *by arrangement.* **www**.obecnidum.cz

Prague's most prominent Art Nouveau building stands on the site of the former Royal Court palace, the King's residence between 1383 and 1485. Abandoned for centuries, what remained was used as a seminary and later as a military college. It was demolished in the early 1900s to be replaced by the present cultural centre (1905–11) with its exhibition halls and auditorium, designed by Antonín Balšánek assisted by Osvald Polívka.

The exterior is embellished with stucco and allegorical statuary. Above the main entrance there is a huge semi-circular mosaic entitled *Homage to Prague* by Karel Špillar. Inside, topped by an impressive glass dome, is Prague's principal concert venue and the core of the entire building, the Smetana Hall, sometimes also used as a ballroom. The interior of the building is decorated with works by leading Czech artists of the first decade of the century, including Alfons Mucha *(see p149)*.

There are numerous smaller halls, conference rooms and offices, as well as cafés and restaurants where visitors can relax and enjoy the centre's flamboyant Art Nouveau decoration at their leisure. On 28 October, 1918, Prague's Municipal House was the scene of the momentous proclamation of the new independent state of Czechoslovakia.

Decorative deta by Alfons Much

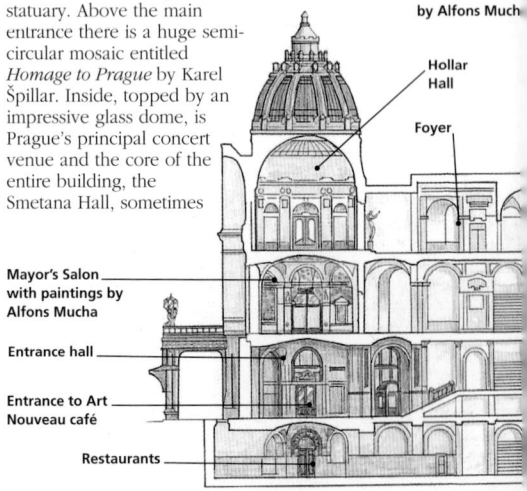

Celetná Street ❸

CELETNÁ ULICE

Map 3 C3. *Náměstí Republiky, Můstek.* **House of the Black Madonna** ***Tel*** *22 42 11 732.* ***Open*** *10am–6pm Tue–Fri.*

One of the oldest streets in Prague, Celetná follows an old trading route from eastern Bohemia. Its name comes from the plaited bread rolls that were first baked here in the Middle Ages. It gained prestige in the 14th century as a section of the Royal Route *(see p172)* used for coronation processions. Foundations of Romanesque and Gothic buildings can be seen in some of the cellars, but most of the houses with their picturesque signs are Baroque remodellings.

At No. 34, the House of the Black Madonna is home to a small but interesting collection of Czech Cubism, including paintings, sculpture, furniture, architectural plans and applied arts.

Church of St James ❹

KOSTEL SV. JAKUBA

Malá Štupartská. **Map** 3 C3. *Můstek, Náměstí Republiky.* ***Open*** *in the season, 10am–noon, 2–3:45pm Mon–Sat.*

This attractive Baroque church was originally the Gothic presbytery of a Minorite monastery. The order (a branch of the Franciscans) was invited to Prague by King Wenceslas I in 1232. It was rebuilt in the Baroque style after a fire in 1689, allegedly started by agents of Louis XIV. Over 20 side altars were added, decorated with works by painters such as Jan Jiří Heinsch, Petr Brandl and Václav Vavřinec Reiner. The tomb of Count Vratislav of Mitrovice (1714–16), designed by Johann Bernhard Fischer von Erlach and executed by sculptor Ferdinand Brokof, is the most beautiful Baroque tomb in Bohemia. The count is said to have been accidentally buried alive – his corpse was later found sitting up in the tomb. Hanging on the right of the entrance is a mummified forearm. It has been there for over 400 years, ever since a thief tried to steal the jewels from the Madonna on the high altar. But the Virgin grabbed his arm and held on so tightly it had to be cut off.

Because of its long nave, the church's acoustics are excellent and many concerts and recitals are given here. There is also a magnificent organ built in 1702.

Baroque organ loft in the Church of St James

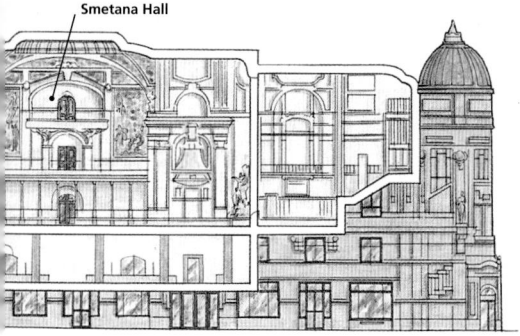

Estates Theatre ❺

STAVOVSKÉ DIVADLO

Ovocný trh 1. **Map** 3 C4. ***Tel*** *22 42 28 503.* *Můstek.* ***Foyer open*** *for performances only.* **www**.narodni-divadlo.cz

Built by Count Nostitz in 1783, the theatre is one of the finest examples of Neo-Classical elegance in Prague. It is a mecca for Mozart fans *(see p220)*. On 29 October 1787, Mozart's opera, *Don Giovanni* had its debut here with Mozart at the piano conducting the orchestra. In 1834 the musical *Fidlovačka* premiered here. One of the songs, *Kde domov můj?* (Where is my Home?), became the Czech national anthem.

Carolinum ❻

KAROLINUM

Ovocný trh 3. **Map** 3 C4. ***Tel*** *22 44 91 111.* *Můstek.* ***Closed*** *to the public.* ***Open*** *for special exhibitions.*

At the core of the university founded by Charles IV in 1348 is the Carolinum. The chapel, arcade and walls still survive, together with a fine oriel window, but in 1945 the courtyard was reconstructed in Gothic style. In the 15th and 16th centuries the university played a leading role in the movement to reform the church. After the Battle of the White Mountain *(see pp30–31)*, the university was taken over by the Jesuits.

Old Town Square ❼

STAROMĚSTSKÉ NÁMĚSTÍ

See pp66–9.

Old Town Square: East and North Sides ❼

STAROMĚSTSKÉ NÁMĚSTÍ

Some of Prague's colourful history is preserved around the Old Town Square in the form of its buildings. On the north side of the Square, the Pauline Monastery is the only surviving piece of original architecture. The east side boasts two superb examples of the architecture of their times: the House at the Stone Bell, restored to its former appearance as a Gothic town palace, and the Rococo Kinský Palace. An array of pastel-coloured buildings completes the Square.

★ House at the Stone Bell
At the corner of the building, the bell is the sign of this medieval town palace.

Kinský Palace
C G Bossi created the elaborate stucco decoration on the façade of this Rococo palace (see p70).

Statues by Ignaz Platzer from 1760–65

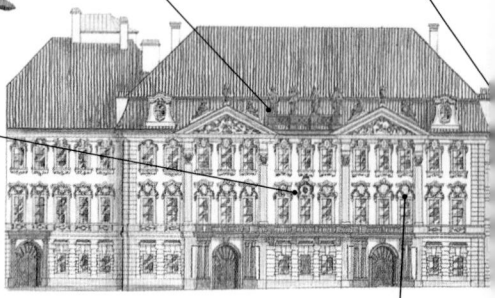

EAST SIDE

Rococo stucco work

NORTH SIDE

★ Church of St Nicholas
Besides its original purpose as a parish church and, later, a Benedictine monastery church, this has served as a garrison church and a concert hall (see p70).

STAR SIGHTS

- ★ Church of Our Lady before Týn
- ★ House at the Stone Bell
- ★ Church of St Nicholas

★ Church of Our Lady before Týn
Astronomer and astrologer Tycho Brahe is buried in Týn Church (see p70).

Týn School
Gothic rib vaulting is a primary feature of this building, which was a school from the 14th to the mid-19th century.

Ministerstvo pro místní rozvoj
Architect Osvald Polívka designed this Art Nouveau building in 1898, with figures of firefighters on the upper façade. It houses the Ministry of Local Development.

Staroměstské náměstí, 1793
The engraving by Filip and František Heger shows the Old Town Square teeming with people and carriages. The Old Town Hall is on the left.

Old Town Square: South Side ❼

STAROMĚSTSKÉ NÁMĚSTÍ

A colourful array of houses of Romanesque or Gothic origin, with fascinating house signs, graces the south side of the Old Town Square. The block between Celetná Street and Železná Street is especially attractive. The Square has always been a busy focal point, and today offers visitors a tourist information centre, as well as a number of restaurants, cafés, shops, and galleries.

FRANZ KAFKA (1883–1924)

The author of two of the most influential novels of the 20th century, *The Trial* and *The Castle*, Kafka spent most of his short life in the Old Town. From 1893 to 1901 he studied in the Golz-Kinský Palace *(see p70)*, where his father later had a shop. He worked as an insurance clerk, but frequented Berta Fanta's literary salon at the Stone Ram, Old Town Square, along with others who wrote in German. Hardly any of his work was published in his lifetime.

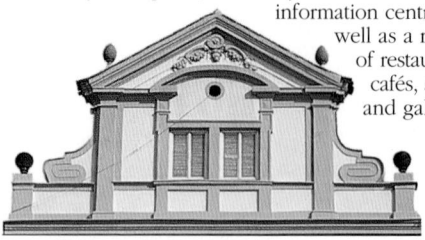

U Lazara (At Lazarus's)
Romanesque barrel vaulting testifies to the house's early origins, though it was rebuilt during the Renaissance. The ground floor houses the Staroměstská restaurace.

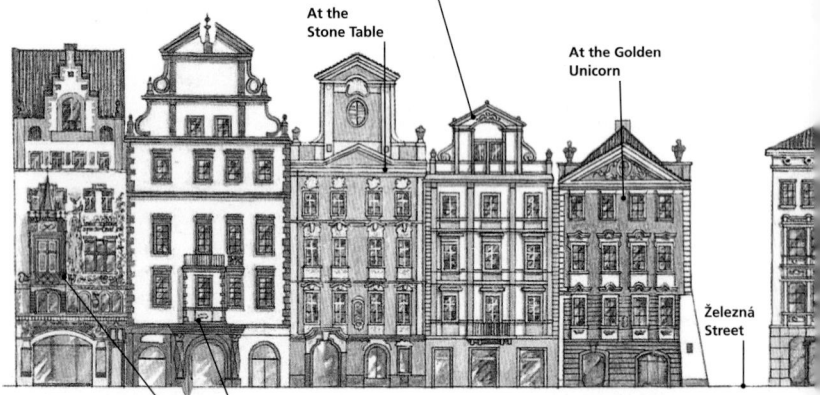

SOUTH SIDE

★ At the Stone Ram
The early-16th-century house sign shows a young maiden with a ram. The house has been referred to as At the Unicorn due to the similarity between the one-horned ram and a unicorn.

★ Štorch House
The late-19th-century painting of St Wenceslas on horseback by Mikuláš Aleš appears on this ornate Neo-Renaissance building, also known as At the Stone Madonna.

STAR SIGHTS

★ Štorch House

★ At the Stone Ram

Melantrichova Passage
Václav Jansa's painting (1898) shows the narrow passageway leading to the Old Town Square.

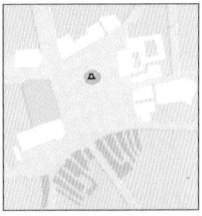

At the Red Fox
A golden Madonna and Child look down from the Baroque façade of an originally Romanesque building.

At The Ox
Named after its 15th-century owner, the burgher Ochs, this house features an early-18th-century stone statue of St Anthony of Padua.

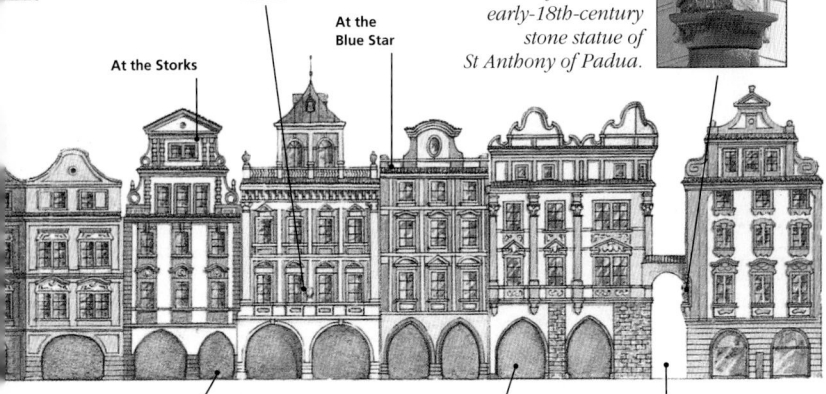

Leopold II's Royal Procession through the Old Town Square in 1791

TIMELINE

1338 Old Town becomes municipality

1735 Church of St Nicholas completed

1948 Klement Gottwald proclaims Communist state from balcony of Golz-Kinský Palace

1300 | 1450 | 1600 | 1750 | 1900

1200 Square is meeting point of trade routes and important market

1365 Building of present Týn Church

1621 Execution of 27 anti-Habsburg leaders in square *(see p31)*

1689 Fire destroys large part of Old Town

1784 Unification of Prague towns

1915 Unveiling of Jan Hus Monument

Hus Monument (detail)

Statue of the Madonna on Our Lady before Týn

Church of Our Lady before Týn 8

KOSTEL MATKY BOŽÍ PŘED TÝNEM

Týnská, Štupartská. **Map** 3 C3. ***Tel*** *22 42 13 475.* *Staroměstská, Můstek.* ***Open*** *9am–noon, 1–2pm Mon–Fri.* ***Closed*** *in winter.* *6pm Wed–Fri, 8am Sat, 9:30am & 9pm Sun.*

Dominating the Old Town Square are the magnificent multiple steeples of this historic church. The present Gothic church was started in 1365 and soon became associated with the reform movement in Bohemia. From the early 15th century until 1620 Týn was the main Hussite church in Prague. The Hussite king, George of Poděbrady, took Utraquist communion *(see Church of St Martin in the Wall p73)* here and had a gold chalice – the Utraquist symbol – mounted on the façade. After 1621 the chalice was melted down to become part of the statue of the Madonna that replaced it.

On the northern side of the church is a beautiful entrance portal (1390) decorated with scenes of Christ's passion. The dark interior has some notable features, including Gothic sculptures of *Calvary*, a pewter font (1414) and a 15th-century Gothic pulpit. Behind the church is the Týn Courtyard, with its numerous architectural styles.

Kinský Palace 9

PALÁC KINSKÝCH

Staroměstské náměstí 12. **Map** 3 C3. ***Tel*** *22 48 10 758.* *Staroměstská.* ***Open*** *10am–6pm Tue–Sun.* **www**.ngprague.cz

This lovely Rococo palace, designed by Kilian Ignaz Dientzenhofer, has a pretty pink and white stucco façade crowned with statues of the four elements by Ignaz Franz Platzer. It was bought from the Golz family in 1768 by Štěpán Kinský, an Imperial diplomat.

In 1948 Communist leader, Klement Gottwald, used the balcony to address a huge crowd of party members – a key event in the crisis that led up to his *coup d'état*. The National Gallery now uses the Kinský Palace for temporary art exhibitions.

Kinský arms on Golz-Kinský Palace

Jan Hus Monument 10

POMNÍK JANA HUSA

Staroměstské náměstí. **Map** 3 B3. *Staroměstská.*

At one end of the Old Town Square stands the massive monument to the religious reformer and Czech hero, Jan Hus *(see pp26–7)*. Hus was burnt at the stake after being pronounced a heretic by the Council of Constance in 1415. The monument by Ladislav Šaloun was unveiled in 1915 on the 500th anniversary of his death. It shows two groups of people, one of victorious Hussite warriors, the other of Protestants forced into exile 200 years later, and a young mother symbolizing national rebirth. The dominant figure of Hus emphasizes the moral authority of the man who gave up life rather than his beliefs.

Church of St Nicholas 11

KOSTEL SV. MIKULÁŠE

Staroměstské náměstí. **Map** 3 B3. ***Tel*** *22 41 90 991.* *Staroměstská.* ***Open*** *10am–4pm daily and for evening concerts Apr–Nov.* *10:30am Sun.*

There has been a church here since the 12th century. It was the Old Town's parish church and meeting place until Týn Church was completed in the 14th century. After the Battle of the White Mountain in 1620 *(see pp30–31)* the church became part of a Benedictine monastery. The present church by Kilian Ignaz Dientzenhofer, was completed in 1735. Its dramatic white façade is studded with statues by Antonín Braun.

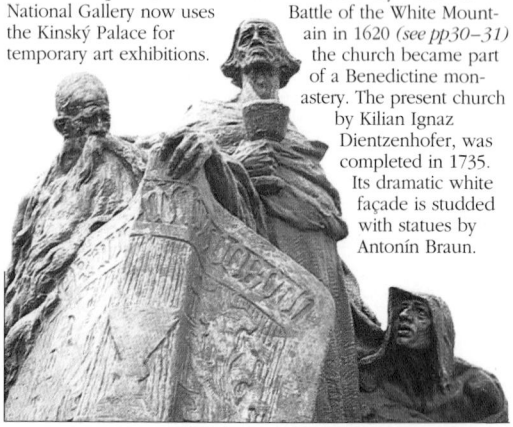

Defiant Hussites on the Jan Hus Monument in Old Town Square

Church of St Nicholas in the Old Town

When in 1781 Emperor Joseph II closed all monasteries not engaged in socially useful activities, the church was stripped bare. In World War I the church was used by the troops of Prague's garrison. The colonel in charge took the opportunity to restore the church with the help of artists who might otherwise have been sent to the front. The dome has frescoes of the lives of St Nicholas and St Benedict by Kosmas Damian Asam. In the nave is a huge crown-shaped chandelier. At the end of the war, the church of St Nicholas was given to the Czechoslovak Hussite Church. Concerts are given now in the church during the summer.

Old Town Hall ⓬

STAROMĚSTSKÁ RADNICE

See pp72–3.

House at the Two Golden Bears ⓭

DŮM U DVOU ZLATÝCH MEDVĚDŮ

Kožná 1. **Map** 3 B4. *Můstek.* ***Closed*** *to the public.*

If you leave the Old Town Square by the narrow Melantrichova Street, make a point of turning into the first alleyway on the left to see the portal of the house called "At the Two Golden Bears". The present Renaissance building was constructed from two earlier houses in 1567. The portal was added in 1590, when a wealthy merchant, Lorenc Štork, secured the services of court architect Bonifaz Wohlmut, who had designed the spire on the tower of St Vitus's Cathedral *(see pp100–3)*. His ornate portal with reliefs of two bears is one of the most beautiful Renaissance portals in Prague. Magnificent arcades, also dating from the 16th century, have been preserved in the inner courtyard. In 1885 Egon Erwin Kisch, known as the "Furious Reporter", was born here. He was a German-speaking Jewish writer and journalist, feared for the force of his left-wing rhetoric.

Church of St Gall ⓮

KOSTEL SV. HAVLA

Havelská. **Map** 3 C4. *Můstek.* ***Tel*** *22 42 13 475.* ***Open*** *only for services. 12:15pm Mon–Fri, 8am Sun.*

Dating from around 1280, this church was built to serve an autonomous German community in the area known as Gall's Town (Havelské Město). In the 14th century this was merged with the Old Town. In the 18th century the church was given a Baroque facelift by Giovanni Santini-Aichel, who created a bold façade decorated with statues of saints by Ferdinand Brokof. Rich interior furnishings include paintings by the leading Baroque artist Karel Škréta, who is buried here. Prague's best-known market has been held in Havelská Street since the middle ages, selling flowers, vegetables, toys, and clothes.

One of nine statues on façade of St Gall's

Carved Renaissance portal of the House at the Two Golden Bears

Old Town Hall ⓬

STAROMĚSTSKÁ RADNICE

One of the most striking buildings in Prague is the Old Town Hall, established in 1338 after King John of Luxemburg agreed to set up a town council. Over the centuries a number of old houses were knocked together as the Old Town Hall expanded, and it now consists of a row of colourful Gothic and Renaissance buildings, most of which have been carefully restored after heavy damage inflicted by the Nazis in the 1945 Prague Uprising. The tower is 69.5 m (228 ft) high and offers a spectacular view of the city.

Old Council Hall
This 19th-century engraving features the well-preserved 15th-century ceiling.

Old Town Coat of Arms
Above the inscription, "Prague, Head of the Kingdom", is the coat of arms of the Old Town, which was adopted in 1784 for the whole city.

Tourist information and entrance to Tower

Temporary art exhibitions

EXECUTIONS IN THE OLD TOWN SQUARE

A bronze tablet below the Old Town Hall chapel records the names of the 27 Protestant leaders executed here by order of the Catholic Emperor Ferdinand on 21 June 1621. This was the humiliating aftermath of the Battle of the White Mountain *(see pp30–31)*. This defeat led to the emigration of Protestants unwilling to give up their faith, a Counter-Reformation drive and Germanization.

★ Old Town Hall Tower
In 1364 the tower was added to what was the private house of Volflin of Kamen. Its gallery provides a fine city view.

Viewing gallery

VISITORS' CHECKLIST

Staroměstské náměstí 1. **Map** 3 C3. ***Tel*** *22 44 82 909.* M *Staroměstská (line A), Můstek (A & B).* 🚋 *17, 18.* ***Open*** *Apr–Oct: 9am–6pm daily (from 11am Mon); Nov–Mar: 9am–5pm daily (from 11am Mon).* 🎫 📷 ♿ 🎟

Oriel Chapel
The original stained-glass windows on the five-sided chapel were destroyed in the last days of World War II, but were replaced in 1987.

Oriel Chapel Ceiling
The chapel, which was built on the first floor of the tower in 1381, has an ornate, recently restored ceiling.

Former house of Volflin of Kamen

Steps to gallery

★ Astronomical Clock
Mechanical figures perform above the zodiac signs in the upper section (see p74)*; the lower section is a calendar.*

Calendar *(see pp32–3)*

Entrance hall decorated with mosaics

Gothic Door
This late Gothic main entrance to the Town Hall and Tower was carved by Matthias Rejsek. The entrance hall is filled with wall mosaics after designs by the Czech painter Mikuláš Aleš.

STAR FEATURES

★ Astronomical Clock

★ Old Town Hall Tower

Town Hall Clock

ORLOJ

Jan Táborský

The Town Hall acquired its first clock at the beginning of the 15th century. According to legend, in 1490, when it was rebuilt by a master clockmaker called Hanuš (real name Jan Z Růže), the councillors were so anxious to prevent him from re-creating his masterpiece elsewhere, that they blinded the poor man. Though the clock has been repaired many times since, the mechanism was perfected by Jan Táborský between 1552 and 1572.

The Apostles

Vanity and Greed

Arabic numerals 1–24

Astronomical Clock with the sun in Aries

Death

Blue, representing the daylight hours

Calendar by Josef Mánes *(see pp32–3)*

The Turk, a symbol of lust

APOSTLES

The centrepiece of the show that draws a crowd of spectators every time the clock strikes the hour is the procession of the 12 Apostles. First the figure of Death, the skeleton on the right of the clock, gives a pull on the rope that he holds in his right hand. In his left hand is an hourglass, which he raises and inverts. Two windows then open and the clockwork Apostles (or to be precise 11 of the Apostles plus St Paul) move slowly round, led by St Peter.

At the end of this part of the display, a cock crows and the clock chimes the hour. The other moving figures are a Turk, who shakes his head from side to side, Vanity, who looks at himself in a mirror and Greed, adapted from the original medieval stereotype of a Jewish moneylender.

Vojtěch Sucharda's Apostles, sculpted after the last set was burnt in 1945

ASTRONOMICAL CLOCK

The clockmaker's view of the universe had the Earth fixed firmly at the centre. The purpose of the clock was not to tell you the exact time but to imitate the supposed orbits of the sun and moon about the Earth. The hand with the sun, which points to the hour, in fact records three different kinds of time. The outer ring of medieval Arabic numerals measures Old Bohemian time, in which a day of 24 hours was reckoned from the setting of the sun. The ring of Roman numerals indicates time as we know it. The blue part of the dial represents the visible part of the sky. This is divided into 12 parts. In so-called Babylonian time, the period of daylight was divided into 12 hours, which would vary in length from summer to winter.

The clock also shows the movement of the sun and moon through the 12 signs of the zodiac, which were of great importance in 16th-century Prague.

The figures of Death and the Turk

Church of St Martin in the Wall ⑮

KOSTEL SV. MARTINA VE ZDI

Martinská. **Map** 3 B5. *Národní třída, Můstek.* *6, 9, 17, 18, 22.* ***Open*** *for concerts.*

This 12th-century church became part of the newly erected town wall during the fortification of the Old Town in the 13th century, hence its name. It was the first church where blessed wine, usually reserved for the clergy, was offered to the congregation as well as bread. This was a basic tenet of belief of the moderate Hussites *(see pp26–7)*, the Utraquists, who took their name from the Latin *sub utraque specie*, "in both kinds". In 1787 the church was converted into workshops, but rebuilt in its original form in the early years of this century.

Náprstek Museum ⑯

NÁPRSTKOVO MUZEUM

Betlémské náměstí. **Map** 3 B4. ***Tel*** *22 22 21 418.* *Národní třída, Staroměstská.* *6, 9, 17, 18, 22.* ***Open*** *9am–5:30pm Tue–Sun.* **www**.aconet.cz/npm

Vojta Náprstek, art patron and philanthropist, created this museum as a tribute to modern industry following a decade of exile in America after the 1848 revolution *(see pp32–3)*. On his return in 1862, inspired by London's Victorian museums, he began his collection. He created the Czech Industrial Museum by joining five older buildings together, and in the process virtually destroyed the family brewery and home – an 18th-century house called At the Haláneks (U Halánků). He later turned to ethnography and the collection now consists of artefacts from Asian, African and Native American cultures, including weapons and ritual objects from the Aztecs, Toltecs and Mayas. The museum is part of the National Museum.

Nearby, on Smetanovo nábřeží is Neo-Gothic Kranners Fountain erected in 1850.

Ceiling fresco by Václav Vavřinec Reiner in Church of St Giles

Church of St Giles ⑰

KOSTEL SV. JILJÍ

Husova. **Map** 3 B4. ***Tel*** *22 42 20 235.* *Národní třída.* *6, 9, 17, 18, 22.* ***Open*** *for services only.* *7am & 6:30pm Mon–Fri, 6:30pm Sat, 9:30am, noon, 6:30pm Sun.* **www**.jilji.po.cz

Despite a beautiful Gothic portal on the southern side, the inside of this church is essentially Baroque. Founded in 1371 on the site of an old Romanesque church, it became a Hussite parish church in 1420. Following the Protestant defeat in 1620 *(see pp30–31)*, Ferdinand II presented the church to the Dominicans, who built a huge friary on its southern side. It has now been returned to the Dominicans, religious orders having been abolished under the Communists.

The vaults of the church are decorated with frescoes by the painter Václav Vavřinec Reiner, who is buried in the nave before the altar of St Vincent. The main fresco, a glorification of the Dominicans, shows St Dominic and his friars helping the pope defend the Catholic Church from non-believers.

Bethlehem Chapel ⑱

BETLÉMSKÁ KAPLE

Betlémské náměstí. **Map** 3 B4. *Národní třída, Staroměstská.* *6, 9, 17, 18, 22.* ***Open*** *Apr–Oct: 10am–6:30pm Tue–Sun; Nov-Mar: 10am–5:30pm Tue–Sun.* *organized by the Prague Information Service* (see p227).

The present "chapel" is a reconstruction of a hall built by the followers of the radical preacher Jan Milíč z Kroměříže in 1391–4. The hall was used for preaching in Czech. Between 1402 and 1413 Jan Hus *(see pp26–7)* preached in the Chapel. Influenced by the teachings of the English religious reformer John Wycliffe, Hus condemned the corrupt practices of the Church, arguing that the Scriptures should be the sole source of doctrine. After the Battle of the White Mountain in 1620 *(see pp30–31)*, when Protestant worship was outlawed, the building was handed over to the Jesuits, who rebuilt it with six naves. In 1786 it was almost demolished. After World War II the chapel was reconstructed following old illustrations.

16th-century illustration showing Jan Hus preaching in Bethlehem Chapel

Street-by-Street: Old Town (West)

The narrow streets near Charles Bridge follow Prague's medieval street plan. For centuries Charles Street (Karlova) was the main route across the Old Town. The picturesque, twisting street is lined with shops and houses displaying Renaissance and Baroque façades. In the 17th century the Jesuits bought up a vast area of land to the north of the street to house the complex of the Clementinum university.

★ Clementinum
This plaque records the founding in 1783 of a state-supervised seminary in place of the old Jesuit university 23

Knights of the Cross Square
From the façade of the Church of the Holy Saviour, blackened statues overlook the small square 25

★ Smetana Museum
A museum devoted to the life and work of composer Bedřich Smetana is housed in this Neo-Renaissance building set on the riverfront, which was once an old waterworks 24

Church of St Francis

St Anne's Convent was abolished in 1782. Some of its buildings are now used by the National Theatre *(see pp156–7).*

The Old Town Bridge Tower *dates from 1380. The Gothic sculptural decoration on the eastern façade was from Peter Parler's workshop. The kingfisher was the favourite personal symbol of Wenceslas IV (son of Charles IV) in whose reign the tower was completed* (see p139).

Charles Street
Among the many decorated houses along the ancient street, be sure to look out for this Art Nouveau statue of the legendary Princess Libuše (see p21) *surrounded by roses at No. 22/24* 21

Mariánské Square
The square used to be flooded so often, it was called "the puddle". The Art Nouveau sculptures on the balcony of the New Town Hall, built here in 1911, are by Stanislav Sucharda 20

LOCATOR MAP
See Street Finder, map 3

Observatory tower

MARIÁNSKÉ NÁMĚSTÍ

Clam-Gallas Palace
One of Prague's grandest Baroque palaces and full of wonderful statuary, the Clam-Gallas has been restored and is open for concerts 19

KARLOVA

To Old Town Square

LILIOVÁ

HUSOVA

ŘETĚZOVÁ

Church of St Giles
Much of the Baroque sculpture, like this angel on the altar (1738), is by František Weiss 17

Palace of the Lords of Kunštát
George of Poděbrady lived here before he became King in 1458 22

Bethlehem Chapel
In this spacious chapel, rebuilt in the 1950s, Hus and other reformers preached to huge congregations 18

0 metres 100
0 yards 100

KEY
— — — Suggested route

STAR SIGHTS
★ Clementinum
★ Smetana Museum

Clam-Gallas Palace ⑲

CLAM-GALLASŮV PALÁC

Husova 20. **Map** 3 B4. ***Tel*** *23 60 02 019.* Ⓜ *Staroměstská.* ***Open*** *for concerts and temporary exhibitions only.* **www**.ahmp.cz

The interior of this magnificent Baroque palace had suffered during its use as a store for the city archives, but has now been lovingly restored. The palace, designed by Viennese court architect Johann Bernhard Fischer von Erlach, was built in 1713–30 for the Supreme Marshal of Bohemia, Jan Gallas de Campo. Its grand portals, each flanked by two pairs of Hercules sculpted by Matthias Braun, give a taste of what lies within. The main staircase is also decorated with Braun statues, set off by a ceiling fresco, *The Triumph of Apollo* by Carlo Carlone. The palace has a theatre, where Beethoven performed some of his works.

Mariánské Square ⑳

MARIÁNSKÉ NÁMĚSTÍ

Map 3 B3. Ⓜ *Staroměstská, Můstek.*

Two statues dominate the square from the corners of the forbidding Town Hall, built in 1912. One illustrates the story of the long-lived Rabbi Löw *(see p88)* finally being caught by the Angel of Death. The other is the Iron Man, a local ghost condemned to roam the Old Town after murdering his mistress. A niche in the garden wall of the Clam-Gallas Palace houses a statue of the River Vltava, depicted as a nymph pouring water from a jug. There is a story that an old soldier once made the nymph sole beneficiary of his will.

Matthias Braun's statues on a portal of the Clam-Gallas Palace (c.1714)

Charles Street ㉑

KARLOVA ULICE

Map 3 A4. Ⓜ *Staroměstská.*

A 19th-century sign on the House at the Golden Snake

Dating back to the 12th century, this narrow, winding street was part of the Royal Route *(see pp174–5)*, along which coronation processions passed on the way to Prague Castle. Many original Gothic and Renaissance houses remain, most converted into shops to attract tourists.

A café at the House at the Golden Snake (No. 18) was established in 1714 by an Armenian, Deodatus Damajan, who handed out slanderous pamphlets from here. It is now a restaurant. Look out for At the Golden Well (No. 3), which has a magnificent Baroque façade and stucco reliefs of saints including St Roch and St Sebastian, who are believed to offer protection against plagues.

Palace of the Lords of Kunštát ㉒

DŮM PÁNŮ Z KUNŠTÁTU

Řetězová. **Map** 3 B4. ***Tel*** *22 22 21 240.* Ⓜ *Národní třída, Staroměstská.* 🚌 *6, 9, 17, 18, 22.* ***Open*** *May–Sep: 11am–9pm daily.* 🔊 📷

The basement of the palace, dating from around 1200, contains three of the best-preserved Romanesque rooms in Prague. It was originally the ground floor, but over the years the surrounding ground level was raised by 3m (10 ft) to prevent flooding. In the 15th century the house was enlarged in Gothic style by its owners, the Lords of Kunštát and Poděbrady. The palace houses a historical exhibition devoted to Bohemia's only Hussite king, George of Poděbrady *(see pp26–7)*, who lived here for a time.

Clementinum ㉓

KLEMENTINUM

Křižovnické náměstí 4, Mariánské náměstí 5, Seminářská 1. **Map** 3 A4. ***Tel*** *22 16 63 111.* *Staroměstská.* *17, 18.* **Library *open*** *9am–10pm Mon–Fri, 8am–2pm Sat.* **Church *open*** *only for services.* *7pm Tue, 2pm & 8pm Sun.* *Mar–Oct: 2–9pm daily (from 10am Sat & Sun).* ***Tel*** *22 22 21 339.*

Former Jesuit Church of the Holy Saviour in the Clementinum

In 1556 Emperor Ferdinand I invited the Jesuits to Prague to help bring the Czechs back into the Catholic fold. They established their headquarters in the former Dominican monastery of St Clement, hence the name Clementinum. This soon became an effective rival to the Carolinum *(see p65)*, the Utraquist university. Prague's first Jesuit church, the Church of the Holy Saviour (Kostel sv. Salvátora) was built here in 1601. Its façade, with seven large statues of saints by Jan Bendl (1659), is dramatically lit up at night.

Expelled in 1618, the Jesuits were back two years later more determined than ever to stamp out heresy. In 1622 the two universities were merged, resulting in the Jesuits gaining a virtual monopoly on higher education in Prague. They believed two-thirds of the population were secret heretics, searched for books in Czech and then burnt them by the thousand. Between 1653 and 1723 the Clementinum expanded eastwards. Over 30 houses and three churches were pulled down to make way for the new complex.

When in 1773 the pope dissolved their order, the Jesuits had to leave Prague and education was secularized. The Clementinum became the Prague University library, today the National Library. Look out for any classical concerts performed in the beautiful Chapel of Mirrors (Zrcadlová kaple).

Smetana Museum ㉔

MUZEUM BEDŘICHA SMETANY

Novotného lávka 1. **Map** 3 A4. ***Tel*** *& **Fax** 22 22 20 082.* *Staroměstská.* *17, 18.* ***Open*** *10am–5pm Wed–Mon.* **www**.nm.cz

On a spit of land beside the Vltava, a former Neo-Renaissance waterworks has been turned into a memorial to Bedřich Smetana, the father of Czech music. The museum contains documents, letters, scores and musical instruments detailing the composer's life and work. Smetana was a fervent patriot and his music helped inspire the Czech national revival. Deaf towards the end of his life, he never heard his cycle of symphonic poems *Má Vlast* (My Country), being performed.

Statue of Charles IV (1848) in Knights of the Cross Square

Knights of the Cross Square ㉕

KŘIŽOVNICKE NÁMĚSTÍ

Map 3 A4. ***Tel*** *22 11 08 200.* *Staroměstská.* *17, 18.* *135, 207.* **Church of St Francis *open*** *only for services.* *7am Mon–Fri, 10am Sun.* **Gallery Křižovníků *open*** *10am–7pm daily.* **www**.guk-prague.cz

This small square in front of the Old Town Bridge Tower offers fine views across the Vltava. On the north side is the Church of St Francis (kostel sv. Františka), once part of the monastery of the crusading Knights of the Cross with the Red Star. To the east is the Church of the Holy Saviour, part of the huge Clementinum complex. On the western side is the Gallery Křižovníků, holding temporary art exhibitions. In the square stands a large bronze Neo-Gothic statue of Charles IV.

Sgraffitoed façade of the Smetana Museum

JEWISH QUARTER

JOSEFOV

In the Middle Ages there were two distinct Jewish communities in Prague's Old Town: Jews from the west had settled around the Old-New Synagogue, Jews from the Byzantine Empire around the Old Shul (on the site of today's Spanish Synagogue). The two settlements gradually merged and were confined in an enclosed ghetto. For centuries Prague's Jews suffered from oppressive laws – in the 16th century they had to wear a yellow circle as a mark of shame. Christians often accused them of starting fires and poisoning wells – any pretext for a pogrom. Discrimination was partially relaxed in 1784 by Joseph II, and the Jewish Quarter was named Josefov after him. In 1850 the area was officially incorporated as part of Prague. In the 1890s the city authorities decided to raze the ghetto slums because the area's complete lack of sanitation made it a health hazard. However, the Town Hall, a number of synagogues and the Old Jewish Cemetery were saved.

Art Nouveau detail on house in Kaprova

SIGHTS AT A GLANCE

Synagogues and Churches
Pinkas Synagogue 4
Klausen Synagogue 5
Old-New Synagogue pp88–9 6
High Synagogue 7
Maisel Synagogue 9
Church of the Holy Ghost 10
Spanish Synagogue 11
Church of St Simon and St Jude 13
Church of St Castullus 14

Concert Hall
Rudolfinum 1

Museums and Galleries
Museum of Decorative Arts 2
St Agnes of Bohemia Convent pp92–3 15

Historic Buildings
Jewish Town Hall 8
Cubist Houses 12

Cemeteries
Old Jewish Cemetery pp86–7 3

GETTING THERE

Staroměstská station on metro line A is close to all the major sights in the Jewish Quarter. The alternative is to take tram 17 or 18 to Náměstí Jana Palacha. For St Agnes of Bohemia Convent, bus 207 is convenient.

0 metres 250
0 yards 250

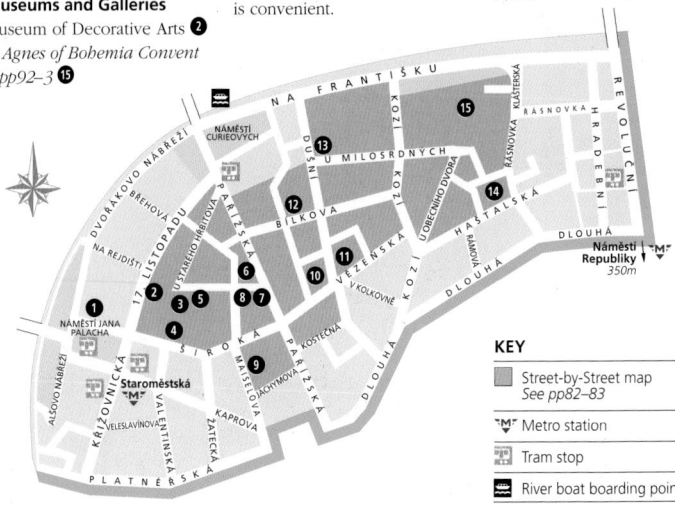

KEY
Street-by-Street map *See pp82–83*
Metro station
Tram stop
River boat boarding point

◁ **Densely-packed gravestones in the Old Jewish Cemetery**

Street-by-Street: Jewish Quarter

Though the old ghetto has disappeared, much of the area's fascinating history is preserved in the synagogues around the Old Jewish Cemetery, while the newer streets are lined with many delightful Art Nouveau buildings. The old lanes to the east of the former ghetto lead to the quiet haven of St Agnes's Convent, beautifully restored as a branch of the National Gallery.

★ Old Jewish Cemetery
Thousands of gravestones are crammed into the ancient cemetery ❸

Cubist Houses
One of the new architectural styles used in the rebuilding of the old Jewish Quarter was based on the ideas of Cubism ⓬

★ Old-New Synagogue
The Gothic hall with its distinctive crenellated gable has been a house of prayer for over 700 years ❻

Klausen Synagogue
The exhibits of the Jewish Museum include this alms box, dating from about 1800 ❺

High Synagogue
The interior has splendid Renaissance vaulting ❼

★ Museum of Decorative Arts
Stained glass panels on the staircase depict the crafts represented in the museum's wide-ranging collection ❷

Pinkas Synagogue
The walls are now a moving memorial to the Czech Jews killed in the Holocaust ❹

To Metro Staroměstská

Jewish Town Hall
The 16th-century building still serves the Czech Jewish community ❽

Maisel Synagogue
The original synagogue was built for Mayor Mordechai Maisel in 1591 ❾

BŘEHOVÁ

17. LISTOPADU

ELIŠKY KRÁSNOHORSKÉ

PAŘÍZSKÁ

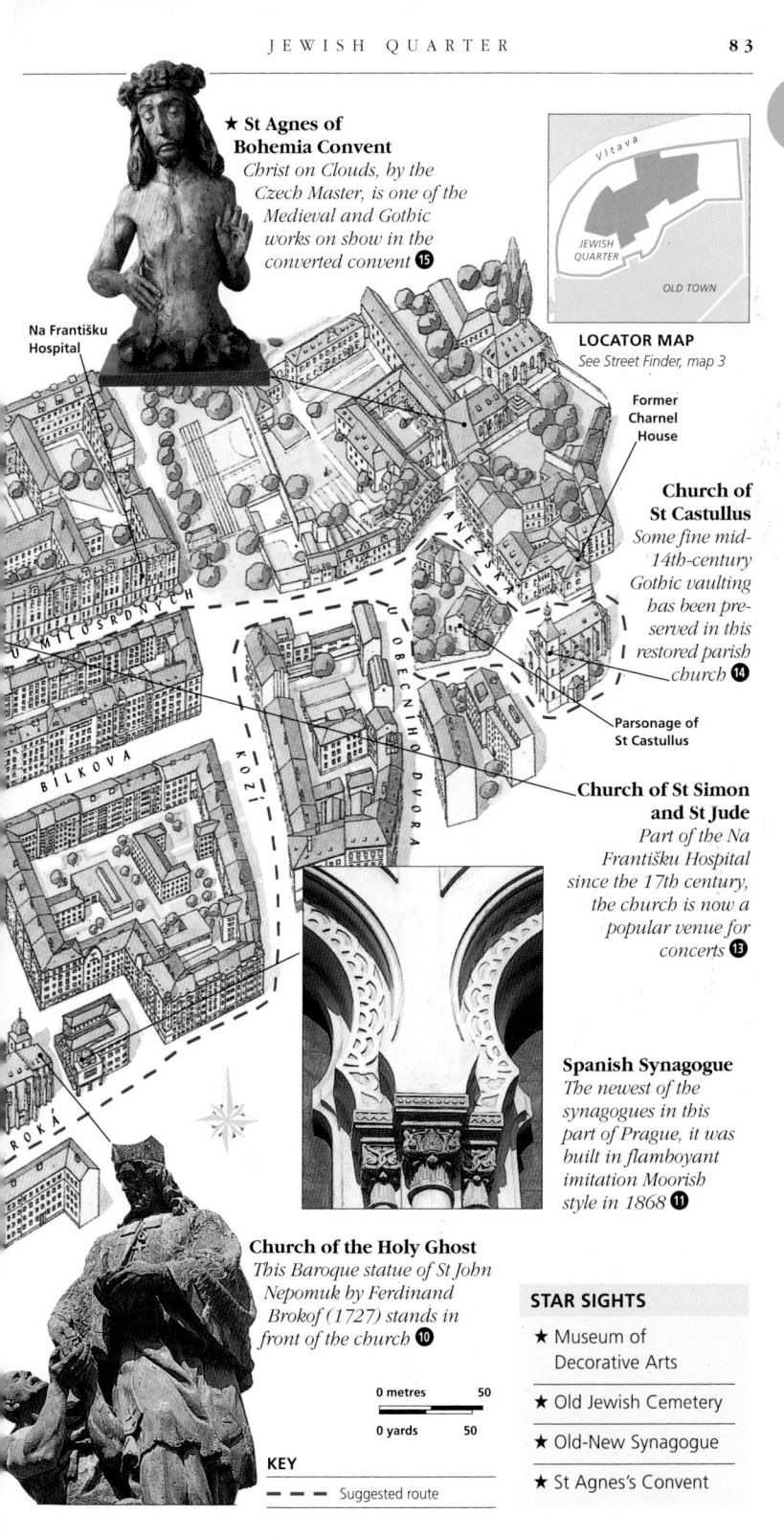
★ St Agnes of Bohemia Convent
Christ on Clouds, by the Czech Master, is one of the Medieval and Gothic works on show in the converted convent 15
Vltava
JEWISH QUARTER
OLD TOWN
LOCATOR MAP
See Street Finder, map 3
Na Františku Hospital
Former Charnel House
Church of St Castullus
Some fine mid-14th-century Gothic vaulting has been preserved in this restored parish church 14
Parsonage of St Castullus
Church of St Simon and St Jude
Part of the Na Františku Hospital since the 17th century, the church is now a popular venue for concerts 13
Spanish Synagogue
The newest of the synagogues in this part of Prague, it was built in flamboyant imitation Moorish style in 1868 11
Church of the Holy Ghost
This Baroque statue of St John Nepomuk by Ferdinand Brokof (1727) stands in front of the church 10
U MILOSRDNÝCH
BILKOVÁ
KOZÍ
U OBECNÍHO DVORA
ANEŽSKÁ
ROKÁ
0 metres 50
0 yards 50
KEY
Suggested route
STAR SIGHTS
★ Museum of Decorative Arts
★ Old Jewish Cemetery
★ Old-New Synagogue
★ St Agnes's Convent

Stage of the Dvořák Hall in the Rudolfinum

Rudolfinum ❶

Alšovo nábřeží 12. **Map** 3 A3. M *Staroměstská.* 🚋 *17, 18.* 🚌 *135, 207.* **Philharmonic** ***Tel*** *22 70 59 352.* **Galerie Rudolphinum** ***Tel*** *22 70 59 204.* ***Open*** *10am–6pm Tue–Sun.* 🚫 ♿ 💻 **www.**rudolfinum.cz

Now the home of the Czech Philharmonic Orchestra, the Rudolfinum is one of the most impressive landmarks on the Old Town bank of the Vltava. Many of the major concerts of the Prague Spring music festival *(see p50)* are held here. There are several concert halls, the sumptuous Dvořák Hall ranking among the finest creations of 19th-century Czech architecture.

The Rudolfinum was built between 1876 and 1884 to a design by Josef Zítek and Josef Schulz and named in honour of Crown Prince Rudolph of Habsburg. Like the National Theatre *(see pp156–7)*, it is an outstanding example of Czech Neo-Renaissance style. The curving balustrade is decorated with statues of distinguished Czech, Austrian and German composers and artists.

Also known as the House of Artists (Dům umělců), the building houses the Gallerie Rudolphinum, a collection of modern art. Between 1918 and 1939, and for a brief period after World War II, the Rudolfinum was the seat of the Czechoslovak parliament.

Museum of Decorative Arts ❷

UMĚLECKOPRŮMYSLOVÉ MUZEUM

17. listopadu 2. **Map** 3 B3. ***Tel*** *25 10 93 111.* M *Staroměstská.* 🚋 *17, 18.* 🚌 *135, 207.* ***Open*** *10am–6pm Tue–Sun.* 🚫 🚫 💻 **www.**upm.cz

For some years after its foundation in 1885, the museum's collections were housed in the Rudolfinum. The present building, designed by Josef Schulz in French Neo-Renaissance style, was completed in 1901.

The museum's glass collection is one of the largest in the world, but only a fraction of it is ever on display. Pride of place goes to the Bohemian glass, of which there are many fine Baroque and 19th- and 20th-century pieces. Medieval and Venetian Renaissance glass are also well represented.

Among the permanent exhibitions of other crafts are Meissen porcelain, the Gobelin tapestries and displays covering fashion, textiles, photography and printing. The furniture collection has exquisitely carved escritoires and bureaux from the Renaissance. On the mezzanine floor are halls for temporary exhibitions and an extensive art library housing more than 100,000 publications.

Old Jewish Cemetery ❸

STARÝ ŽIDOVSKÝ HŘBITOV

See pp86–7.

Pinkas Synagogue ❹

PINKASOVA SYNAGÓGA

Široká 3. **Map** 3 B3. M *Staroměstská.* 🚋 *17, 18.* 🚌 *135, 207.* ***Open*** *Apr–Oct: 9am–6pm Sun–Fri; Nov–Mar: 9am–4:30pm.* 🚫 🚫 ♿ **www.**jewishmuseum.cz

The synagogue was founded in 1479 by Rabbi Pinkas and enlarged in 1535 by his great-nephew Aaron Meshulam Horowitz. It has been rebuilt many times over the centuries. Excavations have turned up fascinating relics of life in the medieval ghetto, including a *mikva* or ritual bath. The core of the present building is a hall with

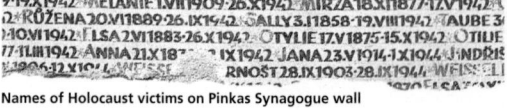

Names of Holocaust victims on Pinkas Synagogue wall

Gothic vaulting. The gallery for women was added in the early 17th century.

The synagogue now serves as a memorial to all the Jewish Czechoslovak citizens who were imprisoned in Terezín concentration camp and later deported to various Nazi extermination camps. The names of the 77,297 who did not return are inscribed on the synagogue walls. The building now houses an exhibition of children's drawings from the Terezín concentration camp.

Klausen Synagogue ❺

KLAUSOVÁ SYNAGÓGA

U starého hřbitova 3a. **Map** 3 B3. *Staroměstská. 17, 18. 135, 207.* ***Open*** *Apr–Oct: 9am–6pm daily; Nov–Mar: 9am–4:30pm.*
www.jewishmuseum.cz

Before the fire of 1689, this site was occupied by a number of small Jewish schools and prayer houses known as *klausen*. The name was preserved in the Klausen Synagogue, built on the ruins and completed in 1694. The High Baroque structure has a fine barrel-vaulted interior with rich stucco decorations. It now houses Hebrew prints and manuscripts and an exhibition of Jewish traditions and customs, tracing the history of the Jews in Central Europe back to the early Middle Ages. Many exhibits relate to famous figures in the city's Jewish community including the 16th-century Rabbi Löw *(see p88)*, who, according to legend, created an artificial man out of clay.

19th-century Torah pointer in Klausen Synagogue

Adjoining the synagogue is a building that looks like a tiny medieval castle. It was built in 1906 as the ceremonial hall of the Jewish Burial Society. In 1944 an exhibition was put on here detailing the history of the Prague ghetto.

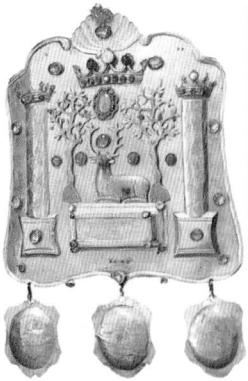

18th-century silver-gilt Torah shield in the High Synagogue

Old-New Synagogue ❻

STARONOVÁ SYNAGÓGA

See pp88–9.

High Synagogue ❼

VYSOKÁ SYNAGÓGA

Červená 4. **Map** 3 B3. *Staroměstská. 17, 18. 135, 207.* ***Open*** *Apr–Oct: 9am–6pm daily; Nov–Mar: 9am–4:30pm.*

Like the Jewish Town Hall, the building of the High Synagogue was financed by Mordechai Maisel, mayor of the Jewish Town, in the 1570s. Originally the two buildings formed a single complex and to facilitate communication with the Town Hall, the main hall of the synagogue was on the first floor. It was not until the 19th century that the two buildings were separated and the synagogue was given a staircase and street entrance. You can still see the original Renaissance vaulting and stucco decoration.

The exhibition in the synagogue includes richly embroidered Torah mantles, curtains and other religious textiles. There are also silver ornaments, such as shields and finials, used to decorate the Ark, where the Torah scrolls are kept. These date from the 16th to the 19th centuries.

Jewish Town Hall ❽

ŽIDOVSKÁ RADNICE

Maislova 18. **Map** 3 B3. ***Tel*** *&* ***Fax*** *22 23 19 002. Staroměstská. 17, 18. 135, 207.* ***Closed*** *to the public.*

The core of this attractive pink and white building is the original Jewish Town Hall, built in 1570–77 by the immensely rich mayor, Mordechai Maisel. In 1763 it acquired a new appearance in the flowery style of the Late Baroque. The last alterations date from 1908, when the southern wing was enlarged.

On the roof stands a small wooden clock tower with a distinctive green steeple. The right to build the tower was originally granted to the Jewish community after their part in the defence of Charles Bridge against the Swedes in 1648 *(see pp30–31)*. On one of the gables there is another clock. This one has Hebrew figures and, because Hebrew reads from right to left, hands that turn in an anti-clockwise direction. The Town Hall is now the seat of the Council of Jewish Religious Communities in the Czech Republic.

Façade and clock tower of the Jewish Town Hall

Old Jewish Cemetery ❸

STARÝ ŽIDOVSKÝ HŘBITOV

This remarkable site was, for over 300 years, the only burial ground permitted to Jews. Founded in 1478, it was slightly enlarged over the years but still basically corresponds to its medieval size. Because of the lack of space people had to be buried on top of each other, up to 12 layers deep. Today you can see over 12,000 gravestones crammed into the tiny space, but an estimated 100,000 people are thought to have been buried here. The last burial was of Moses Beck in 1787.

View across the cemetery towards the western wall of the Klausen Synagogue

David Gans' Tombstone
*The tomb of the writer and astronomer (1541–1613) is decorated with the symbols of his name – a star of David and a goose (*Gans *in German).*

The Pinkas Synagogue is the second-oldest in Prague *(see p84)*.

Jewish printers, Mordechai Zemach (d 1592) and his son Bezalel (d 1589), are buried under this square gravestone.

The oldest tomb is that of the writer Rabbi Avigdor Kara (1439).

Rabbi David Oppenheim (1664–1736)
The chief rabbi of Prague owned the largest collection of old Hebrew manuscripts and prints in the city.

Klausen Synagogue *(see p85)*

The gravestone of Moses Beck

Main entrance

The Nephele Mound was where infants who died under a year old were buried.

★ 14th-Century Tombstones
Embedded in the wall are fragments of Gothic tombstones brought here from an older Jewish cemetery discovered in 1866 in Vladislavova Street in the New Town.

STAR SIGHTS

- ★ Tombstone of Rabbi Löw
- ★ Tombstone of Hendela Bassevi
- ★ 14th-Century Tombstones

Prague Burial Society
Founded in 1564, the group carried out ritual burials and performed charitable work in the community. Members of the society wash their hands after leaving the cemetery.

VISITORS' CHECKLIST

Široká 3 (main entrance). **Map** 3 B3. ***Tel*** *22 23 17 191 (bookings), 22 48 10 099, 22 48 19 456 (Jewish Museum).* Staroměstská. *17, 18 to Staroměstská.* ***Open*** *Apr–Oct: 9am–6pm Sun–Fri; Nov–Mar: 9–4:30pm Sun–Fri (last admission 30 mins before closing).*
www.jewishmuseum.cz

★ Tombstone of Rabbi Löw
The most visited grave in the cemetery is that of Rabbi Löw (1520–1609). Visitors place hundreds of pebbles and wishes on his grave as a mark of respect.

The Museum of Decorative Arts *(see p84)*

The Neo-Romanesque Ceremonial Hall

Mordechai Maisel (1528–1601) was Mayor of Prague's Jewish Town and a philanthropist.

★ Tombstone of Hendela Bassevi
The highly-decorated tomb (1628) was built for the beautiful wife of Prague's first Jewish nobleman.

UNDERSTANDING THE GRAVESTONES

From the late 16th century onwards, tombstones in the Jewish cemetery were decorated with symbols denoting the background, family name or profession of the deceased person.

Blessing hands: Cohen family

A pair of scissors: tailor

A stag: Hirsch or Zvi family

Grapes: blessing or abundance

Old-New Synagogue ❻

STARONOVÁ SYNAGOGA

Star of David in Červená Street

Built around 1270, this is the oldest synagogue in Europe and one of the earliest Gothic buildings in Prague. The synagogue has survived fires, the slum clearances of the 19th century and many Jewish pogroms. Residents of the Jewish Quarter have often had to seek refuge within its walls and today it is still the religious centre for Prague's Jews. It was originally called the New Synagogue until another synagogue was built nearby – this was later destroyed.

The synagogue's eastern side

★ Jewish Standard
The historic banner of Prague's Jews is decorated with a Star of David and within it the hat that had to be worn by Jews in the 14th century.

The 14th-century stepped brick gable

These windows formed part of the 18th-century extensions built to allow women a view of the service.

Candlestick holder

RABBI LÖW AND THE GOLEM

The scholar and philosophical writer Rabbi Löw, director of the Talmudic school (which studied the Torah) in the late 16th century, was also thought to possess magical powers. He was supposed to have created a figure, the Golem, from clay and then brought it to life by placing a magic stone tablet in its mouth. The Golem went berserk and the Rabbi had to remove the tablet. He hid the creature among the Old-New Synagogue's rafters.

Rabbi Löw and the Golem

★ Five-rib Vaulting
Two massive octagonal pillars inside the hall support the five-rib vaults.

Right-hand Nave
The glow from the bronze chandeliers provides light for worshippers using the seats lining the walls.

VISITORS' CHECKLIST

Pařížská and Červená. **Map** 3 B2. ***Tel*** *22 23 17 191.* *Staroměstská.* *17, 18 to Staroměstská, 17 to Law Faculty (Právnická fakulta).* ***Open*** *9:30am–6pm Sun–Fri (to 5pm Nov–Mar).* ***Closed*** *Jewish holidays.* *8am Mon–Fri, 9am Sat.* **www**.jewishmuseum.cz

The tympanum above the Ark is decorated with 13th-century leaf carvings.

★ Rabbi Löw's Chair
A star of David marks the chair of the Chief Rabbi, placed where the distinguished 16th-century scholar used to sit.

The cantor's platform and its lectern is surrounded by a wrought-iron Gothic grille.

Entrance to the Synagogue in Červená Street

The Ark
This shrine is the holiest place in the synagogue and holds the sacred scrolls of the Torah.

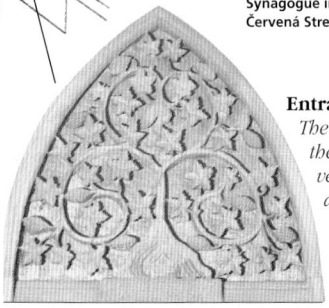

Entrance Portal
The tympanum above the door in the south vestibule is decorated with clusters of grapes and vine leaves growing on twisted branches.

STAR FEATURES

★ Rabbi Löw's Chair

★ Five-rib Vaulting

★ Jewish Standard

18th-century silver Torah crown in the Maisel Synagogue

Maisel Synagogue ❾

MAISELOVA SYNAGÓGA

Maiselova 10. **Map** 3 B3.
Staroměstská. *17, 18.* *135, 207.* ***Open*** *Apr–Oct: 9am–6pm Sun–Fri; Nov–Mar: 9am–4.30pm Sun–Fri.*
www.jewishmuseum.cz

When it was first built, at the end of the 16th century, this was a private house of prayer for the use of mayor Mordechai Maisel and his family. Maisel had made a fortune lending money to Emperor Rudolph II to finance wars against the Turks, and his synagogue was the most richly decorated in the city. The original building was a victim of the fire that devastated the Jewish Town in 1689 and a new synagogue was built in its place. Its present crenellated, Gothic appearance dates from the start of the 20th century. Since the 1960s the Maisel Synagogue has housed a fascinating collection of Jewish silver and other metalwork dating from Renaissance times to the 20th century. It includes many Torah crowns, shields and finials. Crowns and finials were used to decorate the rollers on which the text of the Torah (the five books of Moses) was kept. The shields were hung over the mantle that was draped over the Torah and the pointers were used to follow the text so that it was not touched by readers' hands. There are also objects such as wedding plates, lamps and candlesticks. By a tragic irony, nearly all these Jewish treasures were brought to Prague by the Nazis from synagogues throughout Bohemia and Moravia with the intention of founding a museum of a vanished people.

Church of the Holy Ghost ❿

KOSTEL SV. DUCHA

Dušní, Široká. **Map** 3 B3.
Staroměstská. *17.* *135, 207.* ***Open*** *only for services.* *9:30am Sun.*

This church stands on the narrow strip of Christian soil which once separated the two Jewish communities of the Middle Ages – the Jews of the eastern and western rites. Built in the mid-14th century, the single-naved Gothic church was originally part of a convent of Benedictine nuns. The convent was destroyed in 1420 during the Hussite Wars *(see pp26–7)* and not rebuilt.

The church was badly damaged in the Old Town fire of 1689. The exterior preserves the original Gothic buttresses and high windows, but the vault of the nave was rebuilt in Baroque style after the fire. The furnishings too are mainly Baroque. The high altar dates from 1760, and there is an altar painting of *St Joseph* by Jan Jiří Heintsch (c1647–1712). In front of the church stands a stone statue of St John Nepomuk *(see p83)* distributing alms (1727) by the prolific sculptor of the Czech Baroque Ferdinand Maximilian Brokof. Inside the church there are a few earlier statues, including a 14th-century *Pietà* (the heads of the figures are later, dating from 1628), a Late Gothic statue of St Ann and busts of St Wenceslas and St Adalbert from the early 16th century.

Church of the Holy Ghost

Spanish Synagogue ⓫

ŠPANĚLSKÁ SYNAGÓGA

Vězeňská 1. **Map** 3 B2.
Staroměstská. *17.*
Open *Apr–Oct: 9am–6pm Sun–Fri; Nov–Mar: 9am–4.30pm Sun–Fri.*
www.jewishmuseum.cz

Prague's first synagogue, known as the Old School (Stará škola), once stood on this site. In the 11th century the Old School was the centre of the community of Jews of the eastern rite, who lived strictly apart from the Jews of the western rite, who were concentrated round the Old-New Synagogue. The present building dates from the second half of the 19th century. The exterior and interior are both pseudo-Moorish in

Motif of the Ten Commandments on the Spanish Synagogue's façade

appearance. The rich stucco decorations on the walls and vaults are reminiscent of the Alhambra in Spain, hence the name. Once closed to the public, the Spanish Synagogue now houses a permanent exhibition dedicated to the history of the Jews of Bohemia.

Cubist Houses ⓬

KUBISTICKÉ DOMY

Elišky Krásnohorské, 10–14. **Map** 3 B2. *Staroměstská.* *17, 18.* ***Closed*** *to the public.*

The rebuilding of the old Jewish Quarter at the turn of the 20th century gave Prague's architects scope to experiment with many new styles. Most of the blocks in this area are covered with flowing Art Nouveau decoration, but on the corner of Bílkova and Elišky Krásnohorské there is a plain façade with a few simple repeated geometrical shapes. This is an example of Cubist architecture, a fashion that did not really catch on in the rest of Europe, but was very popular with the avant-garde in Bohemia and Austria before and after World War I. This block was built for a cooperative of teachers in 1919–21.

At No. 7 Elišky Krásnohorské you can see the influence of Cubism in the curiously flattened atlantes supporting the windows. Another interesting Cubist building is the House of the Black Mother of God in Celetná *(see pp174–5).*

Church of St Simon and St Jude ⓭

KOSTEL SV. ŠIMONA A JUDY

U milosrdných. **Map** 3 B2. *Staroměstská.* *17, 18.* *135, 207.* ***Open*** *for concerts.* **www**.festival.cz

Members of the Bohemia Brethren built this church with high Late Gothic windows in 1615–20. The Brethren, founded in the mid-15th century, agreed with the Utraquists *(see p75)* in directing the congregation to receive both bread and wine at Holy Communion. In other respects they were more conservative than other Protestant sects, continuing to practise celibacy and Catholic sacraments such as confession. After the Battle of the White Mountain *(see pp30–31)*, the Brethren were expelled from the Empire.

The church was then given to a Catholic order, the Brothers of Mercy, becoming part of a monastery and hospital. Tradition has it that the monastery's wooden steps were built from the scaffold on which 27 Czechs were executed in 1621 *(see p72).* In the 18th century the city's first anatomy lecture hall was established here and the complex continues to serve as a hospital – the Na Františku. The church is now used as a venue for concerts.

Cubist-style atlantes framing a window in Elišky Krásnohorské Street

Detail of Baroque façade of Church of St Simon and St Jude

Church of St Castullus ⓮

KOSTEL SV. HAŠTALA

Haštalské náměstí. **Map** 3 C2. *5, 8, 14.* *135, 125, 207.* Open *irregularly.* *5pm Sun.*

This peaceful little corner of Prague takes its name – Haštal – from the parish church of St Castullus. One of the finest Gothic buildings in Prague, the church was erected on the site of an older Romanesque structure in the second quarter of the 14th century. Much of the church had to be rebuilt after the fire of 1689, but fortunately the double nave on the north side survived. It has beautiful slender pillars supporting a delicate ribbed vault.

The interior furnishings are mainly Baroque, though there are remains of wall paintings of about 1375 in the sacristy and a metal font decorated with figures dating from about 1550. Standing in the Gothic nave is an impressive sculptural group depicting *Calvary* (1716) from the workshop of Ferdinand Maximilian Brokof.

St Agnes of Bohemia Convent ⓯

KLÁŠTER SV. ANEŽKY ČESKÉ

See pp92–3.

St Agnes of Bohemia Convent ⓯

KLÁŠTER SV. ANEŽKY ČESKÉ

Head of statue of St Agnes by Josef Myslbek

In 1234 a convent of the Poor Clares was founded here by Agnes, sister of King Wenceslas I. She was not canonized until 1989. The convent, one of the very first Gothic buildings in Bohemia, was abolished in 1782 and fell into disrepair. Following painstaking restoration in the 1960s, it has recovered much of its original appearance and is now used by the National Gallery to display a collection of medieval art from Bohemia and Central Europe. The recent enlargement of the exhibition space, has enabled these to be shown in a much broader Central European context.

★ Votive panel of Archbishop Jan Očko of Vlašim
This detailed panel, painted around 1370 by an anonymous artist, shows Charles IV kneeling before the Virgin in Heaven.

★ The Annunciation of Our Lady
Painted around 1350 by the renowned Master of the Vyšší Brod Altar, this panel is one of the oldest and finest works in the museum.

Cloister
The Gothic vaulting around the cloister of the convent dates from the 14th century.

First floor

Ground floor

Steps to first-floor gallery

Terrace café

STAR EXHIBITS

- ★ The Annunciation by the Master of the Vyšší Brod Altarpiece
- ★ Strakonice Madonna
- ★ Votive panel of Archbishop Jan Očko of Vlašim

GALLERY GUIDE

The permanent exhibition is housed on the first floor of the old convent in a long gallery and smaller rooms around the cloister. The works are arranged chronologically.

VISITORS' CHECKLIST

U Milosrdných 17. **Map** 3 C2. ***Tel*** *22 48 10 628.* *Náměstí Republiky, Staroměstská.* *17 to Law Faculty (Právnická fakulta), 5, 8, 14 to Dlouhá třída.* ***Open*** *10am–6pm Tue–Sun (last guided tour: 5pm).* **www**.ngprague.cz

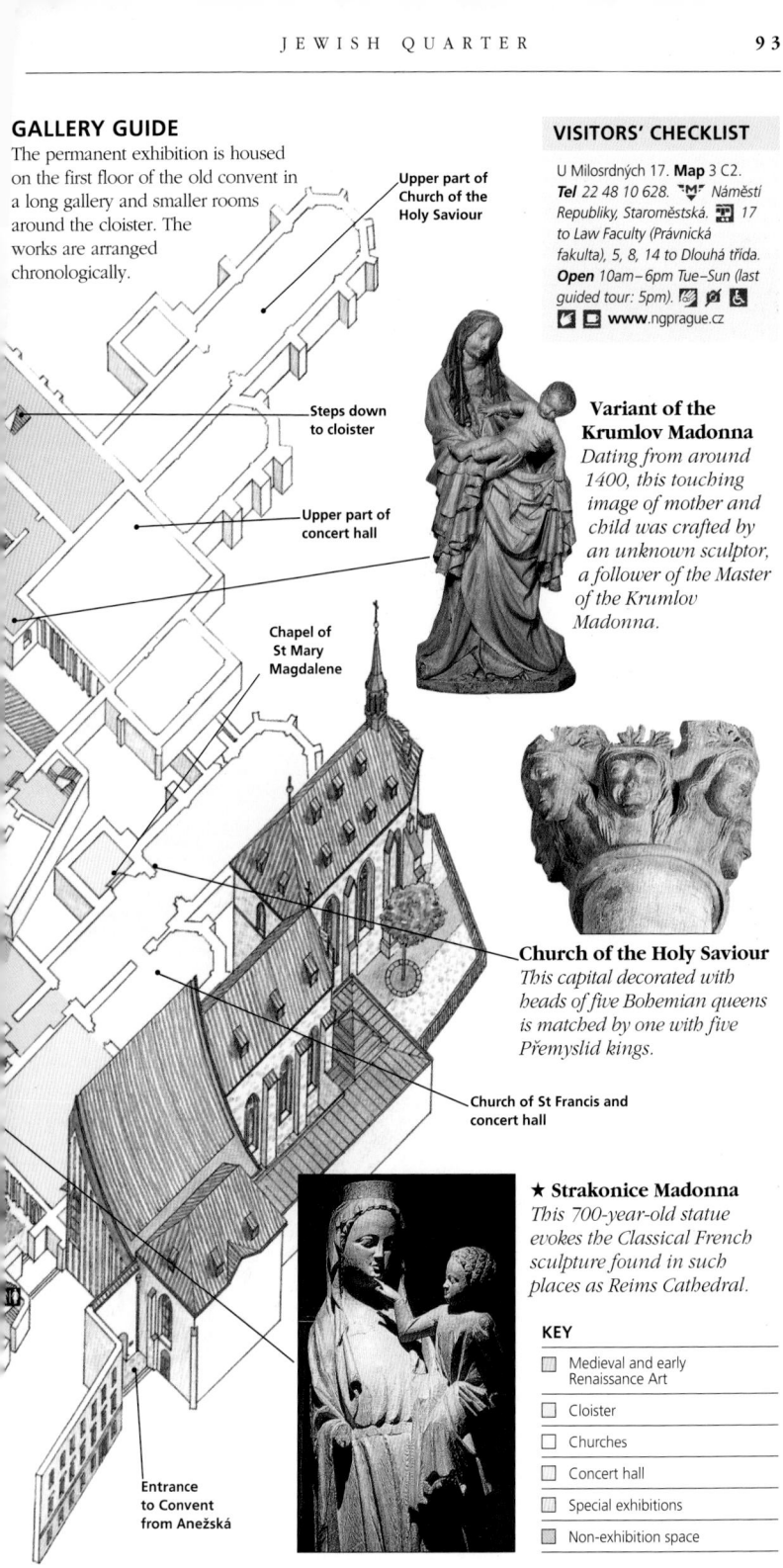

PRAGUE CASTLE AND HRADČANY

PRAŽSKÝ HRAD A HRADČANY

The history of Prague begins with the Castle, founded in the 9th century by Prince Bořivoj. Its commanding position high above the river Vltava soon made it the centre of the lands ruled by the Přemyslids. The buildings enclosed by the Castle walls included a palace, three churches and a monastery. In about 1320 a town called Hradčany was founded in part of the Castle's outer bailey. The Castle has been rebuilt many times, most notably in the reigns of Charles IV and Vladislav Jagiello. After a fire in 1541, the badly damaged buildings were rebuilt in Renaissance style and the Castle enjoyed its cultural heyday under Rudolph II. Since 1918 it has been the seat of the president of the Republic. The Changing of the Guard takes place every hour. At noon the ceremony includes a fanfare.

Stained-glass window in St Vitus's Cathedral

SIGHTS AT A GLANCE

Churches and Monasteries
- *St Vitus's Cathedral pp100–3* 2
- St George's Basilica 5
- Capuchin Monastery 19
- *The Loreto pp116–17* 20
- *Strahov Monastery pp120–21* 23

Palaces
- *Royal Palace pp104–5* 4
- Lobkowicz Palace 8
- Belvedere 11
- Archbishop's Palace 14
- Martinic Palace 16
- Černín Palace 21

Historic Buildings
- Powder Tower 3
- Dalibor Tower 9

Museums and Galleries
- Picture Gallery of Prague Castle 1
- *St George's Convent pp106–9* 6
- Riding School 13
- *Sternberg Palace pp112–15* 15
- Schwarzenberg Palace 17

Historic Streets
- Golden Lane 7
- New World 18
- Pohořelec 22

Parks and Gardens
- South Gardens 10
- Royal Garden 12

KEY
- Street-by-Street map *See pp96–7*
- Metro station
- Tram stop
- Tourist Information
- Castle wall

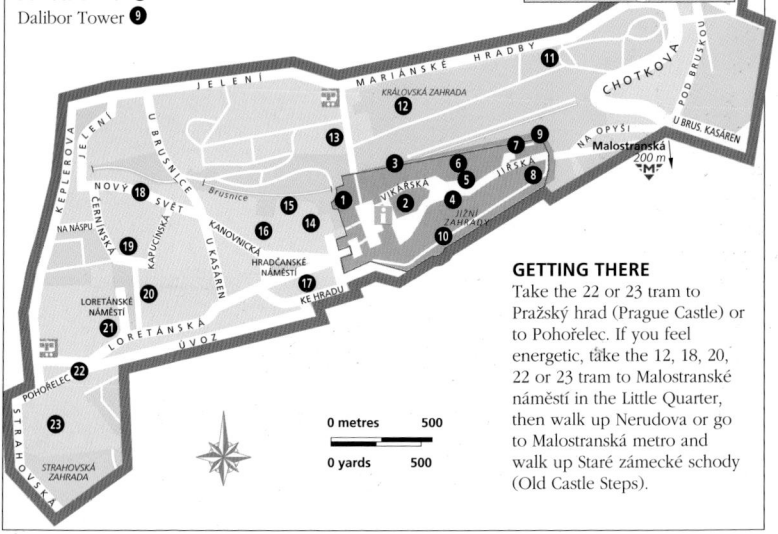

GETTING THERE

Take the 22 or 23 tram to Pražský hrad (Prague Castle) or to Pohořelec. If you feel energetic, take the 12, 18, 20, 22 or 23 tram to Malostranské náměstí in the Little Quarter, then walk up Nerudova or go to Malostranská metro and walk up Staré zámecké schody (Old Castle Steps).

◁ **The main entrance to Prague Castle**

Street-by-Street: Prague Castle

Despite periodic fires and invasions, Prague Castle has retained churches, chapels, halls and towers from every period of its history, from the the Gothic splendour of St Vitus's Cathedral to the Renaissance additions of Rudolph II, the last Habsburg to use the Castle as his principal residence. The courtyards date from 1753–75 when the whole area was rebuilt in Late Baroque and Neo-Classical styles. The Castle became the seat of the Czechoslovak president in 1918, and the current president of the Czech Republic has an office here.

Gothic reliquary of St George's arm in St Vitus's Cathedral

★ St Vitus's Cathedral
The decoration on the fence at St Vitus's Golden Portal ❷

Powder Tower
Used in the past for storing gunpowder and as a bell foundry, the tower is now a museum ❸

Picture Gallery of Prague Castle
Renaissance and Baroque paintings hang in the restored stables of the castle ❶

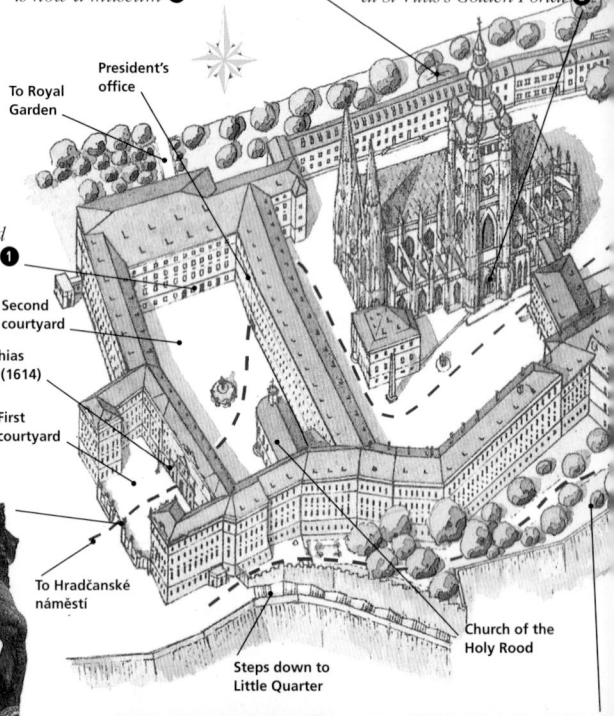

The Castle gates are crowned by copies of 18th-century statues of Fighting Giants by Ignaz Platzer.

South Gardens
18th-century statues decorate the gardens laid out in the old ramparts ❿

★ Golden Lane
The picturesque artisans' cottages along the inside of the castle wall were built in the late 16th century for the Castle's guards and gunners ❼

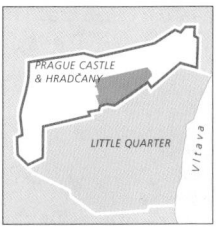

LOCATOR MAP
See Street Finder, map 2

White Tower

Dalibor Tower
This grim tower takes its name from the first man to be imprisoned in it ❾

Old Castle steps to Malostranská Metro

Lobkowicz Palace
The historical collection of the National Museum is housed here ❽

★ St George's Basilica
The vaulted chapel of the royal Bohemian martyr St Ludmilla is decorated with 16th-century paintings ❺

★ St George's Convent
The convent houses Renaissance and Baroque art, such as this 16th-century painting, The Resurrection of Christ *by B. Spranger* ❻

KEY

Suggested route

0 metres 60
0 yards 60

STAR SIGHTS

- ★ St Vitus's Cathedral
- ★ Royal Palace
- ★ St George's Basilica and Convent
- ★ Golden Lane

★ Royal Palace
The uniform exterior of the palace conceals many fine Gothic and Renaissance halls. Coats of arms cover the walls and ceiling of the Room of the New Land Rolls ❹

Picture Gallery of Prague Castle ❶

OBRAZÁRNA PRAŽSKÉHO HRADU

Prague Castle, the second courtyard. **Map** 2 D2. ***Tel*** *22 43 73 368.* *Malostranská, Hradčanská.* *22, 23* ***Open*** *10am–6pm daily* **www**.hrad.cz

The gallery was created in 1965 to hold works of art collected since the reign of Rudolph II *(see pp28–9)*. Though most of the collection was looted by the Swedes in 1648, many interesting paintings remain. Paintings from the 16th–18th centuries form the bulk of the collection, but there are also sculptures, among them a copy of a bust of Rudolph by Adriaen de Vries. Highlights include Titian's *The Toilet of a Young Lady*, Rubens' *The Assembly of the Olympic Gods* and Guido Reni's *The Centaur Nessus Abducting Deianeira*. Master Theodoric, Paolo Veronese, Tintoretto and the Czech Baroque artists Jan Kupecký and Petr Brandl are among other artists represented. The Picture Gallery houses many of Rudolph's best paintings.

You can also see the remains of the Castle's first church, the 9th-century Church of our Lady, thought to have been built by Prince Bořivoj, the first Přemyslid prince to be baptized a Christian *(see pp20–21)*. The historic site was discovered during reconstruction.

St Vitus's Cathedral ❷

CHRÁM SV. VÍTA

See pp100–3.

Powder Tower ❸

PRAŠNÁ VĚŽ

Prague Castle, Vikářská. **Map** 2 D2. ***Tel*** *22 43 73 368.* *Malostranská, Hradčanská.* *22, 23.* ***Open*** *Apr–Oct: 9am–5pm; Nov–Mar: 9am–4pm daily.* **www**.hrad.cz

A tower was built here in about 1496 by the King Vladislav II's architect Benedikt Ried as a cannon bastion overlooking the Stag Moat. The original was destroyed in the fire of 1541, but it was rebuilt as the home and workshop of gunsmith and bell founder Tomáš Jaroš. In 1549 he made Prague's largest bell, the 18-tonne Sigismund, for the bell tower of St Vitus's Cathedral.

During Rudolph II's reign (1576–1612), the tower became a laboratory for alchemists. It was here that adventurers such as Edward Kelley performed experiments that convinced the emperor they could turn lead into gold.

In 1649, when the Swedish army was occupying the Castle, gunpowder exploded in the tower, causing serious damage. Nevertheless it was used as a gunpowder store until 1754, when it was converted into flats for the sacristans of St Vitus's Cathedral. In the 1960s it became a museum with exhibits relating to Jaroš's bell foundry and alchemy practised in the reign of Rudolph II.

View of the Powder Tower from across the Stag Moat

Titian's *The Toilet of a Young Lady* in the Castle Picture Gallery

Royal Palace ❹

KRÁLOVSKÝ PALÁC

See pp104–5.

St George's Basilica ❺

BAZILIKA SV. JIŘÍ

Jiřské náměstí. **Map** 2 E2. ***Tel*** *22 43 73 368.* *Malostranská, Hradčanská.* *22, 23.* ***Open*** *Apr–Oct: 9am–5pm daily; Nov–Mar: 9am–4pm daily.* **www**.hrad.cz

Founded by Prince Vratislav (915–21), the basilica predates St Vitus's Cathedral and is the best-preserved Romanesque church in Prague. It was enlarged in 973 when the adjoining St George's Convent was established here, and rebuilt following a fire in 1142. The massive twin towers and austere interior have been scrupulously restored to give a good idea of the church's original appearance. However, the rusty red façade was a 17th-century Baroque addition.

Buried in the church is St Ludmilla, widow of the 9th-century ruler Prince Bořivoj *(see pp20–21)*. She became Bohemia's first female Christian martyr when she was strangled on the orders of Drahomíra, her daughter-in-law, as she knelt at prayer. Other members of the Přemyslid dynasty buried here include Vratislav. His austere tomb stands on the right-hand side of the nave at the foot of the curving steps that lead up to the choir. The impressive Baroque grille opposite encloses the tomb of Boleslav II (973–99).

Façade and towers of St George's Basilica

St George's Convent ❻

KLÁŠTER SV. JIŘÍ

See pp106–9.

Golden Lane ❼

ZLATÁ ULIČKA

Map 2 E2. *Malostranská, Hradčanská.* *22, 23.*

Named after the goldsmiths who lived here in the 17th century, this short, narrow street is one of the most picturesque in Prague. One side of the lane is lined with tiny, brightly painted houses which were built right into the arches of the Castle walls. They were constructed in the late 1500s for Rudolph II's 24 Castle guards. A century later the goldsmiths moved in and modified the buildings. But by the 19th century the area had degenerated into a slum and was populated by Prague's poor and the criminal community. In the 1950s all the remaining tenants were moved and the area restored to something like its original state. Most of the houses were converted into shops selling books, Bohemian glass and other souvenirs for tourists, who flock to the narrow lane.

Golden Lane has been home to some well-known writers, including the Nobel prize-winning poet, Jaroslav Seifert, and Franz Kafka *(see p68)* who stayed at No. 22 with his sister for a few months in 1916–17.

Because of its name, legends have spread about the street being filled with alchemists huddled over their bubbling alembics trying to produce gold for Rudolph II. In fact the alchemists had laboratories in Vikářská, the lane between St Vitus's Cathedral and the Powder Tower.

One of the tiny houses in Golden Lane

Lobkowicz Palace ❽

LOBKOVICKÝ PALÁC

Jiřská 3. **Map** 2 E2. ***Tel*** *25 75 35 979.* *Hradčanská.* *22, 23.*
Open *9am–5pm Tue–Sun.*
www.nm.cz
Toy Museum *22 43 72 294.*
Open *9:30am–5:30pm daily.*
www.barbiemuseum.cz

This is one of the palaces that sprang up after the fire of 1541, when Hradčany was almost totally destroyed. It dates from 1570, and some original *sgraffito* on the façade has been preserved, but most of the present palace is Carlo Lurago's 17th-century reconstruction for the Lobkowicz family, who had inherited it in 1627. The most splendid room is the 17th-century banqueting hall with mythological frescoes by Fabian Harovník.

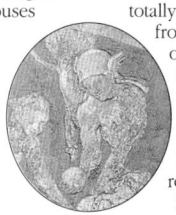
Detail of 16th-century *sgraffito* on façade of Lobkowicz Palace

The palace is part of the National Museum. Its superb permanent exhibition traces Czech history from the first settlements to the revolution of 1848 by means of documents, paintings, jewellery, glass, sculpture and weapons. Copies of the Czech Coronation Jewels, kept in St Vitus's Cathedral, are also on display.

Opposite the palace at No. 6 is a delightful toy museum claiming to be the world's second largest, with toys from ancient Greece to the present.

St Vitus's Cathedral ❷

KATEDRÁLA SV. VÍTA, VÁCLAVA A VOJTĚCHA

Work began on the city's most distinctive landmark in 1344 on the orders of John of Luxembourg. The first architect was the French Matthew of Arras. After his death, Swabian Peter Parler took over. His masons' lodge continued to work on the building until the Hussite Wars. Finally completed by 19th- and 20th-century architects and artists, the cathedral houses the crown jewels and the tomb of "Good King" Wenceslas *(pp20–21)*.

St Vitus's Cathedral
This 19th-century engraving shows how the cathedral looked before the additions made in 1872–1929.

Rose Window
Designed by František Kysela in 1925–7, the window above the portals depicts scenes from the biblical story of the creation.

Gargoyles
On the ornate west front, gutter spouts are given their traditional disguise.

Twin west spires

Triforium

West front

Main entrance

Nave

TIMELINE

c925 Rotunda of St Vitus built by St Wenceslas

1359 Masterbuilder Peter Parler summoned to continue work on the cathedral

Bust of Peter Parler on triforium

1619 Calvinists take over cathedral as house of prayer

1929 Consecration of completed cathedral, nearly 1,000 years after death of St Wenceslas

1000 | 1200 | 1400 | 1600 | 1800

1060 Building of triple-naved basilica begins on orders of Prince Spytihněv

Tomb of Přemysl Otakar II

1421 Hussites occupy St Vitus's

1589 Royal tomb completed

1344 King John of Luxembourg founds Gothic cathedral. French architect Matthew of Arras begins work

1872 Joseph Mocker begins work on west nave

1770 New steeple added to tower after fire

★ Flying Buttresses
The slender buttresses that surround the exterior of the nave and chancel, supporting the vaulted interior, are richly decorated like the rest of the cathedral.

VISITORS' CHECKLIST

Prague Castle, third courtyard. **Map** 2 D2. *Hradčanská, Malostranská.* *22, 23 to Prague Castle (Pražský hrad) or to U Prašného mostu.* **Cathedral open** *Nov–Mar: 9am–4pm daily; Apr–Oct: 9am–5pm (except during services).* **Steeple open** *Apr–Oct: 9am–4:15pm.*

The Renaissance bell tower is capped with a Baroque "helmet".

Chancel

★ Chapel of St Wenceslas
The bronze ring on the chapel's north portal was thought to be the one to which St Wenceslas clung as he was murdered by his brother Boleslav (see pp20–21).

To Royal Palace ***(See pp104–5)***

The tomb of St Wenceslas is connected to an altar, decorated with semi-precious stones.

★ Golden Portal
Until the 19th century this was the main cathedral entrance, and it is still used on special occasions. Above it is a mosaic of The Last Judgment *by 14th-century Venetian craftsmen.*

Gothic Vaulting
The skills of architect Peter Parler are never more clearly seen than in the delicate fans of ribbing that support the three Gothic arches of the Golden Portal.

STAR FEATURES

- ★ Chapel of St Wenceslas
- ★ Golden Portal
- ★ Flying Buttresses

A Guided Tour of St Vitus's Cathedral

West door: St Wenceslas' murder

A walk around St Vitus's takes you back through a thousand years of history. Go in through the west portal to see some of the best elements of the modern, Neo-Gothic style and continue past a succession of side chapels to catch glimpses of religious artefacts such as saintly relics, and works of art from Renaissance paintings to modern statuary. Allow plenty of time to gaze at the richly decorated, jewel-encrusted St Wenceslas Chapel before you leave.

② Chancel
The chancel was built by Peter Parler from 1372. It is remarkable for the soaring height of its vault, counter-pointed by the intricacy of the webbed Gothic tracery.

① Alfons Mucha Window
The cathedral contains many superb examples of 20th-century Czech stained glass, notably St Cyril and St Methodius.

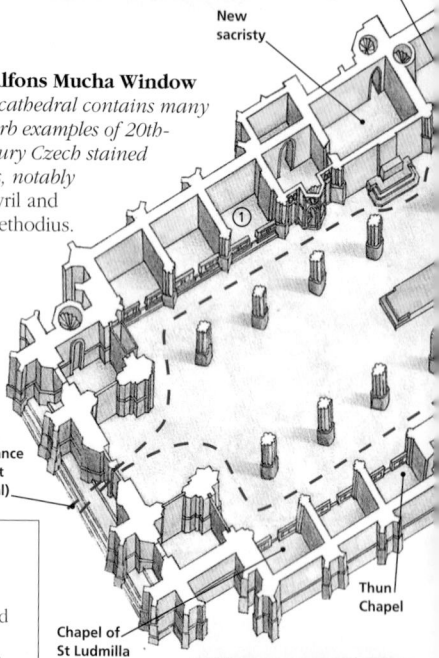

THE FOUR ERAS OF ST VITUS'S

Excavations have revealed sections of the northern apse of St Wenceslas's original rotunda, and architectural and sculptural remains of the later basilica, beneath the existing cathedral. The western, Neo-Gothic end is a faithful completion of the 14th-century plan.

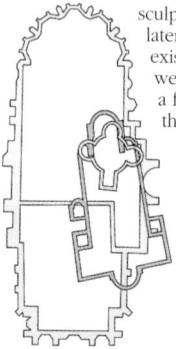

KEY

- Rotunda, 10th century
- Basilica, 11th century
- Gothic cathedral, 14th century
- 19th- and 20th-century additions to cathedral

Leopold II is shown in a contemporary engraving being crowned King of Bohemia at the cathedral in September 1791. Mozart composed an opera, *La Clemenza di Tito*, in honour of the occasion.

③ Flight of Frederick of the Palatinate
In depicting the sad aftermath of the Battle of the White Mountain in 1620 (see p31), *this carved wooden panel shows 17th-century Prague in fascinating detail.*

④ Tomb of St John Nepomuk
Crafted from solid silver in 1736, this elaborate tomb honours the saint who became the focus of a Counter-Reformation cult (see p137).

Chapel of St John the Baptist

Pulpit (1618)

Chapel of the Holy Relics

Chapel of the Holy Rood

Stairs to crypt

Golden Portal

Exit from crypt

⑤ Royal Oratory
The vault of the 15th-century Late-Gothic oratory is carved with branches instead of ribs.

⑥ Crypt
Steps lead down to the royal tombs, including those of Charles IV and his four wives, as well as vestiges of the early rotunda and basilica.

⑦ Royal Mausoleum
Ferdinand I died in 1564. His beloved wife and son, Maximilian II, are buried alongside him in the mausoleum.

⑧ St Wenceslas Chapel
Gothic frescoes with scenes from the Bible and the life of the saint cover the walls, interspersed with a patchwork of polished gemstones and fine gilding. Every object is a work of art – this golden steeple held the wafers and wine for Holy Communion.

KEY

- - - Tour route

Royal Palace ❹

KRÁLOVSKÝ PALÁC

From the time Prague Castle was first fortified in stone in the 11th century *(see pp22–3)*, the palace was the seat of Bohemian princes. The building consists of three different architectural layers. A Romanesque palace built by Soběslav I around 1135 forms the cellars of the present building. Přemysl Otakar II and Charles IV then added their own palaces above this, while the top floor, built for Vladislav Jagiello, contains the massive Gothic Vladislav Hall. During the period of Habsburg rule the palace housed government offices, courts and the old Bohemian Diet (parliament). In 1924 it was extensively restored.

Riders' Staircase
These wide and gently sloping steps, with their Gothic rib vault, were used by knights on horseback to get to Vladislav Hall for indoor jousting competitions.

Vladislav Hall
The 17th-century painting by Aegidius Sadeler shows that the Royal Court was very like a public market. The hall's magnificent rib vaulting was designed by Benedikt Ried in the 1490s.

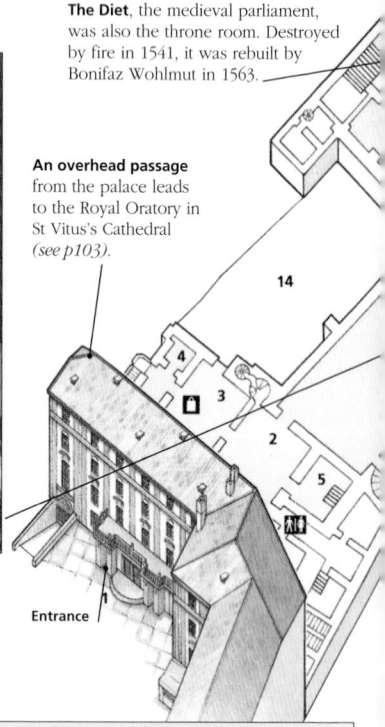

TIMELINE

Přemysl Otakar II, 1230–78

1041 Castle besieged and palace burnt

1253 Palace reconstructed by Přemysl Otakar II

1541 Fire destroys large part of Castle

1618 Defenestration from Bohemian Chancellery

1766–8 Building of Theresian Wing

900 | 1100 | 1300 | 1500 | 1700 | 1900

Late 9th century Founding of Prague Castle by Prince Bořivoj

1135 Rebuilding undertaken by Soběslav I

1340 Charles IV rebuilds palace

1370s Peter Parler rebuilds All Saints' Chapel

1502 Completion of Vladislav Hall by Benedikt Ried after nine years

Decorated door of office in Royal Palace

1924 Palace undergoes extensive restoration

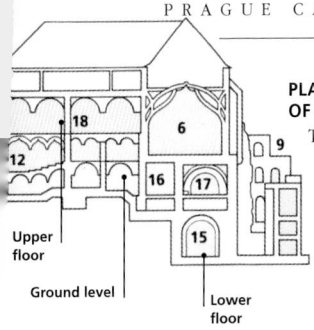

PLAN AND CROSS SECTION OF ROYAL PALACE

The cross section of the palace shows the three distinct levels of the building, all constructed at different times. The plan shows how Vladislav Hall dominates the entire palace structure.

VISITORS' CHECKLIST

Prague Castle, third courtyard. **Map** 2 D2. ***Tel*** *22 43 73 368.* *Hradčanská, up K Brusce, then through the Royal Garden; Malostranská, left up Klárov, then up Old Castle Steps.* *22, 23 to Prague Castle (Pražský hrad).* ***Open*** *9am–4pm daily (to 5pm Apr–Oct; last adm: 1hr before closing).* **www**.hrad.cz

All Saints' Chapel was built by Peter Parler for Charles IV. After the 1541 fire, its vault had to be rebuilt and it was redecorated in the Baroque style.

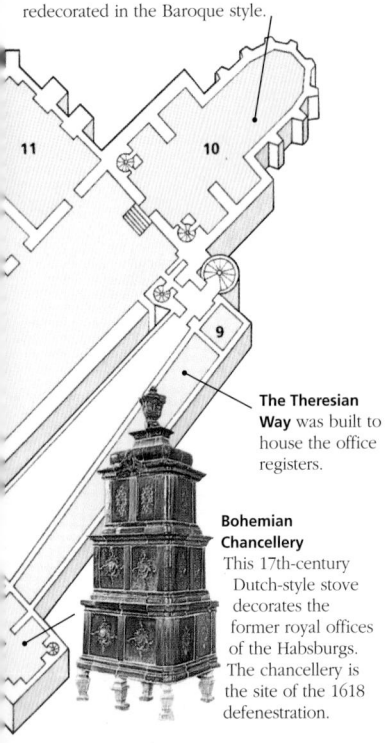

The Theresian Way was built to house the office registers.

Bohemian Chancellery
This 17th-century Dutch-style stove decorates the former royal offices of the Habsburgs. The chancellery is the site of the 1618 defenestration.

KEY TO ROYAL PALACE

- ☐ Romanesque and Early Gothic
- ☐ Late Gothic
- ☐ Rebuilt after 1541 fire
- ☐ Baroque and later

1 Eagle Fountain
2 Vestibule
3 Green Chamber
4 King's Bedchamber
5 Romanesque tower
6 Vladislav Hall
7 Bohemian Chancellery
8 Imperial Council Room steps
9 Terrace
10 All Saints' Chapel
11 Diet Hall
12 Ride taircase
13 Court of Appeal
14 Palace courtyard
15 Hall of the Romanesque palace
16 Old Land Rolls
17 Palace of Charles IV
18 New Land Rolls

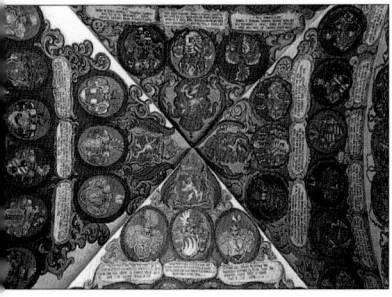

The New Land Rolls
These rooms are decorated with the crests of clerks who worked here from 1561 to 1774.

DEFENESTRATION OF 1618

Painting by Václav Brožík, 1889

On 23 May, 1618, more than 100 Protestant nobles, led by Count Thurn, marched into the palace to protest against the succession to the throne of the intolerant Habsburg Archduke Ferdinand. The two Catholic Governors appointed by Ferdinand, Jaroslav Martinic and Vilém Slavata, were confronted and, after a row, the Protestants threw both the Governors and their secretary, Philipp Fabricius, out of the eastern window. Falling some 15 m (50 ft), they survived by landing in a dung heap. This event signalled the beginning of the Thirty Years' War. The Catholics attributed the survival of the Governors to the intervention of angels.

St George's Convent ❻

KLÁŠTER SV. JIŘÍ

The first convent in Bohemia was founded here close to the Royal Palace in 973 by Prince Boleslav II. His sister Mlada was its first abbess. Rebuilt over the centuries, the convent was finally abolished in 1782 and converted into barracks. In 1962–74 it was reconstructed and today it houses the National Gallery's collection of Bohemian Baroque art. It shows works by some of the Baroque masters, including the painters Karel Škréta, Petr Brandl and Václav Vavřinec Reiner, and the sculptor Matyáš Bernard Braun.

★ Landscape with Orpheus and Animals
This pre-1720 work by Baroque master Václav Vavřinec Reiner represents a departure from his usual landscape frescoes by including a figure from Greek myth.

★ Bust of a Talking Apostle
Painted in about 1725 by Petr Brandl, this painting has since been hailed as one of the greatest examples of Czech art. It is noted for its strong sense of movement.

Stairs to upper floor

Stairs down to exit

Ground floor

Entrance to Gallery from Jiřské náměstí

St George's Basilica *(see pp98–9)*

STAR EXHIBITS

- ★ Bust of a Talking Apostle by Petr Brandl
- ★ Landscape with Orpheus and Animals by V. V. Reiner
- ★ Self Portrait by Jan Kupecký

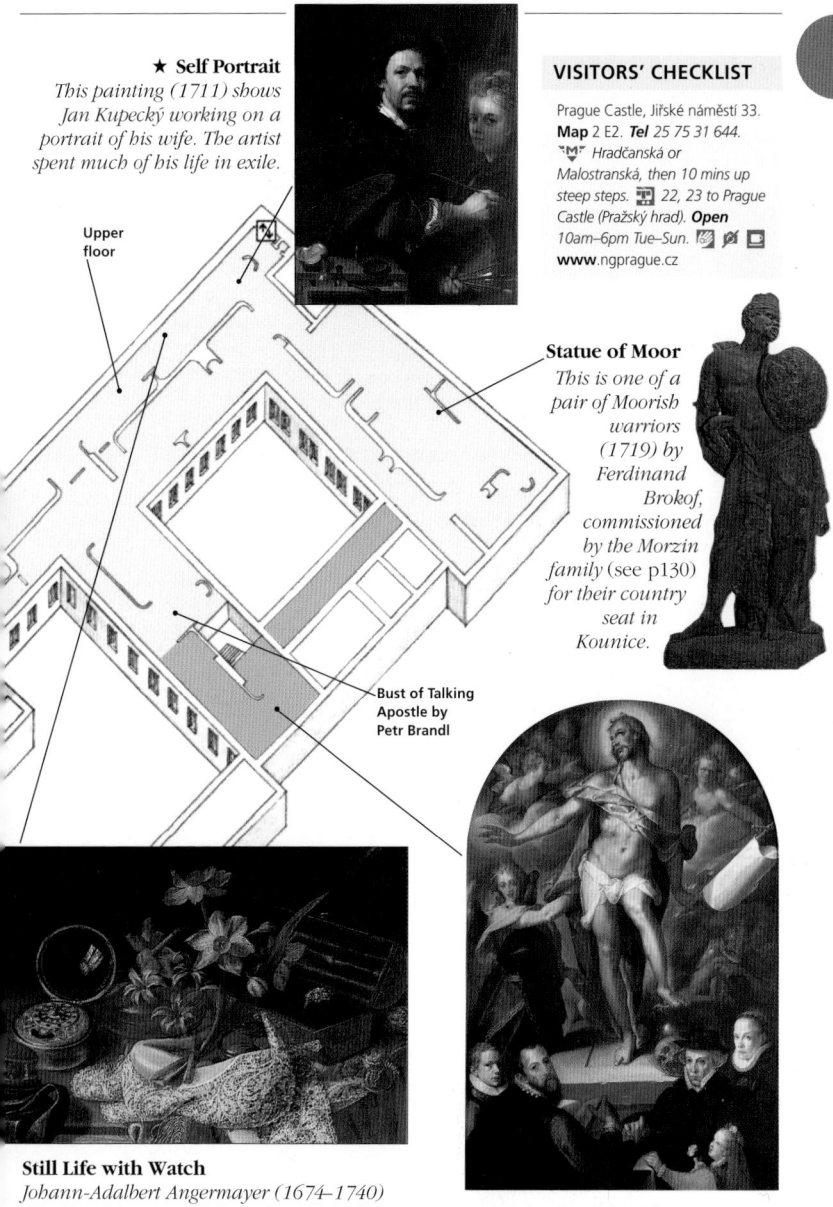

★ Self Portrait
This painting (1711) shows Jan Kupecký working on a portrait of his wife. The artist spent much of his life in exile.

Statue of Moor
This is one of a pair of Moorish warriors (1719) by Ferdinand Brokof, commissioned by the Morzin family (see p130) *for their country seat in Kounice.*

Still Life with Watch
Johann-Adalbert Angermayer (1674–1740) filled his delicate still lifes with symbols of the transience and vanity of human life.

Epitaph of Goldsmith Mikuláš Müller
This work by Bartholomeus Spranger epitomizes the Mannerist style popular in the court of Rudolph II.

VISITORS' CHECKLIST

Prague Castle, Jiřské náměstí 33. **Map** 2 E2. ***Tel*** *25 75 31 644.* *Hradčanská or Malostranská, then 10 mins up steep steps.* *22, 23 to Prague Castle (Pražský hrad).* ***Open*** *10am–6pm Tue–Sun.* **www**.ngprague.cz

KEY

- Rudolphian Mannerism (c1600)
- Czech art of the Baroque
- Chapel of St Anne
- St George's Basilica
- Special exhibitions
- Non-exhibition space

GALLERY GUIDE

The permanent exhibition is located on the first floor of the convent. Beginning with a small collection of Mannerist art, you can follow the development of Czech Baroque painting and sculpture throughout the 17th and 18th centuries.

Exploring the St George's Collection

This wonderful collection gives a fascinating insight into the art and sculpture of one of the periods of Prague's history that is so conspicuous in the city's architecture – the Baroque. The Bohemian school of Baroque art produced dramatic biblical paintings and statues of saints and angels in flamboyant poses. There are also collections of works representing the antecedents of the Baroque: not only the better known late Gothic, but also paintings and sculptures of the Mannerist school that were created under the patronage of Rudolph II.

Wooden statue of St Judas Thaddeus by Matyáš Bernard Braun (1712)

EARLY 16TH-CENTURY CZECH ART

Some of the works in the gallery's collection of late Gothic art show greater similarity with contemporary German and Italian paintings. The finest Bohemian painter of this period is the Master of the Litoměřice Altar, who was active at the beginning of the 16th century. His most impressive works are an altar triptych showing *The Holy Trinity and The Visitation of the Virgin Mary*.

Also on display are some fascinating reliefs by a wood-carver who signed his works with the initials I P. His style is that of the so-called Danube school and his figures are clearly influenced by German painter and engraver Albrecht Dürer. Dating from about 1520, the *Votive Altarpiece of Zlíchov* shows a kneeling knight with the Virgin Mary, St Andrew, Christ and Death.

RUDOLPHIAN MANNERISM (C1600)

Before the Baroque reached Bohemia, there was a short period when Prague was the main centre of Northern Mannerism. This term is used to describe a style that evolved in Italy after the Renaissance. Many 16th-century painters and sculptors strove to outdo the exaggerated poses of Michelangelo's later works just for the sake of creating a startling effect. A typical example of this is *The Last Judgment* by Josef Heintz. A more successful exponent of this style was Bartholomeus Spranger from Antwerp. He died in Prague in 1611 while in the employment of the Imperial Emperor Rudolph II *(see p28–9)*.

With his passion for the unusual and the artificial, Rudolph loved Mannerist artists and invited many to work at his court in Prague. Although the Mannerist style had fallen out of fashion throughout the royal courts of Europe, the paintings made under his patronage represent the last flowering of this dramatic style. They made an impression on the next generation of artists who emerged after the Thirty Years War and who came to define style of the Bohemian school of Baroque art.

Rudolph's great collection was dispersed when Prague Castle was looted in 1648, but the few works on show here give an idea of his tastes. The best are probably the paintings of the German-born Hans von Aachen and the sculptures of the Dutch-born Adriaen de Vries. There are also other sculptures by Hans Mont and Benedict Wurzelbauer.

Not all the works here are typically Mannerist in style. The landscapes of Roelant Savery, for example, show a genuine feeling for the beauty of the Bohemian forests that he gained during an eight-year stay in Prague (1604–12).

Altarpiece of *The Holy Trinity* by Master of the Litoměřice Altar (c1515)

***Stag Hunt* (c1610) by Roelant Savery, artist at the court of Rudolph II**

CZECH ART OF THE BAROQUE

There are many agreeable surprises in this extensive collection of Baroque art.

The founding personality of Czech Baroque painting is Karel Škréta. The five years he spent in Italy early in his career were profoundly influential on his work. He is the prime representative of the realistic trend in Czech Baroque art. Of his religious paintings, *St Charles Borromeo Visiting the Sick* shows realistic types and detail, and this also applies in full measure to the lunette scene of the *Nativity of St Wenceslas*. His large group portrait of Dionysius Miseroni, the Italian cutter of precious stones, and his family, reveals an interesting glimpse into a workshop, and the rare work, a crystal chalice, made there. Much of his later work, both in portraits and altarpieces, reflects a Dutch and Flemish influence.

Of the paintings of religious subjects, the finest are surely those by Petr Brandl. The old men who feature in many of his works are beautifully painted. Particularly moving is the painting known as *Simeon and the Infant Jesus*. The gallery gives a good idea of his work as a portraitist, but unfortunately his work on Prague and country churches is not represented here.

A contemporary of Brandl, Jan Kupecký was Czech by birth but lived abroad for most of his life. He had a large middle-class and aristocratic clientele throughout Central Europe, and his portraits are among the highlights of the exhibition. The large portrait of Karl Bruni, a painter of miniatures, clearly illustrates the form and content of Baroque portraiture at the beginning of the 18th century.

Václav Vavřinec Reiner's most important contribution to the development of Bohemian Baroque paintings were his strikingly coloured frescoes and vivid landscape paintings. The several pictures housed here give an idea of his art, in particular two of his sketches, one for the ceiling painting in the Prague Church of St Giles, and the other for the Loretto Church of the Nativity. The *Landscape with Orpheus and Animals and Landscape with Birds* are highly decorative.

On a smaller scale, look out for the still lifes of flowers and game by the Swiss painter Johann Rudolf Bys and his pupil Johann-Adalbert Angermayer. There are also notable works by Jan Jiří Heinsch, Jan Kryštof Liška and Michal Václav Halbax. The transition to the later Rococo styles is demonstrated in works by Bohemian artists such as Antonín Kern, Norbert Grund and František Xaver Palko.

The sculptures are chiefly by the 18th-century artists whose works decorate so many of the city's Baroque churches: Ferdinand Brokof, Matthias Braun and Ignaz Platzer. Several of the more flamboyant saints and angels are in painted wood, an unexpected link with the early polychrome wood carvings of the Gothic period.

***Hedvika Francesca Wussin* by Jan Kupecký (1710)**

Old prison in the Dalibor Tower

Dalibor Tower ❾

DALIBORKA

Prague Castle, Zlatá ulička. **Map** 2 E2. *Malostranská.* *18, 20, 22, 23.* ***Open*** *on request.*

This 15th-century tower with a conical roof was part of the fortifications built by King Vladislav Jagiello *(see p26–7)*. His coat of arms can be seen on the outer wall. The tower also served as a prison and is named after its first inmate, Dalibor of Kozojedy, a young knight sentenced to death for harbouring some outlawed serfs. While awaiting execution, he was kept in an underground dungeon, into which he had to be lowered through a hole in the floor.

According to legend, while in prison he learnt to play the violin. People sympathetic to his plight came to listen to his playing and provided him with food and drink, which they lowered on a rope from a window – prisoners were often left to starve to death. The story was used by Bedřich Smetana in his opera *Dalibor*. The tower ceased to serve as a prison in 1781. Visitors can see part of the old prison.

South Gardens ❿

JIŽNÍ ZAHRADY

Prague Castle (access from Hradčanské náměstí). **Map** 2 D3. *Malostranská, Hradčanská.* *18, 20, 22, 23.* ***Open*** *Apr–Oct: 10am–6pm daily.* **www**.hrad.cz

The gardens occupy the long narrow band of land below the Castle overlooking the Little Quarter. Several small gardens have been linked to form what is now known as the South Gardens. The oldest, the Paradise Garden (Rajská zahrada), laid out in 1562, contains a circular pavilion built for Emperor Matthias in 1617. Its carved wooden ceiling shows the coloured emblems of the 39 countries of the Habsburg Empire. The Garden on the Ramparts (Zahrada Na valech) dates from the 19th century. It occupies a former vegetable patch and is famous as the site of the defenestration of 1618 *(see p105)*, when two Imperial governors were thrown from a first-floor window. Two obelisks were subsequently erected by Ferdinand II to mark the spots where they landed. Extensive modifications were carried out in the 1920s by Josip Plečnik, who built the Bull Staircase leading to the Paradise Garden and the observation terrace. Below the terrace, in the former Hartig Garden, is a Baroque music pavilion designed by Giovanni Battista Alliprandi. Beside it stand four statues of Classical gods by Antonín Braun.

Alliprandi's music pavilion in the South Gardens

Belvedere ⓫

BELVEDÉR

Prague Castle, Royal Garden. **Map** 2 E1. *Malostranská, Hradčanská.* *18, 20, 22, 23.* ***Open*** *10am–6pm Tue–Sun during exhibitions only.* **www**.hrad.cz

Built by Ferdinand I for his beloved wife Anne, the Belvedere is one of the finest Italian Renaissance buildings north of the Alps. Also known as the Royal Summer Palace

The Belvedere, Emperor Ferdinand I's summer palace in the Royal Garden beside Prague Castle

Antonín Braun's statue of *The Allegory of Night* in front of the *sgraffito* decoration of the Ball Game Hall in the Royal Garden

(Královský letohrádek), it is an arcaded summerhouse with slender Ionic columns topped by a roof shaped like an inverted ship's hull clad in blue-green copper. The main architect was Paolo della Stella, who was also responsible for the ornate reliefs inside the arcade. Work began in 1538, but was interrupted by the great Castle fire of 1541. The Belvedere was eventually completed in 1564.

In the middle of the small geometrical garden in front of the palace stands the Singing Fountain. Dating from 1568, it owes its name to the musical sound the water makes as it hits the bronze bowl, though you have to listen closely to appreciate the effect. The fountain was cast by Tomáš Jaroš, the famous bell founder, who lived and worked in the Powder Tower *(see p98)*.

Many of the Belvedere's works of art were plundered by the occupying Swedish army in 1648. The statues stolen included Adriaen de Vries's 16th-century bronze of *Mercury and Psyche*, which is now in the Louvre in Paris. The Belvedere is now used as an art gallery.

Royal Garden ⓬

KRÁLOVSKÁ ZAHRADA

Prague Castle, U Prašného mostu. **Map** 2 D2. *Malostranská, Hradčanská.* *22, 23.* **Open** *May–Oct: 10am–6pm daily.* **www**.hrad.cz

The garden was created in 1535 for Ferdinand I. Its appearance has been altered over time, but some examples of 16th-century garden architecture have survived, notably the Belvedere and the Ball Game Hall (Míčovna), built by Bonifaz Wohlmut in 1569. The building is covered in beautiful, though much restored, Renaissance *sgraffito*, a form of decoration created by cutting a design through the wet top layer of plaster on to a contrasting undercoat. The garden is a beautiful place for a stroll, especially in spring when thousands of tulips bloom in its immaculate beds. This is where tulips were first acclimatized to Europe.

Příchovský coat of arms

Riding School ⓭

JÍZDÁRNA

Prague Castle. **Map** 2 D2. ***Tel*** *22 43 73 368.* *Malostranská, Hradčanská.* *22, 23.* **Open** *10am–6pm during exhibitions.*

The 17th-century Riding School forms one side of U Prašného mostu, a road which runs to the northern side of Prague Castle via Deer Moat. In the 1920s it was converted into an exhibition hall, which now holds important exhibitions of painting and sculpture. A garden provides excellent views of St. Vitus's Cathedral and the northern fortifications of the castle.

Archbishop's Palace ⓮

ARCIBISKUPSKÝ PALÁC

Hradčanské náměstí 16. **Map** 2 D3. ***Tel*** *22 03 92 111.* *Malostranská, Hradčanská.* *22, 23.* **Not open** *to the public.*

Ferdinand I bought this sumptuous palace in 1562 for the first Catholic Archbishop since the Hussite Wars *(see pp26–7)*. It replaced the old Archbishop's Palace in the Little Quarter, which had been destroyed during the wars, and has remained the Archbishop's seat in Prague ever since. In the period after the Battle of the White Mountain *(see p30–31)*, it was a powerful symbol of Catholic domination of the city and the Czech lands. Its spectacular cream-coloured Rococo façade was designed by Johann Joseph Wirch in the 1760s for Archbishop Antonín Příchovský, whose coat of arms sits proudly above the portal.

Sternberg Palace ⓯

ŠTERNBERSKÝ PALÁC

See pp112–15.

Sternberg Palace ⓯

ŠTERNBERSKÝ PALÁC

Franz Josef Sternberg founded the Society of Patriotic Friends of the Arts in Bohemia in 1796. Fellow noblemen would lend their finest pictures and sculpture to the society, which had its headquarters in the early-18th-century Sternberg Palace. Since 1949, the fine Baroque building has been used to house the National Gallery's collection of European art, with its superb range of Old Masters.

★ Scholar in his Study
In this painting from 1634 Rembrandt used keenly observed detail to convey wisdom in the face of the old scholar.

Cardinal Cesi's Garden in Rome
Henrick van Cleve's painting (1548) provides a valuable image of a Renaissance collections of antiquities. The garden was later destroyed.

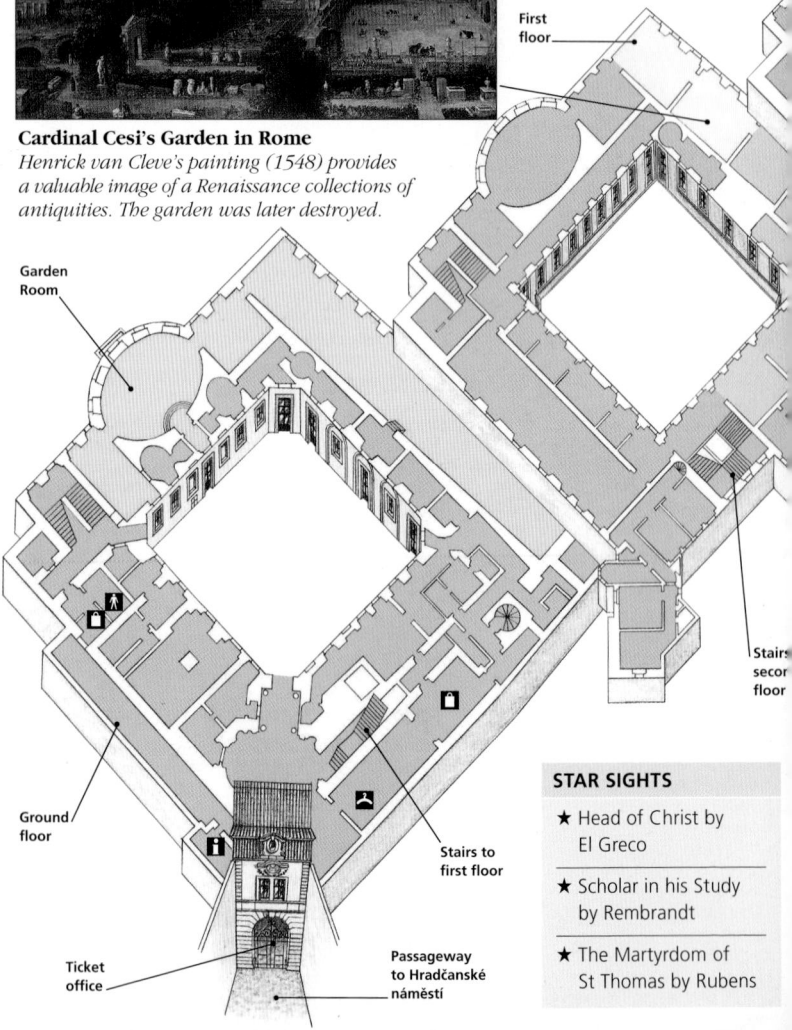

STAR SIGHTS

- ★ Head of Christ by El Greco
- ★ Scholar in his Study by Rembrandt
- ★ The Martyrdom of St Thomas by Rubens

Concerning the Eden *(1618)*
Roelandt Savery studied models of exotic animals, brought to Prague by Persian nobles, at the court of Emperor Rudolf II. He was then able to paint real animals.

VISITORS' CHECKLIST

Hradčanské náměstí 15. **Map** 1 C2. ***Tel*** *20 51 45 98.* *Hradčanská, Malostranská.* *22, 23 to Prague Castle (Pražský hrad) or Pohořelec.* ***Open*** *10am– 6pm Tue–Sun (last tour: 5pm).* **www**.ngprague.cz

★ The Martyrdom of St Thomas
This magnificent work is by Peter Paul Rubens, the foremost Flemish painter of the 17th century.

Chinese Cabinet

Second floor

airs down to
her floors
d exit

★ Head of Christ
Painted by El Greco in the 1590s, this portrait emphasizes the humanity of Christ. At the same time the curious square halo framing the head gives the painting the qualities of an ancient icon.

GALLERY GUIDE

The gallery is arranged on three floors around the central courtyard of the palace. The ground floor, reached from the courtyard, houses German and Austrian art from the 15th to 19th centuries. The stairs to the collections on the upper floors are opposite the ticket office at the main entrance.

The Lamentation of Christ
The frozen, sculptural figures make this one of the finest paintings by Lorenzo Monaco (1408).

KEY

- German and Austrian Art 1400–1800
- Flemish and Dutch Art 1400–1600
- Italian Art 1400–1500
- Roman Art
- Flemish and Dutch Art 1600–1800
- French Art 1600–1800
- Icons, Classical and Ancient Art
- Venice 1700–1800 and Goya
- Spanish Art 1600–1800
- Naples and Venice 1600–1700
- Italian Art 1500–1600
- Non-exhibition space

Exploring the Sternberg Collections

The National Gallery's collection of European art ranks among the best collections of comparable size. Since the transfer of the outstanding 19th- and 20th-century exhibits to Veletržní Palace in 1996 *(see pp164–5)* the Sternberg has been expanding its permanent exhibition, with especially strong representations from Italian medieval art, Neapolitan artists of the 17th and 18th centuries, Dutch and Flemish works, and German art of the 15th to 17th centuries. There is also a fine collection of Renaissance bronzes, and the fascinating Chinese Cabinet is on display again after a restoration lasting several years.

***St John the Baptist* by Rodin**

ICONS, CLASSICAL AND ANCIENT ART

Two small rooms contain an odd assortment of paintings that do not quite fit in with the rest of the collection. These include a *Portrait of a Young Woman* dating from the 2nd century AD, discovered during excavations at Fayoum in Egypt in the 19th century.

The majority of the exhibits, however, are icons of the Orthodox church. These come from a variety of Eastern European countries – some are Byzantine, some Italo-Greek and some Russian. The finest examples are two of the later 16th-century works, *The Lamentation of Christ* from Crete and *Christ's Entry Into Jerusalem* from Russia.

***Christ's Entry into Jerusalem*, a 16th-century Russian icon**

GERMAN AND AUSTRIAN ART (1400–1800)

One of the most celebrated paintings in the Sternberg's collection is Albrecht Dürer's *The Feast of the Rosary*, painted during the artist's stay in Venice in 1506. It has special significance for Prague since it was bought by Emperor Rudolph II. The two figures seen in front of the Virgin and Child are Maximilian I (Rudolph's great-great-grandfather) and Pope Julius II.

There are works by several other important German painters of the Renaissance, including Hans Holbein the Elder and the Younger and Lucas Cranach the Elder. Cranach is represented by works including a striking *Adam and Eve* whose nudes show the spirit of the Renaissance, tempered by Lutheran Reform.

***The Feast of the Rosary* by Dürer (1506)**

ITALIAN ART (1300–1800)

When you enter the Italian galleries, you are greeted by a splendid array of early diptychs, triptychs and other richly gilded panel paintings from the churches of Tuscany and northern Italy. Most came originally from the d'Este collection at Konopiště Castle *(see p169)*. Of particularly high quality are the two triangular panels of saints by the 14th-century Sienese painter Pietro Lorenzetti and a moving *Lamentation of Christ* by Lorenzo Monaco.

A fascinating element of the collection is the display of Renaissance bronze statuettes. Fashionable amongst Italian nobility of the 15th century, these little bronzes were at first cast from famous or newly-discovered works of antiquity. Later, sculptors began to use the medium more freely – Padua, for example, specialized in the depiction of small animals – and producers also adapted items for use as decorative household goods such as oil lamps, ink pots and door knockers. This small collection has representative works from all the major Italian producers except Mantua and, while many variations can be found in other museums throughout the world, there are some pieces here that are both unique and outstanding examples of the craft.

***Don Miguel de Lardizábal* (1815), by Francisco Goya**

Among the 16th-century Italian works on display, there are some delightful surprises. These include *St Jerome* by the Venetian painter, Tintoretto, and *The Flagellation of Christ* and *Portrait of an Elderly Man* by another Venetian, Jacopo Bassano. There is also an expressive portrait by the Florentine mannerist, Bronzino, of *Eleanor of Toledo*, the wife of Cosimo de' Medici.

FLEMISH AND DUTCH ART (1400–1800)

The collections of Flemish and Dutch art are rich and varied, ranging from rural scenes by Pieter Brueghel the Elder to portraits by Rubens and Rembrandt.

Highlights of the former include an altarpiece showing the *Adoration of the Magi* by Geertgen tot Sint Jans. Other early works of great interest include *St Luke Drawing the Virgin* by Jan Gossaert (c1515), one of the first works of art from the Netherlands to show the clear influence of the Italian Renaissance. The collection from the 17th century includes several major works, notably by Peter Paul Rubens who, in 1639, sent two paintings to the Augustinians of the Church of St Thomas *(see p127)* in the Little Quarter. The originals were lent to the gallery in 1896 and replaced by copies. The violence and drama of *The Martyrdom of St Thomas* is in complete contrast to the spiritual calm of *St Augustine*. Two other fine portraits are those of Rembrandt's *Scholar in His Study* and Frans Hals' *Portrait of Jasper Schade*.

Also on display is a wide assortment of paintings by other, less-prominent, artists who nonetheless represent the enormous range and quality of this period.

***Eleanor of Toledo* (1540s) by the Florentine Mannerist painter Agnolo Bronzino**

SPANISH, FRENCH AND ENGLISH ART (1400–1800)

French art is represented chiefly by the 17th-century painters Simon Vouet *(The Suicide of Lucretia)*, Sébastien Bourdon and Charles Le Brun. Spanish painting is even less well represented, but two of the collection's finest works are a haunting *Head of Christ* by El Greco – the only work by the artist on display in the Czech Republic – and a noble half-length portrait of the politician *Don Miguel de Lardizábal by* Goya.

THE CHINESE CABINET

After several years of difficult restoration work, this curiousity is once again open to the public. The richly-decorated little chamber was part of the original furnishings of the Sternberg Palace, and was designed as an intimate withdrawing room away from the bustle of the grand state rooms. In its plethora of decorative styles, Baroque mingles with Far Eastern motifs and techniques, which were fashionable at the turn of the 18th century. The vaulted ceiling features the Star of the Sternbergs among its geometric decorations. Black lacquered walls are embellished with cobalt blue and white medallions in golden frames, while gilded shelves once held rare Oriental porcelain.

The Loreto ⑳

LORETA

Ever since its construction in 1626, the Loreto has been an important place of pilgrimage. It was commissioned by Kateřina of Lobkowicz, a Czech aristocrat who was very keen to promote the legend of the Santa Casa of Loreto *(see opposite)*. The heart of the complex is a copy of the house believed to be the Virgin Mary's. The Santa Casa was enclosed by cloisters in 1661, and a Baroque façade 60 years later by Christoph and Kilian Ignaz Dientzenhofer. The grandiose design and miraculous stories about the Loreto were part of Ferdinand II's campaign to re-catholicize the Czechs *(see pp30–31)*.

Katerina Lobkowicz, founder of the Santa Casa

Bell Tower
Enclosed in this large Baroque tower, is a set of 30 bells cast 1691–94 in Amsterdam by Claudy Fremy.

Chapel of St Joseph

Fountain decorated with a sculpture of the Resurrection

Chapel of St Francis Seraphim

Chapel of St Ann

Entrance from Loretánské náměstí

★ Loreto Treasury
This gold-plated, diamond-encrusted monstrance, for displaying the host, is one of the valuable liturgical items in the Loreto treasury, most of which originated in the 16th–18th centuries.

Baroque Entrance
The balustrade above the Loreto's front entrance is decorated with statues of St Joseph and St John the Baptist by Ondřej Quitainer.

STAR SIGHTS

- ★ Loreto Treasury
- ★ Santa Casa
- ★ Church of the Nativity

★ Santa Casa
Stucco figures of many of the Old Testament prophets and reliefs from the life of the Virgin Mary by Italian artists decorate the chapel.

VISITORS' CHECKLIST

Loretánské náměstí, Hradčany. **Map** 1C3 ***Tel*** *22 05 16 740.* *22, 23 to Pohořelec.* ***Open*** *9am–12:15pm, 1–4:30pm Tue–Sun.* *7:30am Sat, 5pm Sun.* **www**.loreta.cz

★ Church of the Nativity
Gruesome relics, including fully-clothed skeletons with death masks made of wax, line the walls of this 18th-century church. The frescoes are by Václav Vavřinec Reiner.

Chapel of the Holy Rood

Chapel of St Anthony of Padua

Chapel of Our Lady of Sorrows

17th-Century Cloister
Built originally as a shelter for the many pilgrims who visited the shrine, the cloister is covered with frescoes.

Fountain Sculpture
This copy of The Ascension of the Virgin *Mary is taken from Jan Brüderle's 1739 sandstone statue, now in the Lapidarium* (see p162).

LEGEND OF THE SANTA CASA

The original house, said to be where the Archangel Gabriel told Mary about the future birth of Jesus, is in the small Italian town of Loreto. It was believed that angels transported the house from Nazareth to Loreto in 1278 following threats by infidels. After the Protestants' defeat in 1620 *(see pp30–31)*, Catholics promoted the legend, and 50 replicas of the Loreto were built in Bohemia and Moravia. This, the grandest, became the most important in Bohemia, and received many visitors.

The stuccoed Santa Casa

Martinic Palace ⑯

MARTINICKÝ PALÁC

Hradčanské náměstí 8. **Map** 1 C2. ***Tel*** *22 43 08 111.* Ⓜ *Malostranská, Hradčanská.* 🚋 *22, 23.* ***Closed*** *to the public.*

In the course of the palace's restoration in the early 1970s, workmen uncovered the original 16th-century façade decorated with ornate cream and brown *sgraffito (see p111)*. It depicts Old Testament scenes, including the story of Joseph and Potiphar's wife. More *sgraffito* came to light in the courtyard, showing the story of Samson and the Labours of Hercules.

Martinic Palace was enlarged by Jaroslav Bořita of Martinice, who was one of the imperial governors thrown from a window of the Royal Palace in 1618 *(see p105)*.

According to an old legend, between 11pm and midnight the ghost of a fiery black dog appears at the palace and accompanies walkers as far as the Loreto *(see pp116–17)*, where it disappears again. Today the palace houses the city architecture department.

Schwarzenberg Palace ⑰

SCHWARZENBERSKÝ PALÁC

Hradčanské náměstí 2. **Map** 2 D3. ***Tel*** *22 02 02 023; 22 02 02 398.* Ⓜ *Malostranská, Hradčanská.* 🚋 *22, 23.* ***Closed*** *for renovation.* **www**.militarymuseum.cz

From a distance, the façade of this grand Renaissance palace appears to be clad in projecting pyramid-shaped stonework. On closer inspection, this turns out to be an illusion created by *sgraffito* patterns incised on a flat wall. Built originally for the Lobkowicz family by the Italian architect Agostino Galli in 1545–76, the gabled palace is Florentine rather than Bohemian in style. It passed through several hands before the Schwarzenbergs, a leading family in the Habsburg Empire, bought it in 1719. Most of the interior decoration has survived, including four painted ceilings on the second floor dating from1580. Since 1945 the palace has housed the Museum of Military History, a collection of arms and uniforms from the wars in Bohemia from the time of the first Slavs up to 1918.

In the square outside is the statue of Tomáš G Masaryk, Czechoslovakia's first president.

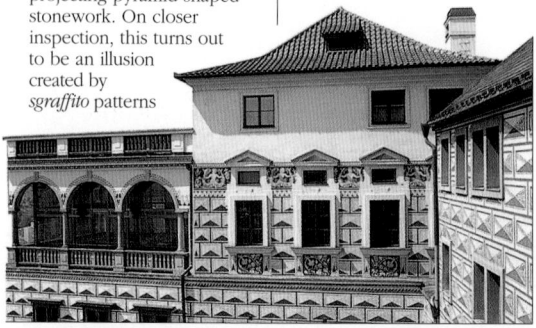

The Carmelite monastery next to the Schwarzenberg Palace

New World ⑱

NOVÝ SVĚT

Map 1 B2. 🚋 *22, 23.*

Now a charming street of small cottages, Nový Svět (New World) used to be the name of this area of Hradčany. Developed in the mid-14th century to provide houses for the castle workers, the area was twice destroyed by fire, the last time being in 1541. Most of the cottages date from the 17th century. They have been spruced up, but are otherwise unspoilt and very different in character from the rest of Hradčany. In defiance of their poverty, the inhabitants chose golden house signs to identify their modest houses – you will see a Golden Pear, a Grape, a Foot, a Bush and an Acorn. Plaques identify No. 1 as the former home of Rudolph II's brilliant court astronomer, Tycho Brahe, and No. 25 as the 1857 birthplace of the great Czech violinist František Ondříček.

Tycho Brahe, Rudolph II's astronomer

Capuchin Monastery ⑲

KAPUCÍNSKÝ KLÁŠTER

Loretánské náměstí 6. **Map** 1 B3. 🚋 *22, 23.* ***Closed*** *to the public except the church.*

Bohemia's first Capuchin monastery was founded here in 1600. It is connected to the neighbouring Loreto *(see pp116–17)* by an overhead roofed passage. Attached to the monastery is the Church of Our Lady Queen of Angels, a single-naved building with plain furnishings, typical of the ascetic Capuchin order.

The church is famous for its miraculous statue of the Madonna and Child. Emperor Rudolph II liked the statue so much he asked the Capuchins to give it to him to place in his private chapel. The monks agreed, but then the statue somehow found its way back to the church. Three times Rudolph had the Madonna brought back but each time she returned to her original position. The Emperor eventually gave up, left her where she was and presented her with a gold crown and a robe. Each year at Christmas the church attracts crowds of visitors to see its delightful Baroque nativity scene of life-sized figures dressed in costumes from the period.

Church of the Capuchin Monastery

The Loreto ⓴

LORETA

See pp116–17.

Černín Palace ㉑

ČERNÍNSKÝ PALÁC

Loretánské náměstí 5. **Map** 1 B3.
Tel *22 41 81 111.* *22, 23.*
Closed *to the public.* **www**.mzv.cz

Built in 1668 for Count Černín of Chudenice, the Imperial Ambassador to Venice, the Černín Palace is 150 m (500 ft) long with a row of 30 massive Corinthian half-columns running the length of its upper storeys. The palace towers over the attractive, small, grassy square that lies between it and the Loreto.

The huge building suffered as a result of its prominent position on one of Prague's highest hills. It was looted by the French in 1742 and badly damaged in the Prussian bombardment of the city in 1757. In 1851 the impoverished Černín family sold the palace to the state and it became a barracks. After the creation of Czechoslovakia in 1918 the palace was restored to its original design and became the Ministry of Foreign Affairs. A few days after the Communist Coup in 1948 the Foreign Minister, Jan Masaryk, the popular son of Czechoslovakia's first President, Tomáš Masaryk, died as the result of a fall from a top-floor window of the Palace. He was the only non-Communist in the government that had just been formed. No-one really knows whether he was pushed or jumped, but he is still widely mourned.

Capital on Černín Palace

Pohořelec ㉒

Map 1 B3. *22, 23.*

First settled in 1375, this is one of the oldest parts of Prague. The name is of more recent origin: Pohořelec means "place destroyed by fire", a fate the area has suffered three times in the course of its history – the last time being in 1741. It is now a large open square on a hill high over the city and part of the main access route to Prague Castle. In the centre stands a large monument to St John Nepomuk (1752) *(see p137)*, thought to be by Johann Anton Quitainer. The houses around the square are mainly Baroque and Rococo. In front of the Jan Kepler grammar school stands a monument to Kepler and his predecessor as astronomer at the court of Rudolph II, Tycho Brahe, who died in a house on the school site in 1601.

Strahov Monastery ㉓

STRAHOVSKÝ KLÁŠTER

See pp120–21.

Kučera Palace, a Rococo building in Pohořelec

Strahov Monastery ㉓

STRAHOVSKÝ KLÁŠTER

The bust of Joseph II over entrance gate

When it was founded in 1140 by an austere religious order, the Premonstratensians, Strahov rivalled the seat of the Czech sovereign in size. Destroyed by fire in 1258, it was rebuilt in the Gothic style, with later Baroque additions. Its famous library, in the theological and philosophical halls, is over 800 years old and despite being ransacked by many invading armies, is one of the finest in Bohemia. Strahov also escaped Joseph II's 1783 dissolution of the monasteries by changing its library into a research institute. It is now a working monastery and museum.

Statue of St John
A Late-Gothic, painted statue of St John the Evangelist situated in the Theological Hall, has the saint's prayer book held in a small pouch.

The Museum of National Literature is devoted to Czech literature.

Refectory

Baroque tower

Entrance to main courtyard of the monastery

Baroque organ on which Mozart played

Entrance to Church of Our Lady

★ Church of Our Lady
The interior of this Baroque church is highly decorated. Above the arcades of the side naves, there are 12 paintings with scenes from the life of St Norbert, founder of the Premonstratensian order, by Jiří Neunhertz.

Church Façade
The elaborate statues, by Johann Anton Quitainer, were added to the western façade of the church when it was remodelled by the architect Anselmo Lurago in the 1750s.

STAR FEATURES

- ★ Church of Our Lady
- ★ Philosophical Hall
- ★ Theological Hall

View from Petřín Hill
A gate at the eastern end of the first courtyard leads to Petřín Hill, part of which was once the monastery's orchards.

VISITORS' CHECKLIST

Královská Kanonie Premonstrátů na Strahově. Strahovské nádvoří 1, Strahovská. **Map** 1 B4. ***Tel*** *22 05 16 671.* 🚌 *22, 23 to Pohořelec.* ***Open*** *9am–noon, 12:30–5pm Tue–Sun.* ***Philosophical Hall, Theological Hall, Church of Our Lady, Picture Gallery open*** *9am–noon, 1–5pm daily,* ***closed*** *Easter Sun, 25 Dec.* 🎫 🏛

★ Theological Hall
One of the 17th-century astronomical globes by William Blaeu that line the hall. The stucco and wall paintings relate to librarianship.

The façade of the Philosophical Hall is decorated with vases and a gilded medallion of Joseph II by Ignaz Platzer.

trance libraries

★ Philosophical Hall
The ceiling fresco depicts the Struggle of Mankind to Know Real History *by Franz Maulbertsch. It was built in 1782 to hold the Baroque bookcases and their valuable books from a dissolved monastery near Louka, in Moravia.*

Strahov Gospel Book
A facsimile of this superb and precious 9th-century volume, is now on display in the Theological Hall.

LITTLE QUARTER

MALÁ STRANA

The Little Quarter is the part of Prague least affected by recent history. Hardly any new building has taken place here since the late 18th century and the quarter is rich in splendid Baroque palaces and old houses with attractive signs. Founded in 1257, it is built on the slopes below the Castle hill with magnificent views across the river to the Old Town.

Sign from At the Golden Horseshoe in Nerudova

The centre of the Little Quarter has always been Little Quarter Square (Malostranské náměstí), dominated by the Church of St Nicholas. The Grand Prior's millwheel at Kampa Island still turns, pilgrims still kneel before the Holy Infant of Prague in the Church of Our Lady Victorious, and music rings out from churches and palaces as it did when Mozart stayed here.

SIGHTS AT A GLANCE

Churches
- Church of St Thomas ❸
- *Church of St Nicholas pp128–9* ❺
- Church of Our Lady Victorious ❾
- Church of Our Lady beneath the Chain ⓭
- Church of St Lawrence ㉒

Parks and Gardens
- Vrtba Garden ❽
- Vojan Park ⓱
- Ledebour Garden ⓳
- Observation Tower ⓴
- Mirror Maze ㉑
- Observatory ㉓
- Petřín Park ㉕
- Funicular Railway ㉖

Museums
- Kampa Museum of Modern Art ⓲
- Museum of Music ㉗

Historic Monuments
- Hunger Wall ㉔

Historic Restaurants and Beer Halls
- At St Thomas's ❷
- At the Three Ostriches ⓯

Historic Streets and Squares
- Little Quarter Square ❹
- Nerudova Street ❻
- Italian Street ❼
- Maltese Square ❿
- Grand Priory Square ⓬
- Bridge Street ⓰

Bridges and Islands
- Kampa Island ⓫
- *Charles Bridge pp136–9* ⓮

Palaces
- Wallenstein Palace and Garden ❶
- Michna Palace ㉘

KEY
- Street-by-Street map *See pp124–5*
- Street-by-Street map *See pp132–3*
- Metro station
- Tram stop
- Funicular railway
- River boat boarding point
- Tourist information
- City wall

0 metres 250
0 yards 250

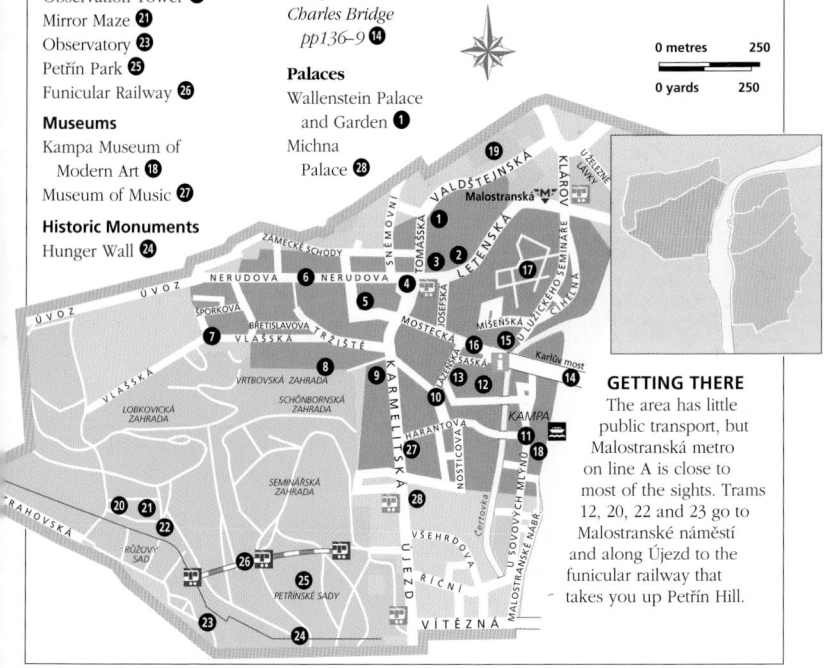

GETTING THERE

The area has little public transport, but Malostranská metro on line A is close to most of the sights. Trams 12, 20, 22 and 23 go to Malostranské náměstí and along Újezd to the funicular railway that takes you up Petřín Hill.

◁ **Charles Bridge and the Little Quarter Bridge Towers**

Street-by-Street: Around Little Quarter Square

The Little Quarter, most of whose grand Baroque palaces now house embassies, has preserved much of its traditional character. The steep, narrow streets and steps have an air of romantic mystery and you will find fascinating buildings decorated with statues and house signs at every turn. Some smart new restaurants have been established in the old buildings.

At the Three Little Fiddles, now a restaurant, acquired its house sign when it was the home of a family of violin makers around 1700.

Thun-Hohenstein Palace (1721–6) has a doorway crowned with two sculpted eagles by Matthias Braun. The palace is now the seat of the Italian embassy.

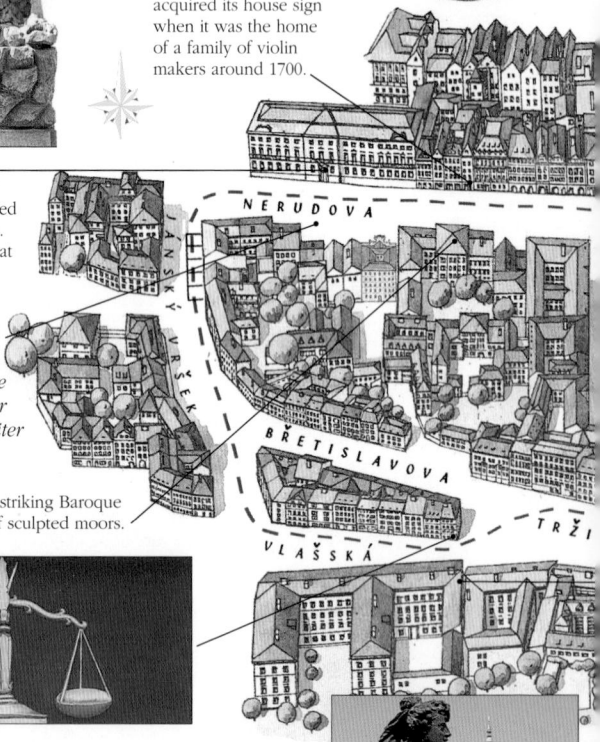

★ **Nerudova Street**
This historic street leading up to Prague Castle is named after the 19th-century writer Jan Neruda ❻

Morzin Palace has a striking Baroque façade with a pair of sculpted moors.

Italian Street
From the 16th to the 18th century, houses in the street, like the House at the Golden Scales, were occupied by Italian craftsmen ❼

Vrtba Garden
Laid out in about 1725 by František Maximilián Kaňka, these fine Baroque terraces provide good views over the rooftops of the Little Quarter ❽

STAR SIGHTS

★ Wallenstein Palace

★ Church of St Nicholas

★ Nerudova Street

★ Wallenstein Palace
On the main hall ceiling, Albrecht von Wallenstein, the great general of the 30 Years' War, appears as the god Mars ❶

LOCATOR MAP
See Street Finder, map 2

To Malostranská Metro

Czech National Assembly

Plague Column

TOMÁŠSKÁ

Wallenstein Gardens

Little Quarter Town Hall

STRANSKÉ NÁMĚSTÍ

At St Thomas's
This traditional beer hall occupies the cellars of a medieval monastery brewery ❷

Church of St Thomas
A statue of St Augustine by Hieronymus Kohl (1684) decorates the church's dramatic Baroque façade ❸

Little Quarter Square
This 18th-century view shows the lower half of the square between the church of St Nicholas and the Town Hall ❹

Schönborn Palace, now the American Embassy, is decorated with caryatids from the 17th century.

★ Church of St Nicholas
The cupola and bell tower of this Baroque church are the best-known landmarks of the Little Quarter ❺

0 metres 100
0 yards 100

KEY

Suggested route

Wallenstein Palace and Garden ❶

VALDŠTEJNSKÝ PALÁC

Valdštejnské náměstí 4. **Map** 2 E3. Malostranská. ***Tel*** *25 70 71 111.* 12, 18, 20, 22, 23. ***Palace open*** *10am–4pm Sat & Sun (subject to change).* ***Riding school open*** *10am–6pm Tue–Sun.* *from Valdštejnská.* ***Garden open*** *Apr–Oct: 10am–6pm dail (to 8pm in Aug).* *from Valdštejnské náměstí.*
www.senat.cz

The first large secular building of the Baroque era in Prague, the palace stands as a monument to the fatal ambition of imperial military commander Albrecht von Wallenstein (1581–1634). His string of victories over the Protestants in the 30 Years' War *(see pp30–31)* made him vital to Emperor Ferdinand II. Already showered with titles, Wallenstein soon started to covet the crown of Bohemia. Finally he dared to begin to negotiate independently with the enemy, and he was killed on the emperor's orders by mercenaries in 1634.

Wallenstein

The main hall of Wallenstein Palace

Wallenstein's intention was to overshadow even Prague Castle with his palace, built between 1624 and 1630. To obtain a suitable site, he had to purchase 23 houses, three gardens and the municipal brick kiln. The magnificent main hall rises to a height of two storeys with a ceiling fresco of Wallenstein himself portrayed as Mars, the god of war, riding in a triumphal chariot. The architect, Andrea Spezza, and nearly all the artists employed in the decoration of the palace were Italians.

Today the palace is used as the home of the Czech Senate, and will be open to the public when restoration work is complete. The gardens are laid out as they were when Wallenstein dined in the huge *sala terrena* (garden pavilion) that looks out over a fountain and rows of bronze statues. These are copies of works by Adriaen de Vries that were stolen by the Swedes in 1648 *(see pp30–31)*. There is also a pavilion with fine frescoes showing scenes from the legend of the Argonauts and the Golden Fleece.

Wallenstein was a holder of the Order of the Golden Fleece, the highest order of chivalry of the Holy Roman Empire. At the far end of the garden is a large ornamental pond with a central statue. Behind this stands the old Riding School, now used to house special exhibitions by the National Gallery. Both gardens and riding school have undergone substantial restoration.

Copy of a bronze statue of Eros by Adriaen de Vries

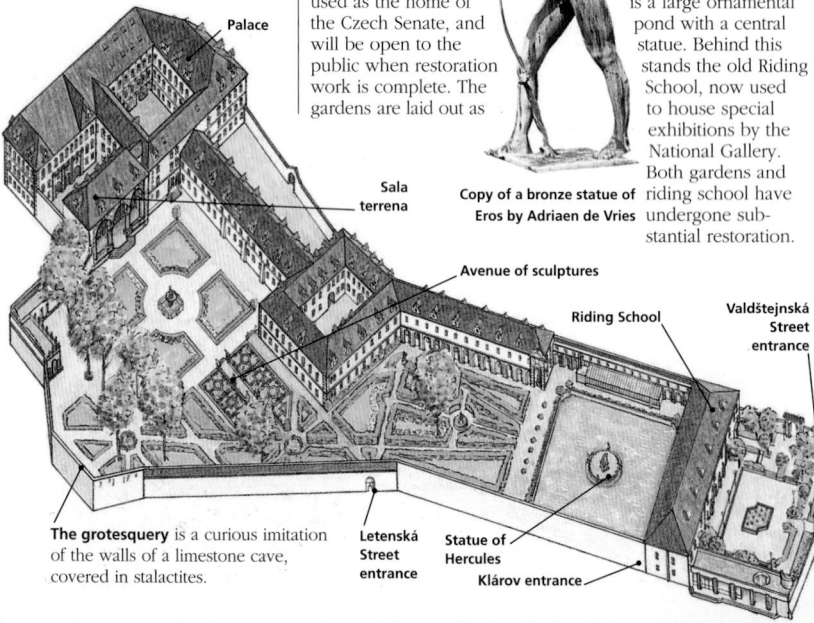

At St Thomas's ❷

U SV. TOMÁŠE

Letenská 12. **Map** 2 E3. ***Tel*** *25 75 33 466.* *Malostranská.* *12, 20, 22, 23.* ***Open*** *11:30am–midnight daily.*

No other beer hall in Prague can match the antiquity of At St Thomas's. Beer was first brewed here in 1352 by Augustinian monks. The brewery gained such renown that it was appointed sole purveyor of beer to Prague Castle. It remained in operation until 1951. Since then a special dark beer from the Braník brewery has been sold here. The basement of the old brewery has three beer halls, the most spectacular being the so-called "Cave", furnished in mock medieval style.

Church of St Thomas ❸

KOSTEL SV. TOMÁŠE

Josefská 8. **Map** 2 E3. ***Tel*** *25 53 26 75.* *Malostranská.* *12, 20, 22, 23.* ***Open*** *for services.* *6:45am, 12:15pm Mon–Sat, 9:30am, 11am (in English), 12:30pm Sun.*

Founded by Wenceslas II in 1285 as the monastery church of the Augustinians, the original Gothic church was completed in 1379. In the Hussite period *(see pp26–7)* this was one of the few churches to remain Catholic. As a result it suffered serious fire damage. During the reign of Rudolph II *(see pp28–9)*, St Thomas's developed strong links with the Imperial court. Several prominent members of Rudolph's entourage were buried here, including court architect Ottavio Aostalli and the sculptor Adriaen de Vries.

In 1723 the church was struck by lightning and Kilian Ignaz Dientzenhofer was called in to rebuild it. The shape of the original church was preserved in the Baroque reconstruction but, apart from the spire, the church today betrays little of its Gothic origins. The interior of the dome and the curving ceiling frescoes in the nave were painted by Václav Vavřinec Reiner. Above the altar are copies of paintings by Rubens – *The Martyrdom of St Thomas* and a picture of St Augustine. The originals are in the Sternberg Palace *(see pp112–15)*. The English-speaking Catholic community of Prague meets in this church.

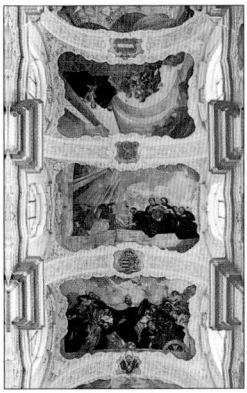

Baroque ceiling in the nave of the Church of St Thomas

Little Quarter Square ❹

MALOSTRANSKÉ NÁMĚSTÍ

Map 2 E3. *Malostranská.* *12, 20, 22, 23.*

The square has been the centre of life in the Little Quarter since its foundation in 1257. It had started life as a large marketplace in the outer bailey of Prague Castle. Buildings sprang up in the middle of the square dividing it in half – a gallows and pillory stood in its lower part.

Most of the houses around the square have a medieval core, but all were rebuilt in the Renaissance and Baroque periods. The centre of the square is dominated by the splendid Baroque church of St Nicholas. The large building beside it was a Jesuit college. Along the upper side of the square, facing the church, runs the vast Neo-Classical façade of Lichtenstein Palace. In front of it stands a column raised in honour of the Holy Trinity to mark the end of a plague epidemic in 1713.

Other important buildings include the Little Quarter Town Hall with its splendid Renaissance façade and the Sternberg Palace, built on the site of the outbreak of the fire of 1541, which destroyed most of the Little Quarter. Beside it stands the Smiřický Palace. Its turrets and hexagonal towers make it an unmistakable landmark on the northern side of the lower square. The Baroque Kaiserstein Palace is situated at the eastern side. On the façade is a bust of the great Czech soprano Emmy Destinn, who lived there between 1908 and 1914. She often sang with the famous Italian tenor Enrico Caruso.

Church of St Nicholas ❺

KOSTEL SV. MIKULÁŠE

See pp128–9.

Arcade in front of buildings on the north side of Little Quarter Square

Church of St Nicholas ❺

KOSTEL SV. MIKULÁŠE

The Church of St Nicholas divides and dominates the two sections of Little Quarter Square. Building began in 1703, and the last touches were put to the glorious frescoed nave in 1761. It is the acknowledged masterpiece of father-and-son architects Christoph and Kilian Ignaz Dientzenhofer, Prague's greatest exponents of High Baroque *(see opposite)*, although neither lived to see the completion of the church. The statues, frescoes and paintings inside the church are by leading artists of the day, and include a fine *Crucifixion* of 1646 by Karel Škréta. Extensive renovation in the 1950s reversed the damage caused by 200 years of leaky cladding and condensation.

★ Pulpit
Dating from 1765, the ornate pulpit is by Richard and Peter Prachner. It is lavishly adorned with golden cherubs.

Altar Paintings
The side chapels hold many works of art. This painting of St Michael is by Francesco Solimena.

Baroque Organ
A fresco of St Cecilia, patron saint of music, watches over the superb organ. Built in 1746, the instrument was played by Mozart in 1787.

Entrance from west side of Little Quarter Square

Chapel of St Ann

Chapel of St Catherine

Façade
St Paul, by John Frederick Kohl, is one of the statues that grace the curving façade. It was completed in 1710 by Christoph Dientzenhofer, who was influenced by Italian architects Borromini and Guarini.

STAR FEATURES

- ★ Dome Fresco
- ★ Pulpit
- ★ Statues of the Church Fathers

The dome was completed by Kilian Ignaz Dientzenhofer in 1751, shortly before his death.

The belfry, added in 1751–6, was the last part to be built. It houses a small museum of musical instruments.

VISITORS' CHECKLIST

Malostranské náměstí. **Map** 2 E3. M *Malostranská*. **Tel** *25 75 34 215*. 🚋 *12, 20, 22, 23 to Malostranské náměstí*. **Open** *Apr–Oct: 9am–5pm daily; Nov–Mar: 9am–4pm daily*. **Concerts**. **www**.psalterium.cz

★ Dome Fresco

Franz Palko's fresco, The Celebration of the Holy Trinity *(1752–3), fills the 70 m (230 ft) high dome.*

High Altar

A copper statue of St Nicholas by Ignaz Platzer surmounts the high altar. Below it, the painting of St Joseph is by Johann Lukas Kracker, who also painted the nave fresco.

Entrance to Belfry

★ Statues of the Church Fathers

The great teachers by Ignaz Platzer stand at the four corners of the crossing. St Cyril dispatches the devil with his crozier.

apel of Francis vier

THE DIENTZENHOFER FAMILY

Christoph Dientzenhofer (1655–1722) came from a family of Bavarian master builders. His son Kilian Ignaz (1689–1751) was born in Prague and educated at the Jesuit Clementinum *(see p79)*. They were responsible for the greatest treasures of Jesuit-influenced Prague Baroque architecture. The Church of St Nicholas, their last work, was completed by Kilian's son-in-law, Anselmo Lurago.

Kilian Ignaz Dientzenhofer

Nerudova Street ❻

NERUDOVA ULICE

Map 2 D3. *Malostranská.* *12, 20, 22, 23.*

A picturesque narrow street leading up to Prague Castle, Nerudova is named after the poet and journalist Jan Neruda, who wrote many short stories set in this part of Prague. He lived in the house called At the Two Suns (No. 47) between 1845 and 1857.

Up until the introduction of numbers in 1770, Prague's houses were distinguished by signs. Nerudova's houses have a splendid selection of heraldic beasts and emblems. As you make your way up Nerudova's steep slope, look out in particular for the Red Eagle (No. 6), the Three Fiddles (No. 12), the Golden Horseshoe (No. 34), the Green Lobster (No. 43) and the White Swan (No. 49) as well as the Old Pharmacy museum (No. 32).

There are also a number of grand Baroque buildings in the street, including the Thun-Hohenstein Palace (No. 20, now the Italian embassy) and the Morzin Palace (No. 5, the Rumanian embassy). The latter has a façade with two massive statues of moors (a pun on the name Morzin) supporting the semicircular balcony on the first floor. Another impressive façade is that of the Church of Our Lady of Unceasing Succour, the church of the Theatines, an order founded during the Counter-Reformation.

Italian Street, heart of the former colony of Italian craftsmen

Italian Street ❼

VLAŠSKÁ ULICE

Map 1 C4. *Malostranská.* *12, 20, 22, 23.*

Italian immigrants started to settle here in the 16th century. Many were artists or craftsmen employed to rebuild and redecorate the Castle. If you approach the street from Petřín, on the left you will see the former Italian Hospital, a Baroque building with an arcaded courtyard. Today it maintains its traditional allegiance as the cultural section of the Italian embassy.

The grandest building in the street is the former Lobkowicz Palace, now the German embassy. One of the finest Baroque palaces in Prague, it has a large oval hall on the ground floor leading out onto a magnificent garden. Look out too for the pretty stucco sign on the house called At the Three Red Roses, dating from the early 18th century.

Sign of Jan Neruda's house, At the Two Suns, 47 Nerudova Street

Vrtba Garden ❽

VRTBOVSKÁ ZAHRADA

Karmelitská 25. **Map** 2 D4. ***Tel*** *25 75 31 480.* *Malostranská.* *12, 20, 22, 23.* ***Open*** *Apr–Oct: 10am–6pm daily.* **www**.vrtbovska.cz

Behind Vrtba Palace lies a beautiful Baroque garden with balustraded terraces. From the highest part of the garden there are magnificent views of Prague Castle and the Little Quarter. The Vrtba Garden was designed by František Maximilián Kaňka in about 1720. The statues of Classical gods and stone vases are the work of Matthias Braun and the paintings in the *sala terrena* (garden pavilion) in the lower part of the garden are by Václav Vavřinec Reiner.

View of the Little Quarter from the terrace of the Vrtba Garden

Church of Our Lady Victorious ❾

KOSTEL PANNY MARIE VÍTĚZNÉ

Karmelitská. **Map** 2 E4. ***Tel*** *25 75 33 646.* *12, 20, 22, 23.* ***Open*** *9am–7pm daily.* *9am, 6pm Mon–Fri, 9am, 6pm Sat, 10am, noon (English), 5pm (French), 6pm (Italian), 7pm Sun.* **www**.karmel.at/prag-jesu

The first Baroque building in Prague was the Church of the Holy Trinity, built for the German Lutherans by Giovanni Maria Filippi. It was finished in 1613 but after the Battle of the White Mountain *(see p31)* the Catholic authorities gave the church to the Carmelites, who rebuilt it and renamed it in honour of the victory. The fabric has survived including the portal. Enshrined on a marble altar in the right aisle is a glass case containing the Holy Infant of Prague (better-known by its Italian name – *il Bambino di Praga*). This wax effigy has a record of miracle cures and is one of the most revered images in the Catholic world. It was brought from Spain and presented to the Carmelites in 1628 by Polyxena of Lobkowicz. A small museum adjacent to the church traces its history.

Maltese Square ⑩

MALTÉZSKÉ NÁMĚSTÍ

Map 2 E4. 🚌 *12, 20, 22, 23.*

The square takes its name from the Priory of the Knights of Malta, which used to occupy this part of the Little Quarter. At the northern end stands a group of sculptures featuring St John the Baptist by Ferdinand Brokof – part of a fountain erected in 1715 to mark the end of a plague epidemic.

Most of the buildings were originally Renaissance houses belonging to prosperous townspeople, but in the 17th and 18th centuries the Little Quarter was taken over by the Catholic nobility and many were converted to flamboyant Baroque palaces. The largest, Nostitz Palace, stands on the southern side. Part of the palace now houses the Dutch embassy. It was built in the mid-17th century, then in about 1720 a balustrade was added with Classical vases and statues of emperors. In summer, concerts are given at the Palace. The Japanese embassy is housed in the Turba Palace (1767), an attractive pink Rococo building designed by Joseph Jäger.

Ferdinand Brokof's statue of John the Baptist in Maltese Square

Čertovka (the Devil's Stream) with Kampa Island on the right

Kampa Island ⑪

KAMPA

Map 2 F4. 🚌 *6, 9, 12, 20, 22, 23.*

Kampa, an island formed by a branch of the Vltava known as the Devil's Stream (Čertovka), is a delightfully peaceful corner of the Little Quarter. The stream got its name in the 19th century, allegedly after the diabolical temper of a lady who owned a house nearby in Maltese Square. For centuries the stream was used as a millrace and from Kampa you can see the remains of three old mills. Beyond the Grand Prior's Mill the stream disappears under a small bridge below the piers of Charles Bridge. From here it flows between rows of houses. Predictably, the area has become known as "the Venice of Prague", but instead of gondolas you will see canoes.

For most of the Middle Ages there were only gardens on Kampa, though the island was also used for washing clothes and bleaching linen. In the 17th century the island became well-known for its pottery markets. There are some enchanting houses from this period around Na Kampě Square. Most of the land from here to the southern tip of the island is a park, created from several old palace gardens.

The island all but vanished beneath the Vltava during the floods of 2002, which caused widespread devastation to homes, businesses and historic buildings, many of which are still being rebuilt and restored.

Grand Priory Square ⑫

VELKOPŘEVORSKÉ NÁMĚSTÍ

Map 2 F4. Ⓜ *Malostranská.* 🚌 *12, 20, 22, 23.*

On the northern side of this small leafy square stands the former seat of the Grand Prior of the Knights of Malta. In its present form the palace dates from the 1720s. The doorways, windows and decorative vases were made at the workshop of Matthias Braun. On the opposite side of the square is the Buquoy Palace, now the French embassy, a delightful Baroque building roughly contemporary with the Grand Prior's Palace.

The only incongruous features are a painting of John Lennon and graffiti exhorting the world to "give peace a chance". These have decorated the wall of the Grand Prior's garden since Lennon's death.

Street-by-Street: Little Quarter Riverside

On either side of Bridge Street lies a delightful half-hidden world of gently decaying squares, picturesque palaces, churches and gardens. When you have run the gauntlet of the trinket-sellers on Charles Bridge, escape to Kampa Island to enjoy a stroll in its informal park, the views across the Vltava weir to the Old Town and the flocks of swans gliding along the river.

The House at the Golden Unicorn in Lázeňská Street has a plaque commemorating the fact that Beethoven stayed here in 1796.

The Church of St Joseph dates from the late 17th century. The painting of *The Holy Family* (1702) on the gilded high altar is by the leading Baroque artist Petr Brandl.

Bridge Street
A major thoroughfare for 750 years, the narrow street leads to Little Quarter Square 16

Grand Priory Square
The Grand Prior's Palace is the former seat of the Knights of Malta and dates from the 1720s. Its street wall features colourful murals and graffitti 12

Church of Our Lady beneath the Chain
Two massive towers survive from when this was a fortified priory 13

Museum of Music
This museum houses a vast collection of beautifully hand-crafted musical instruments 27

Church of Our Lady Victorious
This Baroque church houses the famous effigy, the Holy Infant of Prague 9

Maltese Square
Grand palaces surround the oddly-shaped square. This coat of arms decorates the 17th-century Nostitz Palace, a popular venue for concerts 10

To Little Quarter Square

MOSTECKÁ

LÁZEŇSKÁ

KARMELITSKÁ

NEBOVIDSKÁ

0 metres 100

0 yards 100

KEY

Suggested route

Vojan Park
Quiet shady paths have been laid out under the apple trees of this former monastery garden ⓱

LOCATOR MAP
See Street Finder, map 2

At the Three Ostriches
A restaurant and hotel have kept the sign of a seller of ostrich plumes ⓯

U LUŽICKÉHO SEMINÁŘE

★ Charles Bridge
The approach to this magnificent 14th-century bridge, with its files of Baroque statues, passes under an arch below a Gothic tower ⓮

Čertovka (the Devil's Stream)

NA KAMPĚ

The Grand Priory Mill has had its wheel meticulously restored, though it now turns very slowly in the sluggish water of the Čertovka, the former millrace.

Lichtenstein Palace

★ Kampa Island
This 19th-century painting by Soběslav Pinkas shows boys playing on Kampa. The island's park is still a popular place for children ⓫

STAR SIGHTS

★ Charles Bridge

★ Kampa Island

Church of Our Lady beneath the Chain ⓭

KOSTEL PANNY MARIE POD ŘETĚZEM

Lázeňská. **Map** 2 E4. ***Tel*** *25 75 30 876.* Ⓜ *Malostranská.* 🚋 *12, 20, 22, 23.* ***Open*** *for concerts and services.* ✝ *5pm (4pm in winter) Sat, 11am Sun.*

This church, the oldest in the Little Quarter, was founded in the 12th century. King Vladislav II presented it to the Knights of St John, the order which later became known as the Knights of Malta. It stood in the centre of the Knights' heavily fortified monastery that guarded the approach to the old Judith Bridge. The church's name refers to the chain used in the Middle Ages to close the monastery gatehouse.

A Gothic presbytery was added in the 13th century, but in the following century the original Romanesque church was demolished. A new portico was built with a pair of massive square towers, but work was then abandoned and the old nave became a courtyard between the towers and the church. This was given a Baroque facelift in 1640 by Carlo Lurago. The painting by Karel Škréta on the high altar shows the Virgin Mary and John the Baptist coming to the aid of the Knights of Malta in the famous naval victory over the Turks at Lepanto in 1571.

Charles Bridge ⓮

KARLŮV MOST

See pp136–9.

View along Bridge Street through the tower on Charles Bridge

At the Three Ostriches ⓯

U TŘÍ PŠTROSŮ

Dražického náměstí 12. **Map** 2 F3. ***Tel*** *25 75 32 410.* Ⓜ *Malostranská.* 🚋 *12, 20, 22, 23. See* ***Where to Stay*** *pp182–9,* ***Restaurants*** *pp198–209.* **www**.utripstrosu.cz

Many of Prague's colourful house signs indicated the trade carried on in the premises. In 1597 Jan Fux, an ostrich-feather merchant, bought this house by Charles Bridge. At the time ostrich plumes were very fashionable as decoration for hats among courtiers and officers at Prague Castle. Fux even supplied feathers to foreign armies. So successful was his business, that in 1606 he had the house rebuilt and decorated with a large fresco of ostriches. The building is now an expensive hotel and restaurant.

Fresco that gave At the Three Ostriches its name

Bridge Street ⓰

MOSTECKÁ ULICE

Map 2 E3. Ⓜ *Malostranská.* 🚋 *12, 20, 22, 23.*

Since the Middle Ages this street has linked Charles Bridge with the Little Quarter Square. Crossing the bridge from the Old Town you can see the doorway of the old customs house built in 1591 in front of the Judith Tower. On the first floor of the tower there is a 12th-century relief of a king and a kneeling man.

Throughout the 13th and 14th centuries the area to the north of the street was the Court of the Bishop of Prague. This was destroyed during the Hussite Wars *(see pp26–7)*, but one of its Gothic towers is preserved in the courtyard of the house called At the Three Golden Bells. It can be seen from the higher of the two bridge towers. The street is lined with a mixture of Renaissance and Baroque houses. As you walk up to Little Quarter Square, look out for the house called At the Black Eagle on the left. It has rich sculptural decoration and a splendid Baroque wrought-iron grille. Kaunic Palace, also on the left, was built in the 1770s. Its Rococo façade has striking stucco decoration and sculptures by Ignaz Platzer.

Vojan Park ⑰

VOJANOVY SADY

U lužického semináře. **Map** 2 F3. *Malostranská. 12, 18, 20, 22, 23.* ***Open*** *9am–6pm daily (to 8pm in summer).*

A tranquil spot hidden behind high white walls, the park dates back to the 17th century, when it was the garden of the Convent of Barefooted Carmelites. Two chapels erected by the Order have survived among the park's lawns and fruit trees. One is the Chapel of Elijah, who, because of his Old Testament associations with Mount Carmel, is regarded as the founder of the Order. His chapel takes the form of a stalagmite and stalactite cave. The other chapel, dedicated to St Theresa, was built in the 18th century as an expression of gratitude for the convent's preservation during the Prussian siege of Prague in 1757.

Kampa Museum of Modern Art ⑱

MUZEUM KAMPA

U Sovových mlýnů2. **Map** 2 F4. ***Tel*** 25 72 86 147. *6, 9, 22, 23.* ***Open*** *10am–6pm daily.* **www**.museumkampa.cz

Housed in the historic Sova mill in the heart of the city, the Kampa Museum of Modern Art boasts an impressive collection of Central European art. The museum was founded by the Czech-American couple Jan and Meda Mládková to house their private collection of drawings, paintings and sculptures. Among the artists on display are abstract painter Frantisek Kupka and Czech cubist sculptor Otto Gutfreund.

Ledebour Garden ⑲

LEDEBURSKÁ ZAHRADA

Valdštejnská. **Map** 2 F2. ***Tel*** 25 70 10 401. *Malostranská. 12, 18, 20, 22, 23.* ***Open*** *Apr–Jun, Sep–Oct: 10am–6pm daily; Jul–Aug: 10am–8pm daily.* **www**.palacovezahrady.cz

The steep southern slope below Prague Castle was covered with vineyards and gardens during the Middle Ages. But in the 16th century, when nobles started building palaces here, they laid out larger formal terraced gardens based on Italian Renaissance models. Most of these gardens were rebuilt during the 18th century and decorated with Baroque garden statuary and fountains. Three of the gardens – those belonging to the former Ledebour, Černín and Pálffy Palaces – have been linked together. They have recently undergone a much-needed programme of restoration work, and they again are delighting visitors with their elegant landscaping and attractive plants.

From their terraces, the gardens boast magnificent views of Prague. The Ledebour Garden, designed in the early 18th century, has a fine *sala terrena* (garden pavilion) by Giovanni Battista Alliprandi. The Pálffy Garden was laid out in the mid-18th century with terraces (the second still has its original sundial) and loggias. The most beautiful of the three and architecturally the richest is the Kolowrat-Černín Garden, created in 1784 by Ignaz Palliardi. The highest terrace has a *sala terrena* decorated with statues and Classical urns. Below this there is a wonderful assortment of staircases, archways and balustrades, and the remains of Classical statuary and old fountains.

18th-century statue of Hercules located in the Ledebour Garden

The foot of the Ledebour Garden

Charles Bridge (Little Quarter Side) ⓮

KARLŮV MOST

Prague's most familiar monument, connects the Old Town with the Little Quarter. Although it is now pedestrianized, at one time it could take four carriages abreast. Today, due to wear and tear, many of the statues on the bridge are copies; the originals are kept in the Lapidarium of the National Museum *(see p162)* and at Vyšehrad *(see p181)*. The Gothic Old Town Bridge Tower *(see p139)* is one of the finest buildings of its kind in existence.

★ View from Little Quarter Bridge Tower
The tall pinnacled wedge tower, gives a superb view of the city of 100 spires. The shorter tower is the remains of Judith Bridge.

St Adalbert, 1709
Adalbert, Bishop of Prague, founded the Church of St Lawrence (see p140) *on Petřín Hill in 991. He is known to the Czechs as Vojtěch.*

Little Quarter Bridge Tower

Tower entrance

St Wenceslas, 1858

St Philip Benizi, 1

Steps to Saská Street

Christ between St Cosmas and St Damian, 1709

Judith Bridge Tower, 1158

St John de Matha, St Felix de Valois and the Blessed Ivan, 1714
These saints, sculpted by Ferdinand Brokof, founded the Trinitarian Order of mendicants to collect money to buy the freedom of Christians enslaved by the infidels (represented at the foot of the sculpture).

St Vitus, 1714
This engraving of the statue shows the 3rd-century martyr with the lions which were supposed to maul him, but licked him instead. St Vitus is the patron saint of dancers and often invoked against convulsive disorders.

STAR FEATURES

- ★ Little Quarter Bridge Tower and View
- ★ St John Nepomuk
- ★ St Luitgard

★ St Luitgard, 1710
This statue, regarded as the most artistically remarkable on the bridge, was sculpted by Matthias Braun when he was only 26. It is based on the blind Cistercian nun's celebrated vision when Christ appeared and she kissed his wounds.

VISITORS' CHECKLIST

Map 2 F4. 12, 22, 23 to Malostranské náměstí, then walk down Mostecká. ***Little Quarter Bridge Tower open*** *10am–6pm daily (Jul–Aug: 10am–10pm).*

★ St John Nepomuk, 1683
Reliefs on the bridge depict the martyrdom of St John Nepomuk. Here the saint is polished bright from people touching it for good luck.

St Cajetan, 1709

St Augustine, 1708

St Jude Thaddaeus, 1708

St Anthony of Padua, 1707

Steps to Kampa Island

St Nicholas Tolentino, 1708

St Francis of Assisi, with two angels, 1855

St Ludmilla, 1710

St Vincent Ferrer and St Procopius, 1712
This detail shows a rabbi saddened by St Vincent's success in converting many Jews to Christianity. St Procopius is one of Bohemia's patron saints.

ST JOHN NEPOMUK

The cult of St John Nepomuk, canonized in 1729, was promoted by the Jesuits to rival the revered Jan Hus *(see p27)*. Jan Nepomucký, vicar-general of the Archdiocese of Prague, was arrested in 1393 by Wenceslas IV along with the archbishop and others who had displeased the king over the election of an abbot. The archbishop escaped, but John died under torture. The body was bound and thrown off Charles Bridge. Statues modelled on the one placed here in 1683 can be seen throughout central Europe, especially on bridges.

Charles Bridge (Old Town Side) ⓮

KARLŮV MOST

Until 1741, Charles Bridge was the only crossing over the Vltava. It is 520 m (1,706 ft) long and is built of sandstone blocks, rumoured to be strengthened by mixing mortar with eggs. The bridge was commissioned by Charles IV in 1357 to replace the Judith Bridge and built by Peter Parler. The bridge's original decoration was a simple cross. The first statue – of St John Nepomuk – was added in 1683, inspired by Bernini's sculptures on Rome's Ponte Sant'Angelo.

St Francis Xavier, 1711
The Jesuit missionary is supported by three Moorish and two Oriental converts. The sculptor Brokof is seated on the saint's left.

★ 17th-Century Crucifixion
For 200 years, the wooden crucifix stood alone on the bridge. The gilded Christ dates from 1629 and the Hebrew words "Holy, Holy, Holy Lord", were paid for by a Jew as punishment for blasphemy.

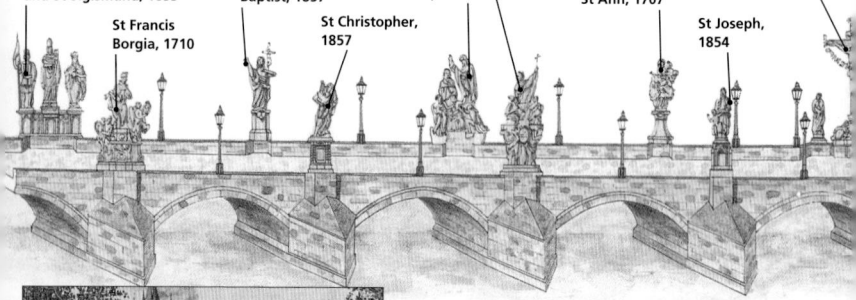

Thirty Years' War
In the last hours of this war, the Old Town was saved from the Swedish army. The truce was signed in the middle of the bridge in 1648.

STAR FEATURES

★ Old Town Bridge Tower

★ 17th-Century Crucifixion

TIMELINE

1342 Judith Bridge destroyed by floods

1357 Charles IV commissions new bridge

1621 Heads of ten Protestant nobles exhibited on the Old Town Bridge Tower

1648 Swedes damage part of the bridge and Old Town Bridge Tower

1890 flood damage

1100 | **1300** | **1500** | **1700** | **1900**

1158 Europe's second medieval stone bridge, Judith Bridge, is built

1393 St John Nepomuk thrown off Bridge on the orders of Wenceslas IV

Sculptor Matthias Braun (1684–1738)

1713 Bridge decorated with 21 statues by Braun, Brokof and others

1890 Three arches destroyed by flood

1938 Karel Dvořák's sculpture of St Cyril and St Methodius

The Madonna, St Dominic and St Thomas, 1708
The Dominicans, (known in a Latin pun as Domini canes, *the dogs of God), are shown with the Madonna and their emblem, a dog.*

VISITORS' CHECKLIST

Map 3 A4. 17, 18 to Křižovnické náměstí. ***Old Town Bridge Tower open*** *10am–5pm daily (Mar: to 6pm; Apr–May & Oct: to 7pm; Jun–Sep: to 10pm).*

Madonna and St Bernard, 1709
Cherubs and symbols of the Passion, including the dice, the cock and the centurion's gauntlet, form part of the statue.

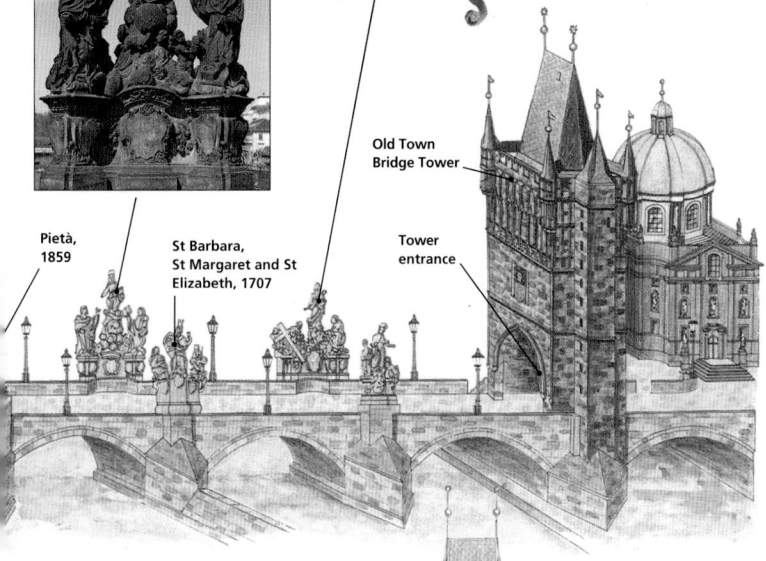

★ OLD TOWN BRIDGE TOWER

This magnificent Gothic tower, designed by Peter Parler, was built at the end of the 14th century. A fitting ornament to the new Charles Bridge, it was also an integral part of the Old Town's fortifications.

Bridge Tower sculptures by Peter Parler include St Vitus, the bridge's patron saint, Charles IV (left) and Wenceslas IV.

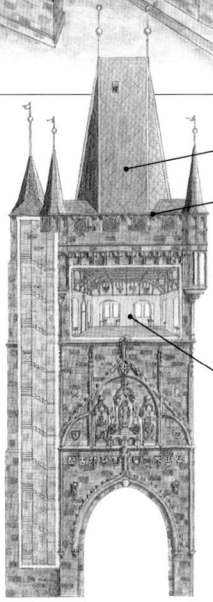

The viewing gallery is a rib-vaulted room, on the tower's first floor. It provides a wonderful view of Prague Castle and the Little Quarter.

Observation Tower ⑳

PETŘÍNSKÁ ROZHLEDNA

Petřín. **Map** 1 C4. *6, 9, 12, 20, 22, 23, then take funicular railway. 132, 143, 149, 217.* ***Open*** *May–Aug: 10am–10pm daily; Apr & Sep: 10am–7pm daily; Oct: 10am–6pm daily; Jan–Mar & Nov–Dec: 10am–5pm Sat & Sun.*

The most conspicuous landmark in Petřín Park is an imitation Eiffel Tower, built for the Jubilee Exhibition of 1891. The octagonal Petřín tower is only 60 m (200 ft), a quarter the height of the Eiffel Tower. A spiral staircase of 299 steps leads up to the viewing platform. A lift is also available. On a clear day, you can see as far as Bohemia's highest peak, Sněžka in the Krkonoše (Giant) Mountains, 150 km (100 miles) to the northeast.

Mirror Maze ㉑

ZRCADLOVÉ BLUDIŠTĚ

Petřín. **Map** 1 C4. ***Tel*** *25 73 15 212. 6, 9, 12, 20, 22, 23, then take funicular railway. 132, 143, 149, 217.* ***Open*** *May–Aug: 10am–10pm daily; Apr & Sep: 10am–7pm daily; Oct: 10am–6pm daily; Jan–Mar & Nov–Dec: 10am–5pm Sat & Sun.*

Like the Observation Tower, the maze, which has walls lined with distorting mirrors, is a relic of the Exhibition of 1891. It is in a wooden pavilion in the shape of the old Špička Gate, part of the Gothic fortifications of Vyšehrad

The 100-year-old Observation Tower overlooking the city

(see pp180–81). This amusement house moved to Petřín at the end of the exhibition.

When you have navigated your way through the maze and laughed at your reflection, your reward is to view the vivid diorama of *The Defence of Prague against the Swedes,* which took place on Charles Bridge *(see p138)* in 1648.

Church of St Lawrence ㉒

KOSTEL SV. VAVŘINCE

Petřín. **Map** 1 C5. *6, 9, 12, 20, 22, 23, then take funicular railway. 132, 143, 149, 217.* ***Closed*** *to the public.*

According to legend, the church was initially founded in the 10th century by the pious Prince Boleslav II and St Adalbert on the site of a pagan shrine. The ceiling of the sacristy is decorated with a painting illustrating this legend. The painting dates from the 18th century when the Romanesque church was swallowed up by a large new Baroque structure, featuring a cupola flanked by two onion-domed towers. The small Calvary Chapel, which dates from 1735, is situated just to the left of the entrance to the church.

Diorama of *The Defence of Prague against the Swedes* in the Mirror Maze

Observatory ㉓

HVĚZDÁRNA

Petřín 205. **Map** 2 D5. ***Tel*** *25 73 20 540. 6, 9, 12, 20, 22, 23, then funicular.* ***Open*** *Tue–Sun year-round; opening hours vary monthly, so phone ahead.* **www**.observatory.cz

Since 1930, Prague's amateur astronomers have been able to enjoy the facilities of this observatory on Petřín Hill. You can use its telescopes to view anything from the craters of the moon to unfamiliar distant galaxies. There is an exhibition of old astronomical instruments and special events for children are held on Saturdays and Sundays.

Hunger Wall ㉔

HLADOVÁ ZEĎ'

Újezd, Petřín, Strahovská. ***Map*** 2 D5. *6, 9, 12, 20, 22, 23, then take funicular railway. 132, 143, 149, 217.*

The fortifications built around the southern edge of the Little Quarter on the orders of Charles IV in 1360–62 have been known for centuries as the Hunger Wall. Nearly 1,200 m (1,300 yards) of the wall have survived, complete with crenellated battlements and a platform for marksmen on its inner side. It runs from Újezd across Petřín Park to Strahov. The story behind the name is that Charles commissioned its construction with the aim of giving employment to the poor during a period of famine. It is true that a great famine did break out in Bohemia in the 1360s and the two events, the famine and the building of the wall, became permanently linked in the people's memory.

Nebozízek, the station halfway up Petřín's funicular railway

Petřín Park ㉕

PETŘÍNSKÉ SADY

Map 2 D5. 🚋 *6, 9, 12, 20, 22, 23, then take funicular railway. See* ***Three Guided Walks*** *pp176–7.*

To the west of the Little Quarter, Petřín hill rises above the city to a height of 318 m (960 ft). The name derives either from the Slavonic god Perun, to whom sacrifices were made on the hill or from the Latin name Mons Petrinus, meaning "rocky hill". A forest used to stretch from here as far as the White Mountain *(see p31)*. In the 12th century the southern side of the hill was planted with vineyards, but by the 18th century most of these had been transformed into gardens and orchards.

Today a path winds up the slopes of Petřín, offering fine views of Prague. In the park is the *Monument to the Victims of Communism* (2002) by the sculptor Olbram Zoubek and a monument to Romantic poet Karel Hynek Mácha.

Statue of Karel Hynek Mácha in Petřín Park

Funicular Railway ㉖

LANOVÁ DRÁHA

Újezd. **Map** 2 D5. 🚋 *6, 9, 12, 20, 22, 23.* ***In operation*** *summer: 9am–11:30pm daily; winter: 9am–11:20pm daily.* 📷 ♿

Built to carry visitors to the 1891 Jubilee Exhibition up to the Observation Tower at the top of Petřín hill, the funicular was originally powered by water. In this form, it remained in operation until 1914, then between the wars was converted to electricity. In 1965 it had to be shut down because part of the hillside collapsed – coal had been mined here during the 19th century. Shoring up the slope and rebuilding the railway took 20 years, but since its reopening in 1985 it has proved a reliable way of getting up Petřín Hill. At the halfway station, Nebozízek, there is a restaurant *(see p205)* with fine views of the Castle and the city.

Museum of Music ㉗

ČESKÉ MUZEUM HUDBY

Karmelitská 2, Praha 1, Malá Strana. **Map** 2 E4. Ⓜ *Malostranská.* 🚋 *12, 20, 22, 23.* ***Open*** *10am–6pm Mon, Wed–Sun.* 📷 ♿

Housed in the former 17th century Baroque Church of St Magdalene, the Museum of Music seeks to present musical instruments not only as fine specimens of craftsmanship and artistry but also as mediators between man and music.

The museum is run by the National Museum *(see p147)* and boasts a magnificent atrium. Exhibits include a look at the diversity of popular 20th century music as preserved in film, television, photographs and sound recordings. Also examined is the production of handcrafted instruments, the history of musical notation and the social occasions on which certain instruments were played. Earphones offer high-quality sound reproduction of original recordings made on the instruments displayed. The museum's collections can be accessed via the study room and there is a listening studio for the library of recordings.

Michna Palace ㉘

MICHNŮV PALÁC

Újezd 40. **Map** 2 E4. ***Tel*** *25 73 11 831.* 🚋 *12, 20, 22, 23.* ***Open*** *9am–5pm Thu, Sat, Sun.* 📷 ♿

In about 1580 Ottavio Aostalli built a summer palace here for the Kinský family on the site of an old Dominican convent. In 1623 the building was bought by Pavel Michna of Vacínov, a supply officer in the Imperial Army, who had grown rich after the Battle of the White Mountain. He commissioned a new Baroque building that he hoped would rival the palace of his late commander, Wallenstein *(see p126)*.

In 1767 the Michna Palace was sold to the army and over the years it became a crumbling ruin. After 1918 it was bought by Sokol (a physical culture association) and converted into a gym and sports centre with a training ground in the old palace garden. The restored palace was renamed Tyrš House in honour of Sokol's founder.

Restored Baroque façade of the Michna Palace (Tyrš House)

NEW TOWN

NOVE MĚSTO

The New Town, founded in 1348 by Charles IV, was carefully planned and laid out around three large central market-places: the Hay Market (Senovážné Square), the Cattle Market (Charles Square) and the Horse Market (Wenceslas Square). Twice as large as the Old Town, the area was mainly inhabited by tradesmen and craftsmen such as blacksmiths, wheelwrights and brewers. During the late 19th century, much of the New Town was demolished and completely redeveloped, giving it the appearance it has today.

Art Nouveau decoration on No. 12 Wenceslas Square

SIGHTS AT A GLANCE

Churches and Monasteries
- Church of Our Lady of the Snows ❷
- Church of St Ignatius ❽
- Church of St Cyril and St Methodius ⓫
- Church of St John on the Rock ⓭
- Slavonic Monastery Emauzy ⓮
- Church of St Catherine ⓰
- Church of St Stephen ⓳
- Church of St Ursula ㉒

Historic Buildings
- Hotel Europa ❹
- Jesuit College ❾
- Faust House ⓬
- New Town Hall ⓴

Theatres and Opera Houses
- State Opera ❻
- *National Theatre pp156–7* ㉓

Historic Squares
- Wenceslas Square ❶
- Charles Square ❿

Museums and Galleries
- National Museum ❺
- Mucha Museum ❼
- Dvořák Museum ⓲

Historic Restaurants and Beer Halls
- Chalice Restaurant ⓱
- U Fleků ㉑

Parks and Gardens
- Franciscan Garden ❸
- Botanical Gardens ⓯

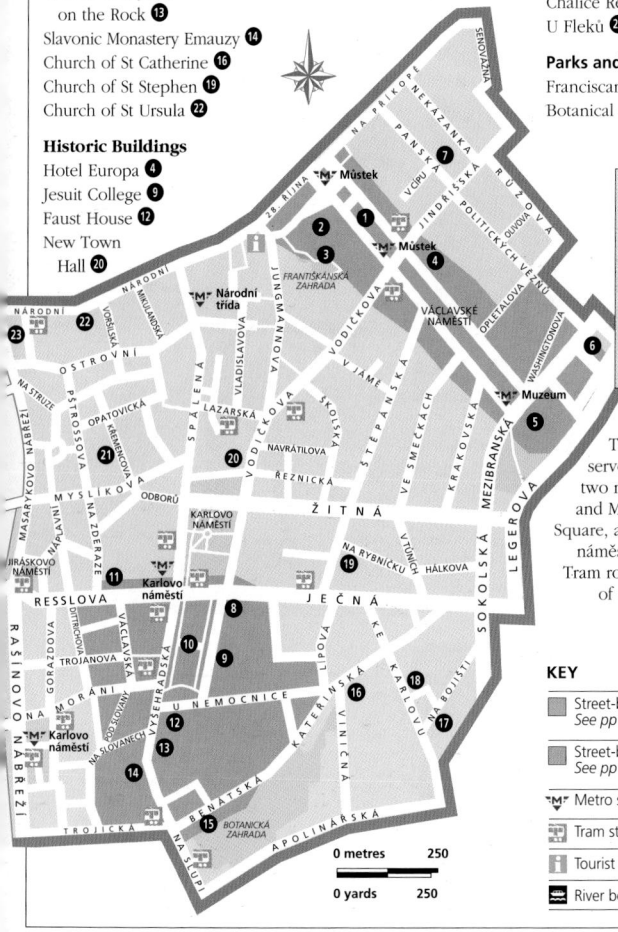

GETTING THERE

The entire area is well served by the metro with two main stations, Můstek and Muzeum in Wenceslas Square, and others at Karlovo náměstí and Národní třída. Tram routes from most parts of the city pass through Karlovo náměstí.

KEY

- Street-by-Street map *See pp144–5*
- Street-by-Street map *See pp150–51*
- Metro station
- Tram stop
- Tourist information
- River boat boarding point

◁ **Art Nouveau sculptures on the Hlahol Choir Building (1905) on Masarykovo nábřeží**

Street-by-Street: Wenceslas Square

Hotels and restaurants occupy many of the buildings around Wenceslas Square, though it remains an important commercial centre – the square began life as a medieval horse market. As you walk along, look up at the buildings, most of which date from the turn of this century, when the square was redeveloped. There are fine examples of the decorative styles used by Czech architects of the period. Many blocks have dark covered arcades leading to shops, clubs, theatres and cinemas.

Koruna Palace (1914) is an ornate block of shops and offices. Its corner turret is topped with a crown (*koruna*).

To Powder Gate

Statue of St Lawrence at U Pinkasů

U Pinkasů became one of Prague's most popular beer halls when it started serving Pilsner Urquell *(see pp200–1)* in 1843.

Church of Our Lady of the Snows
The towering Gothic building is only part of a vast church planned during the 14th century ❷

Jungmann Square is named after Josef Jungmann (1773–1847), an influential scholar of language and lexicographer, and there is a statue of him in the middle. The Adria Palace (1925) used to be the Laterna Magika Theatre *(see p220)*, which was where Václav Havel's Civic Forum worked in the early days of the 1989 Velvet Revolution.

Franciscan Garden
An old monastery garden has been laid out as a small park with this fountain, rose-beds, trellises and a children's playground ❸

Lucerna Palace

Wiehl House, named after its architect Antonín Wiehl, was completed in 1896. The five-storey building is in striking Neo-Renaissance style, with aloggia and colourful *sgraffito*. Mikuláš Aleš designed some of the Art Nouveau figures.

STAR SIGHTS

★ Wenceslas Square

★ Hotel Europa

★ National Museum

★ Wenceslas Square
The dominant features of the square are the bronze, equestrian statue of St Wenceslas (1912) and the National Museum behind it. St Wenceslas, a former prince who was murdered by his brother Boleslav, is the patron saint of Bohemia ❶

LOCATOR MAP
See Street Finder, maps 3, 4 & 6

The Monument to the Victims of Communism is on the spot where Jan Palach staged his protest. Since the Velvet Revolution in 1989 an unofficial shrine has been maintained here.

The Assicurazioni Generali Building was where Franz Kafka *(see p68)* worked as an insurance clerk for 10 months in 1906–7.

★ Hotel Europa
Both the façade and the interior of the hotel (1906) preserve most of their original Art Nouveau features ❹

State Opera
Meticulously refurbished in the 1980s, the interior retains the luxurious red plush, crystal chandeliers and gilded stucco of the original late-19th-century theatre ❻

Café Tramvaj 11

St Wenceslas Monument

VÁCLAVSKÉ NÁMĚSTÍ

OPLETALOVA

SMEČKÁCH

KRAKOVSKÁ

WILSONOVA

Fénix Palace

Muzeum

Muzeum

Memorial to Jan Palach, who died in protest against communism.

★ National Museum
The grand building with its monumental staircase was completed in 1890 as a symbol of national prestige ❺

0 metres 100

0 yards 100

KEY

— — — Suggested route

Wenceslas Monument in Wenceslas Square

Wenceslas Square ❶

VÁCLAVSKÉ NÁMĚSTÍ

Map 3 C5. *Můstek, Muzeum.* *3, 9, 14, 24.*

The square has witnessed many key events in recent Czech history. It was here that the student Jan Palach burnt himself to death in 1969, and in November 1989 a protest rally in the square against police brutality led to the Velvet Revolution and the overthrow of Communism.

Wenceslas "Square" is something of a misnomer, for it is some 750 m (825 yd) long and only 60 m (65 yd) wide. Originally a horse market, today it is lined with hotels, restaurants, clubs and shops, reflecting the seamier side of global consumerism. The huge equestrian statue of St Wenceslas that looks the length of the square from in front of the National Museum was erected in 1912. Cast in bronze, it is the work of Josef Myslbek, the leading Czech sculptor of the late 19th century. At the foot of the pedestal there are several other statues of Czech patron saints. A memorial near the statue commemorates the victims of the former regime.

Church of Our Lady of the Snows ❷

KOSTEL PANNY MARIE SNĚŽNÉ

Jungmannovo náměstí 18. **Map** 3 C5. **Tel** *22 44 90 350.* *Můstek.* **Open** *9am–5:15pm Mon–Sat, 12:30–5:15pm Sun.* *7am, 8am, 6pm Mon–Fri, 9am, 10:15am, 11:30am, 6pm Sun.*

Charles IV founded this church to mark his coronation in 1347. The name refers to a 4th-century miracle in Rome, when the Virgin Mary appeared to the pope in a dream telling him to build a church to her on the spot where snow fell in August. Charles's church was to have been over 100 m (330 ft) long, but was never completed. The towering building we see today was just the presbytery of the projected church. Over 33 m (110 ft) high, it was finished in 1397, and was originally part of a Carmelite monastery. On the northern side there is a gateway with a 14th-century pediment that marked the entrance to the monastery graveyard.

In the early 15th century a steeple was added, but further building was halted by the Hussite Wars *(see pp26–7)*. The Hussite firebrand Jan Želivský preached at the church and was buried here after his execution in 1422. The church suffered considerable damage in the wars and in 1434 the steeple was destroyed. For a long time the church was left to decay. In 1603 Franciscans restored the building. The intricate net vaulting of the ceiling dates from this period, the original roof having collapsed. Most of the interior decoration, apart from the 1450s pewter font, is Baroque. The monumental three-tiered altar is crowded with statues of saints, and is crowned with a crucifix.

Franciscan Garden ❸

FRANTIŠKÁNSKÁ ZAHRADA

Jungmannovo náměstí 18. **Map** 3 C5. *Můstek.* **Open** *6am–7pm daily.*

Originally the physic garden of a Franciscan monastery, the area was opened to the public in 1950 as a tranquil oasis close to Wenceslas Square. By the entrance is a Gothic portal leading down to a cellar restaurant – U františkánů (At the Franciscans). In the 1980s several of the beds were replanted with herbs, cultivated by the Franciscans in the 17th century.

Hotel Europa ❹

HOTEL EVROPA

Václavské náměstí 29. **Map** 4 D5. **Tel** *22 42 28 117.* *Můstek.* *3, 9, 14, 24.* *See* ***Where to Stay*** *pp184–95,* ***Restaurants, Pubs and Cafés*** *pp202–11.* **www**.evropahotel.cz

Though a trifle shabby in places, the Europa Hotel is a wonderfully preserved reminder of the golden age

Art Nouveau decoration on façade of the Hotel Europa

Façade of the State Opera, formerly the New German Theatre

of hotels. It was built in highly decorated Art Nouveau style between 1903 and 1906. Not only has its splendid façade crowned with gilded nymphs survived, but many of the interiors on the ground floor have remained virtually intact, including all the original bars, large mirrors, panelling and light fittings.

National Museum ❺

NÁRODNÍ MUZEUM

Václavské náměstí 68. **Map** 6 E1. ***Tel*** *22 44 97 111.* *Muzeum.* ***Open*** *Oct–Apr: 9am–5pm daily; May–Sep: 10am–6pm (but closed first Tue of month).* *for a fee.* **www**.nm.cz

The vast Neo-Renaissance building at one end of Wenceslas Square houses the National Museum. Designed by Josef Schulz as a triumphal affirmation of the Czech national revival, the museum was completed in 1890. The entrance is reached by a ramp decorated with allegorical statues. Seated by the door are History and Natural History.

Inside, the rich marbled decoration is impressive, but overwhelms the collections devoted mainly to mineralogy, archaeology, anthropology, numismatics and natural history. The museum also has a Pantheon containing busts and statues of Czech scholars, writers and artists. It is decorated with many paintings by František Ženíšek, Václav Brožík and Vojtěch Hynais.

State Opera ❻

STÁTNÍ OPERA

Wilsonova 4. **Map** 4 E5. ***Tel*** *22 42 27 266 (box office).* *Muzeum.* ***Open*** *for performances only. See* ***Entertainment*** *p220 & p222.* **www**.opera.cz

The first theatre built here, the New Town Theatre, was pulled down in 1885 to make way for the present building. This was originally known as the New German Theatre, built to rival the Czechs' National Theatre *(see pp156–7)*. A Neo-Classical frieze decorates the pediment above the columned loggia at the front of the theatre. The figures include Dionysus and Thalia, the muse of comedy. The interior is stuccoed and original paintings in the auditorium and on the curtain have been preserved. In 1945 the theatre became the city's main opera house.

Mucha Museum ❼

MUCHOVO MUZEUM

Panská 7. **Map** 4 D4. ***Tel*** *22 14 51 333.* *Můstek, Náměstí Republiky.* *3, 5, 9, 14, 24, 26.* ***Open*** *10am– 6pm daily.* **www**.mucha.cz

The 18th-century Kaunicky Palace is home to the first museum dedicated to this Czech master of Art Nouveau. A selection of over 80 exhibits include paintings and drawings, sculptures, photographs and personal memorabilia. The central courtyard becomes a terrace for the café in the summer, and there is a museum shop offering exclusive gifts with Mucha motifs.

Main staircase of the National Museum

Art Nouveau in Prague

Façade detail, 10 Masaryk Embankment

The decorative style known as Art Nouveau originated in Paris in the 1890s. It quickly became international as most of the major European cities quickly responded to its graceful, flowing forms. In Prague it was called "Secese" and at its height in the first decade of the 20th century but died out during World War I, when it seemed frivolous and even decadent. There is a wealth of Art Nouveau in Prague, both in the fine and decorative arts and in architecture. In the New Town and the Jewish Quarter *(see pp80–93)*, entire streets were demolished at the turn of the century and built in the new style.

Praha House
This house was built in 1903 for the Prague Insurance Company. Its name is in gilt Art Nouveau letters at the top.

ARCHITECTURE

Art Nouveau made its first appearance in Prague at the Jubilee exhibition of 1891. Architecturally, the new style was a deliberate attempt to break with the 19th-century tradition of monumental buildings. In Art Nouveau the important aspect was ornament, either painted or sculpted, often in the form of a female figure, applied to a fairly plain surface. This technique was ideally suited to wrought iron and glass, popular at the turn of the century. These materials were light but strong. The effect of this, together with Art Nouveau decoration, created buildings of lasting beauty.

Hotel Central
Built by Alois Dryák and Bedřich Bendelmayer in 1900, the façade of this hotel has plasterwork shaped like tree branches.

Hlahol Choir Building, 1905
The architect Josef Fanta embellished this building with mosaics and sculptures by Karl Mottl and Josef Pekárek (see also p142).

Hotel Meran
Finished in 1904, this grand Art Nouveau building is notable for its fine detailing inside and out.

Hlavní nádraží
Prague's main railway station was completed in 1901. With its huge interior glazed dome and elegant sculptural decoration, it shows many Art Nouveau features.

DECORATIVE AND FINE ARTS

Many painters, sculptors and graphic artists were influenced by Art Nouveau. One of the most successful exponents of the style was the artist Alfons Mucha (1860–1939). He is celebrated chiefly for his posters. Yet he designed stained glass *(see p102)*, furniture, jewellery, even postage stamps. It is perhaps here, in the decorative and applied arts, that Art Nouveau had its fullest expression in Prague. Artists adorned every type of object – doorknobs, curtain ornaments, vases and cutlery – with tentacle- and plant-like forms in imitation of the natural world from which they drew their inspiration.

Postage Stamp, 1918
A bold stamp design by Alfons Mucha marked the founding of the Czechoslovak Republic.

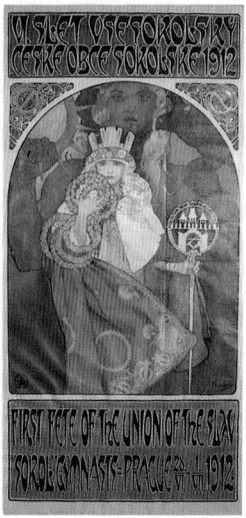

Poster for Sokol Movement
Mucha's colour lithograph for the sixth national meeting of the Sokol gymnastic movement (1912) is in Tyrš's Museum (Physical Culture and Sports).

Záboj and Slavoj
These mythical figures (invented by a forger of old legends) were carved by Josef Myslbek for Palacký Bridge in 1895. They are now in Vyšehrad.

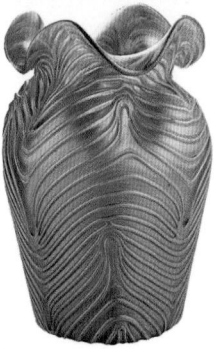

Glass Vase
This iridescent green vase made of Bohemian glass has relief decoration of intertwined threads. It is in the Museum of Decorative Arts.

Curtain Ornament and Candlestick
The silver and silk ornament adorns the Mayor's room of the Municipal House. The candlestick by Emanuel Novák with fine leaf design is in the Museum of Decorative Arts.

WHERE TO SEE ART NOUVEAU IN PRAGUE

Detail of doorway, Široká 9, Jewish Quarter

ARCHITECTURE
Apartment Building, Na příkopě 7
Hanavský Pavilion *p161*
Hlahol Choir Building, Masarykovo nábřeží 10
Hlavní nádraží, Wilsonova
Hotel Central, Hybernská 10
Hotel Evropa *p146*
Industrial Palace *p162* and Four Guided Walks *pp178–9*
Ministerstvo pro místní rozvoj *p67*
Municipal House *p64*
Palacký Bridge (Palackého most)
Praha House, Národní třída 7
Wiehl House *p144*

PAINTING
St Agnes's Convent *pp92–3*

SCULPTURE
Jan Hus Monument *p70*
Vyšehrad Garden and Cemetery *p160* and Four Guided Walks *pp180–1*
Zbraslav Monastery *p163*

DECORATIVE ARTS
Mucha Museum *p147*
Museum of Decorative Arts *p84*
Prague Museum *p161*

Street-by-Street: Charles Square

Detail of house in Charles Square

The southern part of the New Town resounds to the rattle of trams, as many routes converge in this part of Prague. Fortunately, the park in Charles Square (Karlovo náměstí) offers a peaceful and welcome retreat. Some of the buildings around the Square belong to the University and the statues in the centre represent writers and scientists, reflecting the academic environment. There are several Baroque buildings and towards the river stands the historic 14th-century Slavonic Monastery.

The Czech Technical University was founded here in 1867 in a grand Neo-Renaissance building.

Charles Square Centre

Church of St Wenceslas

To the river

RESSLOVA

VÁCLAVSKÁ

NA MORÁNI

KARLOVO

To metro Karlovo náměstí

VYSEHRADSKÁ

POD SLOVANY

TROJICKÁ

★ Church of St Cyril and St Methodius
A plaque and a bullet-scarred wall are reminders of the siege of the church in 1942, when German troops mounted an assault on the Czech and Slovak agents who were hiding there ⓫

★ Charles Square
The centre of the square is a pleasant 19th-century park with lawns, formal flowerbeds, fountains and statues ⓪

Church of St Cosmas and St Damian

Slavonic Monastery Emauzy
In 1965 a pair of modern concrete spires by František Černý were added to the church of the 14th-century monastery ⓮

Church of St John on the Rock
This view of the organ and ceiling shows the dynamic Baroque design of Kilian Ignaz Dientzenhofer ⓭

STAR SIGHTS

★ Charles Square

★ Church of St Cyril and St Methodius

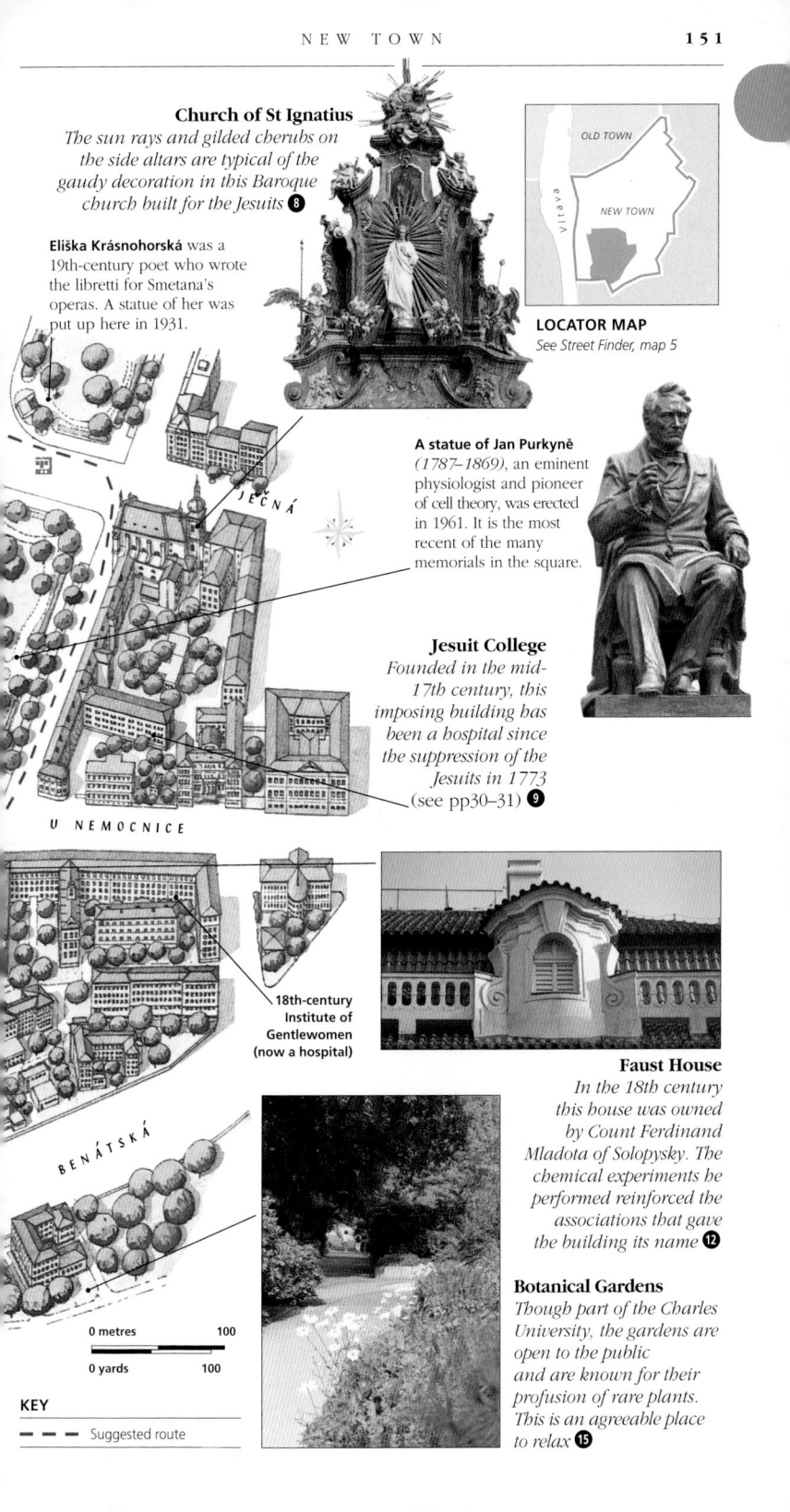

Church of St Ignatius
The sun rays and gilded cherubs on the side altars are typical of the gaudy decoration in this Baroque church built for the Jesuits 8

Eliška Krásnohorská was a 19th-century poet who wrote the libretti for Smetana's operas. A statue of her was put up here in 1931.

LOCATOR MAP
See Street Finder, map 5

A statue of Jan Purkyně *(1787–1869)*, an eminent physiologist and pioneer of cell theory, was erected in 1961. It is the most recent of the many memorials in the square.

Jesuit College
Founded in the mid-17th century, this imposing building has been a hospital since the suppression of the Jesuits in 1773 (see pp30–31) 9

18th-century Institute of Gentlewomen (now a hospital)

Faust House
In the 18th century this house was owned by Count Ferdinand Mladota of Solopysky. The chemical experiments he performed reinforced the associations that gave the building its name 12

Botanical Gardens
Though part of the Charles University, the gardens are open to the public and are known for their profusion of rare plants. This is an agreeable place to relax 15

Sculptures on the façade of the Jesuit College by Tomasso Soldati

Church of St Ignatius ⑧

KOSTEL SV. IGNÁCE

Ječná 2. **Map** 5 C2. ***Tel*** *22 49 21 254.* *Karlovo náměstí.* *3, 4, 6, 10, 14, 18, 22, 23, 24.* ***Open*** *6am–6:30pm daily.* *frequent.*

With its wealth of gilding and flamboyant stucco decoration, St Ignatius is typical of the Baroque churches built by the Jesuits to impress people with the power and glamour of their faith. The architects were the same two men responsible for the adjoining Jesuit College, Carlo Lurago, who started work on the church in 1665, and Paul Ignaz Bayer, who added the tower in 1687.

The painting on the high altar of *The Glory of St Ignatius* (St Ignatius Loyola, the founder of the Jesuit order) is by Jan Jiří Heinsch.

The Jesuits continued to embellish the interior right up until the suppression of their order in 1773, adding stuccowork and statues of Jesuit and Czech saints.

Jesuit College ⑨

JEZUITSKÁ KOLEJ

Karlovo náměstí 36. **Map** 5 B2. *Karlovo náměstí.* *3, 4, 6, 10, 14, 16, 18, 22, 23, 24.* ***Closed*** *to the public.*

Half the eastern side of Charles Square is occupied by the former college of the Jesuit order in the New Town. As in other parts of Prague, the Jesuits were able to demolish huge swathes of the city to put up another bastion of their formidable education system. The college was built between 1656 and 1702 by Carlo Lurago and Paul Ignaz Bayer. The two sculptured portals are the work of Johann Georg Wirch who extended the building in 1770. After the suppression of the Jesuit order in 1773 the college was converted into a military hospital. It is now a teaching hospital and part of Charles University.

Charles Square ⑩

KARLOVO NÁMĚSTÍ

Map 5 B2. *Karlovo náměstí.* *3, 4, 6, 10, 14, 16, 18, 22, 23, 24.*

Since the mid-19th century the square has been a park. Though surrounded by busy roads, it is a pleasant place to sit and read or watch people exercising their dachshunds.

The square began life as a vast cattle market, when Charles IV founded the New Town in 1348. Other goods sold in the square included firewood, coal and pickled herrings from barrels. In the centre of the market Charles had a wooden tower built, where the coronation jewels were put on display once a year. In 1382 the tower was replaced by a chapel, from which, in 1437, concessions made to the Hussites by the pope at the Council of Basle were read out to the populace.

Church of St Cyril and St Methodius ⑪

KOSTEL SV. CYRILA A METODĚJE

Resslova 9. **Map** 5 B2. ***Tel*** *22 49 20 686.* *Karlovo náměstí.* *3, 4, 6, 10, 14, 16, 18, 22, 23, 24.* ***Open*** *Oct–Apr: 10am–4pm Tue–Sun; May–Sep: 10am–5pm Tue–Sun.*

This Baroque church, with a pilastered façade and a small central tower, was built in the 1730s. It was dedicated to St Charles Borromeo and served as the church of a community of retired priests, but both were closed in 1783. In the 1930s the church was restored and given to the Czechoslovak Orthodox Church, and rededicated to St Cyril and St Methodius, the 9th-century "Apostles to the Slavs" *(see pp20–21)*. In May 1942 parachutists who had assassinated Reinhard Heydrich, the Nazi governor of Czechoslovakia, hid in the crypt along with members of the Czech Resistance. Surrounded by German troops, they took their own lives rather than surrender. Bullet holes made by the German machine guns during the siege can still be seen below the memorial plaque on the outer wall of the crypt, which now houses a museum of these times.

Main altar in the Church of St Cyril and St Methodius

Faust House ⓬

FAUSTŮV DŮM

Karlovo náměstí 40, 41. **Map** 5 B3. *Karlovo náměstí.* *3, 4, 14, 16, 18.* ***Closed*** *to the public.*

Prague thrives on legends of alchemy and pacts with the devil, and this Baroque mansion has attracted many. There has been a house here since the 14th century when it belonged to Prince Václav of Opava, an alchemist and natural historian. In the 16th century it was owned by the alchemist Edward Kelley. The chemical experiments of Count Ferdinand Mladota of Solopysky, who owned the house in the mid-18th century, gave rise to its association with the legend of Faust.

Baroque façade of Faust House

Church of St John on the Rock ⓭

KOSTEL SV. JANA NA SKALCE

Vyšehradská 49. **Map** 5 B3. ***Tel*** *22 49 15 371.* *3, 4, 14, 16, 18, 24.* ***Open*** *for services only.* *8am Sun.*

One of Prague's smaller Baroque churches, St John on the Rock is one of Kilian Ignaz Dientzenhofer's most daring designs. Its twin square towers are set at a sharp angle to the church's narrow façade and the interior is based on an octagonal floorplan. The church was completed in 1738, but the double staircase leading up to the west front was not added until the 1770s. On the high altar there is a wooden version of Jan Brokof's statue of St John Nepomuk *(see p137)* which stands on the Charles Bridge.

Slavonic Monastery Emauzy ⓮

KLÁŠTER NA SLOVANECH-EMAUZY

Vyšehradská 49. **Map** 5 B3. ***Tel*** *221 979 296.* *3, 4, 14, 18, 24.* ***Monastery church open*** *7am–7pm Mon–Fri.* ***Cloisters open*** *by appointment.* *noon Mon–Sat, 10am Sun.* **www**.emauzy.cz

Both the monastery and its church were almost destroyed in an American air raid in 1945. During their reconstruction, the church was given a pair of modern reinforced concrete spires.

The monastery was founded in 1347 for the Croatian Benedictines, whose services were held in the Old Slavonic language, hence its name "Na Slovanech". In the course of Prague's tumultuous religious history it has since changed hands many times. In 1446 a Hussite order was formed here, then in 1635 the monastery was acquired by Spanish Benedictines. In the 18th century the complex was given a thorough Baroque treatment, but in 1880 it was taken over by some German Benedictines, who rebuilt almost everything in Neo-Gothic style. The monastery has managed to preserve some historically important 14th-century wall paintings in the cloister, though many were damaged in World War II.

Remains of 14th-century wall paintings in the Slavonic Monastery

Botanical Gardens ⓯

BOTANICKÁ ZAHRADA

Na slupi 16. **Map** 5 B3. ***Tel*** *22 49 18 970.* *18, 24.* *148.* ***Glasshouses open*** *10am–4pm daily.* ***Gardens open*** *Jan–Feb: 10am–5pm daily; Mar–Oct: 10am–6pm daily; Nov–Dec: 10am–4pm daily.*

Charles IV founded Prague's first botanical garden in the 14th century. This is a much later institution. The university garden was founded in the Smíchov district in 1775, but in 1897 it was moved to its present site. The huge greenhouses date from 1938.

Special botanical exhibitions and shows of exotic birds and tropical fish are often held here. One star attraction of the gardens is the giant water lily, *Victoria cruziana,* whose huge leaves can support a small child. During the summer it produces dozens of flowers which only survive for a day.

Entrance to the university's Botanical Gardens

Octagonal steeple of St Catherine's

Church of St Catherine ⑯

KOSTEL SV. KATEŘINY

Kateřinská. **Map** 5 C3. 🚋 *4, 6, 10, 16, 22, 23.* ***Closed*** *to the public.*

St Catherine's stands in the garden of a former convent, founded in 1354 by Charles IV to commemorate his victory at the Battle of San Felice in Italy in 1332. In 1420, during the Hussite revolution *(see pp26–7)*, the convent was demolished, but in the following century it was rebuilt by Kilian Ignáz Dientzenhofer as an Augustinian monastery. The monks remained here until 1787, when the monastery closed. Since 1822 it has been used as a hospital. In 1737 a new Baroque church was built, but the slender steeple of the old Gothic church was retained. Its octagonal shape has gained it the nickname of "the Prague minaret".

Chalice Restaurant ⑰

RESTAURACE U KALICHA

Na bojišti 14. **Map** 6 D3. ***Tel*** *29 61 89 600.* Ⓜ *IP Pavlova.* 🚋 *4, 6, 10, 16, 22, 23.* ***Open*** *11am–11pm daily.* 📷 ♿ *See* ***Restaurants*** *pp202–9.* **www**.ukalicha.cz

This Pilsner Urquell beer hall owes its fame to the novel *The Good Soldier Švejk* by Jaroslav Hašek. It was Švejk's favourite drinking place and the establishment trades on the popularity of the best-loved character in 20th-century Czech literature. The staff dress in period costume from World War I, the era of this novel.

Dvořák Museum ⑱

MUZEUM ANTONÍNA DVOŘÁKA

Ke Karlovu 20. **Map** 6 D2. ***Tel*** *22 49 23 363.* Ⓜ *IP Pavlova.* 🚌 *148.* ***Open*** *10am–5pm Tue–Sun and for concerts.* 🎫 🚫 ♿ **www**.nm.cz

One of the most enchanting secular buildings of the Prague Baroque, this red and ochre villa now houses the Antonín Dvořák Museum. On display are Dvořák scores and editions of his works, plus photographs and memorabilia of the great 19th-century Czech composer, including his piano, his viola and his desk.

The building is by the great Baroque architect Kilian Ignaz Dientzenhofer *(see p129)*. Just two storeys high with an elegant tiered mansard roof, the house was completed in 1720, for the Michnas of Vacínov and was originally known as the Michna Summer Palace. It later became known as Villa Amerika, after a nearby inn called Amerika. Between the two pavilions flanking the house is a fine iron gateway, a replica of the Baroque original. In the 19th century villa and garden fell into decay. The garden statues and vases, from the workshop of Matthias Braun, date from about 1735. They are original but heavily restored, as is the interior of the palace. The ceiling and walls of the large room on the first floor, often used for recitals, are decorated with 18th-century frescoes by Jan Ferdinand Schor.

Church of St Stephen ⑲

KOSTEL SV. ŠTĚPÁNA

Štěpánská. **Map** 5 C2. 🚋 *4, 6, 10, 16, 22, 23.* ***Open*** *only for services.* ✝ *11am Sun.* 🚫

Founded by Charles IV in 1351 as the parish church of the upper New Town, St Stephen's was finished in 1401 with the completion of the multi-spired steeple. In the late 17th century the Branberg Chapel was built on to the north side of the church. It contains the tomb of the prolific Baroque sculptor Matthias Braun.

Most of the subsequent Baroque additions were removed when the church was scrupulously re-Gothicized in the 1870s by Josef Mocker. There are several fine Baroque paintings,

The Michna Summer Palace, home of the Dvořák Museum

Renaissance painted ceiling in the New Town Hall

however, including *The Baptism of Christ* by Karel Škréta at the end of the left hand aisle and a picture of St John Nepomuk *(see p137)* by Jan Jiří Heinsch to the left of the 15th-century pulpit. The church's greatest treasure is undoubtedly a beautiful Gothic panel painting of the Madonna, known as *Our Lady of St Stephen's*, which dates from 1472.

Gothic pulpit in St Stephen's

New Town Hall ⓴

NOVOMĚSTSKÁ RADNICE

Karlovo náměstí 23. **Map** 5 B1. *Karlovo náměstí.* *3, 4, 6, 10, 14, 16, 18, 22, 24.* ***Tel*** *22 49 47 131.* ***Tower open*** *May–Sep: 10am–6pm Tue–Sun.*

In 1960 a statue of Hussite preacher Jan Želivský was unveiled at the New Town Hall. It commemorates the first and bloodiest of many defenestrations. On 30 July 1419 Želivský led a crowd of demonstrators to the Town Hall to demand the release of some prisoners. When they were refused, they stormed the building and threw the Catholic councillors out of the windows. Those who survived the fall were finished off with pikes.

The Town Hall already existed in the 14th century, the Gothic tower was added in the mid-15th century and contains an 18th century chapel. In the 16th century it acquired an arcaded courtyard. After the joining-up of the four towns of Prague in 1784 the Town Hall ceased to be the seat of the municipal administration and became a courthouse and a prison. It is now used for cultural and social events, and its splendid Gothic hall can be hired for wedding receptions.

U Fleků ㉑

Křemencova 11. **Map** 5 B1. ***Tel*** *22 49 34 019.* *Národní třída, Karlovo náměstí.* *6, 9, 17, 18, 22.* **Museum *open*** *10am–4pm Mon–Fri. See* ***Restaurants*** *pp202–9.* **www**.ufleku.cz

Records indicate that beer was brewed here as early as 1459. This archetypal Prague beer hall has been fortunate in its owners, who have kept up the tradition of brewing as an art rather than just a means of making money. In 1762 the brewery was purchased by Jakub Flekovský, who named it U Fleků (At the Fleks). The present brewery, the smallest in Prague, makes a special strong, dark beer, sold only here. The restaurant now also features a small museum of Czech brewing history.

Church of St Ursula ㉒

KOSTEL SV. VORŠILY

Ostrovní 18. **Map** 3 A5. ***Tel*** *22 49 30 502.* *Národní třída.* *6, 9, 18, 22, 23.* *5pm daily. For visits at any other time, contact Prague Information Service (see p227).*

The delightful Baroque church of St Ursula was built as part of an Ursuline convent founded in 1672. The original sculptures still decorate the façade and in front of the church stands a group of statues featuring St John Nepomuk (1747) by Ignaz Platzer the Elder. The light airy interior has a frescoed, stuccoed ceiling and on the various altars there are lively Baroque paintings. The main altar has one of St Ursula.

The adjoining convent has been returned to the Ursuline order and is now a Catholic school. One part of the ground floor is still used for secular purposes – the Klášterní Vinárna (Convent Restaurant).

National Theatre ㉓

NÁRODNÍ DIVADLO

See pp156–7.

U Fleků, Prague's best-known beer hall

National Theatre ㉓

NÁRODNÍ DIVADLO

A bronze sculpture in the foyer

This gold-crested theatre has always been an important symbol of the Czech cultural revival. Work started in 1868, funded largely by voluntary contributions. The original Neo-Renaissance design was by the Czech architect Josef Zítek. After its destruction by fire *(see opposite)*, Josef Schulz was given the job of rebuilding the theatre and all the best Czech artists of the period contributed towards its lavish and spectacular decoration. During the late 1970s and early 80s the theatre was restored and the New Stage was built by architect Karel Prager.

The theatre from Marksmen's Island

A bronze three-horse chariot, designed by Bohuslav Schnirch, carries the Goddess of Victory.

Laterna Magika

The New Stage auditorium

★ Auditorium
The elaborately-painted ceiling is adorned with allegorical figures representing the arts by František Ženíšek.

STAR FEATURES

- ★ Auditorium
- ★ Lobby Ceiling
- ★ Stage Curtain

The five arcades of the loggia are decorated with lunette paintings by Josef Tulka, entitled *Five Songs*.

★ Lobby Ceiling
This ceiling fresco is the final part of a triptych painted by František Ženíšek in 1878 depicting the Golden Age of Czech Art.

★ Stage Curtain
This sumptuous gold and red stage curtain, showing the origin of the theatre, is the work of Vojtěch Hynais.

VISITORS' CHECKLIST

Národní 2, Nové Město. **Map** 3 A5. ***Tel*** *22 49 12 673.* *Národní třída, line B.* *17, 18, 22, 23 to Národní třída.* ***Auditorium open*** *only during performances.* *Sat & Sun.* ***Tel*** *22 17 14 151.*

Façade Decoration
This standing figure on the attic of the western façade is one of many figures representing the Arts sculpted by Antonín Wagner in 1883.

The startling sky-blue roof covered with stars, is said to symbolize the summit all artists should aim for.

The President's Box
The former royal box, lined in red velvet, is decorated with famous historical figures from Czech history by Václav Brožík.

NATIONAL THEATRE FIRE

On 12 August, 1881, just days before the official opening, the National Theatre was completely gutted by fire. It was thought to have been started by metalworkers on the roof. But just six weeks later, enough money had been collected to rebuild the theatre. It was finally opened two years late in 1883 with a performance of Czech composer Bedřich Smetana's opera *Libuše* *(see p79).*

FURTHER AFIELD

Visitors to Prague, finding the old centre packed with sights, tend to ignore the suburbs. It is true that once you start exploring away from the centre, the language can become more of a problem. However, it is well worth the effort, firstly to escape the crowds of tourists milling around the Castle and the Old Town Square, secondly to realize that Prague is a living city as well as a picturesque time capsule. Most of the museums and other sights in the first part of this section are easily reached by Metro, tram or even on foot. If you are prepared to venture a little further, do not miss the grand palace at Troja or the former monastery at Zbraslav, which houses the Asian Art collection of the National Gallery. The Day Trips *(pp168–71)* include visits to castles close to Prague and the historic spa towns of Marienbad and Karlsbad, which attracted the first tourists to Bohemia during the 19th century.

Vaulting in Church of St Barbara, Kutná Hora

SIGHTS AT A GLANCE

Museums and Galleries
Mozart Museum ❶
Prague Museum ❻
National Technical Museum ❽
Trades Fair Palace pp164–5 ❾
Zbraslav Monastery ⓯

Monasteries
Břevnov Monastery ⓭

Historic Districts
Vyšehrad ❷
Žižkov ❹
Náměstí Míru ❺

Cemeteries
Olšany Cemeteries ❸

Historic Sites
White Mountain and Star Hunting Lodge ⓮

Historic Buildings
Troja Palace pp166–7 ⓫

Parks and Gardens
Letná Park ❼
Exhibition Ground and Stromovka Park ❿
Zoo ⓬

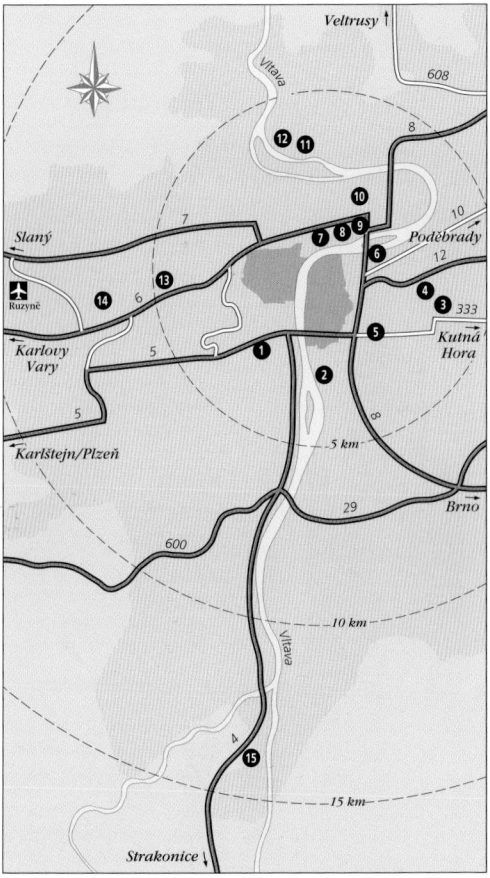

KEY
Central Prague
Greater Prague
Airport
Major road
Minor road

15 km = 10 miles

◁ Part of the garden staircase at the 17th-century Troja Palace

Bertramka, the villa that houses the Mozart Museum

Mozart Museum ❶

BERTRAMKA

Mozartova 169. ***Tel*** *25 73 18 461.* *Anděl.* *4, 7, 9.* ***Open*** *Apr–Oct: 9:30am–6pm daily; Nov–Mar: 9:30am–4pm daily.*
www.bertramka.cz

Though slightly off the beaten track, the museum is well signposted because of Prague's reverence for Mozart. Bertramka is a 17th-century farmhouse, enlarged in the second half of the 18th century into a comfortable suburban villa. Mozart and his wife Constanze stayed here as the guests of the composer František Dušek and his wife Josefina in 1787, when Mozart was working on *Don Giovanni*. He composed the overture to the opera in the garden pavilion just a few hours before its premiere at the Nostitz (now the Estates) Theatre *(see p65)*. The house, with a small exhibition on Mozart, is at its best in the late afternoon when it is quietest. In summer, recitals take place on the terrace.

Vyšehrad ❷

Map 5 B5. *Vyšehrad.* *7, 18, 24.*

A rocky outcrop above the Vltava, Vyšehrad means "castle on the heights" *(see pp180–1)*. It was fortified in the 10th century and, at times, used as the seat of the Přemyslid princes. The area has great historical and mythological significance for the Czech people, and in the 1870s it was chosen as the site for a national cemetery.

Olšany Cemeteries ❸

OLŠANSKÉ HŘBITOVY

Vinohradská 153, Jana Želivského. *Želivského.* ***Tel*** *26 73 10 652.* *5, 6, 10, 11, 16, 19, 26.* ***Open*** *Mar–Sep: 8am–7pm; Oct–Feb: 8am–6pm.*

Well-tended grave in the eastern part of the Olšany Cemeteries

At the northwest corner of the main cemetery stands the small Church of St Roch (1682), protector against the plague – the first cemetery was founded here in 1679 specifically for the burial of plague victims. In the course of the 19th century, the old cemetery was enlarged and new ones developed, including a Russian cemetery, distinguished by its old-fashioned Orthodox church (1924–5), and a Jewish one, where Franz Kafka *(see p68)* is buried. Tombs include those of painter Josef Mánes (1820–71) who worked during the Czech Revival movement *(see pp32–3)*, and Josef Jungmann (1773–1847), compiler of a five-volume Czech-German dictionary.

Žižkov ❹

Jiřího z Poděbrad, Želivského, Flóra. **National Monument**, *Vítkov, U památníku.* *133, 168, 207.*
For visits contact Prague Information Service (see p227).

Equestrian statue of Jan Žižka

This quarter of Prague was the scene of a historic victory for the Hussites *(see pp26–7)* over Crusaders sent by the Emperor Sigismund to destroy them. On 14 July 1420 on Vítkov hill, a tiny force of Hussites defeated an army of several thousand well-armed men. The determined, hymn-singing Hussites were led by the one-eyed Jan Žižka.

In 1877 the area around Vítkov was renamed Žižkov in honour of Žižka's victory, and in 1950 a bronze equestrian statue of Žižka by Bohumil Kafka was erected on the hill. About 9m (30 ft) high, this is the largest equestrian statue in the world. It stands in front of the National Monument (1927–32), built as a symbol of the struggle for independence of the Czechoslovak people. The Monument later served as a mausoleum for Klement Gottwald and other Communist leaders. Their remains have since been removed and the building given to the National Museum *(see p147)* which

Relief by Josef Myslbek on portal of St Ludmilla in Náměstí Míru

plans to open a permanent exhibition on modern Czech history in 2009.

Nearby is a giant television transmitter, 260 m (850 ft) high. Locals are suspicious of the rays emanating from this great tube of reinforced concrete, built in 1984–8.

Náměstí Míru ❺

Map 6 F2. *Náměstí Míru.* *4, 6, 10, 16, 22.* *135, 148, 272.* **Church of St Ludmila** ***open*** *only for services.*

This attractive square, with a well-kept central garden, is the focal point of the Vinohrady quarter. At the top of its sloping lawns stands the attractive, brick Neo-Gothic Church of St Ludmila (1888–93), designed by Josef Mocker, architect of the west end of St Vitus's Cathedral *(see pp100–3)*. Its twin octagonal spires are 60 m (200 ft) high. On the tympanum of the main portal is a relief of Christ with St Wenceslas and St Ludmila by the great 19th-century sculptor Josef Myslbek. Leading artists also contributed designs for the stained-glass windows and the colourful interior.

The outside of the square is lined with attractive buildings, the most conspicuous being the Vinohrady Theatre, a spirited Art Nouveau building completed in 1907. The façade is crowned by two huge winged figures sculpted by Milan Havlíček, symbolizing Drama and Opera.

Prague Museum ❻

MUZEUM HLAVNÍHO MĚSTA PRAHY

Na Poříčí 52. **Map** 4 F3.
Tel *22 48 16 772/22 48 16 773.* *Florenc.* *3, 8, 24, 26.* ***Open*** *9am–6pm Tue–Sun (9am–8pm first Thu of every month).*
www.muzeumprahy.cz

The collection records the history of Prague from primeval times. A new museum was built to house the exhibits in the 1890s. Its Neo-Renaissance façade is rich with stucco and sculptures, and the interior walls are painted with historic views of the city. On display are examples of Prague china and furniture, relics of the medieval guilds and paintings of Prague through the ages.

The most remarkable exhibit is the paper and wood model of Prague by Antonín Langweil. Completed in 1834, it covers 20 sq m (25 sq yards). The scale of the extraordinarily accurate model is 1:500.

Letná Park ❼

LETENSKÉ SADY

Map 3 A1. *Malostranská, Hradčanská.* *1, 8, 12, 18, 20, 22, 23, 25, 26.*

Across the river from the Jewish Quarter, a large plateau overlooks the city. It was here that armies gathered before attacking Prague Castle. Since the mid-19th century it has been a wooded park.

On the terrace at the top of the granite steps that lead up from the embankment stands a curious monument – a giant metronome built in 1991. It was installed after the Velvet Revolution on the pedestal formerly occupied by the gigantic stone statue of Stalin leading the people, which was blown up in 1962. Nobody likes the metronome any more than they did Stalin and it may soon be replaced. A far more durable monument is the Hanavský Pavilion, a Neo-Baroque cast iron structure, built for the 1891 Exhibition. It was later dismantled and erected on its present site in the park, where it houses a popular restaurant and café.

View of the Vltava and bridges from Letná Park

National Technical Museum ❽

NÁRODNÍ TECHNICKÉ MUZEUM

Kostelní 42. ***Tel*** *22 03 99 111.* *1, 8, 25, 26.* ***Open*** *9am–5pm Tue–Fri, 1–6pm Sat, Sun.* **www**.ntm.cz

Though it tries to keep abreast of all scientific developments, the museum's strength is its collection of machines from the Industrial Revolution to the present day, the largest of its kind in Europe. The section that attracts the most visitors is the History of Transportation in the vast central hall. This is filled with locomotives, railway carriages, bicycles, veteran motorcars and motorcycles, with aeroplanes and a hot-air balloon suspended overhead.

The photography and cinematography section is well worth a visit, as is the collection of astronomical instruments. The section on measuring time is also popular, especially on the hour when everything starts to chime at once. In the basement there is a huge reconstruction of a coal mine, with an assortment of tools tracing the development of mining from the 15th to the 19th century.

Trades Fair Palace ❾

VELETRŽNÍ PALÁC

See pp164–5.

Exhibition Ground and Stromovka Park ❿

VÝSTAVIŠTĚ A STROMOVKA

1, 14, 17, 25. **Exhibition Ground** ***open*** *10am–11pm daily.* **Stromovka Park** ***open*** *24hrs daily.* **Lapidarium** ***Tel*** *23 33 75 636.* ***Open*** *noon–5pm Tue–Fri, 10am–5pm Sat, Sun.* **www**.nm.cz

Laid out for the Jubilee of 1891, the Exhibition Ground has been used for trade fairs, sports and artistic events ever since. With its lively funfair, it is great for a day out with the children. All kinds of exhibitions, sporting events, spectacles and concerts are staged throughout the summer. The large park to the west was the former royal hunting enclosure and deer park, first established in the late 16th century. The name Stromovka means "place of trees", a reminder that a large area of the park was once a flourishing tree nursery. Opened to the public in 1804, the park is still a pleasant wooded area and an ideal place for a walk. The Lapidarium holds an exhibition of 11th–19th century sculpture, including some originals from the Charles Bridge *(see pp136–9).*

The Industrial Palace, centrepiece of the 1891 Exhibition Ground

Troja Palace ⓫

TROJSKÝ ZÁMEK

See pp166–7.

Zoo ⓬

ZOOLOGICKÁ ZAHRADA

U trojského zámku 3. ***Tel*** *26 61 12 111.* *Holešovice, then* *112.* ***Open*** *Jun–Aug: 9am–7pm daily; Apr, May, Sep, Oct: 9am–6pm daily; Nov–Feb: 9am–4pm daily; Mar: 9am–5pm daily.* **www**.zoopraha.cz

Attractively situated on a rocky slope overlooking the right bank of the Vltava, the zoo was founded in 1924. It now covers an area of 64 hectares (160 acres) and there is a chair lift to take visitors to the upper part. To travel on the lift, you can use an ordinary metro/tram ticket.

The zoo's 2,500 animals represent 500 species, 50 of them extremely rare in the wild. It is best known for its breeding programme of Przewalski's horses, the only species of wild horse in the world. It has also enjoyed success in breeding big cats, gorillas and orang-utans. In addition there are two pavilions, one for lions, tigers and other beasts of prey and one for elephants.

Red panda, relative of the famous giant panda, in Prague Zoo

Břevnov Monastery ⓭

BŘEVNOVSKÝ KLÁŠTER

Markétská 28. ***Tel*** *22 04 06 111.* *8, 22.* *only, Sat & Sun; tour times vary.* **www**.brevnov.cz

From the surrounding suburban housing, you would never guess that Břevnov is one of the oldest inhabited parts of Prague. A flourishing community grew up here around the Benedictine abbey founded in 993 by Prince Boleslav II *(see p20)* and Bishop Adalbert (Vojtěch) – the first monastery in Bohemia. An ancient well called Vojtěška marks the spot where prince and bishop are supposed to have met and decided to found the monastery.

The gateway, courtyard and most of the present monastery buildings are by the great Baroque architects Christoph and Kilian Ignaz Dientzenhofer *(see p129)*. The monastery Church of St Margaret is the work of Christoph. Completed in 1715, it is based on a floorplan of overlapping ovals, as ingenious as any of Bernini's churches in Rome. In 1964 the crypt of the original 10th-century church was discovered below the choir and is open to the public. Of the other buildings, the most interesting is the abbey's meeting hall, or Theresian Hall, with a painted ceiling dating from 1727.

White Mountain and Star Hunting Lodge ⓮

BÍLÁ HORA A HVĚZDA

8, 22 (White Mountain), 18 (Star Hunting Lodge). **White Mountain enclosure *open*** *24hrs daily.* **Star Hunting Lodge *Tel*** *23 53 57 938.* ***Open*** *Apr, Oct: 10am–5pm Tue–Sun (to 6pm May–Sep).*

The Battle of the White Mountain *(see p31)*, fought on 8 November 1620, had a very different impact for the two main communities of Prague. For the Protestants it was a disaster that led to 300 years of Habsburg domination; for the Catholic supporters of the Habsburgs it was a triumph, so they built a memorial chapel on the hill. In the early 1700s this was converted into the grander Church of Our Lady Victorious and decorated by leading Baroque artists, including Václav Vavřinec Reiner.

Star Hunting Lodge

In the 16th century the woodland around the battle site had been a royal game park. The hunting lodge, completed in 1556, survives today. This fascinating building is shaped as a six-pointed star – *hvězda* means star. In 1950 it was converted into a museum and dedicated to the writer of historical novels Alois Jirásek (1851–1930), and the painter Mikoláš Aleš (1852–1913). The museum also houses exhibits relating to the Battle of the White Mountain and temporary exhibitions about Czech culture.

Zbraslav Monastery ⓯

ZBRASLAVSKÝ KLÁŠTER

Zámek Zbraslav. ***Tel*** *25 79 21 638.* *129, 240, 241, 243, 255, 360.* ***Open*** *10am–6pm Tue–Sun.* **www**.ngprague.cz

In 1279 Wenceslas II founded a monastery to serve as the burial place for the royal family, though only he and Wenceslas IV were ever buried here. Destroyed during the Hussite Wars *(see pp26–7)*, the monastery was rebuilt in 1709–39, only to be abolished in 1785 and made into a factory. Earlier this century it was restored and in 1941 was given to the National Gallery. It now houses a unique collection of Asian art with exhibits including art and artefacts from China, Japan, India, South East Asia and Tibet. A collection of Japanese sculpture is featured which visually impaired visitors are encouraged to touch. The exhibition also includes a section dedicated to Islamic art. Informative guided tours are available.

Zbraslav Monastery, home to the National Gallery's Asian Art Collection

Trades Fair Palace ❾

VELETRŽNÍ PALAC

The National Gallery in Prague opened its Centre for Modern and Contemporary Art in 1995, housed in a reconstruction of a former Trades Fair building of 1929. Its vast, skylit spaces make an ideal backdrop for the collection, which ranges from French 19th-century art through superb examples of Impressionist and Post-Impressionist painting, to works by Munch, Klimt, Picasso and Miró, and a splendid collection of Czech modern art.

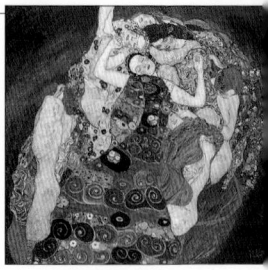

The Virgin *(1913)*
This colourful work epitomizes the distinctive, erotic Art Nouveau style of painter Gustav Klimt.

The Blind *(1926)*
This intriguing work by František Bílek is one of the sculptures on display.

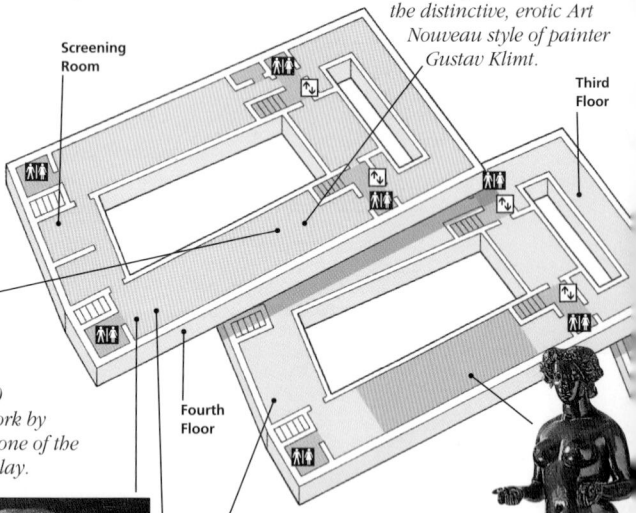

★ George of Poděbrady and Matthias Corvinus
Mikuláš Aleš painted many patriotic historical scenes. Here, Corvinus King of Hungary, signs a treaty with King George in 1469.

Cleopatra *(1942-57)*
This painting by Jan Zrzavy clearly made him a major representative of Czech modern art.

Pomona *(1910)*
Aristide Maillol was a pupil of Rodin. This work is part of an exceptional collection of bronzes.

STAR SIGHTS

- ★ George of Poděbrady and Matthias Corvinus by Aleš
- ★ Evening in Hradčany by Schikaneder
- ★ Torso by Pešánek

★ Evening in Hradčany *(1909-13)*
This incredibly atmospheric painting by Jakub Schikaneder, typically captures the magic and nostalgia of the city of Prague at dusk.

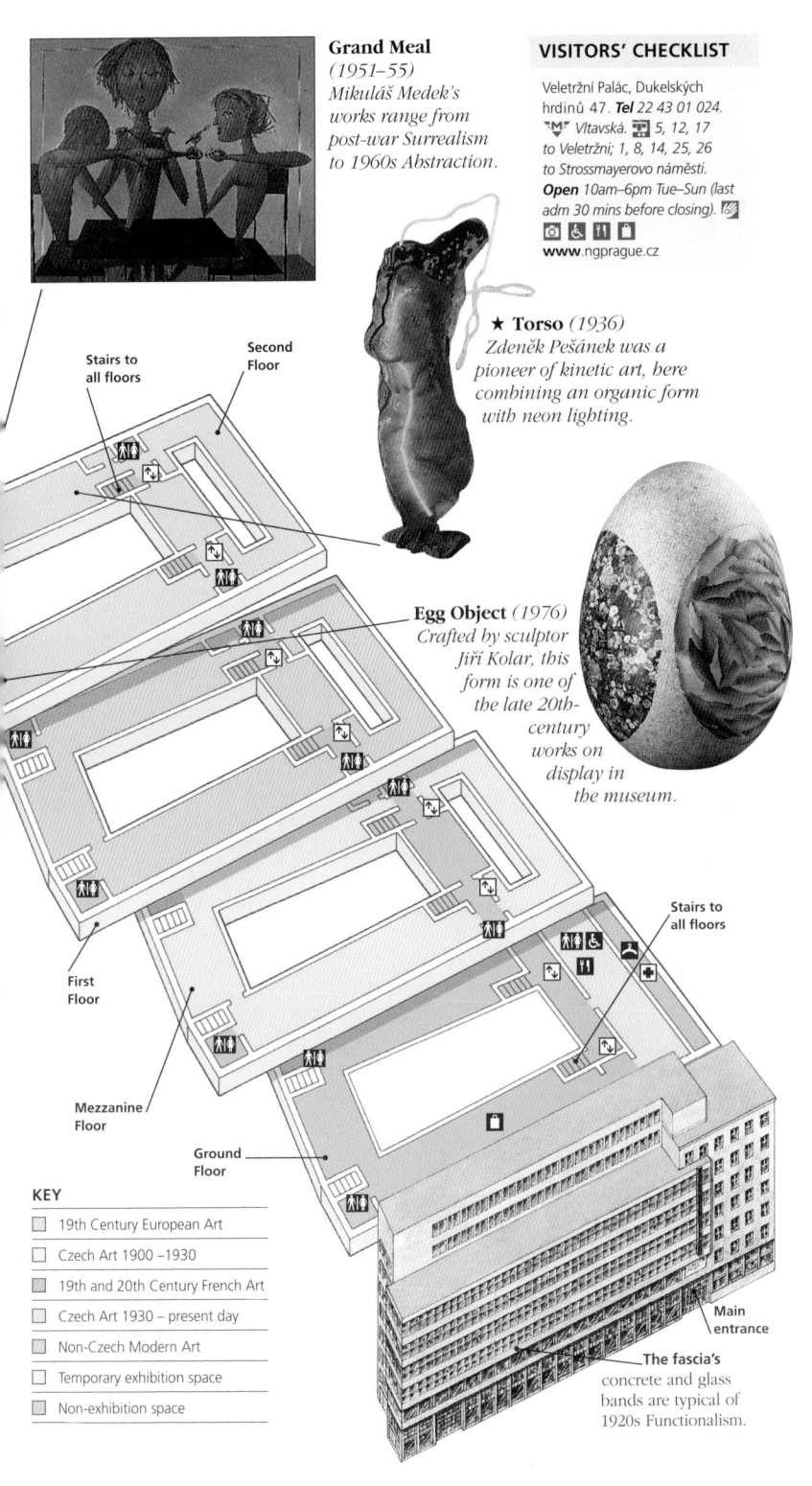
Grand Meal (1951–55)
Mikuláš Medek's works range from post-war Surrealism to 1960s Abstraction.
VISITORS' CHECKLIST
Veletržní Palác, Dukelských hrdinů 47. Tel 22 43 01 024. Vltavská. 5, 12, 17 to Veletržní; 1, 8, 14, 25, 26 to Strossmayerovo náměstí.
Open 10am–6pm Tue–Sun (last adm 30 mins before closing).
www.ngprague.cz
★ Torso (1936)
Zdeněk Pešánek was a pioneer of kinetic art, here combining an organic form with neon lighting.
Stairs to all floors
Second Floor
Egg Object (1976)
Crafted by sculptor Jiří Kolar, this form is one of the late 20th-century works on display in the museum.
First Floor
Mezzanine Floor
Ground Floor
Stairs to all floors
Main entrance
The fascia's concrete and glass bands are typical of 1920s Functionalism.
KEY
19th Century European Art
Czech Art 1900 –1930
19th and 20th Century French Art
Czech Art 1930 – present day
Non-Czech Modern Art
Temporary exhibition space
Non-exhibition space

Troja Palace ⓫

TROJSKÝ ZÁMEK

Terracotta urn on the garden balustrade

One of the most striking summer palaces in Prague, Troja was built in the late 17th century by Jean-Baptiste Mathey for Count Sternberg, a member of a leading Bohemian aristocratic family. Situated at the foot of the Vltava Heights, the exterior of the palace was modelled on a Classical Italian villa, while its garden was laid out in formal French style. The magnificent interior took over 20 years to complete and is full of extravagant frescoes expressing the Sternberg family's loyalty to the Habsburg dynasty. Troja houses a good collection of 19th-century art.

Defeat of the Turks

This turbaned figure, tumbling from the Grand Hall ceiling, symbolizes Leopold I's triumph over the Turks.

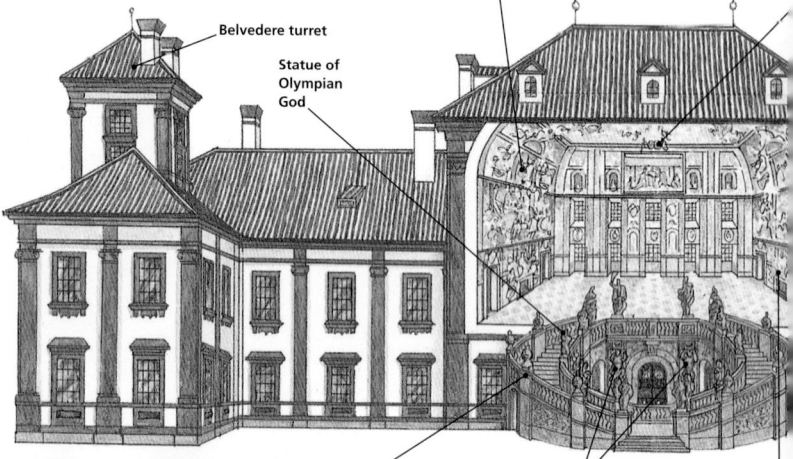

Personification of Justice

Abraham Godyn's image of Justice gazes from the lower east wall of the Grand Hall.

★ Garden Staircase

The two sons of Mother Earth which adorn the sweeping oval staircase (1685–1703) are part of a group of sculptures by Johann Georg Heermann and his nephew Paul, depicting the struggle of the Olympian Gods with the Titans.

VISITORS' CHECKLIST

U trojského zámku 1, Prague 7. **Tel** 283 851614. see p55. 112 from Holešovice. **Open** Apr–Oct: 10am–6pm Tue–Sun; Nov–Mar: 10am–5pm Sat & Sun. **www**.citygalleryprague.cz

★ Grand Hall Fresco
The frescoes in the Grand Hall (1691–7), by Abraham Godyn, depict the story of the first Habsburg Emperor, Rudolph I, and the victories of Leopold I over the archenemy of Christianity, the Sublime Porte (Ottoman Empire).

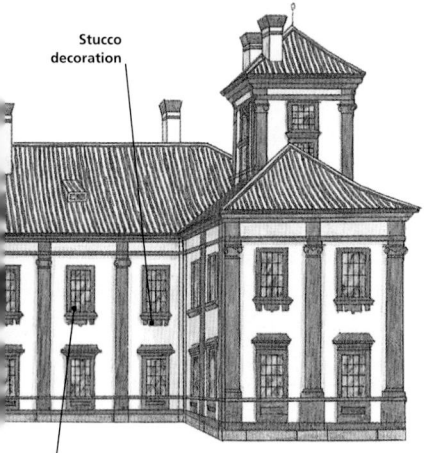

STAR FEATURES

★ Grand Hall Fresco

★ Landscaped Gardens

★ Garden Staircase

Chinese Rooms
Several rooms feature 18th-century murals of Chinese scenes. This room makes a perfect backdrop for a ceramics display.

★ LANDSCAPED GARDENS

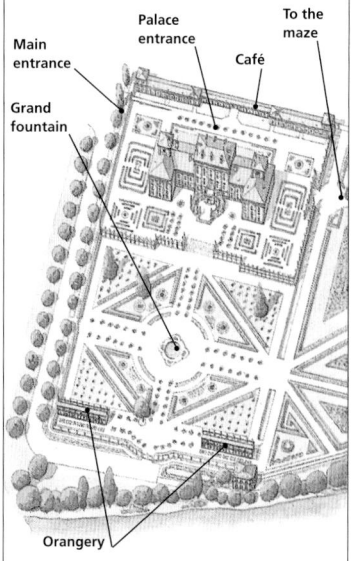

Sloping vineyards were levelled, hillsides excavated and terraces built to fulfil the elaborate and grandiose plans of French architect, Jean-Baptiste Mathey, for the first Baroque French-style formal gardens in Bohemia. The palace and its geometric network of paths, terracing, fountains, statuary and beautiful terracotta vases, is best viewed from the south of the garden between the two orangeries. The gardens have been carefully restored according to Mathey's original plans.

Day Trips from Prague

St George and Dragon, Konopiště

The sights that attract most visitors away from the city are Bohemia's picturesque medieval castles. Karlstein, for example, stands in splendid isolation above wooded valleys that have changed little since the Emperor Charles IV hunted there in the 14th century. We have chosen four castles, very varied in character. There are regular organized tours *(see p227)* to the major sights around Prague, to the historic mining town of Kutná Hora and, if you have more time to spare, to the famous spa towns of Karlsbad and Marienbad in western Bohemia.

SIGHTS AT A GLANCE

Castles
- Veltrusy ❶
- Karlstein ❷
- Konopiště ❸
- Křivoklát ❹

Historic Towns
- Kutná Hora ❺
- Karlsbad ❻
- Marienbad ❼

KEY
- Central Prague
- Greater Prague
- Airport
- Motorway
- Major road
- Minor road

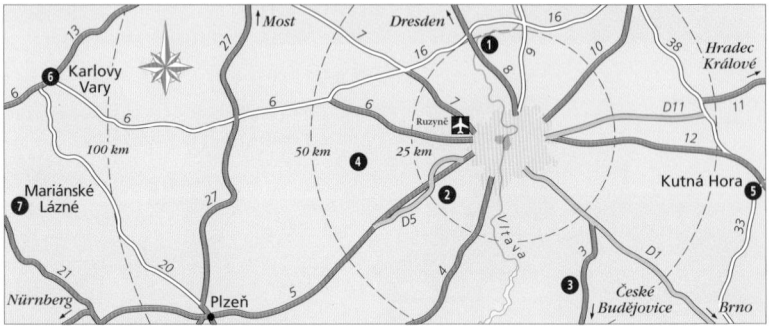

25 km = 16 miles

Veltrusy Château ❶

VELTRUSKÝ ZÁMEK

20 km (12 miles) north of Prague. ***Tel*** *31 57 81 144/146.* *from Smíchov to Kralupy nad Vltavou, then local bus.* ***Open*** *May–Sep: 8am–5pm Tue–Sun (Sep: from 9am); Oct, Nov, Apr: 9am–4pm Sat & Sun.* *(park only).* ***Nelahozeves Castle Tel*** *31 57 09 111.* *from Masarykovo to Nelahozeves–zastávka.* ***Open*** *9am–5pm Tue–Sun (Jun–Aug: to 5pm).*

Veltrusy is a small town beside the Vltava, famous for the 18th-century château built by the aristocratic Chotek family. The building is in the shape of a cross, with a central dome and a grand staircase decorated with statues representing the months of the year and the four seasons.

The estate was laid out as an English-style landscaped deer park, covering an area of 300 hectares (750 acres). Near the entrance there is still an enclosure with a herd of deer. The Vltava flows along one side and dotted around the grounds are several summer houses.

The Doric and Maria Theresa pavilions, the orangery and the grotto date from the late 18th century. The park is planted with some 100 different kinds of tree. The castle was damaged by floods in 2002 and ongoing repairs mean that some rooms will remain closed to the public until 2008.

Just across the river, and easily accessible from Veltrusy by bus or train, is Nelahozeves Castle. This Renaissance castle houses one of the finest private museums in Europe, the Lobkowicz Collection, which includes works by Veronese, Rubens, Canaletto and Velásquez, as well as rare books and manuscripts. The highlight of the collection is *Haymaking*, a painting by Brueghel the Elder. The birthplace of Czech composer Antonin Dvorak is near the castle.

Karlstein Castle, built by Emperor Charles IV in the 14th century

Karlstein Castle ❷

KARLŠTEJN

25 km (16 miles) southwest of Prague. ***Tel*** *27 40 08 154.* *from Hlavní nádraží to Karlštejn (1.5 km/1 mile from castle. The uphill walk takes around 40 minutes).* ***Open*** *Tue–Sun: Apr, Oct: 9am–4pm; May, Jun, Sep: 9am–5pm; Jul–Aug: 9am–6pm; Mar, Nov: 9am–3pm.* *compulsory (book in advance).* **www**.hradkarlstejn.cz

The castle was founded by Charles IV as a country retreat, a treasury for the crown jewels and a symbol of his divine right to rule the Holy Roman Empire. It stands on a crag above the River Berounka. The castle is largely a 19th-century reconstruction by Josef Mocker. The original building work (1348–67) was supervised by French master mason Matthew of Arras, and then by Peter Parler. You can still see the audience hall and the bedchamber of Charles IV in the Royal Palace. On the third floor, the Emperor's quarters are below those of the Empress.

The central tower houses the Church of Our Lady, decorated with faded 14th-century wall paintings. A narrow passage leads to the tiny Chapel of St Catherine, the walls of which are adorned with semiprecious stones set into the plaster.

Konopiště Castle ❸

40 km (25 miles) southeast of Prague. ***Tel*** *31 77 21 366.* *from Hlavní nádraží to Benešov, then local bus.* ***Open*** *Apr, Oct: 9am–3pm, Tue–Fri (to 4pm Sat, Sun); May–Aug: 9am–5pm Tue–Sun; Sep: 9am–4pm Tue–Fri (to 5pm Sat, Sun); Nov: 9am–3pm Sat, Sun (Tue–Fri by reservation only).* **www**.zamek-konopiste.cz

Though it dates back to the 13th century, this moated castle is essentially a late 19th-century creation. In between, Konopiště had been rebuilt by Baroque architect František Kaňka and in front of the bridge across the moat is a splendid gate (1725) by Kaňka and sculptor Matthias Braun.

In 1887 Konopiště was bought by Archduke Franz Ferdinand, who later became heir to the Austrian throne. It was his assassination in 1914 in Sarajevo that triggered off World War I. To escape the Habsburg court's harsh disapproval of his wife, Ferdinand spent much of his time at Konopiště. He amassed arms, armour and Meissen porcelain, all on display in the fine furnished interiors. However, the abiding memory of the castle is of the hundreds of stags' heads lining the walls.

View of the castle at Křivoklát, dominated by the Great Tower

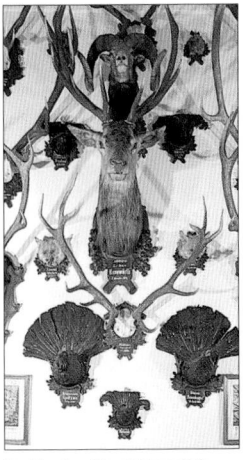

Hunting trophies at Konopiště

Křivoklát Castle ❹

45 km (28 miles) west of Prague. ***Tel*** *31 35 58 120.* *from Smíchov to Křivoklát (1 km /0.6 miles) from castle).* *from Anděl.* ***Open*** *Mar, Nov, Dec: 9am–noon, 1–3pm Sat, Sun; Apr, Oct: 9am–noon, 1–3pm Tue–Sun; May, Sep: 9am–noon, 1–4pm Tue–Sun; Jun–Aug: 9am–noon, 1–5pm Tue–Sun.*

This castle, like Karlstein, owes its appearance to the restoration work of Josef Mocker. It was originally a hunting lodge belonging to the early Přemyslid princes and the seat of the royal master of hounds. In the 13th century King Wenceslas I built a stone castle here, which remained in the hands of Bohemia's kings and the Habsburg emperors until the 17th century.

Charles IV spent some of his childhood here and returned from France in 1334 with his first wife Blanche de Valois. Their daughter Margaret was born in the castle. To amuse his queen and young princess, Charles ordered the local villagers to trap nightingales and set them free in a wooded area just below the castle. Today you can still walk along the "Nightingale Path".

The royal palace is on the eastern side of the triangular castle. This corner is dominated by the Great Tower, 42 m (130 ft) high. You can still see some 13th-century stonework, but most of the palace dates from the reign of Vladislav Jagiello. On the first floor there is a vaulted Gothic hall, reminiscent of the Vladislav Hall in the Royal Palace at Prague Castle *(see pp104–5)*. It has an oriel window and a beautiful loggia that was used by sentries. Also of interest is the chapel, which has a fine Gothic altar carving. Below the chapel lies the Augusta Prison, so-called because Bishop Jan Augusta of the Bohemian Brethren was imprisoned here for 16 years in the mid-16th century. The dungeon now houses a grim assortment of instruments of torture.

Kutná Hora ❺

70 km (45 miles) east of Prague. ***Tel*** *32 75 12 378 (tourist information).* *from Hlavní nádraží, Masarykovo nádraží to Kutná Hora, then bus 1 to Kutná Hora-Město.* *from Florenc.* **Church of St Barbara *open*** *Nov–Mar: 9–noon, 2–4pm Tue–Sun; Apr & Oct: 9–noon, 1–4pm Tue–Sun; May–Sep: 9am–6pm.* **Italian Court *open*** *Nov–Feb: 10am–4pm daily; Mar, Oct: 10am–5pm daily; Apr–Sep: 9am–6pm daily.* **Hrádek *open*** *Apr, Oct: 9am–5pm Tue–Sun; May, Jun, Sep: 9am–6pm Tue–Sun; Jul, Aug 10am–6pm Tue–Sun.* **Stone House *open*** *as Hrádek.* **www**.kutnahora.cz

The town originated as a small mining community in the second half of the 13th century. When rich deposits of silver were found, the king took over the licensing of the mines and Kutná Hora became the second most important town in Bohemia.

In the 14th century five to six tonnes of pure silver were extracted here each year, making the king the richest ruler in Central Europe. The Prague *groschen*, a silver coin that circulated all over Europe, was minted here in the Italian Court (Vlašský dvůr), so-called because Florentine experts were employed to set up the mint. Strongly fortified, it was also the ruler's seat in the town. In the late 14th century a superb palace was constructed with reception halls and the Chapel of St Wenceslas and St Ladislav, below which lay the royal treasury.

When the silver started to run out in the 16th century, the town began to lose its importance; the mint finally closed in 1727. The Italian Court later became the town hall. On the ground floor you can still see a row of forges. Since 1947 a mining museum has been housed in another building, the Hrádek, which was originally a fort. A visit includes a tour of a medieval mine. There is museum in the Stone House (Kamenný dům), a restored Gothic building of the late 15th century.

To the southwest of the town stands the Church of St Barbara, begun in 1380 by the workshop of Peter Parler, also the architect of St Vitus's Cathedral *(see pp100–3)*. The presbytery (1499) has a fine net vault and windows with intricate tracery. The slightly later nave vault is by royal architect Benedikt Ried. Catch the murals in the nave, many of which show mining scenes. The cathedral, with its three massive and tent-shaped spires rising above a forest of flying buttresses, is a wonderful example of Bohemian Gothic.

The Italian Court, Kutná Hora's first mint

The three steeples of Kutná Hora's great Church of St Barbara

Karlsbad ❻

KARLOVY VARY

140 km (85 miles) west of Prague. *from Masarykovo nádraží or Holešovice.* *from Florenc.*

Legend has it that Charles IV *(see pp24–5)* discovered one of the sources of mineral water that would make the town's fortune when one of his staghounds fell into a hot spring. In 1522 a medical description of the springs was published and by the end of the 16th century over 200 spa buildings had been built there. Today there are 12 hot mineral springs – *vary* means hot springs. The best-known is the Vřídlo (Sprudel), which rises to a height of 12 m (40 ft). At 72°C, it is also the hottest. The water is good for digestive disorders, but you do not have to drink it; you can take the minerals in the form of salts.

The town is also known for its Karlovy Vary china and Moser glass, and for summer concerts and other cultural events. The race course is popular with the more sporting invalids taking the waters.

Outstanding among the local historic monuments is the Baroque parish church of

Mary Magdalene by Kilian Ignaz Dientzenhofer (1732–6). More modern churches built for foreign visitors include a Russian church (1896) and an Anglican one (1877). The 19th-century Mill Colonnade (Mlýnská kolonáda) is by Josef Zítek, architect of the National Theatre *(see pp156–7)* in Prague. There have been many royal visitors over the centuries – from Peter the Great of Russia in 1711 to England's Edward VII in 1907.

Marienbad ❼

MARIÁNSKÉ LÁZNĚ

170 km (105 miles) west of Prague.
from Hlavní nádraží.
from Florenc.

The elegance of Marienbad's hotels, parks and gardens has faded considerably since it was the playground of kings and princes at the turn of the century. The area's health-giving waters – *lázně* means bath (or spa) – have been known since the 16th century, but the spa was not founded until the beginning of the last century. The waters are used to treat all kinds of disorders; mud baths are also popular.

Most of the spa buildings date from the latter half of the 19th century. The great cast-iron colonnade with frescoes by Josef Vyletěl is still an impressive sight. In front of it is a "singing fountain", its jets of water now controlled by computer. Churches were provided for visitors of all denominations, including an Evangelical church (1857), an Anglican church (1879) and the Russian Orthodox church of St Vladimír (1902). Visitors can learn the history of the spa in the house called At the Golden Grape (U zlatého hroznu), where the German poet Johann Wolfgang von Goethe stayed in 1823. Musical visitors during the 19th century included the composers Weber, Wagner and Bruckner, while writers such as Ibsen, Gogol, Mark Twain and Rudyard Kipling also found its treatments beneficial. King Edward VII came here frequently. In 1905 he agreed to open the golf course (Bohemia's first), even though he hated the game.

There are many pleasant walks in the countryside around Marienbad, especially in the protected Slavkov Forest.

Bronze statue of a chamois at Jeleni skok (Stag's Leap), with a view across the valley to the Imperial Sanatorium, Karlsbad

The cast-iron colonnade at Marienbad, completed in 1889

FOUR GUIDED WALKS

Prague offers some good opportunities for walking. In the centre of the city, many streets are pedestrianized and the most important sights are confined to quite a small area *(see pp14–15)*. Here are four guided walks of varied character. The first passes through a main artery of the city, from the Powder Gate on the outskirts of the Old Town to St Vitus's Cathedral in Prague Castle, crossing Charles Bridge at its mid-point. This is the Royal Coronation Route, followed for centuries by Bohemian kings. Away from the busy centre, the second and third of the walks takes in the peace and tranquility of two of Prague's loveliest parks – Petřín and the Royal Enclosure. Petřín Park is rewarding for its spectacular views of the city. The Royal Enclosure is outside the centre in the old royal hunting park. The final walk is in Vyšehrad – an ancient fortress which is steeped in history and atmosphere. The views from Vyšehrad of the Vltava and Prague Castle are unparalleled.

House sign in Celetná Street
(See Royal Route Walk pp174–5)

The Lapidarium *(See the Royal Enclosure Walk pp178–9)*

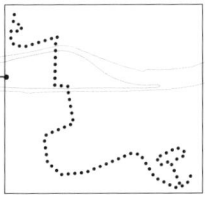

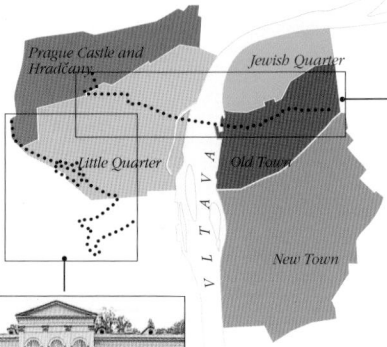

Royal Route
(See pp174–5)

Leopold Gate, Vyšehrad
(See Vyšehrad Walk pp180–81)

Kinský Summer Palace
(See Petřín Park Walk pp176–7)

KEY

•••• Walk route

0 kilometres 1
0 miles 0.5

◁ View of the New Town from Petřín Park with the Church of St Lawrence in the foreground

A 90-Minute Walk along the Royal Route

The Royal Route originally linked two important royal seats; the Royal Court – situated on the site of the Municipal House and where the walk starts – and Prague Castle, where the walk finishes. The name of this walk derives from the coronation processions of the Bohemian kings and queens who passed along it. Today, these narrow streets offer a wealth of historical and architecturally interesting sights, shops and cafés, making the walk one of Prague's most enjoyable. For more details on the Old Town, the Little Quarter and Hradčany turn to pages 60–79; 122–41 and 94–121 respectively.

Figural *sgraffito* covers the façade of the Renaissance House at the Minute

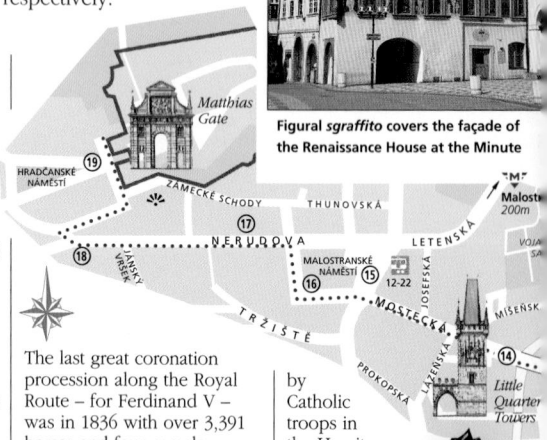

History of the Royal Route

The first major coronation procession to travel along this route was for George of Poděbrady *(see p26)* in 1458. The next large procession took place in 1743, when Maria Theresa was crowned with great pomp – three Turkish pavilions were erected just outside the Powder Gate. September 1791 saw the coronation of Leopold II. This procession was led by cavalry, followed by mounted drummers, trumpeters and soldiers and Bohemian lords. Some 80 carriages came next, carrying princes and bishops. The most splendid were each drawn by six pairs of horses, flanked by servants with red coats and white leather trousers, and carried the ladies-in-waiting. The last great coronation procession along the Royal Route – for Ferdinand V – was in 1836 with over 3,391 horses and four camels.

From the Powder Gate to Old Town Square

At Náměstí Republiky turn towards the Municipal House *(see p64)* and walk under the Gothic Powder Gate ① *(see p64)*. Here, at the city gates, the monarch and a large retinue of church dignitaries, aristocrats, and foreign ambassadors were warmly welcomed by leading city representatives. The gate leads into one of Prague's oldest streets, Celetná *(see p65)*. It was here the Jewish community and the crafts guilds, carrying their insignia, greeted their king.

The street is lined with Baroque and Rococo houses. At house No. 36 was the Mint ②. It moved here after the mint at Kutná Hora *(see p170)* was occupied by Catholic troops in the Hussite Wars *(see pp26–7)*. It minted coins from 1420 to 1784. The House of the Black Madonna ③ contains a museum of Czech Cubist art *(see p65)*. Revellers would watch processions from the taverns At the Spider ④ and At the Vulture ⑤.

The distinct Baroque façade of the House at the Golden Well in Karlova Street ⑪

House at the Black Madonna ③

At the end of Celetná Street is the Old Town Square ⑥ *(see pp66–9)*. Here, the processions halted beside Týn Church ⑦ *(see p70)* for pledges of loyalty from the university. Keep to the left of the square, past No. 17, At the Unicorn ⑧, then No. 20, Smetana House, where the composer began a music school in 1848. Proceed to the Old Town Hall ⑨ *(see pp72–4)*.

Here, the municipal guard and a band waited for the royal procession and city dignitaries cheered from the temporary balcony around the hall.

Along Karlova Street and across Charles Bridge

Walk past the sgraffitoed façade of the House at the Minute and into Malé náměstí ⑩, where merchants waited with members of the various religious orders. Bear left off the square, then turn right into gallery-filled Karlova Street. Beyond Husova Street is an attractive Baroque house, At the Golden Well ⑪. Further on is the 16th-century Clementinum *(see p79)*, where the clergy stood. You then pass into Knights of the Cross Square *(see p79)*. When Leopold II's procession passed through here the clouds lifted, which was considered to be a good omen. But only a few months later he died. Walk under the Old Town Bridge Tower ⑫ and over Charles Bridge ⑬ and then under the Little Quarter Towers ⑭ *(see pp136–9)*.

The Old Town from Charles Bridge ⑬

The Little Quarter

The walk now follows Mostecká Street. On entering the Little Quarter the mayor handed the city keys to the king and the artillery fired a salute. At the end of this street is Little Quarter Square ⑮ *(see p124)* and the Baroque church St Nicholas's ⑯ *(see pp128–9)*. The procession passed the church to the sound of its bells ringing.

Leave this picturesque square by Nerudova Street ⑰ *(see p130)*. Poet and writer Jan Neruda, who immortalized hundreds of Little Quarter characters in books like *Mala Strana Tales*, grew up and worked at No. 47, The Two Suns ⑱. Cross the street, turn sharp right and walk up the Castle ramp, which leads you to Hradčanské Square. The route ends at the Castle's Matthias Gate *(see p48)* ⑲. The procession ended with the coronation held at St Vitus's Cathedral.

Sculpture of Moor by Ferdinand Brokof on Morzin Palace

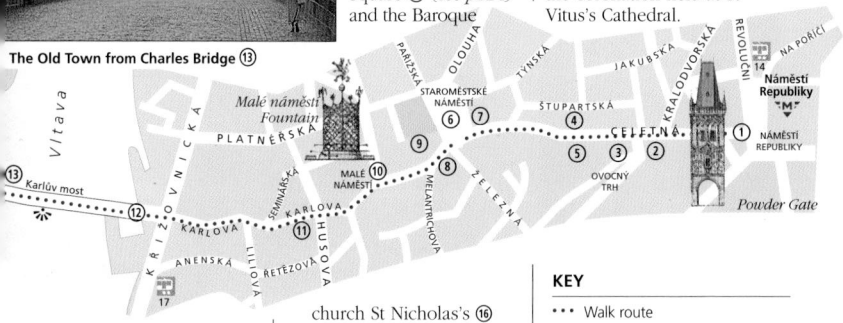

KEY

- Walk route
- Good viewing point
- Metro station
- Tram stop
- City wall

0 metres 300

0 yards 300

TIPS FOR WALKERS

Starting point: *Náměstí Republiky.*
Length: *2.4 km (1.5 miles).*
Getting there: *Line B goes to Náměstí Republiky metro station. At Hradčany you can get tram 22 back into town.*
Stopping-off points: *Rest beneath the sunshades of the outdoor cafés on Old Town Square or Karlova Street in the summer. On Malostranské náměstí you can enjoy the restaurant Square and in Karlova the café Clementin (at Hotel Clementin).*

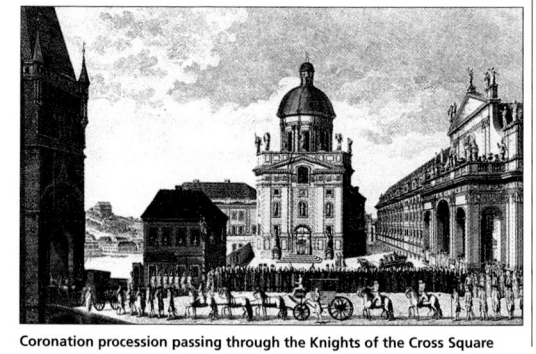

Coronation procession passing through the Knights of the Cross Square

A Two-Hour Walk through Petřín Park

Part of the charm of this walk around this large and peaceful hillside park are the many spectacular views over the different areas of Prague. The Little Quarter, Hradčany and the Old Town all take on a totally different aspect when viewed from above. The tree-covered gardens are dotted with châteaux, pavilions and statues and crisscrossed by winding paths leading you to secret and unexpected corners. For more on the sights of Petřín Hill see pages 140–41.

One of the gateways in the Hunger Wall ⑤

Actress Hana Kvapilová's statue, near Kinský Summer Palace ①

Kinský Square to Hunger Wall

The walk starts at náměstí Kinských in Smíchov. Enter Kinský Garden through a large enclosed gateway. This English-style garden was founded in 1827 and named after the wealthy Kinský family, supporters of Czech culture in the 19th century.

Take the wide cobbled and asphalt path on your left to the Kinský Summer Palace ①. This 1830s pseudo-classical building was designed by Jindřich Koch and its façade features Ionic columns terminating in a triangular tympanum. Inside the building is a large hall of columns with a triple-branched staircase beautifully decorated with statues. The Ethnographical Museum, housed here, holds a permanent exhibition of folk art.

Next to the museum is a 1913 statue of the actress Hana Kvapilová.

About 50 m (150 ft) above the palace is the lower lake ②, where a small waterfall trickles into a man-made pond. Keep going up the hill until you reach the Church of St Michael ③, on your left. This 18th-century wooden folk church was moved here from a village in the Ukraine.

Follow the path up the hill for about 20 m (60 ft), then go to the top of the steps to a wide asphalt path known as the Observation Path for its beautiful views of the city. Turn right and further on your left is the small upper lake ④ with a 1950s bronze statue of a seal at its centre. Keep following the Observation Path; ahead of you stands a Neo-Gothic gate. This allows you to pass through the city's old Baroque fortifications.

Hunger Wall to Observation Tower

Continue along the path to the Hunger Wall ⑤ *(see pp140–41).* This was a major part of the Little Quarter's fortifications; the wall still runs from Újezd

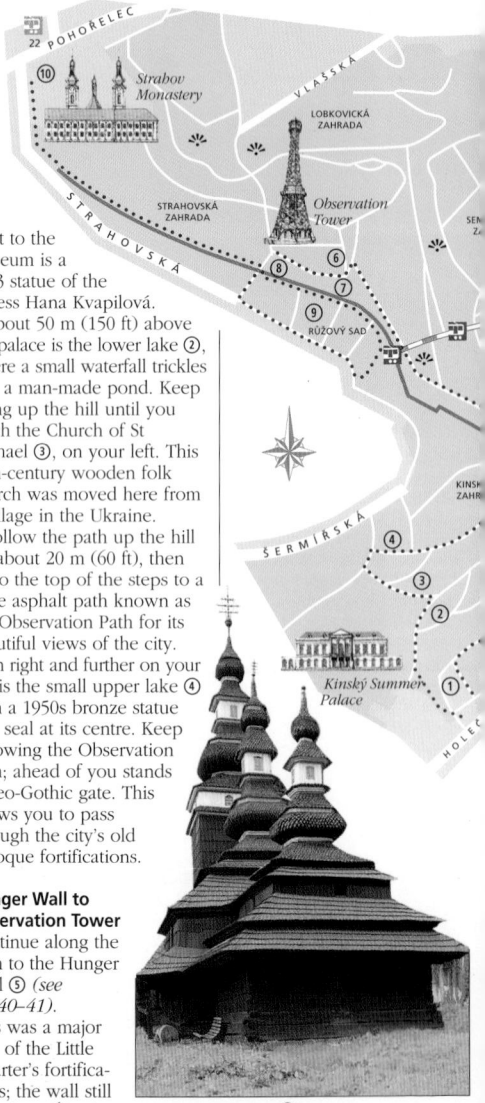

Church of St Michael ③

Street across Petřín Hill and up to Strahov Monastery. Passing through the gate in the wall brings you to Petřín Park. Take the wide path to the left below the wall and walk up the hill beside the wall until you cross the bridge which spans the funicular railway *(see p141)*. Below on your right you can see the

Sunbathers on Petřín Hill

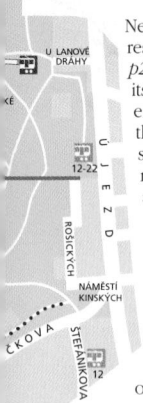

Nebozízek restaurant *(see p206)* famed for its views. On either side of the path are small sandstone rockeries. Most are entrances to reservoirs, built in the 18th and 19th centuries, to bring water to Strahov Monastery; others are left over from the unsuccessful attempts at mining the area. Walk up to the summit of the hill. On your right is the Mirror Maze ⑥ *(see p140)*. Facing the maze is the 12th-century St Lawrence's Church ⑦ *(see p140)*, renovated in 1740 in the Baroque style.

KEY

- ••• Walk route
- Good viewing point
- Tram stop
- Funicular railway
- Hunger wall

0 metres 300

0 yards 300

Observation Tower to Strahov Monastery

A little further on stands the Observation Tower ⑧ *(see p140)*. This steel replica of the Eiffel Tower in Paris is 60 m (200 ft) high. Opposite the tower is the main gate of the Hunger Wall. Pass through, turn left and follow the path to the Rose Garden ⑨.

The garden was planted by the city of Prague in 1932, and features a number of attractive sculptures. When you look down to the far end of the garden you can see The Observatory *(see p140)*. This was rebuilt from a municipal building in 1928 by the Czech Astronomical Society and was then modernized in the 1970s. It now houses a huge telescope and is open in the evenings to the public.

Returning to the Observation Tower, follow the wall on the left, passing some chapels of the Stations of the Cross dating from 1834. Then pass through a gap in the Hunger Wall, turn right, and walk past a charming Baroque house. About 50 m (150 ft) beyond this, you pass through another gap in the Hunger Wall on your right. Turn left into a large orchard above Strahov Monastery ⑩ *(see pp120–21)* for spectacular views of the city. Leave by the same hole in the wall that you came in by, turn right, and walk downhill along the wall, through the orchard and past tennis courts to the Strahov Monastery courtyard. You can catch tram 22 from here, or linger in the peaceful monastery grounds. If you feel energetic you can walk back down the hill.

Sgraffitoed façade of the Calvary Chapel next to the Church of St Lawrence ⑦

TIPS FOR WALKERS

Starting point: *náměstí Kinských in Smíchov.*
Length: *2.7 km (1.7 miles). The walk includes steep hills.*
Getting there: *The nearest metro station to the starting point is Anděl. Trams 6, 9 and 12 go to náměstí Kinských (Kinský Square).*
Stopping-off points: *There is a restaurant, Nebozízek, half way up Petřín Hill and during the summer a few snack bars are open at the summit of the Hill near the Observation Tower.*

Hradčany and the Little Quarter from the summit of Petřín Hill

A 90-Minute Walk in the Royal Enclosure

The royal enclosure, more popularly called Stromovka, is one of the largest parks in Prague. It was created around 1266 during the reign of Přemysl Otakar II, who fenced the area in and built a small hunting château in the grounds. In 1804 it was opened to the public and became Prague's most popular recreational area. The large park of Troja Palace and the zoological garden are on the opposite river bank.

A bust on the Academy of Fine Arts ⑥

The Exhibition Ground (Výstaviště)

From U Výstaviště ① pass through the gate to the old Exhibition Ground. This was created for the 1891 Jubilee Exhibition. Since the late 19th century it has been used for exhibitions and entertainment.

The large Lapidarium of the National Museum ② is on your right. This Neo-Renaissance exhibition pavilion was rebuilt in 1907 in the Art Nouveau style, and decorated with reliefs of figures from Czech history. Many architectural monuments and sculptures from the 11th to the 19th centuries are also housed here.

Facing you is the Industrial Palace ③, a vast Neo-Renaissance building constructed of iron. It is now only open for concerts and events. Walk to the right of the building and you will come to Křižík's Fountain ④. This was restored in 1991 in honour of the Czechoslovakia Exhibition. It was designed by the great inventor František Křižík (1847–1941), who established Prague's first public electric lighting system. From March to September the fountain is illuminated at night by computer-controlled lights which synchronize with the music *(see p51)*.

Behind the fountain there is a permanent fairground. On the left of the Industrial Palace is a circular building which houses Marold's Panorama ⑤. This was painted by Luděk Marold in 1898 and depicts the Battle of Lipany. As you walk back to the Exhibition Ground entrance, you pass the Academy of Fine Arts ⑥, decorated with 18 busts of artists. On leaving the

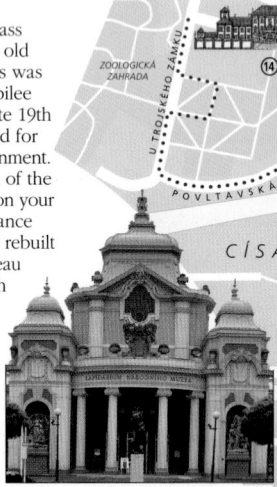

The Art Nouveau Lapidarium ②

The summer palace created from a medieval Hunting Château ⑩

ZOOLOGICKÁ ZAHRADA
U TROJSKÉHO ZÁMKU
⑭ Troja
POD HAVRÁNKOU
POVLTAVSKÁ
⑬
POVLTAVSKÁ
CÍSAŘSKÝ OSTROV
Vltava
jezdecké závodiště
⑫
průplav
ZA ELEKTRÁRNOU
STROMOVKA
⑪
Hunting Château
⑧
⑨
⑩

0 metres 300
0 yards 300

KEY

- Walk route
- Good viewing point
- Tram stop
- Railway line

Exhibition Ground, turn sharp right. Following the outer edge of the Ground you will pass the Planetarium ⑦ on your left; walk straight ahead, then take the road down the slope until you can turn left into a wide avenue of chestnut trees.

The Royal Enclosure

Continue for some way along the avenue until you reach a simple building among trees, on your left. Behind this is the Rudolph Water Tunnel ⑧, a grand monument of the age of Rudolph II *(see pp28–9)*. Hewn into rock, the aqueduct is over 1,000 m (3,000 ft) long. It was built in 1584 to carry water from the Vltava to Rudolph's newly constructed lakes in the Royal Park.

The grand facade of Troja Palace *(see pp166-167)* ⑭

Statue of lovers in the 16th century gardens of the Enclosure ⑪

Continue along the path until you reach the derelict Royal Hall ⑨. Built in the late 17th century, it was converted into a restaurant, then rebuilt in 1855 in Neo-Gothic style.

Beyond the Royal Hall, at the bend in the main path, take a steep left fork up through woods to the former Hunting Château ⑩. This medieval building was built for the Bohemian kings who used the park as a hunting reserve. The Château was then later enlarged, and in 1805 was changed again by Jiří Fischer into a Neo-Gothic summer palace. Until 1918, this was a residence of the Governor of Bohemia. Today it is used to house the extensive library of newspapers and magazines of the National Museum.

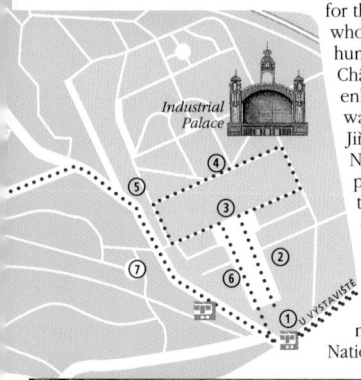

Disused entrance to the Rudolph Water Tunnel ⑧

Retrace your steps to the main path, walk ahead and take the first small path on the right into a late-16th-century formal garden with a modern statue of lovers ⑪.

Return to the main path and turn right. At the fork, take the path which bends to the right along the railway embankment. Continue for a short way then turn left under the railway line to a canal ⑫.

Walk over the bridge, turn left along the canal, then right across the island. Cross the Vltava ⑬ and turn left into Povltavská Street where a wall marks the boundary of Troja Park. Carry along to the south entrance of the gardens of Troja Palace ⑭ *(see pp166–7)*, and then wander through them up to the palace itself.

TIPS FOR WALKERS

Starting point: *U Výstaviště in Holešovice.*

Length: *5 km (3 miles). The walk goes up a very steep incline to the former Hunting Château.*

Getting there: *Trams 5, 12, 14 and 17 run to the starting point. The nearest metro stations are Vltavská or Nádraží Holešovice on line C, ten minutes walk away. At the end of the walk you can get on bus No. 112 at Troja to Nádraží Holešovice metro station.*

Stopping-off points: *There are a number of restaurants and kiosks in the Exhibition Ground. All the gardens are tranquil spots in which to rest. If you feel like a boat trip down the Vltava, there are often trips starting from the bridge over the canal to Palacký Bridge* (see p55).

A 60-Minute Walk in Vyšehrad

According to ancient legend, Vyšehrad was the first seat of Czech royalty. It was from this spot that Princess Libuše is said to have prophesied the future glory of the city of Prague *(see pp20–21)*. However, archaeological research indicates that the first castle on Vyšehrad was not built until the 10th century. The fortress suffered a turbulent history and was rebuilt many times. Today, it is above all a peaceful place with parks and unrivalled views of the Vltava valley and Prague. The fascinating cemetery is the last resting place of many famous Czech writers, actors, artists and musicians.

Decorative sculpture on the Baroque Leopold Gate ⑤

The ruin of Libuše's Baths on the cliff face of Vyšehrad Rock ⑩

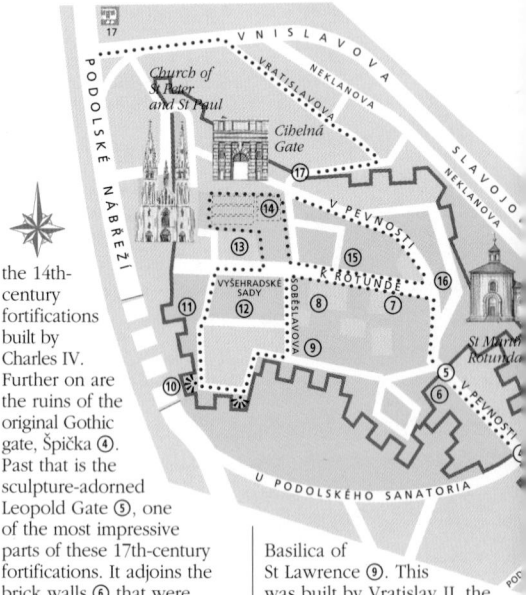

V Pevnosti

From Vyšehrad metro ① make your way up the steps facing the metro exit to the Congress Centre Prague ② straight ahead. Walk west along its large granite terrace, go down the incline and straight ahead into the quiet street Na Bučance. Cross the road, turn right at the end, and you find yourself on V Pevnosti, facing the brick walls of the original Vyšehrad Citadel. Ahead of you is the west entrance to the fortress, the mid-17th-century Tábor Gate ③. Past this gate on the right are the ruins of the 14th-century fortifications built by Charles IV. Further on are the ruins of the original Gothic gate, Špička ④. Past that is the sculpture-adorned Leopold Gate ⑤, one of the most impressive parts of these 17th-century fortifications. It adjoins the brick walls ⑥ that were widened during the French occupation of 1742.

18th-century engraving by I G Ringle, showing Vyšehrad and the Vltava

K rotundě to Soběslavova Street

Turn right out of the gate and just after St Martin's Rotunda, turn left into K rotundě. A few metres on your left, almost concealed behind high walls, is the New Deanery ⑦. Situated at the corner of K rotundě and Soběslavova streets is the Canon's House ⑧. Turn left down Soběslavova to see the excavations of the foundations of the Basilica of St Lawrence ⑨. This was built by Vratislav II, the first Bohemian king, in the late 11th century, but was destroyed by the Hussites *(see pp26–7)* in 1420. About 20 m (65 ft) past the basilica, turn right on to the fortified walls for a stunning view of Prague.

KEY

- Walk route
- Good viewing point
- Metro station
- Tram stop
- Castle wall

0 metres 200

0 yards 200

Vyšehrad Rock

The wooded outcrop of rock on which Vyšehrad was built drops in the west to form a steep rock wall to the river – a vital defensive position. On the summit of the rock are the Gothic ruins of the so-called Libuše's Baths ⑩. This was a defence bastion of the medieval castle. To the left of the bastion is a grassy patch where the remains of a 14th-century Gothic palace ⑪ have been found.

The elaborate memorial to the composer Antonín Dvořák in Vyšehrad Cemetery ⑭

Vyšehrad Park

The western part of Vyšehrad has been transformed into a park. Standing on the lawn south of the Church of St Peter and St Paul are four groups of statues ⑫ by the 19th-century sculptor Josef Myslbek. The works represent figures from early Czech history – including the legendary Přemysl and Libuše *(see pp20–21)*. The statues were originally on Palacký Bridge, but were damaged during the US bombardment of February 1945. After being restored, they were taken to Vyšehrad Park. The park was the site of a Romanesque palace, which was connected to the neighbouring church by a bridge. Another palace was built here in the reign of Charles IV *(see pp24–5)*.

Statue of Přemysl and Princess Libuše by Josef Myslbek in Vyšehrad Park ⑫

The Church of St Peter and St Paul

This twin-spired church ⑬ dominates Vyšehrad. It was founded in the latter half of the 11th century by Vratislav II and was enlarged in 1129. In the mid-13th century it burned down and was replaced by an Early Gothic church. Since then it has been redecorated and restored many times in a variety of styles. In 1885, it was finally rebuilt in Neo-Gothic style, the twin steeples being added in 1902. Note the early-12th-century stone coffin, thought to be of St Longinus, and a mid-14th-century Gothic panel painting *Our Lady of the Rains* on the altar in the third chapel on the right.

Vyšehrad Cemetery and the Pantheon

The cemetery ⑭ was founded in 1869 as the burial place for some of the country's most famous figures, such as Bedřich Smetana *(see p79)*. Access is through a gate at the front. On the east side of the cemetery is the Slavín (Pantheon) – built in 1890 for the most honoured citizens of the Czech nation, including the sculptor Josef Myslbek.

Leave the cemetery by the same gate and return down K rotundě. On your left is the Devil's Column ⑮, said to be left by the devil after losing a wager with a priest. At the end is St Martin's Rotunda *(see p44)* ⑯, a small Romanesque church built in the late 11th century and restored in 1878. Turn left, walk downhill to Cihelná (Brick) Gate ⑰, built in 1741 and home to a small museum that houses six of the original statues from Charles Bridge. Go down Vratislavova Street to Výtoň tram stop on the Vltava Embankment.

The Neo-Gothic Church of St Peter and St Paul ⑬

TIPS FOR WALKERS

Starting point: *Vyšehrad metro station, line C.*
Length: *1.5 km (1 mile).*
Getting there: *The walk starts at Vyšehrad metro station and ends at Výtoň tram stop. Trams 3, 17 and 19 go back to the city centre.*
Stopping-off points: *Relax in the park next to the church of St Peter and St Paul. There is a café in front of the Basilica of St Lawrence and more outdoor cafés in the summer.*

TRAVELLERS' NEEDS

WHERE TO STAY 184–195

RESTAURANTS, CAFES AND PUBS 196–211

SHOPPING IN PRAGUE 212–217

ENTERTAINMENT IN PRAGUE 218–223

WHERE TO STAY

Since the "Velvet Revolution" of 1989, Prague has become one of the most visited cities in Europe. Thanks to investment in new hotels, helped by huge injections of foreign capital, Prague has developed enough accommodation to meet every tourist need. Many old hotels have been rebuilt, while others have been fully re-vamped. Most of the renovated hotels are as smart as any in Europe – and they are often just as expensive. Unfortunately there is little scope for the budget traveller.

Doorman at the exclusive Palace hotel *(see p193)*

The few cheap hotels tend to be old-fashioned places in the centre of the city, or smaller, pension-type hotels located in the suburbs. We have inspected over 100 hotels in every price bracket in Prague, and on pages 188–95 we recommend 30 of those that offer especially good value. A cheap alternative is to stay in a flat or a room in a private home, which is usually booked by an agency *(see p186)*. Hostels and campsites offer other budget options *(see p187)*.

The Ungelt hotel *(see p189)*

WHERE TO LOOK

As Prague is such a small city, it is best to stay near the centre close to all the main sights, restaurants and shops. Most hotels are found around Wenceslas Square. Here you are at the hub of everything, and the prices of some (but not all) of the hotels reflect this. Another popular area is the nearby Náměstí Republiky, but the best area is around Old Town Square, a few minutes' walk from Charles Bridge. Hotels here include large, international establishments, old-fashioned Czech places, and some small, much more exclusive hotels.

To the south, in the New Town, there are a few cheaper hotels only a few metro stops from Old Town Square. But the area is less picturesque and some of the streets suffer from heavy volumes of traffic. For a view of the river Vltava, stay in the Jewish Quarter, although most hotels here are new and expensive. There are also a few botels (floating hotels) moored along the embankments away from the city centre. They are a bit cheaper, but the small cabins are very cramped and uncomfortable, and most of the boats would benefit from some renovation.

Over Charles Bridge, in the Little Quarter, you will find a handful of interesting hotels in delightful surroundings, but there are far fewer by Prague Castle in Hradčany. Further north of this area, there are some large and particularly unappealing hotels. The city's suburbs too, have a number of rather nondescript places a few of these being new. These have some good facilities, but are often as expensive as their equivalents in the centre with the added inconvenience of travelling time and cost – the metro stops at midnight and taxis can become expensive.

HOW TO BOOK

To reserve a room you can book online or send a letter by fax (the best deals are often done online; a popular website is www.HRS.com). It is important to receive written confirmation of your booking by letter or fax in advance, something that will save you time and trouble when you arrive. Most hotel receptionists speak English, so you can always ring them for advice, otherwise ask your tour operator for help;

Pool-side bar at the luxury Praha Renaissance *(see p193)*

a number of UK operators specialize in Prague *(see p186)*. When arriving by car, park in the hotel garage or ask at reception about secure parking in the area.

FACILITIES

Following the large investment in many of Prague's hotels, most rooms now have en suite WC and shower or bath, telephone and TV, which may also offer video and satellite channels. Many hotels offer a reasonably-priced laundry service, and the larger hotels usually have 24-hour room service and mini bars. Guests are expected to vacate rooms by midday, but most hotels are happy to keep luggage safe if you are leaving later.

Foreign-owned hotels sometimes import managers, but the Czech staff generally speak good English so you should encounter few communication problems.

DISCOUNT RATES

The price structure for hotels in Prague is fairly flexible. One way to get a cheap rate is to turn up at the hotel and negotiate, although this practice is being phased out. The popular seasons are Christmas, New Year and Easter, when rooms are often hard to find. For cheap rooms in summer it is worth looking at student houses. Most of these have two bedrooms and a kitchen on the same floor, plus a small shop selling hot and cold drinks.

HIDDEN EXTRAS

All hotels include tax (currently at 19%) and service charges in their tariff, but do check these details when you book. Telephone charges can be a shock when you receive your bill so be aware of the mark-up rate. All telephone boxes in the city take phone cards and many take credit cards; phone cards are much cheaper than using cash *(see p232)*. Some expensive hotels charge an extra fee for breakfast, others include a continental breakfast, but hot dishes cost extra. Buffet-style continental breakfasts are popular, and usually offer fresh fruit, cereals, yogurt, muesli, cold meat and cheese, and juice, jugs of coffee and tea.

Tipping is now common and is expected in many hotels. As in most countries, single travellers receive no favours. There are few single rooms, particularly in newer hotels, and a supplement is charged for single occupancy of a double room; expect to pay about 70–80% of the standard rate.

The Pařiž is a national monument *(see p189)*

The modern Praha Hilton hotel dominates the area *(see p195)*

DISABLED TRAVELLERS

Most of the newer hotels in Prague have wheelchair access. For information on accomodation suitable for the disabled, contact the **Czech Association of Persons with Disabilities**, the **Prague Association of Wheelchair-Users** *(see p234)* or the Embassy of the Czech Republic in your country.

TRAVELLING WITH CHILDREN

Children are accommodated by most hotels, either in family rooms or with extra beds, but Prague is not geared to their needs. Hotel breakfasts offer plenty of choice, and although all the fresh milk is pasteurized, hotels also provide long life milk. Few places offer high-chairs or baby-sitters. It is worth asking if there are discounts, or if children can stay free in parents' rooms.

DIRECTORY

UK AGENCIES

British Airways Holidays
London Road,
Crawley, West Sussex
RH10 2XA.
Tel *0870 243 4224.*
www.baholidays.com

Čedok Travel
Suite 22–23,
Morley House,
314–322 Regent Street,
London W1B 3BG.
Tel *020 7580 3778.*
www.cedok.co.uk/prague

Cresta Holidays
Tabley Court,
32 Victoria St, Altrincham,
Cheshire WA14 1E2.
Tel *0870 238 7711.*
www.cresta holidays.co.uk

Crystal Holidays
Kings Place,
Wood Street,
Kingston-upon-Thames,
Surrey KT1 1JY.
Tel *0870 160 90 30.*
www.crystal holidays.co.uk

Czech Tourist Centre
Morley House,
320 Regent Street,
London W1B 3BG.
Tel *020 7631 0427.*
www.czechtourism.com

Osprey Holidays
Broughton Market,
Edinburgh EH3 6NU.
Tel *0870 56 05 605.*
www.osprey-holidays.co.uk

Page & Moy Ltd.
136 & 140 London Road,
Leicester LE2 1EN.
Tel *8708 32 70 00.*
Fax *0870 01 06 449.*
www.page-moy.co.uk

Prospect Music and Art Tours
36 Manchester Street,
London W1M 5PE.
Tel *020 7486 5704.*
Fax *020 7486 5868.*
www.prospecttours.com

Thomson
Greater London House,
Hampstead Road, London
NW1 7SD.
Tel *0870 888 0225.*
www.thomsoncities.co.uk

US AGENCIES

Friends of Czech Greenways
Suite 1B, 515 Avenue I
Brooklyn, NY 11230.
Tel *718 258 54 68.*
Fax *718 258 56 32.*
www.praguevienna greenways.org

FLATS AND ROOMS IN PRIVATE HOMES

IN UK

The Czechbook
Jopes Mill,
Trebrownbridge,
Nr. Liskard,
Cornwall PL14 3PX.
Tel & ***Fax*** *01503 240 629.*
@ agnes.michael@czechbook.com
www.czechbook.com

Regent Holidays
15 John Street,
Bristol BS1 2HR.
Tel *01179 211 711.*
Fax *01179 254 866.*
www.regent-holidays.co.uk

IN PRAGUE

Akasi
Jungmannovo náměstí 9.
Map 3 C5.
Tel *22 22 42 354.*
Fax *22 42 37 235.*

American Express Travel Service
Václavské náměstí 56.
Map 3 C5.
Tel *22 22 10 106.*
www.american express.cz

Autoturist Travel Agency
Londýnská 62.
Map 6 F4.
Tel *22 25 12 053.*
Fax *22 25 20 242.*
www.autoturist.cz

AVE Ltd
Hlavní nádraží (main station). **Map** 4 E5.
Tel *22 42 23 226.*
Fax *22 42 30 783.*
www.avetravel.cz

Čedok
Na Příkopě 18. **Map** 4 D4.
Tel *22 41 97 616.*
www.cedok.cz

Estec
Vaníčkova 5, Prague 6.
Tel *25 72 10 410.*
Fax *25 72 15 253.*
www.estec.cz

Pragotur
Za Poříčskou branou 7.
Map 4 D3.
Tel *22 17 14 130.*
www.prague–info.cz

Prague Information Service (PIS)
Na příkopě 20.
Map 3 C4.
Tel *22 17 14 130.*
www.pis.cz

Staroměstské náměstí 1.
Map 3 B3.
Tel *22 17 14 130.*
www.pis.cz

Hlavní nádraží (main station).
Map 4 E5.
Tel *22 17 14 130.*
Fax *22 17 14 127.*
www.pis.cz

e.travel.cz
Ostrovní 7.
Map 3 B5.
Tel *22 49 90 990, 020 7681 2362 (UK), 1 800 707 7819 (US).*
www.e.travel.cz

Top Tour
Revoluční 24.
Map 4 D2.
Tel *22 48 13 172.*
Fax *22 48 12 386.*
www.toptour.cz

Travel Agency of České Dráhy
V Celnici 6.
Map 3 C4.
Tel *22 42 39 464.*
Fax *22 42 32 191.*
www.cdrail.cz

HOSTELS

CKM Youth Agency
Václavské Náměstí 56.
Map 4 D5.
Tel *22 27 21 595.*
www.ckm-praha.cz

Dlouhá
Dlouhá 33. **Map** 3 C3.
Tel *22 48 26 662.*
www.travellers.cz

Koleje a Menzy
Opletalova 38. **Map** 4 D5.
Tel *22 49 30 010.*

Petros
Hilbertova 69, Louny.
Tel *41 56 58 580.*
Fax *41 56 58 497.*
www.hostels.cz

CAMPING

Aritma Džbán
Kemp Džbán 3, Vokovice.
Tel & ***Fax*** *23 53 59 007.*
www.dzban.cz

Kotva Braník
U ledáren 55, Braník.
Tel *24 44 61 712.*

Troja
Trojská 129, Troja.
Tel *28 38 50 487.*
www.volny.cz/campdana

DISABLED TRAVELLERS

Czech Association of Persons with Disabilities
Karlínské náměstí 12,
Prague 8.
Tel *22 48 15 915.*
@ puszdp@braill.net.cz

Embassy of the Czech Republic
26 Kensington Palace Gardens,
London W8 4QY.
Tel *020 7243 1115.*
www.mzv.cz/london

Pension Páv, in a quiet street of a historic neighbourhood ***(see p192)***

PRIVATE ROOMS AND SELF-CATERING APARTMENTS

Over the past few years, the number of private rooms to rent in Prague has grown enormously. Although cheap and popular, they may be some distance from the centre. Private rooms in homes start at about Kč600 per person per night, usually with breakfast. There are also self-contained apartments – a fairly central one-bedroom apartment costs about Kč1,600 per night. Most agencies that offer private rooms also rent out apartments *(see Directory opposite)*.

To book a room or apartment, tell the agency exactly what you want, for how many, when and in which area. The agency will suggest places. Find out the exact location and the nearest metro before accepting; if you are in Prague, see it yourself. Make sure you receive written, faxed or emailed confirmation of a booking to take with you. On arrival in Prague, pay the agency in cash; they give you a voucher to take to the room or apartment (sometimes you can pay the owner directly). If the agency requires advance payment by banker's draft go direct to the accommodation with your receipt. Agencies may ask for a deposit on bookings from abroad, or charge a registration fee payable in Prague.

HOSTELS

There are also many hostels in Prague, and the **CKM Youth Agency** in the New Town provides up-to-date information on availability. Useful websites include www.hotelldiscount.cz, www.bed.cz, and www.travellers.cz.

Whilst some hostels are open all year round, many only open during the high season. A few hostels operate curfews, so it's worth checking this before you book. Also, it's often a good idea to bring your own sleeping bag, despite linen usually being available for hire. Sometimes it can be better value to choose a hostel further away from the city centre, as some of the more central establishments can cost just as much as a cheap hotel.

If you are visiting between June and mid-September, it's worth investigating the thousand or so very basic student rooms available to the public in the summer holidays at Prague's university, the Karolinum (Tel: 224 913 692). These, whilst unluxurious, offer an excellent option for the budget traveller. Some other Czech colleges also offer a similar service.

CAMPING

Most campsites in or near Prague are closed from November to the start of April. They are very cheap with basic facilities, but are well served by transport. The largest site is at **Troja**, 3 km (1.5 miles) north of the centre. **Aritma Džbán**, 4 km (2.5 miles) west, is open all year for tents, and **Kotva Braník** is 6 km (4 miles) south of the city on the banks of the Vltava. For details contact the PIS *(see Directory opposite)*.

USING THE LISTINGS

The hotels on pages 188–95 are listed according to area and price category. The symbols summarize the facilities at each hotel.

- air-conditioning in all rooms
- gym/fitness facilities
- swimming pool in hotel
- facilities for children, including cots and sometimes, babysitting
- lift
- hotel parking available
- restaurant
- credit cards not accepted

Price categories for a standard double room per night, including breakfast, tax and service:

- Kč up to 3,000
- Kč3,000–4,500
- Kč4,500–6,000
- Kč6,000–8,000
- over Kč8,000

Entrance of the Domus Henrici hotel ***(see p191)***

Choosing a Hotel

The hotels in this guide have been selected across a wide range of price categories for the excellence of their facilities, location or character. The chart below lists the hotels in price categories within each particular area, starting with the Old Town and moving on to hotels further outside the city centre.

PRICE CATEGORIES
The following price ranges are for a standard double room and taxes per night during the high season. Breakfast is included.
Ⓚ up to Kč3000
ⒸⒸ Kč3000–4500
ⒸⒸⒸ Kč4500–6000
ⒸⒸⒸⒸ Kč6000–8000
ⒸⒸⒸⒸⒸ Over Kč8000.

OLD TOWN

Central
P 🍴 ⒸⒸ

Rybná 8, Praha 1 **Tel** *22 48 12 041* **Fax** *22 32 84 04* **Rooms** *69* **Map** *3 C2*

An old-style hotel, the lobby and reception have had a cursory facelift, but this fades as you climb the stairs. The bedrooms, though old-fashioned, are clean and the bathrooms immaculate. The location, on the border of the Jewish Quarter and Old Town, is great and explains the high prices. **www.orfea.cz**

Cloister Inn
P 🍴 ⒸⒸ

Konviktská 14, Praha 1 **Tel** *22 42 11 020* **Fax** *22 42 10 800* **Rooms** *75* **Map** *3 B5*

Just a few minutes' walk from Charles Bridge, the Cloister Inn is, despite the name, a modern hotel offering large, well-furnished rooms with en suite bathrooms. A good buffet breakfast is served in a high-ceilinged dining room, while tea and coffee is on offer all day in the lobby. **www.cloister-inn.com**

Best Western Meteor
P 🍴 ⒸⒸⒸ

Hybernská 6, 110 00 Praha 1 **Tel** *22 41 92 559* **Fax** *22 42 20 681* **Rooms** *82* **Map** *4 D3*

Though part of the international Best Western group, the Meteor still has a cosy, old-fashioned feel so rare in chain hotels. Some parts of the hotel are slightly scruffy, but most of it has been modernised while retaining character. Most bedrooms are small, and the celler has a nice restaurant. **www.hotel-meteor.cz**

Betlem Club
P ⒸⒸⒸ

Betlémské náměstí 9, Praha 1 **Tel** *22 22 21 574* **Fax** *22 22 20 580* **Rooms** *21* **Map** *3 B4*

Beautiful, pastel-green medieval house on a quiet square, a short distance from the Old Town Square. Rooms are rather small and blandly decorated, but all have a private bath and WC. There is much character in the building, especially the original vaulted cellar where the excellent buffet breakfast is served. **www.betlemclub.cz**

U Zlatého Stromu
P 🍴 ⒸⒸⒸ

Karlova 6, Praha 1 **Tel** *22 22 20 441* **Fax** *22 22 20 441* **Rooms** *22* **Map** *3 B4*

Set in a 13th-century house, this charming hotel has smallish rooms with real character. Furniture and fittings are all tasteful and classic, including wooden, beamed ceilings. While the garden out back is a haven of peace and quiet, some of the rooms facing the busy street are not. **www.zlatystrom.cz**

Apostolic Residence
🍴 ⒸⒸⒸⒸ

Staroměstské náměstí 25, Praha 1 **Tel** *22 16 32 206* **Fax** *22 16 32 204* **Rooms** *31* **Map** *3 C3*

With marvellous views of the Old Town Square it is no wonder that the large rooms and apartments are often fully-booked. Rooms are furnished classically and simply, but all have the necessary amenities the modern world demands. Breakfast is served in the historical U Orloje restaurant and beerhouse. **www.prague-residence.cz**

Clementin
🍴 ⒸⒸⒸⒸ

Seminářská 4, 110 00 Praha 1 **Tel** *22 22 21 798* **Fax** *22 22 21 768* **Rooms** *9* **Map** *3 B4*

Located at the crossroads of ancient and modern Prague, this hotel is an ideal starting point for discovering and enjoying the city. It is housed in the narrowest and greenest building and dates to 1360, though it has only been recently converted to hotel use. Rooms are small but all have en suite bathrooms. **www.clementin.cz**

Élite
P 🍴 ⒸⒸⒸⒸ

Ostrovní 32, 110 00 Praha 1 **Tel** *22 49 32 250* **Fax** *22 49 30 787* **Rooms** *79* **Map** *3 B5*

The Élite is housed in a building which dates from the late-14th century. Its cosy atmosphere is aptly augmented by a stylish grill club on the ground floor, offering excellent Mediterranean and Argentinian cuisine, as well as a cocktail bar providing jazz and Latino music. An open atrium contains a day-bar with a small garden. **www.hotelelite.cz**

Metamorphis
P 🍴 ⒸⒸⒸⒸ

Malá Štupartská 5, Praha 1 **Tel** *22 17 71 011* **Fax** *22 17 71 099* **Rooms** *24* **Map** *3 C3*

In the centre of Old Town, in the wonderful Tyn Courtyard, the Metamorphis offers rather strangely-styled but large rooms, with en suite bathrooms. Many rooms retain original features from the 14th century, when the building was built. The hotel's restaurant makes great pizzas. **www.metamorphis.cz**

Key to Symbols *see back cover flap*

U Prince

Staroměstské náměstí 29, Praha 1 **Tel** *22 42 13 807* **Fax** *22 42 13 807* **Rooms** *24* **Map** *3 C3*

Great views of the Old Town Square from every room make this a popular choice for visitors. While the building itself is centuries old, the decoration and facilities inside are thoroughly modern, the hotel having only opened in 2001. The terrace (served by a glass lift) is a favourite feature of this little jewel. **www.hoteluprince.cz**

Ungelt

Štupartská 7, 110 00 Praha 1 **Tel** *22 48 28 686* **Fax** *22 48 28 181* **Rooms** *10* **Map** *3 C3*

Tucked away in a quiet street behind the Old Town Square, this elegant hotel has more than just an air of exclusivity. The accommodation is in suites, simple yet stylish, and some rooms feature magnificent wooden ceilings. The restaurant is simple and there is a shady terrace. **www.ungelt.cz**

Four Seasons

Veleslavínova 2a, 110 00 Praha 1 **Tel** *22 14 27 000* **Fax** *22 14 26 977* **Rooms** *79* **Map** *3 A3*

This luxury hotel, located close to the Charles Bridge needs no introduction. There are a variety of rooms and suites to choose from, and all have stunning views over the Vltava. The hotel's Allegro restaurant is often rated the best in the Czech Republic. **www.fourseasons.com**

Pařiž

U Obecního domu 1, 110 00 Praha 1 **Tel** *22 21 95 195* **Fax** *22 42 25 475* **Rooms** *86* **Map** *4 D3*

This Neo-Gothic building with a number of Art Nouveau elements was built by the celebrated architect Jan Vejrych, and was declared a historic monument in 1984. The rooms have been modernised in international style and everything is in pristine condition. **www.hotel-paris.cz**

Savoy

Keplerova 6, Praha 1 **Tel** *22 43 02 430* **Fax** *22 43 02 128* **Rooms** *61* **Map**

Splendid period building inside which a luxury, modern hotel plays host to the great and good. The list of famous people who have stayed here is as endless as the services that the hotel offers. Rooms are large and plush, all with what are probably the largest bathrooms in Prague. **www.hotel-savoy.cz**

Ventana

Celetná 7, Praha 1 **Tel** *22 17 76 600* **Fax** *22 17 76 603* **Rooms** *29* **Map** *3 C3*

Classic Prague hotel in the heart of Old Town. A narrow building that makes great use of the space available, such as the modern lift inside the old staircase. The rooms are imaginatively designed, some on two levels, and all have rather grand four-poster beds. The reception area is an Art Deco treat. **www.ventana-hotel.com**

JEWISH QUARTER

Bellagio

U Milosrdných 2, Praha 1 **Tel** *22 17 78 999* **Fax** *22 17 78 900* **Rooms** *46* **Map** *3 B2*

Wonderful, pastel-hued hotel on a quiet street minutes from the river. The tastefully decorated bedrooms are large and all have well-sized bathrooms. While the lobby bar is one of the city's trendiest drinking locations, the Isabella restaurant downstairs is also becoming a popular attraction in its own right. **www.bellagiohotel.cz**

Casa Marcello

Řásnovka 783, Praha 1 **Tel** *22 23 11 230* **Fax** *22 23 13 323* **Rooms** *32* **Map** *3 C2*

Beautiful, rather exclusive hotel alongside St Agnes's Convent. The rooms, in two buildings surrounding lovely gardens, are not so much large as grand, with enormous bathrooms and luxurious furnishings. Sauna and small fitness room onsite. The vaulted lobby bar is a great place for an evening drink. **www.casa-marcello.cz**

Josef

Rybná 20, Praha 1 **Tel** *22 17 00 111* **Fax** *22 17 00 999* **Rooms** *110* **Map** *3 C3*

This ultra-modern hotel is a wonderful contrast to the historic Jewish Quarter. Well furnished rooms, with probably the best showers in Prague, are situated in two bulidings: the Orange House and the Pink House, separated by a lovely courtyard with manicured lawn. Breakfast is served all morning. **www.hoteljosef.com**

Maximilian

Haštalská 14, 110 00 Praha 1 **Tel** *22 53 03 118* **Fax** *22 53 03 119* **Rooms** *71* **Map** *3 C2*

Total renovation and redecoration in early 2005 makes this one of the most up-to-date and fashionable places to stay in the city. Exquisitely furnished rooms with over-sized beds are the order of the day at the Maximilian. Each room has classical drapes from Venice, a large en suite bathroom and internet access. **www.maximilianhotel.com**

President

Curieových námesti 100, Praha 1 **Tel** *23 46 14 100* **Fax** *23 46 14 110* **Rooms** *130* **Map** *3 B2*

Totally refurbished after the 2002 floods, the President now boasts an executive floor, a casino and health spa, and fabulously furnished rooms and suites. Unique amongst Prague's hotels you can select from one of four great views: the Castle, river, Old Town or St Agnes's Convent. **www.hotelpresident.cz**

Rott

Malé náměstí 4/138, Praha 1 **Tel** *22 41 90 901* **Fax** *22 42 16 761* **Rooms** *84* **Map** *3 B3*

This central, but nevertheless quiet, hotel near the Old Town Square delights all with its charm, evocative architecture and original wooden furniture. Rooms are large and all have super-sized beds. The glass-roofed reception area and atrium is a joy, as is the adjacent restaurant specialising in game. **www.hotelrott.cz**

Grand Hotel Bohemia

Králodvorská 4, Praha 1 **Tel** *23 46 08 111* **Fax** *22 23 29 545* **Rooms** *78* **Map** *4 D3*

A mustard-coloured Art Nouveau hotel, as grand and as imperial as the name would suggest. Rooms are enormous, staff are friendly and the hotel's café is one of the city's most popular meeting points. The buffet breakfast is equally famous amongst regular visitors to Prague. **www.grandhotelbohemia.cz**

Inter-Continental

Náměstí Curieových 43–45, Praha 1 **Tel** *29 66 31 111* **Fax** *22 48 11 296* **Rooms** *372* **Map** *3 B2*

An imposing 1970s building set on the banks of the Vltava, this hotel has health and fitness facilities and a swimming pool. There is nothing Czech about the place, but it is a good example of a five-star international hotel. WiFi in all public areas, high-speed broadband in all rooms. **www.prague.interconti.com**

PRAGUE CASTLE AND HRADČANY

U Zlaté Studně

U Zlaté studně 166, Praha 1 **Tel** *25 70 11 213* **Fax** *25 75 33 320* **Rooms** *20* **Map** *2 E2*

Luxury rooms in a former house which is almost as old as Prague itself, just minutes from the castle. Views of Prague from the rooftop restaurant and terrace are stunning, and the rooms are well furnished with original touches. Bathrooms, too, are comfortable, which is something of a rarity in these parts. **www.zlatastudna.cz**

Hoffmeister

Pod Bruskou 7, Praha 1 **Tel** *251 01 71 11* **Fax** *251 01 71 20* **Rooms** *37* **Map** *2 F2*

The closest, quality hotel to Prague Castle, the imposing Hoffmeister offers a spa and fitness centre alongside its individually furnished rooms. Views from the rooms of the river towards the old town are terrific. The location, half-way up Chotkova, is not a great choice for the elderly or disabled, however. **www.hoffmeister.cz**

LITTLE QUARTER

Residence Malá Strana

Mělnická 9, Praha 5 **Tel** *25 15 10 372* **Fax** *25 15 10 406* **Rooms** *35* **Map**

Smart hotel in a lovely Neo-Classical building in the Little Quarter. Rooms are large, more like suites, and have small kitchens and a separate dining area. A filling breakfast is included in the price. There is a nice lounge with garden view on the ground floor, perfect for relaxing after a day's sightseeing. **www.hotelresidence-mala-strana.com**

Sax

Jánský vršek 3, Praha 1 **Tel** *25 75 31 268* **Fax** *25 75 34 101* **Rooms** *22* **Map** *2 D3*

With a great location close to Prague Castle, the Sax and its classical white façade, is ideal for serious sightseers who want to be among the first up Hradčany hill in the morning. The rooms are simple but immaculate, overlooking a courtyard, and the common areas are well kept. **www.sax.cz**

U Žluté boty

Jánský vršek 11, Praha 1 **Tel** *25 75 32 269* **Fax** *257 53 41 34* **Rooms** *9* **Map** *2 D3*

The sparsely furnished but tasteful and elegant rooms at U Žluté boty are all individually decorated, some with lots of wood, others with a more modern feel. The rooms are large and have well-sized bathrooms. The courtyard at the back is very pleasant during the summer. **www.zlutabota.cz**

Best Western Kampa

Všehrdova 16, Praha 1 **Tel** *25 74 04 444* **Fax** *25 74 04 333* **Rooms** *84* **Map** *2 E5*

A 17th-century armoury, the Kampa is minutes from Charles Bridge, tucked away on a peaceful side street surrounded by lovely gardens. In the large reception hall, a bar and restaurant are combined under a huge Baroque-vaulted ceiling. The furnishings are simple and bedrooms are clean. **www.euroagentur.cz**

Pod Věží

Mostecká 2, Praha 1 **Tel** *25 75 32 041* **Fax** *25 75 32 069* **Rooms** *12* **Map** *2 F3*

In the heart of the historical centre, this is a delightful, family-run hotel. Pod Věží offers a peaceful ambience, highlighted by the charming roof garden and the sidewalk café, which is open – and usually full – all day. Rooms are well appointed if not huge, and breakfast is included in the price. **www.podvezi.com**

Key to Price Guide *see p188* **Key to Symbols** *see back cover flap*

U Brány

Nerudova 21, Praha 1 **Tel** *25 75 34 050* **Fax** *25 75 32 767* **Rooms** *17* **Map** *2 D3*

With one of the best addresses in Prague, U Brány is a popular spot, often full at busy times. Reserving your room well ahead is essential. The rooms, all of which are in fact two-, three- or four-roomed suites, are large and luxuriously decorated. The bathrooms are splendid. **www.ubrany.cz**

Biskupský Dům

Dražického náměstí 6, Praha 1 **Tel** *25 75 32 320* **Fax** *25 75 31 840* **Rooms** *45* **Map** *2 F3*

Completely refurbished in the 1990s, this upmarket hotel is located in an old house overlooking the Royal Route. Rooms are classically furnished, evoking a bygone age. Those on the upper floor have stunning high ceilings with wooden beams and all sorts of awkward but enchanting nooks and crannies. **www.starshotelsprague.com**

Constans

Břetislavova 309, Praha 1 **Tel** *23 40 91 818* **Fax** *23 40 91 860* **Rooms** *32* **Map** *2 D3*

Located on a quiet, medieval street below the castle, this recently-renovated hotel combines old-world class and taste with modern amenities. Rooms are large, with big beds and classic but simple furniture. The charming restaurant is a fine place to spend long evenings with friends. **www.hotelconstans.cz**

Domus Henrici

Loretánská 11, Praha 1 **Tel** *22 05 11 369* **Fax** *22 05 11 502* **Rooms** *8* **Map** *1 C3*

Part of the Hidden Places hotel group, you may have trouble finding this establishment. It's difficult to get much closer to the castle than this, so sightseers will love the location. Rooms are enormous and tastefully decorated. An excellent buffet breakfast is served on the terrace during the summer. **www.hidden-places.com**

Dům U Červeného lva

Nerudova 41, Praha 1 **Tel** *25 75 33 832* **Fax** *25 75 35 131* **Rooms** *21* **Map** *2 F3*

With views of the Royal Route, Prague Castle or the serene Petrin Hill Orchards, the Red Lion is absolutely ideal for sightseers. Add in the hand-painted Renaissance ceilings, original period furniture and parquet floors and you have a real historical treat. There is a traditional Czech beer hall too. **www.hotelredlion.com**

U Páva

U Lužického semináře 32, Praha 1 **Tel** *25 75 33 573* **Fax** *25 75 30 919* **Rooms** *27* **Map** *2 F3*

Located in a quiet part of the Little Quarter, U Páva provides visitors with stylish surroundings during their stay. Historical features are enhanced by traditional, wooden furniture, crystal chandeliers and attractive rugs. Personal touches give the hotel an individual feel, and the bedrooms are spacious.

U Tří Pštrosů

Dražického náměstí 12, Praha 1 **Tel** *25 75 32 410* **Fax** *25 75 33 217* **Rooms** *18* **Map** *2 F3*

Just beside Charles Bridge, the hotel "At The Three Ostriches" began life as the home of Jan Fux, an ostrich-feather dealer. It is one of the best-known hotel/restaurants in Prague. Family run, it has an intimate atmosphere, and children are especially welcome. The bedrooms have recently been refurbished. **www.utripstrosu.cz**

Aria

Tržiště 9, Praha 1 **Tel** *22 53 34 111* **Fax** *22 53 34 666* **Rooms** *52* **Map** *2 E3*

A charming, unusual little hotel where each of the fantastic, though not large, rooms are modelled to honour a particular musical legend, be it Dizzy Gillespie, Puccini or Mozart. The hotel even has a musical director who will recommend music to suit your mood, while also advising on concerts that you may attend. **www.ariahotel.net**

Waldstein

Valdštejnské náměstí 6, Praha 1 **Tel** *25 75 33 938* **Fax** *25 75 31 143* **Rooms** *15* **Map** *2 E3*

The rooms in this historical hotel are furnished with superb antique furniture, yet all come with modern amenities, including internet connections and satellite TV. Some rooms even have mosaics on the ceilings. The breakfast, served in an original vaulted cellar, is excellent. **www.avehotels.cz**

NEW TOWN

Junior

Senovážné náměstí 21, Praha 1 **Tel** *22 42 31 754* **Fax** *22 42 21 579* **Rooms** **Map** *4 E4*

Expect excellent value-for-money if you stay at this cheap hotel, just a few minutes' walk from the top of Wenceslas Square. Rooms are not luxurious but are well equipped with private bathrooms. A good pizzeria downstairs does a roaring trade, and there is a bowling alley onsite too. **www.euroagentur.cz**

Luník

Londýnská 50, 120 00 Praha 2 **Tel** *22 42 53 974* **Fax** *22 42 53 986* **Rooms** *35* **Map** *6 E2*

Located in a quiet street lined with trees, this good value, historic hotel is in immaculate condition. The decor is simple, with whitewashed walls and good-quality wooden furnishings. Rooms are small but have en suite bathrooms with bath, shower and WC. A buffet breakfast is included in the price. **www.hotel-lunik.cz**

Pension Březina

Legerova 41, Praha 2 **Tel** *22 42 66 779* **Fax** *22 42 66 777* **Rooms** *35* **Map** *6 D2*

A somewhat faded exterior belies a super bed-and-breakfast hidden within. Rooms are modern if somewhat simple, and many have views of the small garden at the rear of the building. Two apartments ideal for families are available. Breakfast is served in the small dining room. **www.brezina.cz**

U Klenotníka

Rytířská 3, Praha 1 **Tel** *22 42 11 699* **Fax** *22 42 21 025* **Rooms** *11* **Map** *3 B4*

A small, but lovely hotel and restaurant in a converted house halfway between the Old Town Square and Wenceslas Square. Rooms are reasonably sized and offer great value for money. There is a small paternoster elevator for luggage. Excellent buffet breakfast is served in the downstairs restaurant. **www.uklenotnika.cz**

U Medvídků

Na Perštýně 7, Praha 1 **Tel** *22 42 11 916* **Fax** *22 42 20 930* **Rooms** *33* **Map** *3 B5*

Classic Czech restaurant, beerhouse and pension. The more expensive rooms have wooden beams and a definite medieval flavour, but all are large and full of character, and have private facilities. U Medvídků is one of the few hotels, which have a brewing museum in the basement. **www.umedvidku.cz**

Axa

Na poříčí 40, Praha 1 **Tel** *22 48 12 580* **Fax** *22 42 14 489* **Rooms** *132* **Map** *4 E3*

This block-style hotel is slightly dispiriting in appearance, yet reasonably priced and centrally located. Inside, things are much better, and all the recently-renovated rooms have a private bath and WC. There is also a large fitness complex in the hotel, including an indoor swimming pool, sauna and solarium. **www.hotelaxa.com**

Evropa

Václavské náměstí 25, 110 00 Praha 1 **Tel** *22 42 28 215* **Fax** *22 42 24 544* **Rooms** *90* **Map** *4 D5*

The Evropa is Prague's most beautiful – and possibly most famous – hotel, with superb Art Nouveau decor, and a ground-floor terrace-café that is in itself a major attraction, boasting stunning glasswork. The rooms are not as fancy or impressive, but are large and all have private bathrooms. **www.evropahotel.cz**

Harmony

Na poříčí 31, Praha 1 **Tel** *22 23 19 807* **Fax** *22 23 10 009* **Rooms** *60* **Map** *4 E3*

The rather bleak looking Harmony is, in fact, in pristine condition after reconstruction. A compact place, it is run by young, friendly staff. Two small restaurants, one with tables on the pavement, give a choice of cuisine. Ask for a room away from the busy central street, which can be noisy at night. **www.hotelharmony.cz**

Na Zlatém Kříži

Jungmannovo náměstí 2, Praha 1 **Tel** *22 42 19 501* **Fax** *22 22 45 418* **Rooms** *8* **Map** *3 C5*

A challenger for the narrowest hotel in Prague award, the charming Golden Cross offers deceptively large, and rather luxurious double rooms and apartments, all with private bathrooms. A good buffet breakfast is served in the hotel's Gothic-style cellar. Transfers to and from the airport are possible. **www.goldencross.cz**

Opera

Těšnov 13, Praha 1 **Tel** *22 23 15 609* **Fax** *22 23 11 477* **Rooms** *67* **Map** *4 F2*

Although nowhere near the opera, this hotel is a classy Neo-Renaissance affair built in the late-19th century. Rooms are classically furnished and all have enormous windows with views of the small park opposite. The hotel bar is pure kitsch, with its 1950s-style booths, and shouldn't be missed. **www.hotel-opera.cz**

Pension Museum

Mezibranská 15, Praha 1 **Tel** *29 63 25 186* **Fax** *29 63 25 188* **Rooms** *12* **Map** *6 D1*

Large rooms, most with separate bedrooms and a small living area, are what distinguish the Pension Museum. Great service, an excellent breakfast and a super location at the top of Wenceslas Square, make this converted school just about the best value bed-and-breakfast in central Prague. **www.pension-museum.cz**

Pension Páv

Křemencova 13, 110 00 Praha 1 **Tel** *22 49 33 760* **Fax** *22 49 33 080* **Rooms** *8* **Map** *5 B1*

Situated in a tranquil street in the historic part of Prague, this hotel is a compact but attractive place with just a few rooms and apartments. The rooms are simple and stylish, but those facing the street can be noisy. The pension has its own bar and a reasonable French restaurant, U Páva. Next door is the U Fleků brewery. **www.pension-pav.cz**

Tchaikovsky

Ke Karlovu 19, Praha 1 **Tel** *22 49 12 121* **Fax** *22 49 12 123* **Rooms** *19* **Map** *5 C2*

Ten-minutes' walk from Wenceslas Square on a quiet side street, the smart, Neo-Classical Tchaikovsky hits all the right notes with its simple charm and elegance. Rooms are well sized if low on frills, and bathrooms are huge and wonderfully decorated. A buffet breakfast is included in the price. **www.hoteltchaikovsky.com**

Elysee

Václavské náměstí 43, Praha 1 **Tel** *22 14 55 111* **Fax** *22 42 25 773* **Rooms** *70* **Map** *4 D5*

If you are looking for a good value, but not luxury hotel on Wenceslas Square, then this place could be your best choice. The large, tastefully decorated rooms are fine for all but the fussiest visitors, and the location is perfect. Good insulation keeps noise from the busy street below to a minimum. **www.europehotels.cz**

Key to Price Guide *see p188* **Key to Symbols** *see back cover flap*

Adria

Václavské náměstí 26, Praha 1 **Tel** *22 10 81 111* **Fax** *22 10 81 300* **Rooms** *87* **Map** *4 D5*

The Adria is bright and chic with an entrance on Wenceslas Square. Clever use of glass and mirrors makes the reception seem bigger than it is, and with plenty of gleaming brass the impression is light and up-beat. The bedrooms are bright, cheerful and smartly furnished. **www.adria.cz**

Carlo IV

Senovážné náměstí 13, Praha 1 **Tel** *22 45 93 111* **Fax** *22 42 23 960* **Rooms** *152* **Map** *4 E4*

This magnificently decorated hotel with shimmering marble floors, intricate hand-painted frescos in a Neo-Classical building, is in the heart of the city. Part of the Boscolo Group, it is all startlingly wonderful, from the Box Block restaurant to the cigar bar, while the spa features Europe's best hotel swimming pool. **www.boscolohotels.com**

Liberty

28. října 11, Praha 1 **Tel** *22 42 39 598* **Fax** *22 42 37 694* **Rooms** *32* **Map** *3 C4*

Simple elegance meets modern efficiency in this fine boutique hotel in the centre of Prague. Spacious rooms and bathrooms, wonderful halls and luxurious services make this a popular choice with the well-heeled. The hotel's Relax Club offers fitness equipment, sauna, whirlpool, massage and solarium. **www.hotelliberty.cz**

Praha Renaissance

V celnici 7, Praha 1 **Tel** *22 18 22 100* **Fax** *22 18 22 200* **Rooms** *310* **Map** *4 E3*

The gleaming glass front of this relatively new hotel has taken over one entire corner of Náměstí Republiky. The opulent bedrooms include soft furnishings, plump bedcovers, plush carpets and fluffy bathrobes. There is a choice of fantastic restaurants, a beer hall and health club with a swimming pool. **www.renaissancehotels.com**

Seven Days

Žitná 46, Praha 2 **Tel** *22 29 23 111* **Fax** *22 29 23 222* **Rooms** *50* **Map** *6 D2*

Fabulous Neo-Classical hotel in the centre of Prague's New Town. Rooms are all large and superbly furnished with good taste, while the stylish common areas are impressively opulent. A sauna and whirlpool are available to guests for a small fee. Internet TV in all rooms. **www.hotelsevendays.cz**

Esplanade

Washingtonova 19, Praha 1 **Tel** *22 45 01 111* **Fax** *22 42 29 306* **Rooms** *74* **Map** *4 E5*

This imposing six-storey hotel opposite the opera house is known for its long history of luxury. The Art Nouveau façade hides an elegant interior, and all the rooms are well furnished. The hotel's café has a summer terrace, while the onsite French restaurant is world class. Service is exceptional. **www.esplanade.cz**

Marriott

V celnici 8, Praha 1 **Tel** *22 28 88 888* **Fax** *22 28 88 889* **Rooms** *293* **Map** *4 E3*

The Prague Marriott is one of the best hotels in the Marriott chain, and has a great location close to the Old Town gate. Every amenity and luxury imaginable is on offer in all the rooms. There is a great health club with a swimming pool, free to guests. The restaurants here are considered to be among the best in the city. **www.marriott.com**

Palace

Panská 12, 110 00 Praha 1 **Tel** *22 40 93 111* **Fax** *22 42 21 240* **Rooms** *124* **Map** *4 D4*

Located on a quiet side street close to Wenceslas Square, the mixture of styles – modern, Art Nouveau and traditional – with lashings of brass, glass, mirrors and fake flowers, may not be to everyone's taste, but the hotel succeeds in providing any luxury guests may require. Rooms are enormous. **www.palacehotel.cz**

Radisson SAS Alcron

Štěpánská 40, Praha 1 **Tel** *22 28 20 000* **Fax** *22 28 20 100* **Rooms** *211* **Map** *6 D1*

The views from the upper floors of this exquisite hotel could be an attraction in themselves. But that would be to forget the other joys of staying at this Radisson hotel, including enormous bathrooms, divine chocolates at bedtime and plush carpets. Expensive but worth every penny. **www.radissonsas.com**

FURTHER AFIELD

Anna

Budečská 17, Praha 2 **Tel** *22 25 13 111* **Fax** *22 25 15 158* **Rooms** *22*

Housed in an elegant Neo-Classical building with Art Nouveau interiors, this excellent value hotel is only a 10-minute walk from Wenceslas Square. Rooms are spacious and have large, comfortable beds, but some of the bathroms can be small. Staff are helpful, multilingual and very friendly. **www.hotelanna.cz**

Apollo

Kubišova 23, Praha 8 **Tel** *28 46 80 628* **Fax** *28 46 84 570* **Rooms** *42*

Modern, non-descript hotel offering small, simple rooms with en suite facilities and satellite TV at reasonable prices. Situated in a quiet residential area in the north of the city, it is a tram or a metro ride away from the centre. A buffet breakfast is included in the price. **www.avetravel.cz**

Carol

Kurta Konráda 12, Praha 9 **Tel** *28 40 19 911* **Fax** *28 40 19 977* **Rooms** *52*

This hotel is Dutch-owned, and the atmosphere is relatively relaxed for Prague. Bedrooms feature minimalist decor, but are immaculate and comfortable. The indoor swimming pool and sauna are a real treat. The only disadvantage is the distance from the city centre. **www.carol.cz**

Julián

Elišky Peškové 11, Praha 5 **Tel** *25 73 11 144* **Fax** *25 73 11 149* **Rooms** *32*

Good value hotel where, though the rooms are on the small side, everything is done to make up for that one drawback. Service is fantastic, there is a sauna, solarium and a small fitness room, and children are especially welcome. All rooms are accesible by wheelchairs, and one room has a specially adapted bathroom. **www.julian.cz**

Kafka

Cimburkova 24, Praha 3 **Tel** *22 42 25 769* **Fax** *22 42 25 769* **Rooms** *59*

A simple, clean but somewhat Spartan and soulless hotel a short walk away from Old Town. The building is a classic though, and a large number of triple and quad rooms make it a good choice for families on a budget. If you want to park in the hotel's carpark you need to pre-book a space. **www.ckvesta.cz**

Kavalír

Plzeňská 177, Praha 5 **Tel** *25 72 16 565* **Fax** *25 72 10 085* **Rooms** *50*

Cheapest hotel in the good value H&Hotels chain, this place is not without charm. Rooms are impressively large – some have two large double beds – and all the common areas are well kept, bright and breezy. Staff are friendly and communicate in a number of languages. It is some way from the city centre though. **www.europehotels.cz**

U Tří Korunek (Three Crowns)

Cimburkova 28, Praha 3 **Tel** *22 27 81 112* **Fax** *22 27 80 189* **Rooms** *58*

It may today cost rather more than three crowns to stay here, but the value for money is good, even if the location – out in the less than salubrious suburb of Žižkov – isn't. Rooms are simple and without any fuss but well appointed with everything you'll need. Service from the friendly staff is always good. **www.3korunky.cz**

Abri

Jana Masaryka 36, Praha 2 **Tel** *22 25 11 568* **Fax** *22 42 54 240* **Rooms** *26*

Comfortable hotel in a quiet residential area of Prague, Vinohrady. Smallish rooms are well furnished and decorated, and all have private bathrooms. A small garden terrace is a pleasant place to unwind with a drink after a long day of sightseeing. Guarded parking and onsite restaurant. **www.abri.cz**

Ariston

Seifertova 65, Praha 3 **Tel** *22 27 82 517* **Fax** *22 27 80 347* **Rooms** *61*

Great value three-star hotel not too far from the city centre in a quiet residential area. Rooms are simple but clean and well-sized, with high ceilings and sturdy wooden desks. All have private bathrooms, and some larger rooms take a third bed. Non-smoking and disabled-friendly rooms are also available. **www.europehotels.cz**

Best Western Alta

Ortenovo náměstí 22, Praha 7 **Tel** *22 04 07 011* **Fax** *22 04 07 091* **Rooms** *87*

It may be some distance from the city centre, but the Alta is close to the metro and offers large, very good value, if plain and somewhat formulaic rooms. As part of Best Western, however, you can be assured that service is very good and always comes with a smile. Excellent breakfast included in the price. **www.hotelalta.com**

Duo

Teplická 492, Praha 9 **Tel** *26 61 31 111* **Fax** *28 38 80 141* **Rooms** *553*

Massive hotel cum mini-resort on the northern edge of town, the Duo offers large rooms and super services at great prices. It also has the best sports centre in Prague, with a swimming pool, fitness centre, whirlpool, sauna and bowling alley. There are also three restaurants, a beer garden and an internet café. **www.hotelduo.cz**

Green Garden

Fügnerovo náměstí 4, Praha 2 **Tel** *22 42 61 181* **Fax** *22 42 62 182* **Rooms** *55* **Map** *6 D3*

Comfortable if not luxurious hotel situated somewhat uncomfortably between the main Prague-Brno highway. It does overlook a small, green garden, however, and pricewise it is competitive. The large, airy and bright terrace is its best asset, where lazy afternoons maybe spent while drinking coffee. **www.hotelgreengarden.cz**

U Blaženky

U Blaženky 1, Praha 5 **Tel** *25 15 64 532* **Fax** *25 15 63 529* **Rooms** *13*

You are guaranteed to feel special just arriving at this villa conversion in one of Prague's best residential districts. The excellent value – though by no means cheap – rooms are modern and spacious, full of extras and nice touches, while the dining room is home to fine local cuisine and an excellent winelist. **www.ublazenky.cz**

Arcotel Teatrino

Bořivojova 53, Praha 3 **Tel** *22 14 22 111* **Fax** *22 14 22 222* **Rooms** *73*

Once a theatre, this design hotel is a well-priced, high-quality alternative to more expensive retreats. Located in residential Žižkov, its finest feature, besides the large, well-furnished rooms, is the spendid restaurant – situated in what was once the stalls – overlooked by the theatre's original balconies and boxes. **www.arcotel.at**

Art Hotel Praha

Nad Královskou oborou 53, Praha 7 **Tel** *23 31 01 331* **Fax** *23 31 01 311* **Rooms** *24*

With its permanent display of Czech modern art, the Art Hotel is a cool, quiet place to escape the capital's tourist trail. Rooms are individually decorated, all with panache and taste. The lighting is a big feature: subtle and designed to catch your mood. Excellent buffet breakfast included in the price. **www.arthotel.cz**

Barceló

Na Strži 32, Praha 4 **Tel** *24 14 40 022* **Fax** *24 14 41 023* **Rooms** *213*

Situated some distance from the city centre, the Barceló – part of the Spanish hotel chain of the same name – is a fine, high-rise hotel catering mainly to large tour groups and business travellers. There is much to enjoy however, as rooms are large and those on higher floors have stunning views of the city. **www.barcelo.com**

Carlton

Táborítská 18, Praha 3 **Tel** *22 27 11 177* **Fax** *22 27 11 199* **Rooms** *49*

Not perfectly located, the Carlton is nevertheless a stylish, good-value hotel, offering large rooms at reasonable prices. The lofty celings and wooden beams make the top-floor rooms a preferred choice. Buffet breakfast served in a small cellar restaurant. One room is specially adapted for disabled visitors. **www.europehotels.cz**

Praha Hilton

Pobřežní 1, 186 00 Praha 8 **Tel** *22 48 41 111* **Fax** *22 48 42 378* **Rooms** *788* **Map** *4 F2*

French-owned and designed, this is the biggest hotel in the country, and despite the huge size, it does have a certain style. The bedrooms are tastefully decorated with all the comforts you would expect to find in a large international hotel, while the cost of staying in one is far lower than you may have thought. **www.prague.hilton.com**

Praha Hotel

Sušická 20, Praha 6 **Tel** *22 43 41 111* **Fax** *22 43 11 218* **Rooms** *124*

When the Praha opened in 1981, it was regarded by its architects as the height of modernity, with its unique design, all curves and waves. Built to accommodate visiting heads of state and dignitaries, it is today open to all, though its secluded location still makes it a favourite of VIPs. **www.htlpraha.cz**

Ametyst

Jana Masaryka 11, Praha 2 **Tel** *22 29 21 921* **Fax** *22 22 91 999* **Rooms** *84* **Map** *6 F3*

Fine, modern townhouse-style hotel with air-conditioned rooms, all with private bath or shower and internet access. The attic rooms with sloping, beamed ceilings are especially attractive. Sauna and massage also available. Ametyst has a small restaurant with some fine decor. **www.hotelametyst.cz**

Corinthia Towers

Kongresová 1, Praha 4 **Tel** *26 11 91 218* **Fax** *26 12 11 673* **Rooms** *544*

Situated beside the Vyšehrad metro stop, the Corinthia Towers is only a few minutes from the city centre. Built in 1988 as a modern high-rise filled with glass, brass and marble, it has an impressive health centre and a beautiful indoor swimming pool. The good-sized bedrooms are well decorated and comfortable. **www.corinthia.cz**

Diplomat Praha

Evropská 15, Praha 6 **Tel** *29 65 59 213* **Fax** *29 65 59 207* **Rooms** *398*

This hotel is located right at the end of metro line A, but is only 12 minutes from the city centre. It opened in 1990 and still feels very new. Efficiently run by Austrians, it offers excellent facilities including a nightclub, numerous restaurants, shops and even a whirlpool in the health club. **www.diplomatpraha.cz**

Mövenpick

Mozartova 1, Praha 5 **Tel** *25 71 51 111* **Fax** *25 71 53 131* **Rooms** *502*

Though not centrally located, this luxurious hotel situated in two buildings linked by a funicular is wonderful. All of the rooms – some of which are split over two levels – are large, comfortable and cater to all needs. The hotel's restaurants are well regarded, and it's also famous for ice cream. **www.movenpick-prague.com**

Mucha

Sokolovská 26, Praha 8 **Tel** *22 23 19 047* **Fax** *22 48 16 641* **Rooms** *39* **Map** *4 F2*

Perhaps a little overpriced, the Mucha is nevertheless a good hotel, in a great location, minutes from the city centre. The legacy of Czech painter Alphonse Mucha for whom the hotel is named is not forgotten, with reproductions of his work all over the building, which is also something of an Art Deco masterpiece. **www.avehotels.cz**

Andel's

Stroupežnického 21, Praha 5 **Tel** *29 68 89 688* **Fax** *29 68 89 999* **Rooms** *239*

Designed by the same team who came up with the multi-award winning One Aldwych in London, this is a modernist fusion of elegance and practicality. Rooms are spacious, bathrooms have separate shower and bath, and the onsite Delight restaurant is one of the city's best. The hotel is a metro ride from the city centre. **www.andelshotel.com**

Riverside

Janáčkovo nábřeží 15, Praha 5 **Tel** *22 59 94 611* **Fax** *22 59 94 622* **Rooms** *45*

Classy, and – as the name suggests – handy for the river, this hotel is not cheap but is certainly impressive, with small touches of elegance and fine living at every turn. From the basket of complimentary high-end toiletries in the bathrooms to the original, contemporary Czech art on the wall, your stay here will be enjoyable. **www.riversideprague.com**

RESTAURANTS, CAFÉS AND PUBS

Restaurants in Prague, just like the economy, seem to be getting better. For 40 years state-licensed eating and drinking establishments had little incentive to experiment or improve. But attitudes are rapidly changing. Fuelled by the booming tourist industry, new restaurants are opening constantly, many of them foreign-owned, offering the discerning eater an ever-increasing choice. The restaurants described in this section reflect the change, though many only serve a limited range of standard Western dishes as well as staple Czech meals. *Choosing a Restaurant* on pages 202–3 summarizes the key features of the restaurants and cafés, listed by area. Full listings can be found on pages 202–7 and information on pubs, beer halls and bars appears on page 208–9. Compared to Western prices, eating out in Prague is still cheap.

The Good Soldier Švejk at U Kalicha *(see p207)*

TIPS ON EATING OUT

Because of the huge influx of tourists, eating out has changed in character. The lunch hour is still early – between 11am and 1pm, and for most Czechs the normal time for the evening meal is around 7pm. However, many of the restaurants stay open late and it is possible to get a meal at any time from 10am until 11pm. Kitchens close 30 minutes to one hour earlier than stated closing times.

During spring and summer, the large numbers of visitors tend to put a strain on many of Prague's more popular restaurants. To be certain of a table, especially in the very well-known restaurants, it is advisable to book in advance. The city centre is full of restaurants, and there are several off the normal tourist track. Prices also tend to be lower the further you go from the centre.

PLACES TO EAT

The importance of a stylish yet comfortable setting, and food which is inspired rather than just prepared, is slowly beginning to trickle down to Prague's better and more innovative restaurants. The places which follow this maxim are generally the best.

One of the simplest places to eat is the sausage stand, a utilitarian establishment which is very common in Central Europe. It offers Czech sausages, which can either be eaten standing at the counter or taken away cold. For a late-night meal your best bet is often a snack bar *(bufet)*.

Modern Czech restaurant

For greater comfort, head for a café *(kavárna)*. Cafés range from loud, busy main street locations to quieter bookstore establishments. All have fully stocked bars and serve a variety of food from simple pastries and sandwiches to full-blown meals. Opening hours differ widely, but many open early in the morning and are good for a quick, if not quite a Western-style, breakfast.

A restaurant may be called a *restaurace* or a *vinárna* (one that sells wine). The best are those geared to non-Czech clientele. While usually cheap by Western standards, they are pricier than Czech places, but in return offer better service and higher quality food.

Plain Czech food is normally available at the local beer hall or pub *(pivnice)*, though the emphasis there is normally on drinking rather than eating.

Diners enjoying their meal at U Kalicha *(see p207)*

Tourists eating at the outdoor cafés in the Old Town Square

READING THE MENU

Never judge a restaurant by the standard of its menu translations – mistakes are common in every class of restaurant. Many menus still list the weight of meat served (a relic of communist rationing). Bear in mind that most main courses come with potatoes, rice or dumplings. Salads and other side dishes must be ordered separately. *(See pp198–9 for The Flavours of Prague.)*

Restaurant sign

THINGS TO BEWARE OF

In some restaurants or bars the waiter may bring nuts to your table. Yes, they are for you to eat, but at a price equal to, or higher than, an appetizer. You will not insult anybody by telling the waiter to take them away. The same applies to appetizers brought round by the waiter.

Check your bill carefully, because extra charges are often added – this is quite a common practice in Prague. However, legitimate extra costs do exist. Cover charges range from Kč10–25 and such basic items as milk, ketchup, bread and butter might be charged for. Finally, a 19% tax, normally included in the menu.

Severe cases of food poisoning are rare in Prague, but mild cases are more common. Avoid stands selling food in the street, as the ingredients are exposed to bacteria and may not be cooked thoroughly. In general, restaurants in Prague have a high standard of hygiene, equal to the rest of Europe.

Fine dining amid stained-glass Art Deco splendour

ETIQUETTE

You don't have to wait to be seated in snack bars and smaller eateries. It is also quite normal for others to join your table if there is any room. No restaurant has an official dress code, but people tend to dress up when dining in up-market restaurants.

PAYMENT AND TIPPING

The average price for a full meal in the centre of Prague is about Kč360. In some restaurants the waiter may write your order on a piece of paper and then leave it on your table for the person who comes around when you are ready to pay. Levels of service vary, but generally a 10% tip is appropriate. Add the tip to the bill, do not leave the money on the table. More and more restaurants now accept major credit cards, but always ask before the meal to make sure. Traveller's cheques are not accepted.

VEGETARIANS

Even vegetarians are well catered for in Prague. Fresh vegetables are available throughout the year, including winter, and numerous restaurants offer vegetarian and vegan options. Nevertheless, even when a dish is described as meatless, it's always worth double-checking. Vegetarians should particularly beware of menu sections called *bezmasa* as, whilst the literal translation of this word is "without meat", its actual meaning is that meat is not the main ingredient in the dishes listed.

DISABLED

Restaurants do not cater specifically for the disabled. The staff will almost always try and help, but Prague's ubiquitous stairs and basements will defeat all but the most determined.

USING THE LISTINGS

Key to symbols in the listings on pp202–207.

- formal dress
- live music
- outdoor tables
- credit cards not accepted
- children welcome
- wheelchair access

Price categories for a three-course meal including a half-bottle of house wine, tax and service:

- Kč under Kč250
- KčKč Kč250–450
- KčKčKč Kč450–650
- KčKčKčKč over Kč650

The Flavours of Prague

While no visitor comes to Prague for the food, there is far more to contemporary Czech cuisine than the Central European norm of meat, potatoes and rice. Czech food remains based on seasonally available ingredients, while a simple, no-fuss approach allows natural flavours to dominate most dishes. The staples of Czech cooking are pork, beef, game and carp, which tend to be served grilled or roasted, accompanied by a light sauce and vegetables. They are also used in sour soups, known as *polevky*. It is also unlikely that you will leave Prague without tasting *knedliky* (dumplings), either savoury or sweet.

Blueberries

Atmospheric U Pinkasů cellar bar and restaurant ***(see p206)***

MEAT

The Czech favourite is pork *(vepřové)*. It appears in countless dishes, including soups, goulash and sausages, or can be served on its own, either grilled or (more commonly) roasted. It is invariably served on the bone, just slightly the burnt side of well-done. It also appears in other forms, notably as Prague ham *(Pražska šunka)*, a succulent, lightly smoked meat usually eaten with bread at breakfast or with horseradish as a starter at suppertime.

Veal, usually served in the form of breadcrumbed, fried Wiener schnitzel *(smažený řízek)*, is popular and good.

Beef in the region has never been up to international standards, and needs to be prepared well to be edible. The Prague favourite is *Pražská hovězí pečeně*, roast beef stuffed with bacon, ham, cheese, onion, and eggs. If cooked well it can be tender and delicious. Beef is also used in goulash and stews. Most of the beef served in top restaurants is likely to be imported. Czech lamb *(jehněčí)* is not the best in the world, either, though for a short period from mid-March to mid-May

Selection of typical Czech cakes and pastries

LOCAL DISHES AND SPECIALITIES

Knedliky (dumplings), either savoury *(spekové)* in soups or sweet *(obocně)* with fruits and berries, are perhaps Bohemia's best-known delicacy. Once a mere side dish they have now become a central feature of Czech cuisine, as Postmodern chefs rediscover their charms and experiment with new and different ways of cooking and serving them. Other specialities of the region include *Drstkova polevka*, a remarkably good tripe soup, which – although an acquired taste – has also seen something of a revival in recent years as better restaurants add it to their menus. Duck and pheasant remain popular in Prague and, with the city surrounded by fine hunting grounds, such game is always of top quality. Pork, though, is the city's (and the nation's) most popular food, served roasted on the bone, with red cabbage.

Stuffed eggs

Polévka s játrovými knedlíčky
Soup with liver dumplings is the most common dish in the Czech Republic.

Wild chanterelle mushrooms from the forests around the city

there is good lamb available in Prague's markets, where it is usually sold whole, complete with the head which is used to make soup.

GAME

There is a wide variety of game to be found in the forests around Prague. Depending on the season (the best time is autumn) you will find duck, pheasant, goose, boar, venison, rabbit and hare on many menus. Duck is probably the most popular game dish, usually roasted with fruits, berries or sometimes with chestnuts, and served with red cabbage. Small pheasants, roasted whole with juniper and blueberries or cranberries, are also popular, while venison is often served grilled with mushrooms. Rabbit and hare are usually presented in spicy, goulash-style sauces.

VEGETABLES

Czech vegetables can be fabulous, if strictly seasonal. Note, however, that Czechs tend to boil their vegetables into oblivion before serving them. While more and more imported, out-of-season produce is finding its way into supermarkets, many Czechs are unwilling to pay the higher prices these goods demand. As a result, the hardy cabbage remains the country's top vegetable, used in numerous different ways, such as raw as a salad, or boiled as an accompaniment to roast meats. The Czech version of *sauerkraut*, *kyselé zel*, is ubiquitous. Mushrooms, too, are well liked, and find their way in to many sauces, especially those served with game.

Fresh vegetables on a Prague market stall

BEST LOCAL SNACKS

Sausages Street stalls and snack bars all over the city sell traditional sausages (*klobásy* and *utopence*), frankfurters (*párky*) or bratwurst, served in a soft roll with mustard.

Chlebíčky Open sandwiches on sliced baguette are found in any delicatessen or snack bar in Prague. Toppings are usually ham, salami or cheese, always accompanied by a gherkin (*nakládaná okurka*).

Pivní sýr Beer cheese is soaked in ale until it becomes soft. It is served spread on bread and eaten with pickles or onions.

Sýrečky These tasty cheese rounds have a pungent aroma and are served with beer and onions.

Palačinky Pancakes are filled with ice cream and/or fruits and jam, and are topped with lashings of sugar.

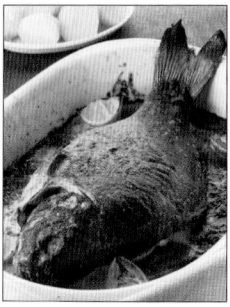

Pečeny kapr s kýselou omackou *Carp with sour cream and lemon is popular, especially at Christmas.*

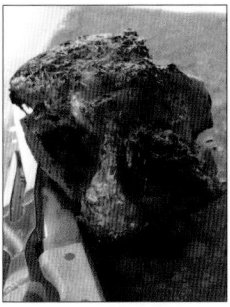

Vepřové s krenem *Pork is served roasted, on the bone, with red cabbage and either sauerkraut or horseradish.*

Ovocné knedlíky *Sweet dumplings are filled with fruits or berries, usually blueberries or plums.*

What to Drink in Prague

'Golden Tiger' beer mat

Czech beers are famous around the world, but nowhere are they drunk with such appreciation as in Prague. The Czechs take their beer *(pivo)* seriously and are very proud of it. Pilsner and its various relations originate in Bohemia. It is generally agreed that the best Pilsners are produced close to Pilsen – and all the top producers are not far from Prague. Beers can be bought in cans, in bottles, and best of all, on draught. Canned beer is made mostly for export, and no connoisseur would ever drink it. The Czech Republic also produces considerable quantities of wine, both red and white, mainly in Southern Moravia. Little of it is bottled for export. Mineral water can be found in most restaurants; Mattoni and Dobrá voda (meaning good water) are the two most widely available brands.

Gambrinus, legendary King of Beer, and trademark of a popular brand of Pilsner

Traditional copper brew-kettles in Plzeň

PILSNER AND BUDWEISER

The best-known Czech beer is Pilsner Urquell. Clear and golden, with a strong flavour of hops, Pilsner is made by the lager method: bottom-fermented and slowly matured at low temperatures. The word "Pilsner" (now a generic term for similar lagers brewed all over the world) is derived from Plzeň (in German, Pilsen), a town 80 km (50 miles) southwest of Prague, where this type of beer was first made in 1842. The brewery that developed the beer still makes Plzeňské pivo as well as the slightly stronger Plzeňský prazdroj (original source), better known as Pilsner Urquell. A slightly sweeter beer, Budweiser Budvar is brewed 150 km (100 miles) south of Prague in the town of České Budějovice (in German, Budweis). The American Budweiser's first brewer adopted the name after a visit to Bohemia in the 19th century.

Budweiser logo

Pilsner Urquell logo

This higher percentage refers to the original gravity, not the alcohol content

Světlé means light

Alcohol content

Reading a Beer Label

The most prominent figure on the label (usually 10% or 12%) does not refer to the alcohol content. It is a Czech measure of original gravity, indicating the density of malt and other sugars used in the brew. The percentage of alcohol by volume is usually given in smaller type. The label also states whether it is a dark or a light beer.

BEER AND BEER HALLS

Staropramen

Gambrinus

Velkopopovický kozel

Budweiser Budvar

Plzeňský prazdroj (Pilsner Urquell)

The real place to enjoy Czech beer is a pub or beer hall *(pivnice)*. Each pub is supplied by a single brewery *(pivovar)*, so only one brand of beer is available, but several different types are on offer. The major brands include Plzeňské and Gambrinus from Plzeň, Staropramen from Prague, and Velkopopovické from Velké Popovice, south of Prague. The usual drink is draught light beer *(světlé)*, but a number of beer halls, including U Fleků *(see p155)* and U Kalicha *(see p154)* also serve special strong dark lagers (ask for *tmavé*). Another type you may encounter is *kozel*, a strong light beer like a German *bock*.

A half litre of beer (just under a pint) is called a *velké* (large), and a third of a litre (larger than a half pint) is called a *malé* (small). The waiters bring beers and snacks to your table and mark everything you eat and drink on a tab. In some pubs there is a tacit assumption that all the customers want to go on drinking until closing time, so don't be surprised if more beers arrive without your ordering them. If you don't want them, just say no. The bill is totted up when you leave.

People enjoying a drink in one of Prague's beer gardens

WINES

Czech wine producers have not yet emulated the success of other East European wine-makers. The main wine-growing region is in Moravia, where most of the best wine is produced for local consumption. Some wine is also made in Bohemia, around Mělník, just north of Prague. The whites are made mostly from Riesling, Müller-Thurgau or Veltliner grapes (*polosuché* is demi-sec and *suché* is sec). Rulandské (Pinot) is an acceptable dry white. The reds are slightly better, the main choices being Frankovka and Vavřinecké. In the autumn, a semi-fermented young, sweet white wine called *burčák* is sold and drunk across the capital.

Rulandské, white and red

CZECH SPIRITS AND LIQUEURS

In every restaurant and pub you'll find Becherovka, a bitter-sweet, amber herbal drink served both as an aperitif and a liqueur. It can also be diluted with tonic. Other local drinks include Borovička, a juniper-flavoured spirit, and plum brandy or Slivovice. The latter is clear and strong and rather an acquired taste. Imported spirits and cocktails are more expensive.

Becherovka

Choosing a Restaurant

These restaurants have been selected across a wide price range for their good value or exceptional cuisine; they are listed area by area, starting with Old Town and moving on to restaurants further outside the city. The entries appear alphabetically within each price category, and any special features are indicated by the symbols.

PRICE CATEGORIES
These have been calculated to represent the cost of an average three-course meal for one, including half a bottle of wine, and all unavoidable charges.
Ⓚ Under Kč250
ⓀⓀ Kč250–450
ⓀⓀⓀ Kč450–650
ⓀⓀⓀⓀ Over Kč650.

OLD TOWN

Bohemia Bagel

Masná 2, Praha 1 **Tel** *22 48 12 560* **Map** *3 C3*

The best breakfast deal in Prague is available until late in the morning at this always-busy bagel shop and café. High-speed Internet is also provided at reasonable rates throughout the day. It's become so popular that a second Bohemia Bagel has opened across the Vltava at Újezd 16. Others are to follow.

Beas

Týnská 19, Praha 1 **Tel** *77 71 65 478* **Map** *3 C3*

Spartan, cheap and tremendously popular vegetarian curry house. Food is served on rather utilitarian trays, yet it is good, hotter than the Prague norm, and comes with free water to alleviate the effect of the spices. As cheap as they come, this place attracts rich, poor and anyone who likes real Indian food.

Country Life

Melantrichova 15, Praha 1 **Tel** *22 42 13 366* **Map** *3 B4*

This is part of the international group of vegetarian restaurants, but few others anywhere in the world can compete with its sublimely picturesque setting. It gets crowded at lunchtimes with vegetarians and non-vegetarians alike, all hungry to try their excellent pizzas, salads, soups and desserts.

Dahab

Dlouhá 33, Praha 1 **Tel** *22 48 73 375* **Map** *3 C3*

Right in the heart of the Old Town, Dahab is perhaps the only place in Prague where you can puff on a genuine *hookah* pipe after your meal. The combination of tearoom, patisserie, café and restaurant works well, and it has a nice selection of Middle Eastern dishes, including several vegetarian options.

Klub Architekt

Betlémské nám 5A, Praha 1 **Tel** *22 44 01 214* **Map** *3 B4*

This hidden jewel is tucked away in a warren of tunnels and arches, reached through a discreet courtyard close to the Bethlehem Chapel. The servings are hearty, and, unusual for an inexpensive Prague dining room. The menu includes a good, varied vegetarian selection.

Patriot X

V Celnici 3, Praha 1 **Tel** *22 42 35 158* **Map** *4 D3*

This is a Czech restaurant, café and bar which, quite distinctively, takes a Scandinavian "less is more" approach to decor, yet keeps the portions traditionally ample. The café is upstairs, while the restaurant and bar are downstairs. It has a terrace with great views of the Old Town.

Restaurace Století

Karolíny Světlé 21, Praha 1 **Tel** *22 22 20 008* **Map** *3 A4*

Arched ceilings, sepia prints and old china all evoke a gentler era in this quiet, intimate restaurant. The menu is inspired by the famous of yesteryear; for example, you can order a Marlene Dietrich (stuffed avocado with whipped Roquefort and marzipan) or an Al Capone (roast chicken leg with hot salsa and papaya).

Chez Marcel

Haštalská 12, Praha 1 **Tel** *22 23 15 676* **Map** *3 C2*

Chez Marcel is a touch of real France in the centre of Prague. This is where business people and students alike come for regional *plats du jour*, as well as steak *au poivre*, fresh mussels and probably the best French fries in the city. Surprisingly for such a good establishment, the food is reasonably priced.

Don Giovanni

Karolíny Světlé 34, Praha 1 **Tel** *22 22 22 060* **Map** *3 A4*

This, the first upscale Italian restaurant in Prague to open after 1989, was named after the opera which Mozart debuted a few blocks away in the National Opera House. Besides excellent contemporary Italian dishes, the seafood selection includes lobster and crab, fresh from the in-house aquarium.

James Joyce

Liliová 10, Praha 1 **Tel** *22 42 48 793* **Map** *3 B4*

The James Joyce was the first Irish pub in Prague, and it's still just about the best, catering mainly to expats, not stag parties. Home to hearty meals, including enormous Irish breakfasts, "door-stopper" sandwiches and the best Irish stew in Prague. The staff is friendlier than at most other Irish pubs in town.

Kinski Palace

Týnská 3, Praha 1 **Tel** *22 48 10 750* **Map** *3 C3*

Fine cellar restaurant in the Kinski Palace, one of Prague's finest buildings. The upmarket Czech food, wine and immaculate service are all in keeping with the surroundings. Prices, when you consider the quality of the food, are of remarkably good value, though not cheap.

La Provence

Štupartská 9, Praha 1 **Tel** *25 75 35 050* **Map** *3 C3*

It's well worth taking the trip down the winding staircase from the lively Banana Bar to this reasonably priced French provincial restaurant. The menu includes the usual countryside game favourites such as rabbit, pheasant and duck (in season), while the cluttered, original, rustic decor has a charm of its own.

Red, Hot and Blues

Jakubská 12, Praha 1 **Tel** *22 23 23 364* **Map** *3 C3*

Located in what were the royal stables some 500 years ago, this place is renowned for good, hometown New Orleans and Creole cooking; chilli, chowder, burgers with all the trimmings, and *étouffé*. There's live jazz or blues on most nights, and it's popular with a trendy crowd. A real Bohemian hangout.

Reykjavik

Karlova 20, Praha 1 **Tel** *22 22 21 218* **Map** *3 A4*

This is an Icelandic restaurant serving dependably good seafood favourites such as *frutti di mare*, shrimp cocktails and Icelandic salmon – in this case grilled *á la Norvegienne*. The service is unobtrusively efficient and it's a pleasantly cosy nook on a cold winter's day. During the summer there is alfresco dining.

Bellevue

Smetanovo nábřeží 2, Praha 1 **Tel** *22 22 14 49* **Map** *3 A5*

Situated by the river, Bellevue has a stunning view of the castle. The interior is an Art Deco triumph, all inlaid wood walls and marble floors. The menu includes Antipodean delicacies such as *carpaccio* with New Zealand lamb, which is yet to be seen on any other menu in Prague.

Kamenný Most

Smetanovo nábř. 195, Praha 1 **Tel** *22 40 97 100* **Map** *3 A4*

The menu here, at what is probably Prague's most adventurous Czech restaurant, will have even the most seasoned and jaded foodie in rapture. To complement the excellent cuisine there is an equally adventurous winelist, and the terrace – with its superb view of the Charles Bridge – is a jewel.

Le Saint-Jacques

Jakubská 4, Praha 1 **Tel** *22 23 22 685* **Map** *3 C3*

Le Saint-Jacques is managed by a French proprietor who is as attentive as his cuisine is sumptuous. Try any fish dish from the constantly evolving menu. A pianist and violinist gently serenade patrons every night, making this one of the city's top romantic locations.

Mlýnec

Novotného lávka 9, Praha 1 **Tel** *22 10 82 208* **Map** *3 A4*

Chef Marek Purkart was the first man in the Czech Republic to receive the Michelin Bibendum twice, so expect only the best food and the highest prices here. Crispy roasted duck with red and white cabbage and Karlovy Vary dumplings are recommended. Traditional Czech food – but with a twist.

Opera Grill

Karolíny Světlé 35, Praha 1 **Tel** *22 22 20 518* **Map** *3 A4*

There are only seven tables here, which gives it the feel of a private dining room. It also means it's a good idea to book ahead. The menu features excellent international dishes, such as lamb, pasta and steak, as they are all superbly cooked and presented. The desserts are to die for.

Pravda

Pařížská 17, Praha 1 **Tel** *22 23 26 203* **Map** *3 B2*

A wonderful blend of old and new encompassing elegant gilt-and-white dining rooms and waiters in chic uniforms, Pravda will tempt the diner with its Asian- and Scandinavian-inspired fare. This includes relatively expensive seafood dishes such as Cajun crawfish and poached cod. The desserts are excellent.

Seven Angels

Jilská 20, Praha 1 **Tel** *22 42 34 381* **Map** *3 B4*

There has been a restaurant on this spot since the 13th century, but whatever the changes of management have been since then, Seven Angels remains one of the most charming, small dining rooms in Central Europe. The house specialty is traditional Bohemian cuisine, with a particular focus on game.

U Modré Růže (The Blue Rose)

Rytířská 16, Praha 1 **Tel** *22 42 25 873* **Map** *3 B4*

There's something for everyone on the Czech and international menu of this upscale but very much underground restaurant, with beef, lamb, game, seafood and vegetarian dishes all vying for space. The setting is certainly unique, in beautifully restored 15th-century catacombs.

JEWISH QUARTER

Orange Moon

Rámová 5, Praha 3 **Tel** *22 23 25 119* **Map** *3 C2*

Immensely popular since its opening, Orange Moon bucks the local propensity for toning down traditionally spicy food by having its dishes listed with a one-, two- or three-red pepper rating – that's spicy, very spicy or burning. Rest assured there are also a number of dishes with a "no pepper" rating.

U Sádlů

Klimentská 2, Praha 1 **Tel** *22 48 13 874* **Map** *4 D2*

The rather kitsch aspects of this medieval-themed restaurant are achieved with much aplomb. Every dish has a thematic name, including several under the heading "Meat from an Apocalyptic Piglet!" Cheerful staff, and a lively crowd most evenings make this a good choice for small groups of friends.

Barock

Pařížská 24, Praha 1 **Tel** *22 23 29 221* **Map** *3 B2*

An eclectic and excellent range of Thai and Japanese cuisine is served by efficient staff in this perennially fashionable restaurant. But it's not merely a trendy venue; the food really is authentic, and more than up to international standards. Popularity means you should reserve a table to be sure of getting in.

Dinitz

Bílkova 12, Praha 1 **Tel** *22 23 13 308* **Map** *3 B2*

Café, bar and casual bistro-influenced restaurant in the Jewish Quarter, owned by Israelis yet not serving kosher food. Instead you'll find a good mix of light meals, desserts and snacks in an easy going atmosphere. Very popular with trendy shoppers taking a break from pounding the streets of nearby Pařížska.

Les Moules

Pařížska 19, Praha 1 **Tel** *22 23 15 022* **Map** *3 B2*

Czechs claim otherwise, but the best beer in Prague is served here, and it's Belgian, not Bohemian. What really brings in the crowds though are the pots of tasty, steaming fresh mussels, flown in daily from Belgium. Other treats on the menu include young tender racks of lamb cooked in beer.

King Solomon

Široká 8, Praha 1 **Tel** *22 48 18 782* **Map** *3 B3*

The light, pleasant interior of the King Solomon, in the heart of the Jewish Quarter, extends to its winter garden. The food is impeccably prepared and presented, complemented by kosher wines from the Czech Republic and beyond. They also deliver special Shabbat meals to hotels throughout Prague.

La Bodeguita del Medio

Kaprova 5, Praha 1 **Tel** *22 48 13 922* **Map** *3 B3*

Papa Hemingway stares down at diners enjoying seafood and Creole delights at this eclectic place. Once dinner is over in the downstairs restaurant, you can then head upstairs to enjoy original and classic cocktails and a great selection of Havana cigars until the early hours.

PRAGUE CASTLE AND HRADČANY

Palffy Palace Restaurant

Valdštejnská 14, Praha 1 **Tel** *25 75 30 522* **Map** *2 E2*

Enter at Valdštenjská 14, then climb the stone staircase to this wonderfully alternative restaurant, in what feels like an aristocrat's private rooms. Soft melodies seep through the walls from a musical academy on the premises, providing the perfect accompaniment to a regularly changing menu.

Peklo (Hell)

Strahovské nádvoří 1, Praha 1 **Tel** *22 05 16 652* **Map** *1 B4*

Peklo is near the Strahov Monastery, which belongs to the order of the Premonstratensians. They've been keeping wine in the cellars here since the 14th century. The restaurant offers fine Czech and international cuisine and, as you may expect, a fabulous array of wines.

Key to Price Guide *see p202* **Key to Symbols** *see back cover flap*

LITTLE QUARTER

Hungarian Grotto

Tomášská 12, Praha 1 **Tel** *25 75 32 344* **Map** *2 E3*

The land of Tokay, Bull's Blood, goulash and paprika has inspired this reasonably priced, romantically rustic cellar restaurant with a pleasant outdoor courtyard. To add to the atmosphere, the premises are supposedly haunted by a cuckolded baker from the 17th century.

Cantina

Újezd 38, Praha 1 **Tel** *25 73 17 173* **Map** *2 E5*

Everything is super-sized here, from the enormous margaritas to the massive portions of good value Tex-Mex food. All the usual favourites are on the menu, including super *burritos* and authentic tacos. The usual Czech problem of "not spicy enough" persists, ask for extra spices if you like hot food.

Mount Steak

Josefská 1, Praha 1 **Tel** *25 75 32 652* **Map** *2 E3*

Very much a place for meat-lovers only, this restaurant offers over 60 different steaks, including boar, venison, kangaroo, shark and ostrich. All are cooked as you wish, either roasted on the bone or grilled, and served with hearty portions of potatoes and vegetables. Good side salads too.

Nebozízek (Little Auger)

Petřínské sady 411, Praha 1 **Tel** *25 73 15 329* **Map** *2 D5*

During spring and summer, the outdoor patio at this renowned restaurant half-way up the Petřín funicular is very popular, offering wonderful views of Old and New Town. Inside, it is cosy and elegant. The menu is diverse, with seafood, Chinese and Czech dishes, steaks and more.

Bazaar

Nerudova 40, Praha 1 **Tel** *25 75 35 050* **Map** *2 D3*

This is a sprawling complex of bars and dining rooms, serving slightly overpriced but always enjoyable Mediterranean food against a lavishly eccentric decor. The upper terrace, however, affords diners one of the best views of central Prague and fills up quickly in spring and summer. Reservations needed.

David

Tržiště 21, Praha 1 **Tel** *25 75 33 109* **Map** *2 E3*

It's a steep incline up a cobblestone lane to David, but gourmets will find it worth the exertion. The set lunch is a serious two to three hour affair, with an interesting selection of Czech, European and New World wines on offer with which to wash down the supreme and intense flavours.

Kampa Park

Na Kampě 8b, Praha 1 **Tel** *25 75 32 685* **Map** *2 F4*

The most famous contemporary restaurant in Prague, Kampa Park has been playing host to the great and good. If you want to impress someone, then this is the place to come, if you can get a reservation. The fusion cuisine is mildly adventurous and always good.

Square

Malostranské nám. 5/28, Praha 1 **Tel** *25 75 32 109* **Map** *2 E3*

There has been a hostelry on this site since 1874, though today Square is as contemporary as restaurants come. It serves inventive Italian and Mediterranean cuisine to Prague's jetset. Check out the daily specials – always good value – on the chalkboard as you make your way inside.

U Malířů (At the Painter's)

Maltézské náměstí 11, Praha 1 **Tel** *25 75 30 318* **Map** *2 E4*

There has been a restaurant on this spot since 1543. Even back then, U Malířů received high praise: King Rudolf II's foodtasters gave it three Royal stars. Today you can expect equally high quality, traditional and contemporary French cuisine in superb, sumptious surroundings still fit for a king.

U Tři Pštrosů (At the Three Ostriches)

Dražického náměstí 12, Praha 1 **Tel** *25 75 32 410* **Map** *2 E3*

The dining room of At The Three Ostriches is somewhat reminiscent of a Bavarian hunting lodge, but the cuisine is 100 per cent bona-fide Czech. Adventurous diners may wish to try their ostrich specialities of goulash and *roulade* "Prague style", while there are simpler but equally good dishes for the less brave.

Valdštejnská Hospoda (Waldstein Inn)

Valdštejnské náměstí 7, Praha 1 **Tel** *25 75 31 759* **Map** *2 E3*

The Waldstein Inn, as it sounds, was once a typical local pub, but renovations and redecorations have exposed the original features of this 15th-century building, such as painted ceilings and stonework. The menu of Czech favourites has an emphasis on game. There is a good hotel above *(see p191)*.

NEW TOWN

Fish & Chips

Rytířská 19, Praha 1 **Tel** *22 42 26 105* **Map** *3 C4*

Reasonably authentic though not brilliant, British Fish & Chips comes to Prague to cater primarily for the marauding English stag parties who eschew sophisticated cuisine. Locals appear to have taken to it too, judging by the long queues at weekends. Cod, plaice and rock salmon available.

Buffalo Bill's

Vodičkova 9, Praha 1 **Tel** *22 49 48 624* **Map** *5 C1*

Quite the sensation when it opened 10 years ago, Buffalo Bill's Wild West-memorabilia covered cellar still draws locals, expat and tourists alike with its great mixture of Tex-Mex dishes and its wide range of ribs and wings from the American grill. Definitely child-friendly, with some of the best waiting staff in town.

Café Imperial

Na Poříčí 15, Praha 1 **Tel** *22 23 16 012* **Map** *4 D3*

This high-ceilinged café is laden with original Art Deco tilework. This is affordable elegance, however, with light breakfasts, lunches, suppers and snacks all served in the atmosphere of a traditional Continental coffeehouse. Staff are polite and formal, though the place can get a little smoky.

Hotel Evropa Café

Václavské náměstí 25, Praha 1 **Tel** *22 42 28 117* **Map** *3 C5*

The café that remains perenially popular is an Art Nouveau classic, even if it is now slightly shabby around the edges. Still a favourite with the Prague literati, it simply oozes character, and the small terrace is one of the city's most popular. The food is distinctly average, but that is not why people come here.

Jáma

V jámě 7, Praha 1 **Tel** *22 42 22 383* **Map** *5 C1*

Popular lunchtime spot serving great burgers – probably the city's best – and *burritos* to office workers and tourists alike. The evenings are very lively, when this becomes one of the city's top drinking spots, and getting a table can be difficult without a reservation. There's a small terrace at the rear.

Radost FX Café

Bělehradská 120, Praha 1 **Tel** *22 42 54 776* **Map** *6 E2*

Good vegetarian food is a rarity in Prague, but the food is so good that many non-vegetarians come here for business and working lunches. Beyond the restaurant is a bar serving lethal absinthe cocktails and an art gallery. Downstairs is Prague's most upmarket disco, home to extravagant theme parties.

U Fleků

Křemencova 11, Praha 1 **Tel** *22 49 34 019* **Map** *5 B1*

This cavernous and often raucous brewery and restaurant with its many rooms and lounges is thought to have been founded in 1499, though nobody seems to know for sure. What's certain is that there's been an onsite brewery since the early 1900s, and the food is good, reliable upmarket Czech pub fare.

U Pinkasů

Jungmannovo nám. 16, Praha 1 **Tel** *22 11 11 150* **Map** *3 C5*

This has been a cheap and great value Czech beer hall since 1843. The food is simple but hearty, making this a very popular lunchtime destination. There are three levels: a traditional beerhouse in the basement, a bar area for light meals and snacks on the ground floor, and a more formal dining room upstairs.

Beograd

Vodičkova 5, Praha 1 **Tel** *22 49 46 063* **Map** *5 C1*

For years there was a Serb restaurant on this patch, and though the latest incarnation is pure Czech, the owners have kept the old name out of respect for the past. Somewhat more upmarket than the average Czech hostelry, prices are somewhat higher than the norm. The food is good, however, with game featured on the menu.

Café Restaurant Louvre

Národní třída 20, Praha 1 **Tel** *22 49 30 912* **Map** *3 B5*

An excellent place for a late and lazy breakfast on the terrace, Louvre has been in business since the early 1900s. A full restaurant menu of Czech and European cuisine, they also have an excellent selection of cakes, pastries and coffees. There's a smart billiards room on the premises.

Casablanca

Na Příkopě 10, Praha 1 **Tel** *24 21 05 19* **Map** *3 C4*

This is an authentic halal Moroccan restaurant within the classy Savarin Palace hotel. The adventurous Mediterranean- and African-influenced cuisine is served by charming staff. The best and most authentic selection of *kefta*, *harira*, *couscous* and *pastilla* in Prague.

Key to Price Guide *see p202* **Key to Symbols** *see back cover flap*

Cicala

Žitná 43, Praha 1 **Tel** *22 22 10 375* **Map** *6 D5*

Owned and run by a friendly Italian chap who knows no English and little Czech, this place is a truly great Italian restaurant. Admire photos on the walls of famous diners as you enjoy fine food just as mamma used to make. The *zuppa di cozze* is about the best in Prague. The actual restaurant is downstairs.

Marie Teresie

Na Příkopě 23, Praha 1 **Tel** *22 42 29 869* **Map** *3 C4*

A fluorescently lit shopping arcade is left behind on entering this spacious cellar restaurant, named after an Austrian Habsburg princess, who spent a great deal of time in these parts. The fare is traditional Czech, served with a silver service flourish. You can feel like royalty for very little money.

U Kalicha (At the Chalice)

Na bojišti 12–14, Praha 1 **Tel** *29 61 89 600* **Map** *6 D2*

The look of this restaurant, including its cartooned walls, is based on the famous Czech novel *The Good Soldier Švejk*. Author Jaroslav Hašek was a frequent visitor and set some of his novel's pivotal scenes here. Traditional Czech cuisine is available at prices aimed more at Western tourist budgets.

U Korbele

V celnici 7 (Renaissance Prague Hotel), Praha 1 **Tel** *22 18 22 433* **Map** *4 E3*

Heaps of traditional wood panelling, decorative Moravian plates and surprisingly affordable prices make this restaurant in the Renaissance hotel a great choice for genuine Czech food. Seasonal specialities come and go, refreshing the menu every couple of months. Every Czech beer imaginable is also on the menu.

El Gaucho

Václavské náměstí 11 – Kenvelo Centre, Praha 1 **Tel** *22 16 29 410* **Map** *3 C5*

Step downstairs from a mini mall (devoted to just one fashion house and its offspring) and into a surprisingly genuine Argentine restaurant. Huge, juicy steaks are cooked on an authentic "asado" grill, waiters are dressed as gauchos, and there is a good selection of South American wines.

La Perle de Prague

Rašín Building, Rašínovo nábřeží 80, Praha 1 **Tel** *22 19 84 160* **Map** *5 A2*

Situated on the seventh floor of the Rašín Building (also known as the Dancing House), with views of the Vltava and Prague Castle, this is a reasonably priced, upscale French restaurant. The wine menu is quite extensive and the knowledgeable staff can help you choose. There's a well-stocked cocktail bar too.

FURTHER AFIELD

Ambiente

Mánesova 59, Praha 3 **Tel** *22 27 27 851* **Map** *6 E1*

This eclectic restaurant, which features everything from American Southwestern to Italian cuisine, is renowned for its salads, and probably serves the best Caesar salad in Prague. A second Ambiente, at Na Příkopě 22 (inside the Slovanský Dům shopping centre) serves the same mix of dishes.

Koliba Praha

Gregorova 8, Praha 11 **Tel** *27 29 41 340*

The open-plan cooking and dining area of this panoramic restaurant, up in the hills above Prague, fills up most evenings during the summer as genuine gypsy musicians lead the locals and tourists alike in a sing-song. Simple, but very good steak and fish dishes bolster what is otherwise standard Czech cuisine.

Krásná Řeka

Anglická 6, Praha 3 **Tel** *22 42 18 154* **Map** *6 E2*

Open for what seems an eternity, this is still the best Chinese restaurant in Prague, although with small portions, you may decide to order an additional main course. Everything is good and authentic, with dishes ranging from tofu to duck. There is a refreshingly large variety of vegetarian options as well.

Taj Mahal

Škrétova 10, Praha 3 **Tel** *22 42 25 566* **Map** *6 E1*

On a small street behind the National Museum, this Indian restaurant is popular with Prague's expat community. The menu is quite extensive, and its Oriental decor and sitar player add to the exotic atmosphere. Food is authentic though it may not be as hot as you are used to. Ask for extra spices if you feel the need.

U Marčanů

Veleslavínská 14, Praha 6 **Tel** *23 53 60 623*

Folk music, dancing and singing every night make this a favourite of visitors to Prague. A taxi-ride from the city centre, it is a pleasant villa in a residential area serving real Czech food to diners seated at long tables, enjoying huge portions and even bigger glasses of beer. Good times guaranteed. You will need to make a reservation.

Pubs, Beer Halls and Bars

Prague suits practically everyone's taste, from sophisticated cocktail bars to traditional Czech cellar pubs. A new breed of pub, the themed Irish, English or sports bar caters to the large number of young English men who travel to Prague on so-called stag weekends. The real charm of drinking in Prague is that it's possible to stroll around the Old Town and find places to drink and fraternize with Czechs and expatriates alike, regardless of the time. If you sit at an empty table, don't be surprised if others join you. In traditional Czech pubs a waiter will automatically bring more beer as soon as you appear close to finishing, unless you indicate otherwise. It pays to expect the unexpected in Prague – in some supposedly upmarket places, the waiters' attitude can be surly and unhelpful, while in the humblest pub you may find service to be efficient and courteous.

TRADITIONAL PUBS AND BEER HALLS

Traditionally, Czech pubs either serve food or are large beer halls dedicated to the mass consumption of beer. The words *hostinec* and *hospoda* used to indicate a pub with food, whereas a *pivnice* served only beer, but over time the distinctions have faded.

Recommended for the brave, **U Zlatého tygra** (The Golden Tiger) is a loud Czech literati pub, wall-to-wall with, mostly male, regulars. (This is where the Czech president, Vaclav Havel took Bill Clinton to show him local beer culture.) **U Fleků** has brewed its unique beer, Flekovské, since 1499. For authenticity, and Budvar, try **U Medvídků** which is not far away from the National Theatre *(see pp156–7)* and the Old Town Square. The traditional *hospoda* scarcely comes more so than **U Pinkasů**, hidden behind Wenceslas Square in a quaint courtyard. **Pivovarský dům** brews its own beer, and is a slightly more up-market take on the usual Czech pub.

COCKTAIL BARS

Prague now has almost more cocktail bars than you could shake a swizzle stick at, but there are some that stand out. On Pařížská, Prague's Fifth Avenue, you'll find **Bugsy's**. This bar has even printed their own cocktail bible, though towards the end of the week it does become somewhat overtaken by burly men in long coats. That fate has yet to befall the neighbouring **Barock**, a cocktail bar and restaurant with a noticeably chic clientele. Nearby **Tretters** combines smart looks with a slightly more down-to-earth attitude.

IRISH PUBS AND THEME BARS

Prague now has theme bars in all shapes and sizes, with still the most common being the ubiquitous Irish pub. **Caffreys** is one of Prague's most popular – and pricier – Irish bars, located off the Old Town Square. **Rocky O'Reilly's** is the biggest Irish pub in town, and a rowdy place, packed to the rafters if there is a big football match on the television. The **James Joyce** is but a stone's throw away from Charles Bridge, and is probably Prague's most upmarket Irish pub. Its neighbour is possibly the only Irish-Cuban hybrid pub anywhere, the noisy and fun **O'Che's**.

There are Cuban dancers at the **Tendr Club**, while **La Casa Blu** is a South American bar which is frequently home to a carnival-type atmosphere. **Prace** is another world away; homage is paid to the good old, bad old days of Stalin and communism, festooned with relics from that bygone era.

BOHEMIAN HANGOUTS

Not only in the geographical heart of Bohemia, these bars also represent the unconventional side of Prague city-life. **Chapeau** is one of the most famous, not to say notorious, drinking dens in the Old Town, host to a parade of visitors and locals. The large, red velvet drinking emporium that is the **Marquis de Sade** also epitomizes that spirit, built as it is in a 19th-century brothel. Over the Vltava in the Castle district you'll find **U Malého Glena** which translates roughly to Glen's house, and is one of the longest surviving expatriate bars in the city. Not far away is **Jo's Bar & Garáž**, which has also stood the test of time as an expat hangout. It's a small, cavernous pub, Mexican eatery and disco, and becomes quickly packed. Over in Žižkov is the large converted cinema and cultural centre **Akropylis**, home to an ever-changing programme of live music and DJs.

SPORTS BARS

Sports bars have taken off in Prague, with places like **Legends**, a long, polished cellar bar with a deck of TV screens. **Jágr's Sports Bar** is also for sports enthusiasts, owned as it is by Czech ice hockey hero Jaromír Jágr.

CAFÉ SOCIETY

The city is embedded in café society, ranging from old-fashioned smoky joints to cafés within bookstores, boutiques and billiard halls. Some are restaurants, others focus on drinking, but all serve alcohol. **Lávka** has the finest setting in the city. Situated at the foot of the Charles Bridge, it offers a great view of the castle. Other places to see and be seen are **Ebel** in the Old Town and **Slavia**, by the river opposite the National Theatre. For a perfect meeting place, try the **Grand Café Praha** opposite the clock tower in Old Town Square. **Globe** café and bookstore is a legend amongst Prague's expat community and serves the best cappuccino.

DIRECTORY

TRADITIONAL PUBS AND BEER HALLS

Lávka
Novotného lávka 1.
Map 3 A4.
Tel *222 222 156.*
www.lavka.cz

The Beer House
PIVOVARSKÝ DŮM
Lípová 15.
Map 5 C2.
Tel *296 216 666.*
www.gastroinfo.cz

Tribolit
Palackého 15.
Map 3 C5.
Tel *224 946 065.*

The Black Bull
U ČERNÉHO VOLA
Loretánské nám 1.
Map 1 B3.
Tel *220 513 481.*

The Golden Tiger
U ZLATÉHO TYGRA
Husova 17.
Map 3 B4.
Tel *222 221 111.*

The Shot Out Eye
U VYSTŘELENÝHO OKA
U Božích bojovníků 3.
Tel *222 540 465.*

U Fleků
Křemencova 11.
Map 5 B1.
Tel *224 934 019.*
www.ufleku.cz

U Kalicha
Na Bojišti 12–14.
Map 6 D3.
Tel *296 189 600.*
www.ukalicha.cz

U Medvídků
Na Perštýně 7.
Map 3 B5.
Tel *224 211 916.*

U Pinkasů
Jungmannovo náměstí 15/16.
Map 3 C5.
Tel *221 111 150.*
www.upinkasu.cz

COCKTAIL BARS

Alcohol Bar
Dušní 6.
Map 3 B2.
Tel *224 811 744.*
www.alcoholbar.cz

Bar Bar
Všehrdova 17.
Map 2 E5.
Tel *257 312 246.*
www.bar-bar.cz

Barock
Pařížská 24.
Map 3 B2.
Tel *22 32 92 21*

Bond's
Polska 7, Praha 2.
Tel *222 733 871.*
www.jamesbondcafe.cz

Bugsy's
Pařížská 10.
Map 3 B2.
Tel *224 810 287.*
www.bugsybar.cz

Tretters
Kolkovně 3.
Map 3 C5.
Tel *24 81 11 65.*
www.tretters.cz

Ultramarin
Ostrovní 32.
Map 3 B5.
Tel *224 932 249.*
www.ultramarin.cz

Zanzibar
Lázeňská 6. **Map** 2 E4.
Tel *602 780 076.*
www.monin.cz

IRISH PUBS AND THEME BARS

Caffreys
Staroměstské nám. 10.
Map 3 B3.
Tel *24 82 80 31.*
www.caffreys.cz

George & Dragon
Staroměstské nám. 11.
Map 3 B3.
Tel *222 326 137.*
www.jamesjoyce.cz

James Joyce
Liliová 10.
Map 3 B4.
Tel *224 248 793.*
www.jamesjoyce.cz

J.J. Murphy's
Tržiště 4. **Map** 2 E3.
Tel *257 535 575.*
www.jjmurphys.cz

La Casa Blu
Kozí 15.
Map 3 C2.
Tel *24 81 82 70.*
www.lacasablu.cz

Molly Malone's
U Obecního dvora 4.
Map 4 D3.
Tel *24 81 88 51.*
www.mollymalones.cz

O'Che's
Liliová 14. **Map** 3 C3.
Tel *222 221 178.*
www.oches.cz

Rocky O'Reilly's
Štěpánská 32.
Map 3 A5.
Tel *22 23 10 60.*
www.rockyoreillys.cz

Tendr Club
Pařížská 6.
Map 3 B2.
Tel *24 81 36 05.*

Work
PRÁCE
Kamenická 9.
Tel *220 571 232.*

BOHEMIAN HANGOUTS

Chateau
Jakubská 2.
Map 3 C3.
Tel *222 316 328.*
www.chateau-bar.cz

Confessions
U Milosrdných 4.
Map 3 B2.

Duende
Karolíny Světlé 30.
Map 3 A4.
Tel *604 269 731.*
www.duende.cz

Jet Set
Radlická 1, Prague 5.
Tel *257 327 251.*

Jo's Bar & Garáž
Malostranské nám 7.
Map 2 E3.
Tel *57 53 33 42.*

Marquis de Sade
Templová 8.
Map 3 C3.
Tel *224 817 505.*

Merlin
Bělehradská 68A.
Map 6 E2.
Tel *222 522 054.*

Mu Café
Mánesova 87.
Map 6 F1.

U Malého Glena
Karmelitská 23.
Map 2 E4.
Tel *257 535 150.*
www.malyglen.cz

SPORTS BARS

Jágr's
Václavské nám. 56 - Palác Blaník. **Map** 3 C5.
Tel *224 032 481.*
www.jagrsportbar.cz

Legends
Týn 1.
Map 3 C3.
Tel *224 895 432.*
www.legends.cz

Sportbar Sparta ve Slavii
Smetanovo nábř. 1012/2.
Map 3 A5.
Tel *224 218 493.*
www.spartabar.cz

Zlata Hvezda
Ve smečkách 12.
Map 6 D1.
Tel *296 222 292.*
www.sportbar.cz

CAFÉ SOCIETY

Café Imperial
Na Poříčí 15.
Map 4 D3.
Tel *222 316 012.*
www.hotelimperial.cz

Ebel
Řetězova 9.
Map 3 B4.
Tel *222 222 018.*
www.ebelcoffee.cz

Globe
Pštrossova 6.
Map 5 A1.
Tel *224 934 203.*
www.globebookstore.cz

Grand Café Praha
Staroměstské nám. 22.
Map 3 B3.
Tel *221 632 602.*

Hotel Evropa Café
Václavské náměstí 25.
Map 3 C5.
Tel *224 228 117.*

Slavia
Smetanovo nábř 2.
Map 3 A5.
Tel *224 220 957.*

Nightlife

Nightlife in Prague is now as lively as in other European cities. A constant stream of visitors and a spirited local crowd has seen to that. Cheap drink, cutting-edge performers, liberal gambling and prostitution laws all help pull in the crowds. Prague is also now firmly established as a tour-stop for major American and UK pop and rock acts, with arenas such as the T-Mobile and Sazka playing host to big names at least once a month.

On a more local level, Prague's club scene is a proven testing ground for up-and-coming bands, and the dance/music events, heavily influenced by that of nearby Berlin, is renowned for being experimental. Prague's gay and lesbian scene is buzzing, and the local population, despite its deep catholic roots, is among the most tolerant in mainland Europe. For similar reasons, Prague is also now well known for its adult venues.

DISCOS AND NIGHTCLUBS

The biggest club in the city is the **Lucerna Bar**, which offers a varied programme – either live local bands or a DJ playing classic hits – in an unusual basement ballroom in the beautiful, but run down, Lucerna building. It fills up quickly however, so make sure you get there early. **Karlovy Lazne** is another large club, which sometimes has live bands. **Zlatý Strom** offers techno/house together with 1970s, 80s and 90s dance tunes until 5am in a spectacular medieval cellar setting.

The trendier clubs, more likely to be playing cutting-edge music, include **Celnice** and **Radost FX**, where the city's most affluent are attracted by a constant diet of house music and plush decor, together with **Guru** and **Obvodní Kulturní dům Vltavská**. The **Double Trouble** is popular with visiting stag parties, which means it can get quite rowdy. For genuinely experimental and original hardcore house and techno music, the best place to go is **Roxy**, where sets are often accompanied by art house video projections. Roxy regularly hosts live rock bands, including a number of big named bands.

If it is cabaret you are after, try **Tingl Tangl**, a club well known for its lively transvestite shows.

ROCK AND POP CLUBS

Lovers of live rock music are well served in Prague. One school of thought feels that the anarchic influence of Prague's pioneering 1980s rock bands helped – however inadvertently – bring down the communist regime. There are today a large number of popular rock venues – generally small clubs and cafés – which host a variety of different groups. The indigenous scene continues to thrive – Prague's own rock bands play both their own compositions as well as cover versions of more famous numbers, many singing in English. Higher-profile, more internationally renowned Western bands play in Prague regularly, usually at the **T-Mobile Arena** or the new **Sazka Arena** *(see p223)*.

The **Rock Café** and the **UZI Rock Bar**, both very popular venues, offer regular concerts followed by discos. Other venues include the **Futurum Rock Club**, open till the early hours. The Lucerna Bar and Roxy also hosts regular bands.

JAZZ

The roots of jazz in Prague can be traced not only to the American tradition but also to the pre-war heyday of Prague's famous jazz players, such as Jaroslav Ježek. Even during the communist period, Prague was an internationally renowned centre of jazz, never failing to attract the biggest names. Dizzy Gillespie, Stan Getz, Duke Ellington and Buddy Rich all played in Prague during the 1960s and 1970s.

Today, Prague's many jazz clubs play all forms, from Dixieland to swing. One of the leading and most popular jazz venues in the city is the **Jazz Club Reduta**, which has daily jazz concerts at around 9pm. When former US President Bill Clinton asked his Czech counterpart Vaclav Havel if he could play some jazz during a state visit to Prague in January 1994, the Czech president took him to the Jazz Club Reduta. The popular **Metropolitan Jazz Club** holds late-night concerts until 3 or 4am. At the **AghaRTA Jazz Centrum**, you can hear a high standard of playing while eating in its café. **U Malého Glena** has regular live blues, jazz and funk, while **Por Favore** is a new venue dedicated to more traditional jazz. For serious enthusiasts, the International Jazz Festival *(see p52)* during October attracts talent from all over the world. For a more bluesy experience, head to **Ungelt Jazz & Blues Club** or **Red Hot & Blues**.

GAY AND LESBIAN VENUES

With even mainstream clubs such as **Radost FX** and **Mecca** holding regular gay nights, it is no wonder that Prague is considered Europe's hottest gay destination. The scene is liberal and diverse. Clubs are split into various categories, with **Alcatraz** a popular, hardcore leather and rubber venue, specialising in special events and theme parties. **Drake's Club** is a less in-your-face venue, and popular with visitors, while the city's most famous gay venue, **Friends**, has recently re-opened in a new venue after the previous location was ruined in the 2002 floods. As Prague's best gay cocktail bar, Friends has a steady following among expat and local men who are less interested in cruising than in just having a drink with like-minded folks. **Pinocchio**, a gay centre, features a bar, disco, sex shop and hotel on the same premises.

The website www.prague.gayguide.net is a valuable resource for all things gay in Prague, including gay-friendly hotels, guesthouses and groups and associations.

ADULT PRAGUE

Like it or not, Prague has seen itself become the sex tourism capital of Europe since 1989, a result of cheap beer and the mistaken assumption that prostitution in the Czech Republic is legal. The law is, in fact, deliberately opaque, though the country's liberal ministers are keen to remove all doubt from the law and fully legalise the practice. For the time being, the emphasis remains on tolerance, and visitors are free to indulge themselves at any number of what are known as "Relax Clubs". Some are more respectable than others, and many are tourist traps which should be avoided.

DIRECTORY

DISCOS AND NIGHTCLUBS

Celnice
V Celnici 4. **Map** 4 D3.
Tel *224 212 240.*
www.celnice.com

Double Trouble
Melantrichova 17.
Map 3 B4.
Tel *221 632 414.*
www.doubletrouble.cz

Guru
Rokycanova 29, Prague 3.
Tel *222 783 463.*
www.guruclub.cz/cz

Karlovy Lazne
Novotného lávka.
Map 3 A4.
Tel *222 220 502.*
www.karlovylazne.cz

La Fabrique
Uhelný trh 2. **Map** 3 B4.
Tel *224 233 137.*
www.lafabrique.cz

Lucerna Bar
Vodičkova 36.
Map 3 C5
Tel *224 217 108.*
www.musicbar.cz

Obvodní Kulturní dům Vltavská
Bubenská 1.
Tel *220 879 683.*
www.vltavska.cz

Radost FX
Bělehradská 120.
Map 6 E2.
Tel *603 181 500.*
www.radostfx.cz

Tingl Tangl
Karolíny Světlé 12.
Map 3 A5.
Tel *224 238 278.*
www.tingltangl.cz

Ujezd
Újezd 18. **Map** 2 E5.
Tel *257 316 537.*

XT3
Pod plynojemem 5, Prague 8.
Tel *284 825 826.*
www.xt3.cz

Zlatý Strom
Karlova 6.
Map 3 A4.
Tel *222 220 441.*
www.zlatystrom.cz

ROCK AND POP CLUBS

Futurum Music Bar
Zborovská 7, Prague 5.
Map 2 F5.
Tel *257 328 571.*
www.musicbar.cz

Klub Lávka
Novotného lávka 1.
Map 3 A4.
Tel *222 222 156.*
www.lavka.cz

Meloun
Michalská 12.
Map 3 B4.
Tel *224 230 127.*
www.meloun.cz

Rock Café
Národní 20.
Map 3 B5.
Tel *224 933 947.*
www.rockcafe.cz

Roxy
Dlouhá 33. **Map** 3 C3.
Tel *224 826 296.*
www.roxy.cz

T-Mobile Arena
See p223.

UZI Rock Bar
Legerova 44.
Map 6 D3.
Tel *777 637 989.*
www.demon.barr.cz/uzi

JAZZ CLUBS

AghaRTA Jazz Club
Zelezna 16.
Map 3 C4.
Tel *222 211 275.*
www.agharta.cz

Jazz Club Reduta
Narodni 20.
Map 3 B5
Tel *224 933 487.*
www.redutajazzclub.cz

Metropolitan Jazz Club
Jungmannova 14.
Map 3 C5.
Tel *224 947 777.*

Por Favore
Tomasska 14.
Map 2 E3.
Tel *257 535 220.*
www.porfavore.cz

Red Hot & Blues
Jakubská 12.
Map 3 C3.
Tel *222 323 364.*

U Malého Glena
Karmelitská 23.
Map 2 E4.
Tel *257 531 717.*
www.malyglen.cz

U Stare Pani
Michalska 9.
Map 3 B4.
Tel *603 551 680.*
www.jazzinprague.com

Ungelt Jazz & Blues Club
Týnská 2. **Map** 3 C3.
Tel *224 895 748.*
www.jazzblues.cz

GAY AND LESBIAN VENUES

Alcatraz
Bořivojova 58, Prague 3.
Tel *222 711 458.*
www.run.to/alcatraz

Drake's Club
Zborovská 50, Praha 5.
Map 2 F5
Tel *257 326 828.*

Friends
Bartoleméjska 11.
Map 3 B5.
Tel *224 236 772.*
www.friends-prague.cz

Gejzeer
Vinohradská 40.
Map 6 F1.
Tel *222 516 036.*
www.gejzeer.cz

Pinocchio
Seifertova 3, Praha 3.
Tel *222 710 773.*
www.volny.cz/pinocchio

Termix
Třebízského 4a
Tel *222 710 462.*
www.club-termix.cz

SHOPPING IN PRAGUE

With its wide, pedestrianised streets, classy shopping malls, souvenir shops and antiques *bazars*, Prague is now established as one of Europe's leading shopping destinations. Almost all of the major US and West European retailers have estalished outlets in the city, and since 1989's Velvet Revolution, the quality of goods manufactured in the Czech Republic – always good – has improved considerably. Most of Prague's best shopping areas are in the centre of the city, and you can spend a whole day just diving in and out of small speciality shops and large department stores. For a different shopping experience, the few traditional markets in the city offer everything from vegetables to fresh fruit and to imported Russian caviar, toys, clothes, furniture, Czech crafts, electrical spare parts and even second-hand cars. Larger out-of-town malls are now also springing up, and are proving to be very popular.

Bohemian crystal

OPENING HOURS

Most of Prague's shops open from 9am to 6pm Monday to Saturday, although supermarkets are open till late. However, shops are often more flexible than that, as many rely almost entirely on tourists for their trade. The more expensive gift shops have adapted their opening hours to the needs of their Western customers and tourists, often opening at 10am and closing much later in the evening. Many also open on Sundays as well.

Food stores open earlier, most of them at 7am – reflecting the early working day of many locals – and close at around 7pm. A few shops also take a break for lunch, which can vary from any time between noon and 2pm. Department stores and the big shopping centres and malls also open early but tend to close later, often around 10pm. Some open on Sundays.

All the shops are at their most crowded on Saturdays and for stress-free shopping it's often better to wander around them during the week. Prague's markets are generally open early every weekday morning but have varied closing times.

One of the many antique shops in Bridge Street in the Little Quarter

HOW TO PAY

Most staple goods, such as food, are cheaper than comparable items in the West, as long as they do not need to be imported. However, with more and more multinationals, such as Boss and Pierre Cardin, moving into the city, prices are slowly starting to rise.

The total price of goods should always include Value Added Tax (this is 19 per cent of the total price, depending on what is being sold), although all food is exempt from this. Cash payments can usually only be made in Czech crowns, though some shops now take Euros, albeit at extortionate exchange rates. Smaller shops appreciate it if you pay the exact amount and at times may refuse to accept banknotes above Kč1,000. All major credit and charge cards are widely accepted, except American Express *(see p230)*.

Global Refund is a programme for non-EU residents that allows tax-free shopping for purchases exceeding Kč2,000. When you make a purchase at a shop displaying the Global Refund sign, ask at the cash till for a tax-free cheque. On leaving the country, show your items, receipts and cheques to customs officials, who will stamp the cheques, and you will get your VAT back. For more details, go to the Global Refund website (www.globalrefund.com).

A set of Russian dolls available from one of the many street shops

SALES AND BARGAINS

Following the examples of the Western stores, sales are becoming more popular. As a result, it is now quite normal for clothes to be sold off cheaper at the end of each season. There is also an increasing number of post-Christmas sales in the shops found around Old Town Square, Wenceslas Square, Na Příkopě and 28. října.

If you want vegetables, fruit, meat or other perishable produce, buy them at the beginning of the day, when the best quality goods are still on sale. There is no point in waiting till the end of the day in the hope of getting bargains, as is the case in Western shops that reduce prices to get rid of perishable items.

WHERE TO SHOP

Most of Prague's best shops are conveniently located in the city centre, especially in and around Wenceslas Square, though the souvenir shops lining Nerudova on the way up to the castle are also well worth your time. Many of these shopping areas have been pedestrianized, making for leisurely window-shopping, although they can get rather crowded. There are a number of department stores which sell an eclectic range of Czech and Western items, with more opening all the time. The best-known department store, **Kotva** (The Anchor), lies in the centre of the city. It was built in 1975 and its four storeys offer a wide range of Western goods, particularly fashion and electronics, with the bonus of an underground car park. But compared to Western department stores, Kotva has a smaller selection of goods than you may be accustomed to – with the exception of food such as smoked meats, for example. Prices for some of the more luxurious items on sale, such as perfumes, can often be equivalent to the Western ones.

Another popular store is **Tesco**. This has a good selection of Czech and Western products in a bland 1970s building in the centre of town. The city's oldest department store is **Bílá Labuť** (The White Swan) in Na Poříčí. It was opened shortly before the occupation of Czechoslovakia in 1939 and was the first building in Prague to have an escalator. It has since been refurbished, and now specializes in furniture and interior accessories. **Debenhams**, another famous name from Western Europe, recently opened an enormous store on Wenceslas Square, and its home furnishings department on the third floor is very popular with locals. **Detsky dům**, on Na Příkopé, is a department store dedicated exclusively to children.

The outskirts of Prague are now home to massive shopping parks, with large hypermarkets. Tesco has a huge branch at Zličín (at the end of metro line B), next to the equally enormous **IKEA**.

A second-hand bookshop in Karlova Street

DIRECTORY

DEPARTMENT STORES

Bílá Labuť
Na Poříčí 23.
Map 4 E3.
Tel *224 811 364.*

Debenhams
Václavské nám. 21.
Map 4 D5.
Tel *221 015 022.*

Dům módy
Václavské nám. 58.
Map 6 D1.
Tel *224 217 005.*

Kotva
Nám. Republiky 8.
Map 4 D3.
Tel *224 801 111.*

Marks & Spencer
Na Příkopě 19/21.
Map 3 C4.
Tel *224 235 735.*

Tesco
Národní 26.
Map 3 B5.
Tel *224 227 971.*

MARKETS AND MALLS

Prague city centre is not blessed with a great market for most of the year, though the Christmas Gift Market in Old Town Square is well worth visiting. The city's major central market, **Havel**, sells mainly fresh produce. A better option for something surprising is **Holešivice** in the north of the city (take the metro to Vltavska). The best of Prague's flea markets, however, is **Bustehrad Collectors Market**, a glorified car-boot sale close to Lidice.

Western-style shopping malls are now a common sight in Prague. The centre of the city is home to **Slovansky dům** *(see p217)* and **Cerna ruže**, while further afield **Flora Palace** *(see p217)* and the **Vinohradský Pavilion** *(see p217)* provide a genuinely Western European retail-therapy experience. Flora Palace is probably the better of the two, offering three levels of stores and direct access from Flora metro station. There is also a large mall at Zličín, the **Metropole Mall**.

What to Buy in Prague

The massive selection of goods available in Prague's shops means that everyday items, such as food, books, camera film and toiletries are ubiquitous. Prague's more traditional products, such as Bohemian crystal, china, wooden toys and antiques, make great souvenirs, and there are still some real bargains to be picked up, though you will need to shop around. Increasingly popular are the more unusual goods which are sold by many of Prague's street shops. These include Soviet army medals, Red Army uniforms, Russian dolls, wooden puppets, ceramics and a wide selection of jewellery.

GLASS AND CHINA

Bohemian glass and china have always been ranked among the finest in the world. From huge, decorative vases to delicate glass figurines, the vast selection of glass and china items for sale is daunting. Crystal, glass and china can be quite different depending on where they are made. Lead crystal ranges in lead content from 14 to 24 per cent, for example. Always make sure you are fully aware of what you are buying.

Some of the best glass and china in Bohemia is produced at the Moser glassworks at Karlovy Vary and sold at the **Karlovy Vary China** shop and **Moser**. The large Crystalex glassworks at Nový Bor and Poděbrady produce some of the most highly-decorated glass, sold at **Crystal**.

Other shops which sell a good selection of glass and china include **Bohemia Art Crystal, Dana-Bohemia** and two outlets called **Glass**. **Artel** is a store selling mouth-blown glassware – designed by Karen Feldman – while **Arzenal** is another popular shop, with glass from the Czech's leading designer, Boris Šipek, whose collections are found in institutions ranging from MOMO in New York to the Design Museum in London. Billing itself as a cross-culture junction, there is a Thai restaurant on-site too.

However, prices for certain goods, especially classically designed vases, decanters and bowls are starting to reflect the increasing popularity of Bohemian crystal. The days when such goods could be purchased in Prague for half the Western European price are over. Yet, value for money remains high, and you can still pick up bargains if you shop around carefully. Remember that many of the modern pieces are just as lovely and much cheaper.

Bohemian porcelain, while not as celebrated as Bohemian crystal, also makes an excellent gift or souvenir. **Cesky Porcelan**, the country's most famous factory, is in the town of Teplice, an hour's drive towards the German border from Prague, and its factory shop offers wonderful bargains. Other names worth looking out for include **Royal Dux Bohemia**, **Haas & Czjzek**, **A. Ruckl & Sons** and **Toner**.

Because of the fragile nature of the goods, many shops will pack anything you buy there. But if you go for a more expensive piece, it is worth looking into insurance before you leave Prague.

ANTIQUE SHOPS

Given its history as a major city in the Hapsburg empire, Prague is a great place to hunt for antiques. Hidden treasures seemingly lurk around every corner, and prices are still generally lower than in the West. Most of the city's shopping districts have a large number of antique shops: Old Town is full of them, as is the Royal Route from the castle. Look out for Bohemian furniture, glass and porcelain, as well as military and Soviet memorabilia.

Antique shops that are well worth exploring include **Dorotheum** and **Starožitnosti**. **Antique Clocks** sells exactly what it says and **Military Antiques** is a haven for all army fanatics. For goods over Kč1,000, check with the shop whether you will need a licence to export them. You should watch out for an increasing number of fakes which are now appearing in the market.

Prague also has several *bazar* shops which stock a range of items at cheaper prices. Items are often unusual and good bargains can be found. **Bazar B & P** is a small, popular shop full of second-hand goods. For furniture bargains **Bazar nábytku** is well worth a visit.

TRADITIONAL CRAFTS

The traditional manufacture of high-quality, hand-crafted goods still survives. The variety of the merchandise available in the shops – hand-woven carpets, wooden toys, table mats, beautifully-painted Easter eggs, baskets, figurines in folk costumes and ceramics – are all based on Czech and Moravian folk crafts and then enriched with modern elements. You can buy them from many market stalls as well as a fair number of shops.

Czech Traditional Handicrafts offers a huge choice of hand-carved decorative items. Other arts and crafts shops include **Pottery Keramika Tupesy**. You should also look out for a new chain of shops called **Manufaktura** (Handmade), which sells goods made only in the Czech Republic. A number of street vendors around Old Town Square also sell a range of handmade items including jewellery and puppets. Czech wooden items are also of the highest quality (*see* Speciality Shops, *pp216–17*).

BOOKS

There are numerous bookshops in Prague, reflecting its literary heritage, and many sell English-language books. Indeed,

Prague is now a popular centre for young American novelists. One of the main bookshops is **U Černé Matky Boží**. Here, you'll find a range of English-language books (including Czech works which have been translated into English) as well as a fair number of German and French editions. Another well-stocked outlet is the **Big Ben Bookshop**. Maps and guides to Prague in English can be bought at **Academia**. Other specialist bookshops include **Palác knih, Kanzelberger, Arbes Bookshop** and **Fišer's Bookshop**.

Prague also has second-hand bookshops – look in Golden Lane and Karlova Street – which stock some English-language books, and they all offer the visiting bibliophile hours of enjoyable browsing. **Antikvariát Meissner** is one of the best and has a vast selection. The legendary **Globe** café and bookstore is a good place to find second-hand English books and enjoy the city's best cappuccino since 1993, when the shop opened in a poorer part of the capital by five entrepreneurial Americans. Now relocated to the city centre, the Globe hosts regular literary events, and art exhibitions, as does the newer **Shakespeare & Sons**, out in Zhizkov, which is attempting to repeat the success of the Globe. The owner of **Anagram**, in Týn, claims to be able to order any book you want.

DIRECTORY

GLASS AND CHINA

Artel
Vinohradská 164.
Map 6 F1.
Tel *271 732 161.*
www.artelglass.com

Arzenal
Valentinská 11.
Map 3 B3.
Tel *224 814 099.*
www.arzenal.cz

Bohemia Art Crystal
ČESKÝ KŘIŠTÁL
Zelena 14.
Tel *224 227 118.*
One of several branches.

Cesky Porcelan
Tovarni 17.
417 01 Dubi.
Tel *417 518 111*
www.cesky.porcelan.cz

Crystal
Karlova 5. **Map** 3 A4.
Tel *222 220 064.*
One of several branches.

Dana-Bohemia
GLASS, CHINA, CRYSTAL
Národní 43. **Map** 3 A5.
Tel *224 214 655.*
One of several branches.

Dum Porcelanu
Jugoslavska 16.
Tel *221 505 320.*

Glass
SKLO
Malé náměstí 6.
Map 3 B4.
Tel *224 229 221.*
Staroměstské náměstí 26–27.
Map 3 C3.
Tel *224 229 755.*

Karlovy Vary China
KARLOVARSKÝ PORCELÁN
Pařížská 2.
Map 3 B2.
Tel *224 811 023.*

Moser
Na příkopě 12.
Map 3 C4.
Tel *224 828 822.*
www.moser-glass.com

ANTIQUE SHOPS

Antique Clocks
STAROŽITNOSTI UHLÍŘ
Mikulandská 8.
Map 3 B5.
Tel *224 930 572.*

Antique Kaprova
Kaprova 12.
Map 3 B3.

A.D. Starožitnosti
Skořepka 8, Prague 1.
Map 3 B4.
Tel *224 234 696.*

Bazar B & P
Nekázanka 17.
Map 4 D4.
Tel *224 210 550.*

Bazar nábytku
Libenský ostrov.
Tel *266 311 278.*

Dorotheum
Ovocný trh 2.
Map 3 C4.
Tel *224 222 001.*
www.dorotheum.cz

Military Antiques
Charvátova 11.
Map 3 C5.
Tel *296 240 088.*
One of several branches.

Starožitnosti
Náměstí Kinských 7.
Tel *257 311 245.*
www.antique-shop.cz

GIFTS AND SOUVENIRS

Czech Traditional Handicrafts
Karlova 26.
Map 3 A4.
Tel *221 111 064.*
Melantrichova 17.
Map 3 B4.
Tel *222 220 433.*

Handmade
MANUFAKTURA
Melantrichova 17.
Map 3 B4.
www.manufaktura.biz
One of several branches.

Pottery Keramika Tupesy
Truhlářská 9.
Map 4 D3.
Tel *222 311 156.*

BOOKS

Anagram
Týn 4.
Map 3 C3.
Tel *224 895 737.*
www.anagram.cz

Antikvariát Meissner
Karlova 2.
Map 3 A4.
Tel *222 220 286.*

Arbes Bookshop
ARBESOVO KNIHKUPECTVÍ
Štefánikova 26.
Prague 5.
Tel *257 329 171.*

Big Ben Bookshop
Malá Štupartská 5.
Map 3 C3.
Tel *224 826 565.*

Fišer's Bookshop
FIŠEROVO KNIHKUPECTVÍ
Kaprova 10.
Map 3 B3.
Tel *222 320 733.*

Franz Kafka Bookshop
Staroměstské nám. 11-12.
Map 3 B3.

Globe
Pštrossova 6.
Map 5 A1.
Tel *224 934 203.*
www.globebookstore.cz

Kanzelberger
Václavské náměstí 4.
Map 4 D5.
Tel *224 219 214.*

Knihkupectoí Academia
Václavské náměstí 34.
Map 4 D5.
Tel *224 223 511.*

Palác knih
Václavské náměstí 41.
Map 4 D5.
Tel *224 216 201.*

Shakespeare & Sons
Krymska 10, Prague 2.
Tel *271 740 839.*
www.shakes.cz

U Černé Matky Boží
Celetná 34.
Map 4 D5.
Tel *224 211 155.*

Markets, Malls and Speciality Shops

Take your pick – super-modern mall or traditional market. Prague has them both, although do remember that Prague's main market is at some distance from the city centre at Holešovice. Malls are springing up everywhere in the city, and Prague has made a name for itself as a leading place to find all sorts of odd bits and pieces in any number of speciality stores. From Faberge eggs to Jewish *yarmulkas*, you'll find it in Prague.

MARKETS

Prague's markets offer a vast range of goods in a very friendly atmosphere where bargaining is all part of the fun. The largest market in the city, **Prague Market**, is in Holešovice. It was converted from a former slaughter-house. The market now sells fresh fruit and vegetables, all kinds of poultry as well as fish, textiles, flowers, electronics and even second-hand cars and vehicle parts. These are all sold in several large halls and in outdoor stalls. The market is generally open from Monday to Friday, 6am to 5pm.

In Havelská, right in the centre of the city, is the small **Havel Market**, which mainly sells fruit and vegetables. Other well-known markets in Prague include the **Smíchov Market** and a small one on the street V kotcích. Remember that some of the goods sold at all these markets, especially clothes and shoes, can be of very poor quality. Nevertheless, they are an excellent place to hunt for a bargain.

You will also enjoy foraging through the junk, antiques, furniture and military memorabilia (none of which comes with a promise of a refund or guarantee) at the out-of-town **Bustehrad Collectors Market**, allegedly the third-largest market of its kind in Europe. You can get there by public transport, taking a bus from Dejvická metro station. The market is only open on the second and fourth Saturday of the month, from 8am to noon.

Old Town Square plays host to an excellent and very popular Christmas Gift Market from the end of November to the middle of January. Besides the stalls selling gifts and toys, there are others selling hot wine and sausages, and there is also a small children's play area. The Square also hosts the city's Christmas tree (which fell down in 2003 causing great damage) and a number of open-air winter concerts.

MALLS

There is an increasing number of Western-style shopping malls in Prague, which are more popular and often much better than the old department stores, offering better value and a greater range of high-quality goods. **Vinohradský Pavilion** has been re-opened as a shopping mall, following extensive modernisation, as has **Koruna Palace**. In the very centre of the town, on Na příkopé, the upmarket **Slovansky dům** is home to a great number of chic boutiques, jewellery stores, the fabulous Kogo restaurant and a multiplex cinema, while **Myslbek**, across the road, is a deceptively large shopping centre with a better range of shops that are more accessible to the average pocket. Other shopping arcades include the enormous **Flora Palace** (Palác Flora: take the metro to Flora), which is home to hundreds of shops, and the slightly smaller **Novy Smichov** (metro Andel) home to Carrefour and more.

Just outside Prague, at the Zličín terminus of the metro line B, is **Metropole**, Prague's biggest mall. It offers hundreds of stores, including a huge C&A, the biggest Kenvelo in Prague and a special children's area. There is also a ten-screen cinema, **Cinema City** *(see p221)*.

STREET STALLS

Street stalls and wandering vendors are not officially allowed to operate in most areas of Prague, though a number of vendors are permitted to sell souvenirs around Charles Bridge. Street stalls are allowed near the entrance to the Old Jewish Cemetery in the Jewish Quarter, and they also line the Old Castle Steps from Malostranská metro station up to the castle's eastern gate.

As most of these sellers are well vetted, the goods on sale tend to be reasonably good quality, though you are unlikely to find any real bargains, and much of what is on sale can be bought cheaper in souvenir stores. At the Old Town's largest outdoor market, **Havelská tržnice**, stalls are crowded with produce as well as handicrafts and textiles, on sale Monday through Friday.

SPECIALITY SHOPS

Bohemia and Moravia have long been known for their fine wooden toys. You will find a number of shops selling them throughout the city, especially in Old Town, but beware cheap imports. You can be sure of the genuine article at **Hracky** in Little Quarter, Beruška in New Town and **Sparky's House of Toys**, just off Na Příkopě, a veritable treasure trove for children of all ages. Older children might also like **Games & Puzzles** on Jungmannova, which specializes in all sorts of mind teasers, including exquisite hand-made wooden labyrinths.

If you are looking for something a little quirky, but very Czech, try **Dr. Stuart's Botanicus** on Old Town Square, which sells all-natural and all-Czech health and beauty products, from soap to massage oil. Another popular store is **Qubus**, which sells anything and everything, as long as it is the height of modern design.

Most of the weird and wonderful things on sale

were designed by young Czechs. There are a number of other weird and wonderful stores in Prague. The **Spanish Synagogue Gift Shop** sells torah pointers, *yarmulkas*, watches and other Jewish gifts. **Le Patio** on Pařížská is a shop specializing in original illuminations and candelabra, as well as top-quality restored furniture imported from India, and tables and chairs made by some outstanding Czech blacksmiths. Another favourite for design fans is **de.fakto**, an upmarket version of IKEA, in the centre of the city. More practical perhaps for souvenir hunters is **Philharmonia**, a music store on Pařížská stocking every great work in the Czech musical lexicon. Yet, the prize for most bizarre shop in Prague must go to **American Heating**, a store specializing in the restoration of historic stoves.

FOOD AND DELICATESSENS

Prague's supermarkets are well stocked with the basic foodstuffs. **Delicacies-lahůdky** is a small shop with meat and fish counters. A specialist food shop, selling smoked sausage, cheeses and other local delicacies, is **Jan Paukert**. For freshly baked bread visit the bakers around Wenceslas Square and Karmelitská Street. **Paneria** shops sell a good selection of patisseries and sandwiches.

For the best selection of local and international delicacies, however, try the **Fruit de France** store on Jindřišska, just off Wenceslas Square. Fine French and Czech foods and ingredients make it popular with the city's better chefs. You can meet them here if you arrive early enough in the day.

DIRECTORY

MARKETS AND MALLS

Bustehrad Collectors Market
Bustehrad.

Flora Palace
PALÁC FLORA
Vinohradska 151.
Map 6 F1.

Havel Market
Havelske náměsti.
Map 3 C4.

Havelská tržnice
Havelský trh.
Map 3 C3.

Koruna Palace
Václavské náměsti 1.
Map 3 C5.
Tel *224 219 526.*

Metropole Mall
Zličín.
Tel *800 876 076.*
www.metropole.cz

Myslbek
Na příkopě.
Map 3 C4
Tel *224 239 550.*

Novy Smichov
Plzenská 8.
Tel *257 284 111.*

Prague Market
Bubenské nábřeži 306.
Praha 7.
Tel *220 800 945.*

Slovansky dům
Bubenské nábřeži 306.
Praha 7.
Tel *220 800 945.*

Smíchov Market
Náměsti 14, rijna 15.
Map 3 C4.
Tel *257 321 101.*

Vinohradský Pavilion
Vinohradská 50.
Map 6 F1.
Tel *222 097 111.*

SPECIALITY SHOPS

American Heating
Jansky vrsek 2.
Map 2 D3.
Tel *257 531 378.*

Beruška
Vodičkova 30.
Map 3 C5.
Tel *221 014 607.*
www.beruska-praha.cz

de.fakto
Perlová 6.
Map 3 B4.
Tel *224 218 326.*
www.defakto.cz

Dr. Stuart's Botanicus
Týnská 3.
Map 3 C3.
Tel *224 895 446.*
One of several outlets around the city.

Games & Puzzles
Jungmannova 8.
Map 3 C5.
Tel *224 009 500.*

Hracky Traditional Toys
Pohořelec 24.
Map 1 B3.
Tel *603 515 745.*

Le Patio
Pařížská 20.
Map 3 B3.
Tel *222 320 260.*
www.patium.com

Philharmonia
Pařížská 13.
Map 3 B3.

Qubus
Rámova 3.
Map 3 C2.
Tel *222 313 151.*
www.qubus.cz

Spanish Synagogue Gift Shop
Věžeňská 1.
Map 3 B2.

Sparky's House of Toys
Havirska 2.
Map 3 C4.
Tel *224 930 257.*
www.sparkys.cz

FOOD AND DELICATESSENS

Bakeshop
Kozi 1.
Map 3 C2.
Tel *222 320 195.*

Delicacies-lahůdky
ZLATÝ KŘÍŽ
Jungmannova 34.
Map 3 C5.
Tel *221 191 801.*

Fruit de France
Jindřišska 9.
Map 4 D4.
Tel *224 220 304.*
www.fdf.cz

Jan Paukert
Národní 17.
Map 3 B5.
Tel *224 214 968.*

Paneria Pekarstvi
Valentinská 10/20.
Map 3 B3.
Tel *224 827 912.*
www.paneria.cz

PHARMACIES

It is not usual for pharmacies to have individual names, so look out for ***Léky*** *(drugs) or* ***Lékárna*** *(pharmacy).*

Belgická 37.
Map 6 E2.
Tel *224 593 396.*

Národní 35.
Map 3 B5.
Tel *224 230 086.*

Vaclavske náměsti 64.
Map 3 C5.
Tel *222 211 423.*

Lékárna u Anděla
Stefanikova 6,
Prague 5.
Tel *257 320 918.*
Open 24 hours.

ENTERTAINMENT IN PRAGUE

Since the Velvet Revolution in 1989, Prague's range of entertainment has become increasingly varied. Whether you prefer opera to jazz or mini-golf to a football match, the city has plenty to offer. Movie buffs can choose from many of the latest Hollywood blockbusters, a lot of them in English with subtitles. For the adventurous, mime and fringe theatre are both thriving. Prague has a superb musical tradition, which includes symphony orchestras, opera, musicals, jazz and folk music. Concerts are performed throughout the year, in venues which range from Baroque palaces to public parks and gardens. Even if you don't speak Czech, you can still enjoy the city's cultural offerings. Some plays can be seen in English, and for many types of entertainment, music, dance and sport, a knowledge of the language isn't necessary at all.

Street musicians entertaining the crowds

PRACTICAL INFORMATION

The best place to look for information about what's on and where in Prague, is in the English-language newspaper *The Prague Post (see p235)*. This provides details of the best entertainment and cultural events which will be of interest to an English-speaking audience. Those events that are in English or have translation facilities are marked. Other sources of information are the leaflets and City Guides given out at the ticket agencies in the city, such as **Ticketpro** or **PIS** *(see p226)*, as well as the many weekly alternative newspapers. These are generally printed in Czech, English and German. You can also use the free booklet *Přebled*, printed in English and available from any PIS office. For a comprehensive rundown of events, buy *Culture in Prague*, a detailed monthly publication listing information on a variety of local exhibitions, concerts and theatre.

A performance of *Cosí Fan Tutte* at the Mozart Festival

BOOKING TICKETS

Tickets can be bought in advance from the box office at most venues. You can also book tickets in advance by writing to, or ringing, the venue. Remember that many of the city's box offices may not have any English speakers available. Tickets for the opera or for the National Theatre can also be booked online; visit www. opera.cz or www. narodni-divadlo.cz respectively. The more popular events tend to become heavily booked up in advance by tour groups – particularly during the summer – and by season-ticket holders. However, standby tickets are usually available about an hour before the show. If this isn't practical and you want to

PUPPET THEATRE

Puppetry has a long tradition in Prague and is still strongly represented. The most famous puppet show in the city is held at the **Spejbl and Hurvínek Theatre** *(see p221)*. The show revolves around Daddy Spejbl and his reprobate son Hurvínek. Other puppet theatres include the **National Marionette Theatre** *(see p221)*, which uses all-string marionettes featured in regular performances for children at weekends. The **Theatre in the Old Town** *(see p221)* and the **Puppet Empire** *(see p221)* also put on puppet shows occasionally. Check listings *(see p226)*.

Theatre puppets

be sure of a ticket on a particular day, it is better to buy them at a booking agency. The drawback to using agencies, however, is that commission on these tickets can be high, sometimes doubling the original price. Your hotel receptionist may also be able to get you tickets.

TICKET PRICES

Ticket prices are very cheap compared to Western prices, except for certain performances, most notably during the Prague Spring Music Festival *(see p50)*. Prices range from around Kč100 for a small fringe production or puppet theatre to up to Kč1,500 for a performance by an internationally famous orchestra. Paying by credit card is rarely acceptable.

TICKET TOUTS

There has been a recent spate of counterfeit tickets on sale, especially for the larger rock concerts. To be safe, always buy your tickets at reputable agencies or at the venue itself.

LATE-NIGHT TRANSPORT

Prague's metro *(see p242)* stops running shortly after midnight, while the normal bus and tram service ends around 11:30pm. Then the city's extensive night bus and tram service takes over. Timetables are displayed at each stop. Night trams and buses are regular and efficient and it is likely that there will be a tram or bus stop near your hotel. Taxis provide the most certain form of late-night transportation, but beware of unscrupulous drivers trying to overcharge you *(see p245)*.

A view of the Rudolfinum auditorium *(see p223)*

The Neo-Classical Estates Theatre (Stavovské divadlo)

Sparta Stadium *(see p223)*

Try to walk a little way from the theatre before you hail a cab; the fare will probably be a lot cheaper. Ask your hotel before you go out what the best transport options are.

MUSIC FESTIVALS

The most famous music festival of all is the Prague Spring Music Festival, held between May and June. Hundreds of international musicians come to Prague to take part in the celebrations. Other music festivals include the Mozart Festival *(see p51)*, held in the summer, the Prague Autumn Music Festival *(see p52)* and the International Jazz Festival *(see p52)*, that takes place in the autumn.

BOOKING AGENTS

Bohemia Ticket International
Malé Náměstí 13. **Map** 3 B4.
Tel *22 42 27 832.*

Na Příkopě 16. **Map** 4 D4.
Tel & ***Fax*** *22 42 15 031.*
www.ticketsbti.cz

Lucerna
Štěpánská 61. **Map** 5 C1.
Tel *22 42 12 003.*

Pragotur
Staroměstské nám.1. **Map** 3 B3.
Tel *22 17 14 128/130.*
Fax *22 17 14 127.*
www.prague-info.cz

Prague Information Service (PIS)
Staroměstské náměstí 1. **Map** 3 B3.
Tel *12 444.*

Na Příkopě 20. **Map** 4 D4.
Tel *12 444.*
www.pis.cz

Ticketpro
Klimentská 22. **Map** 4 D2.
Tel *296 329 999.*
Fax *234 704 204.*
www.ticketpro.cz

Top Theatre Tickets
Žatecká 1. **Map** 3 B3.
Tel *22 48 19 322.*
Fax *22 48 19 324.*

Týnská Galerie
Staroměstké náměstí 14.
Map 3 B3.
Tel *22 23 14 936.*

The Performing Arts

Prague has always been known for its artistic heritage. Theatre has played an important role in the city's cultural development, and recently the range of entertainment has expanded considerably. Even during the communist period Prague remained a centre of experimental theatre, not least the emergence of Black Light Theatre in the 1960s. Today, this tradition continues, with new theatre groups emerging all the time, ever more experimental. In general, the theatre season runs from September to June. During the summer, open-air performances are given in Prague's gardens and parks. For those who prefer to dance till dawn, relax to the sound of jazz or take in a movie – you will find plenty to entertain you in this city.

ENGLISH-LANGUAGE PERFORMANCES

Many theatres in Prague have started to stage a number of English-language productions, especially in the summer months. Even if the play is not performed in English, many venues have installed simultaneous translation facilities. For details, check the listings *(see p227)*.

MAJOR THEATRES

Prague's first permanent theatre was built in 1738, but the city's theatrical tradition dates from the Baroque and Renaissance periods.

The National Theatre *(see pp156–7)* is Prague's main venue for opera, ballet and plays. The neighbouring New Stage is another important venue. It is also the main stage for the multimedia **Laterna Magika** company, which is one of Prague's best-known theatre groups as well as being at the forefront of European improvisational theatre.

Other major theatres in the city include the "stone theatres." These gained importance during the 19th century and include the **Vinohrady Theatre**, the **Estates Theatre** *(see p65)* – one of the most respected in Prague – and the **Prague Municipal Theatre**, an acting company whose plays appear in turn at the **ABC Theatre**, the **Comedy Theatre** and the **Rokoko Studio of Drama**. The **Kolowrat Theatre** is based in the Kolowrat Palace.

FRINGE THEATRES

These originated during the 1960s and won renown for their fight against the status quo. The groups are still very innovative and largely experimental. They perform in small theatres, and many of Prague's best actors and actresses have developed their skills while working for some of these companies.

Fringe theatres include the **Dramatic Club**, well known for its supporting ensemble; the **Ypsilon Studio**, with one of the finest acting companies in the city; **Theatre Na Fidlovačce**, which stages a mix of musicals and straight drama; the large **Theatre Below Palmovka**, renowned for its mix of classical and modern plays; and the **Theatre in Celetná**. One of Prague's most spectacular theatrical and music venues is **Křižík's Fountain**, at the Exhibition Ground, where classical concerts are held and full orchestras perform to stunning lightshows. The **Semafor Theatre** is the home of the tremendously popular comedian, Jiří Suchý.

PANTOMIME, MIME AND BLACK LIGHT THEATRE

Some of the most popular theatre entertainment in Prague is Black Light Theatre, where black-clad actors move objects against a dark stage without being seen – a stunning visual spectacle, pantomime and mime. None of the three requires any understanding of Czech and all are strongly represented.

Jiří Srnec's Black Light Theatre is one of the major venues for Black Light Theatre performance. Others, including **Ta Fantastika** and **WOW**, are listed in the directory *(see p221)*.

DANCE

In Prague, opera and ballet companies traditionally share the National Theatre, where the Czech Republic's best permanent ballet company is based. The **Prague State Opera** also has a resident ballet ensemble, and has in recent years, been keen to usurp the reputation of the National Theatre company as the city's best, something it came close to achieveing in 2003, when it incorporated the now defunct Prague Chamber Ballet. This new company has since set high standards of innovative dance, and with two such fine companies competing so fiercely, ballet fans are in for a treat in Prague. The tickets for the ballet at both major venues are even lower than for opera performances. You can also watch ballet performances at the **Estates Theatre**.

CINEMAS

Although Prague doesn't show all the latest Hollywood blockbusters, more than 80 per cent of the films shown are recent US productions and a third of them have Czech subtitles. Out-of-town multiplex cinemas are now big business. The largest of these – the **Cinema Cities** at Flora and Zličin – boasts 10 screens.

The listings magazines *(see p227)* show which films are on and in what language. There are still some major cinemas situated around Wenceslas Square, including **Hvězda**, **Lucerna**, **Slovanský Dům** and **Blaník**; others are listed in the directory. The **Bio Konvikt Ponrepo** cinema shows old films.

DIRECTORY

THEATRES

Animato Black Light Theatre
ČERNE DIVADLO ANIMATO
Na příkopě 10.
Map 3 C4.
***Tel** 28 19 32 665.*
www.volny.cz/black.theatre

Dramatic Club
ČINOHERNÍ KLUB
Ve Smečkách 26.
Map 6 D1.
***Tel** 29 62 22 123.*
www.cinoherniklub.cz

Estates Theatre
STAVOVSKE DIVADLO
Ovocný trh. **Map** 3 C3.
***Tel** 22 42 15 001.*
www.narodni-divadlo.cz

Jiří Srnec's Black Theatre
ČERNE DIVADLO JIŘÍHO SRNCE
U Lékárny 597, 15600 Prague 5.
***Tel** 25 79 21 835.*
www.blacktheatresrnec.cz

Kolowrat Theatre
DIVADLO KOLOWRAT (IN ESTATES THEATRE)
Ovocný trh.
Map 3 C3.
***Tel** 22 49 01 448.*
www.narodni-divadlo.cz

Křižík's Fountain
KŘIŽÍKOVA FONTÁNA
Výstaviště, Praha 7.
***Tel** 22 01 03 280/295.*
www.krizikovafontana.cz

Laterna Magika
Národní 4.
Map 3 A5.
***Tel** 224 931 482.*
www.laterna.cz

National Theatre
NÁRODNÍ DIVADLO
Národní 2.
Map 3 A5.
***Tel** 22 49 01 448.*
www.narodni-divadlo.cz

National Marionette Theatre
NÁRODNÍ DIVADLO MARIONET
Žatecká 1.
Map 3 B3.
***Tel** 22 48 19 322.*

Prague Municipal Theatre, ABC Theatre
MĚSTSKÁ DIVADLA PRAŽSKÁ, DIVADLO ABC
Vodičkova 28.
Map 3 C5.
***Tel** 22 42 15 943.*
www.ecn.cz/abc

Prague Municipal Theatre, Comedy Theatre
MĚSTSKÁ DIVADLA PRAŽSKÁ, DIVADLO KOMEDIE
Jungmannova 1.
Map 5 B1.
***Tel** 22 42 22 734.*
www.divadlokomedie.cz

Prague Municipal Theatre, Rokoko Studio of Drama
MĚSTSKÁ DIVADLA PRAŽSKÁ, DIVADLO ROKOKO
Václavské náměstí 38.
Map 4 D5.
***Tel** 22 42 12 837.*
www.rokoko.cz

Puppet Empire
ŘÍSE LOUTEK
Žatecká 1.
Map 3 B3.
***Tel** 22 23 24 562.*
www.riseloutek.cz

Reduta Theatre
DIVADLO REDUTA
Národní 20.
Map 3 B5.
***Tel** 22 49 12 246.*

Semafor Theatre
Divadlo Semafor, Křižíkova 10.
Map 4 F3.
***Tel** 22 18 68 151.*

Spejbl and Hurvínek Theatre
DIVADLO SPEJBLA A HURVÍNKA
Dejvická 38.
***Tel** 233 341 241.*
www.spejbl-hurvinek.cz

Ta Fantastika
Karlova 8. **Map** 3 A4.
***Tel** 22 22 21 366.*
www.tafantastika.cz.

Theatre Below Palmovka
DIVADLO POD PALMOVKOU
Zenklova 34, Praha 8.
***Tel** 283 011 172.*
www.divadlopodpalmovkou.cz.

Theatre in Celetná
DIVADLO V CELETNE
Celetná 17.
Map 3 C3.
***Tel** 22 23 26 843.*

Theatre in the Old Town
DIVADLO V DLOUHÉ
Dlouhá 39.
Map 3 C3.
***Tel** 22 48 26 807.*
www.divadlovdlouhe.cz

Theatre Na Fidlovačce
DIVADLO NA FIDLOVAČCE
Křesomyslova 625.
Map 6 E5.
***Tel** 26 12 15 722.*
www.fidlovacka.cz

Vinohrady Theatre
DIVADLO NA VINOHRADECH
Náměstí Míru 7.
Map 6 F2.
***Tel** 296 550 111.*
www.dnv-praha.cz

Wow
Václavské nám. 43.
Map 3 C5.
***Tel** 77 67 50 000.*
www.wow-show.com.

Ypsilon Studio
STUDIO YPSILON
Spálená 16.
Map 3 B5.
***Tel** 22 49 47 119.*
www.ypsilonka.cz

DANCE

Prague State Opera
STÁTNÍ OPERA PRAHA
Wilsonova 4.
Map 6 E1.
***Tel** 22 42 27 266.*
www.opera.cz

CINEMAS

Bio Konvikt Ponrepo
Bartolomějská 11.
Map 3 B5.
***Tel** 22 42 37 233.*

Blaník
Václavské náměstí 56.
Map 6 D1.
***Tel** 22 40 32 172.*

Budějovická Broadway
Budějovická 1667, Prague 4.
***Tel** 26 13 82 297.*

Cinema City Flóra
Vinohradská 149. Prague 3.
***Tel** 25 57 42 021.*
www.cinemacity.cz

Cinema City Zličín
Řevnická 1. Prague 5.
***Tel** 25 79 50 966.*

Evald
Národní 28.
Map 3 B5.
***Tel** 22 11 05 225.*
www.evald.cinemart.cz

Hvězda
Václavské náměstí 38.
Map 4 D5.
***Tel** 22 42 16 822.*

Kotva
Náměstí Republiky 8.
Map 4 D3.
***Tel** 22 48 11 482.*

Lucerna
Vodičkova 36.
Map 3 C5.
***Tel** 22 42 16 972.*

Multiplex Cinema Nový Smíchov
Plzeňská 8.
***Tel** 25 71 81 212.*

Perštýn
Na Perštýně 6.
Map 3 B3.
***Tel** 22 16 68 432.*

Praha
Václavské náměstí 17.
Map 4 D5.
***Tel** 22 22 45 881.*

Slovanský Dům
Na Příkopě 22.
Map 3 C4.
***Tel** 25 71 81 212.*
www.stercentury.cz

Village Cinemas Anděl
Radlická 1.Praha 5.
***Tel** 25 11 15 111.*
www.villagecinemas.cz

Music and Sport

Prague may not match the vibrancy of Vienna or Budapest, but it certainly can hold its own among Europe's leading cultural destinations. Opera and ballet are well represented, while music is provided by some excellent orchestras. Prices offer good value.

Sports fans are well served too, with top-class ice hockey and Champions League football, both attracting crowds during the season, from September to May.

OPERA

Since Richard Wagner's *The Mastersingers of Nurnburg* officially opened Prague's State Opera House on 5 January 1888, Prague has been a centre of operatic excellence. Today, two highly competitive world-class opera companies give opera top billing on Prague's cultural calendar. And while the low Soviet-era prices of yore are now long gone, top-price seats range from Kč1,000 to 1,200, which makes opera in Prague more accessible than most cities in Europe.

The two major companies, the National and the State, both perform exclusively in their own theatres – the National Opera Company in the **National Theatre** *(see pp156–7)*; the State Opera Company at the **State Opera**. The latter presents a predominantly classical Italian repertoire, always in the orginal language, and performances are always popular. Tickets should be bought in advance. The National Opera Company has a more experimental repertoire, and most of its operas are performed in Czech.

To view a Czech opera, by Czech composers Smetana or Dvořák, the National Theatre is your best opportunity to do so. A lesser known opera company based at the **Estates Theatre** *(see p221)* performs mainly classical, Italian operas in the original language.

CLASSICAL MUSIC

The Czech Philharmonic Orchestra (CPO) has been based at the magnificent **Rudolfinum** *(see p84)* since giving its first concert there in January 1896, when it was conducted by no less a personality than Anton Dvořák, whose name the Rudolfinum's grand hall now carries. Finding immediate success with the public in Prague and abroad (the Philharmonic travelled to London on tour as early as 1902), the orchestra is today recognised by music lovers as one of the finest in the world.

The post of chief conductor of the CPO is one of the most competed for appointments in classical music; the post is currently held by Zdeněk Mácal, appointed in 2003. Almost all contemporary Czech music, including the celebrated recent work *Requiem* by Milan Slavický, premiered at the Rudolfinum, though the programme is varied, and the works of Czech composers share the limelight with those of their foreign counterparts.

Besides the Rudolfinum, the main concert venue for classical music is the Smetana Hall, found in the **Municipal House** *(see p64)*. Other permanent concert halls include the **Atrium in Žižkov**, a converted chapel, the **Clementinum** and the imposing **Congress Centre Prague**. **Bertramka** is another venue with the added attraction of being the place where Mozart stayed when he was in Prague.

MUSIC IN CHURCHES AND PALACES

Concerts performed in the numerous churches and palaces around Prague are extremely popular. Many of these buildings are normally closed to the public, so this is the only chance to see them from inside. Major churches include the **Church of St James** *(see p65)*; the **Church of St Nicholas** *(see pp128–9)* in the Little Quarter; the **Church of St Nicholas** *(see p70)* in the Old Town; the **Church of St Francis** in Knights of the Cross Square *(see p79)*; St Vitus's Cathedral *(see p100)* and **St George's Basilica** *(see p98)*. Other important venues are the **National Museum** *(see p147)*; the **Lobkowicz Palace** *(see p99)* and the **Sternberg Palace** *(see pp112–13)*. It's worth checking the listings magazines *(p226)* for the specific dates and timings of concerts.

ETHNIC MUSIC

A small number of clubs and bars in Prague offer ethnic music. The **Palác Akropolis** hosts diverse performances daily in an atmospheric, converted 1920s-theatre building. The Akropolis hosts the likes of Ani Difranco, Apollo 440 and Transglobal Underground. A variety of bands can be seen from around the world in an unusual setting, at the **House of Culture**. Some of the better jazz clubs *(see pp210–11)* also feature ethnic musicians and bands on a regular basis. Another place worth checking out is **La Bodequita del Medio**, a Cuban restaurant that features Cuban performers most weekend evenings.

SPORTS

Czechs are crazy about most sports, and given their habit of winning international competitions in any number of events on a regular basis, it is not surprising. The biggest spectator sports are ice hockey and football, in that order of importance.

Czech ice hockey has long been rated second only to the US NHL, and the 2004–2005 season saw a large number of NHL players in action in the Czech league, a result of a season-long strike in the NHL. Prague has two teams in the top division, Sparta and Slavia. Sparta plays its home games at the **T-Mobile Arena**, where tickets cost from Kč50 onwards. Slavia play at the new **Sazka Arena**, built for the 2004 Ice Hockey World Championship, held in, but surprisingly not won by, the Czech Republic. Tickets here cost Kč140 and up. There are three games a week throughout the season, from September to May, so you should be able to catch a game.

Czech football has long been admired throughout the world, and the national team has often been among the world's best. It should have won the 2004 European Championship in Portugal, but was beaten in the semi-final by the eventual surprise winners, Greece. The domestic league is less admired, as almost all of the country's top stars play in richer leagues elsewhere in Europe. The country's leading team, Sparta Prague, though is a perennial qualifier for the European Champions League, guarantees a procession of big-name opponents. Tickets for Champions League games (played September to December, depending on Sparta's progress) sell out quickly. Home matches of the Czech Republic are also played at **Sparta Stadium**, also known as the Toyota Arena.

If you want to get active yourself, you may have to travel a little further out of town, as sports facilities are not extensive in central Prague. Squash, however, is currently all the rage, and there are number of courts in the city centre, including **ASB** on Wenceslas Square. Golf, mini-golf or tennis are on offer at the **Motol**, the **Exhibition Ground** *(see p162)* and **Štvanice Island**. Swimming pools are also out of the city centre, including two at **Divoká Šárka** and **Kobylisy**. There are beautiful natural lakes at **Lhotka** and **Šeberák** and a whole range of watersports is now on offer at **Hostivař Reservoir** and **Imperial Meadow**.

DIRECTORY

MUSIC VENUES

Academy of Music
HUDEBNÍ FAKULTA AMU
Malostranské náměstí 13.
Map 2 E3.
Tel *257 534 206.*

Atrium in Žižkov
ATRIUM NA ŽIŽKOVĚ
Čajkovského 12, Praha 3.
Tel *222 721 838.*

Bertramka
BERTRAMKA MUZEUM W A MOZARTA
Mozartova 169, Praha 5.
Tel *257 318 461.*

La Bodeguita del Medio
Kaprova 5.
Map 3 B3.
Tel *224 813 922.*
www.bodeguita.cz

Church of St James
KOSTEL SV. JAKUBA
Málá štupartská.
Map 3 C3.

Church of St Nicholas (Old Town)
KOSTEL SV. MIKULÁŠE
Staroměstské náměstí.
Map 3 B3.

Church of St Nicholas
KOSTEL SV. MIKULÁŠE
Malostranské náměstí.
Map 2 E3.

Church of St Francis
KOSTEL SV. FRANTIŠKA
Křižovnické náměstí.
Map 3 A4.

Church of Sts Simon and Jude
KOSTEL SV. ŠIMONA A JUDY
Dušní ulice.
Map 3 B2.

Clementinum
ZRCADLOVÁ SÍŇ KLEMENTINA
Mariánské náměstí 10.
Map 3 B3.

Congress Centre Prague
KONGRESOVÉ CENTRUM PRAHA
5. května 65, Prague 4.
Tel *261 171 111.*
www.kcp.cz

Lichtenstein Palace
Malostranské náměstí 13.
Map 2 E3.

Lobkowicz Palace
LOBKOVICKÝ PALÁC
Jiřská 1, Pražský hrad.
Map 2 E2.
Tel *257 534 578.*

Music Theatre in Karlín
HUDEBNÍ DIVADLO V KARLÍNĚ
Křižíkova 10.
Map 4 F3.
Tel *261 171 111.*

National Museum
NÁRODNÍ MUZEUM
Václavské náměstí 68.
Map 6 D1.
Tel *224 497 111.*

Prague State Opera
STÁTNÍ OPERA PRAHA
Wilsonova 4.
Map 6 E1.
Tel *224 227 266.*
www.opera.cz

Rudolfinum – Dvořák Hall
RUDOLFINUM – DVOŘÁKOVA SÍŇ
Alšovo nábřeží 12.
Map 3 A3.
Tel *224 893 111.*

St George's Basilica
BAZILIKA SV. JIŘÍ
Jiřské náměstí,
Pražský hrad.
Map 2 E2.

St Vitus's Cathedral
KATEDRÁLA VÍTA
Pražský hrad.
Map 2 D2.

Sternberg Palace
ŠTERNBERSKÝ PALAC
Hradčanské náměstí 15.
Map 1 C3.
Tel *233 250 068.*

ETHNIC MUSIC

House of Culture
OBVODNÍ KULTURNÍ DŮM VLTAVSKÁ
Bubenská 1.
Tel *220 879 683.*
www.vltavska.cz

Palác Akropolis
Kubelíkova 27.
Tel *296 330 913.*
www.palacakropolis.cz

SPORTING VENUES

Divoká Šárka
Praha 6.

Exhibition Ground
VÝSTAVIŠTĚ
Sports stadium, Prague 7.

Hostivař Reservoir
Praha 10.

Imperial Meadow
CÍSAŘSKÁ LOUKA
Prague 5.

Kobylisy
Praha 8.

Lhotka
Praha 4.

Motol
V Úvalu 84,
Praha 5.

Sazka Arena
Oceláříksá 460/2,
Praha 9.
Tel *266 121 122.*

Šeberák
Praha 4.

Sparta Stadium
TOYOTA ARENA
Milady Horákové,
Praha 7.
www.sparta.cz

Štvanice Island
Ostrov Štvanice 1125,
Praha 7.

T-Mobile Arena
Za Elektrárnou 419,
Praha 7.
Tel *266 727 475.*

SURVIVAL GUIDE

PRACTICAL INFORMATION 226–235
GETTING TO PRAGUE 236–239
GETTING AROUND PRAGUE 240–245

PRACTICAL INFORMATION

Over the last ten years, Prague has become more and more open to visitors. The city has responded well to the enormous influx of tourists, and facilities such as hotels, banks, restaurants and information centres have improved considerably. Even so, a little forward planning is always worthwhile. Reading up about a sight, checking it is open and how best to get there, can save a lot of time and inconvenience.

A Martin Tour sightseeing bus

Prague's transport system is straightforward and most of the city's sights are within walking distance. In general, prices are still considerably lower than in the West, but a few of the more up-market restaurants and hotels are priced according to Western rather than Czech wallets. Despite a small increase in petty crime, especially pickpocketing, Prague is still safer than the majority of Western cities.

TOURIST INFORMATION

There are a number of tourist information offices and specialized agencies. These can provide advice on anything from accommodation and travel to restaurants and guided tours. Many employ English speakers and print English language publications. The efficient **Prague Information Service (PIS)** is the city's best tourist information point. It has three offices in the city centre and it provides visitors with maps, advice, listings *(see pp218–9)* and other types of information in English, German and Czech. To help you find your way around the city, **Kiwi** has a large selection of maps and guides in English.

Čedok street sign

TIPS FOR TOURISTS

In Prague, there are enough English speakers to make booking a room, buying a ticket or ordering a meal relatively simple. A smattering of German may also help, as many Czechs have a working knowledge of the language.

One of the best times to visit Prague is during the summer, although it can be rather crowded. Other busy times of the year are Easter and major Catholic festivals *(see pp50–53)*. The main sights, such as the Old Town Square, are always packed during these periods, but the crowds give Prague a carnival atmosphere. Street entertainers, buskers and small street stalls spring up around the most popular attractions. If the crowds do get too much, just turn off into one of the smaller streets and you are almost guaranteed peace and quiet. Bring a light raincoat for the summer and some warm, woolly clothes for the rest of the year.

OPENING HOURS

This guide lists the opening hours for the individual museums, galleries and churches. Most of the city's major sights can be seen throughout the year, but many of Prague's gardens and the castles outside the city are only open from 1 April to 31 October. Visiting hours are normally from 9am to 5pm, daily, but the final admission times can often be as much as an hour earlier. All museums and several castles are also closed every Monday, so be sure to check before visiting them. The National Museum is closed on the first Tuesday of the month and the Jewish Museum is closed on Friday afternoons and on Saturdays.

Entry tickets for some of Prague's major tourist sights

Opening hours of Prague's shops vary widely. Some businesses are open between 7am and 6pm, Monday to Friday, and 8am to noon on Saturdays. Some department stores are open until 7pm on Saturdays and Sundays.

The main office of the Prague Information Service in the street Na příkopě

A horse-drawn carriage in the Old Town Square

Prague does not have any standard late-night shopping, although many of the more expensive tourist shops stay open until around 10pm. Banks open from 8am to 4pm, Monday to Friday. Restaurants, cafés and bars all have varied opening hours *(see pp196–7)*. Most of the city's bars open from 10am and as there are no licensing laws, often stay open until everyone leaves.

LISTINGS AND TICKETS

There are some 160 galleries and 40 museums scattered throughout the city, and to find out what's on it is best to look in a listings paper. The English-language newspaper *The Prague Post* gives detailed listings of most events and exhibitions. Available from newsstands in the city centre, it also give tips for the visitor and informative articles on Prague, its politics and its people. The **PIS** has a free monthly English-language listings book.

The price of entry tickets for museums varies widely, from Kč60 to around Kč300. Most churches are free, with a collection box at the door. Tickets for entertainment events can be bought from the booking agencies in the city, or at the venue itself. Some of Prague's hotels can get you tickets, or try a large travel agent in the centre.

SIGHTSEEING TIPS

A good way to see Prague is to take a sightseeing tour. Many firms offer trips around Prague's major sights as well as outings to castles such as Karlstein and Konopiště *(see pp168–9)*. Tours usually start from Náměstí Republiky (Republic Square) and from the upper part of Václavské náměstí (Wenceslas Square). These trips can be expensive but prices vary, so it is worth checking what's on offer before you make a booking.The Jewish Museum *(see p87)* organizes trips around the Jewish Quarter. For those on a tight budget, **PIS** offers some of the cheapest tours.

A trip on tram No. 91, run by the Museum of Municipal Mass Transport, is one of the cheapest and best city centre tours. It starts off at the Exhibition Ground *(see pp178–9)* and travels around the Old Town, the New Town and the Jewish Quarter. It runs from Easter to the middle of November every weekend and public holiday. Tickets can be bought on board. Sightseeing trips in horse-drawn carriages (fiacres) are run from the Old Town Square, and in summer, a "fun train" from Mostecká Street runs through some of the loveliest parts of Hradčany and the Little Quarter.

A street sign showing the services offered by Pragotur

INFORMATION CENTRES AND TOUR OPERATORS

Akasi
28.října. **Map** 3 C5.
Tel *22 22 43 067.*
Na Příkopě 3–5. **Map** 3 C4.
Tel *22 42 36 118.*
Fax *22 42 37 235.*

American Express
Václavské náměstí 56. **Map** 6 D1.
Tel *22 28 00 111.*
Fax *22 22 11 131.*
www.americanexpress.com

Best Tour
Václavské náměstí 27. **Map** 6 D1.
Tel *28 48 14 141.*
Fax *28 48 14 144.*
www.besttour.cz

Čedok
Na Příkopě 18. **Map** 3 C4.
Tel *22 41 87 777.*
Fax *22 42 24 421.*
Rytířská 16. **Map** 3 C4.
Tel *24 22 77 23.*
www.cedok.cz

Cityrama
Štěpánská 21. **Map** 5 C1.
Tel *22 22 30 208.*
Fax *22 22 32 429.*
www.cityrama.cz

Kiwi
Jungmannova 23. **Map** 3 C5.
Tel *22 49 48 455.*
Fax *29 62 45 555.*
www.kiwick.cz

Martin Tour Praha
Štěpánská 61. **Map** 5 C1.
Tel *22 42 12 473.*
Corner of Staroměstské náměstí/ Pařížská 1. **Map** 3 B5.
www.martintour.cz

Pragotur
Staroměstské náměstí 1. Map 3 B3. ***Tel*** *22 44 82 562.*
Fax *22 44 82 380.*
Arbesovo náměstí 4.
Tel *22 17 14 130.*
Fax *22 17 14 127.*
www.prague-info.cz

Prague Information Service – PIS
Na Příkopě 20. **Map** 3 C4.
Tel *12 444.*
Main station, Hlavní Nádraží. **Map** 4 E5.
www.pis.cz

Personal Security and Health

Compared to many Western cities, Prague is relatively safe. Though you may not need emergency help from the police, you should feel free to approach them at any time for advice of any kind; they are generally very helpful to the tourist population. If you should need emergency medical care during you stay in Prague, it will be given free. There is also a number of English-speaking services available, including health centres, pharmacies and dentists, as well as US and British information centres.

ADVICE FOR VISITORS

Prague is a safe and unthreatening city to walk around. Violent crimes against tourists in the city centre are rare. The main crime problems that affect tourists are petty pilfering from cars, hotels and pockets; violence with robbery is very unusual. Using your common sense should help you to avoid Prague's only real plague – its pickpockets. The crowded summer months are a favourite time for these thieves. Always remember to keep your bag in sight and avoid carrying your passport, wallet and valuables in your back pocket or an open bag. Thieves do tend to operate around the popular sights, such as Charles Bridge, and many use diversionary tactics, one knocking into you while the other steals your belongings. It is very unlikely that anything stolen will ever be recovered. Never leave anything of value in your car. Car alarms have proved not to be a deterrent. Try and park your car in an underground car park, especially if you are driving a foreign make. Always take out adequate insurance before visiting Prague, as it is difficult to arrange once there. Report any thefts to the police for future insurance claims. Avoid getting drawn into a street card game known as shells. It is a classic con game.

Women may encounter a few stares and comments, but this is about as far as sexual harassment will go.

Municipal police badge

State police badge

A male state police officer

A municipal police officer

A female state police officer

A "black sheriff"

A Prague police sign

However, one place to try and avoid at night if you are a woman alone is Wenceslas Square. Most men will assume you are one of the city's prostitutes. Unfortunately, Prague has too few reputable bars and cafés that stay open into the early hours. The words "non-stop" and "herna" are synonymous with shady characters; the latter are filled with slot-machines and gambling addicts. See our bars and cafés listings for recommended places *(see pp208–9)*.

It is an unwritten law that you should carry your passport at all times and although you are unlikely to be asked to produce it, having it could save a lot of problems. Before you travel take photocopies of all essential documents as replacing them can be difficult and time-consuming.

THE POLICE AND SECURITY SERVICES

In Prague you will come across several kinds of policemen and women and members of various security services. Report any problems to a uniformed state police officer at a police station. The main stations are marked on the Street Finder maps *(see pp246–57)*. The state police carry guns and can arrest a suspect. They patrol the streets on foot or drive green and white patrol cars. The municipal police are the other main security force, have greater powers, and are divided into different sections. Traffic police ensure the smooth running of traffic and regulate parking, speeding and drink driving. Fines for illegal parking and speeding are huge. It is illegal to drive with any alcohol in your

State police patrol car

Prague ambulance

bloodstream. Occasionally the police have a clamp down on drink driving and if you are caught, the penalties are severe. The traffic police are also responsible for car clamping and collecting the fines *(see pp240–1)*. Finally, if you have a traffic accident, you must immediately ring **Road Accidents**. It is against the law to move anything before the police get there.

There are also a number of private security guards. These are often called "black sheriffs" (many of them actually wear black uniforms) and tend to guard banks and be used as security at football matches and so on. They are not armed.

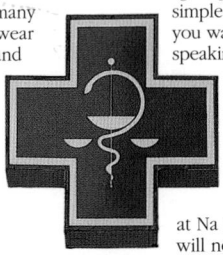

Pharmacy sign

HEALTH CARE

Any EU national who falls ill in the Czech Republic is entitled to free health care. To claim medical treatment, visitors must have a European Health Insurance Card (formerly form E111) which should be presented to the physician along with a valid form of identification. However, not all treatments are covered by the card so additional medical insurance is a good idea.

Your hotel should be able to put you in touch with a local doctor, but if you need more prompt service, Prague's emergency services are on call 24 hours a day and you can call an ambulance if necessary. Hospitals with casualty units are marked on the Street Finder maps at the back of this book *(see pp246–57)*.

There are also 24-hour pharmacies (lékárna) *(see p217)* and a **First Aid/ Emergency Dental Care Centre** giving advice and simple remedies. If you want an English-speaking doctor, visit **Vojenská Nemocnice**, (Army Hospital), or else go to the **Diplomatic Health Centre** for foreigners at Na Homolce. You will need to take a passport and a means of payment if you use either of these.

Those with respiratory problems should be aware that between October and March, sulphur dioxide levels in Prague regularly exceed the World Health Organization's accepted levels – often by up to three times. With increasing car ownership and a lack of money for alternative fuels, this seems unlikely to decrease in the near future.

DIRECTORY

EMERGENCY NUMBERS

Ambulance
Rychlá lékařská pomoc
Tel *155.*

Police
Tísňové volání policie
Tel *158.*

Fire
Tísňové volání hasičů
Tel *150.*

Emergency Operator
Tel *112 (in English).*

MEDICAL CENTRES

Diplomatic Health Centre
Nemocnice Na Homolce
Roentgenova 2.
Tel *25 72 72 146.*
www.homolka.cz

First Aid/Emergency Dental Care
První pomoc zubní
Palackého 5. **Map** 3 C5. *(7pm–7am Mon–Fri, 24hrs Sat, Sun.)*
Tel *22 49 46 981.*

General Health Care Corporation
Krakovská 8. **Map** 6 D1.
Ⓜ Muzeum.
Tel *22 22 10 178.*
www.ghc.cz

24-hour Pharmacy
Štefánikova 6. Ⓜ Anděl.
Tel *25 73 20 918.*
Palackého 5. **Map** 3 C5.

Vojenská Nemocnice
U Vojenské Nemocnice 1200.
Tel *97 32 03 203.* **www**.uvn.cz

GENERAL HELP

American Centre
Americké středisko
US Embassy, Tržiště 15. **Map** 2 E3.
Tel *25 75 30 663.*
www.usembassy.cz

British Council
Britské kulturní středisko
Politických Vězňů13. **Map** 4 D5.
Tel *22 19 91 160.*
www.britishcouncil.cz

Car Breakdown Service/Road Accidents
Tel *1230, 1240.*

Lost and Found
Ztráty a nálezy
Karoliny Světlé 5. **Map** 3 A5.
Tel *22 42 35 085.*

Money, Banks and Currency Exchange Offices

A bureau de change sign in Prague

Compared to many European cities, Prague is a relatively cheap city to visit. Hundreds of banks and bureaux de change have been established, some staying open all night. For the lowest charges and, unfortunately, the longest queues, it is best to change money in a bank. Credit cards are becoming more and more accepted. Traveller's cheques can only be changed in banks.

BANKING

Hundreds of private banks and bureaux de change have been opened in Prague since 1989. The large, modern banks – generally found in the city centre – all open between 8am and 5pm Monday to Friday. The banks may not close at lunch. There are always long queues at the exchange tills so make sure you get there well before closing time. Hundreds of Bureaux de change are found in tiny shops throughout the city. However, despite offering much better exchange rates than the banks, their commission charges are huge, often as high as 12% compared to the bank's 1–5%. But there is a minimum bank commission of Kč20–50. The main advantage of these exchange offices is their convenience. Many are open late every day, some offer a 24-hour service, and queues are rare.

Most of the larger hotels will also change foreign currency for you, but again commission rates may be very high. If you find you have some Czech currency left over from your stay, you can reconvert your money. All banks will reconvert your extra crowns for a small commission. Finally, never change your money on the black market. As well as being illegal the rate is not any higher than banks or exchanges and it is likely you'll be given notes that are not legal tender.

There are also may ATM machines in the centre of Prague. Some of these are in the entrance to banks and are open even when the branch is closed. They accept Mastercard, Visa and Eurocard, and information is in English, German, French or Czech.

An automatic teller machine for dispensing cash

CREDIT CARDS

Paying by credit card is becoming more popular. Even if a shop or restaurant window sports a credit card sign, do not assume they will take them as payment; always ask before you eat your meal. The cards most often accepted are: American Express, VISA, MasterCard and Access. Most banks will allow cash advances (up to your limit) on your card. Only a few restaurants, shops and hotels accept American Express.

Façade of the Československá Obchodní bank

DIRECTORY

BANKS

HVB-Bank
Revoluční 7. **Map** 4 D2.
Tel *22 11 19 761.*
Fax *22 11 19 762.*
W www.HVB.cz

Česká Národní Banka
Na příkopě 28. **Map** 3 C4.
Tel *22 44 11 111.*
Fax *22 44 13 708.*
www.cnb.cz

Česká Spořitelna
Rytířská 29. **Map** 3 C4.
Tel *22 41 01 111.*
www.csas.cz

Czechoslovak Commercial Bank
ČESKOSLOVENSKÁ OBCHODNÍ BANKA
Na příkopě 14. **Map** 3 C4.
Tel *22 41 11 111.*
www.csob.cz

Commercial Bank
KOMERČNI BANKA
Spálená 51. **Map** 3 B5.
Tel *22 19 03 111.*
www.kb.cz
One of several branches.

GE Capital Bank
Opletalova 4. **Map** 4 D5.
Tel *22 44 90 631.*
www.gecapital.cz

BUREAUX DE CHANGE

American Express
Václavské náměstí 56.
Map 3 C5.
Tel *22 28 00 237.*
Fax *22 22 11 131.*
www.aexp.com
One of several branches.

Čekobanka Chequepoint Rapid
Železná 2. **Map** 3 C4.
Tel *22 42 14 370.*
One of several branches.

Exact Change
Na Poříčí 13.
Map 4 D3.
Tel *22 48 19 744.*
One of several branches.

CASH AND TRAVELLER'S CHEQUES

Currency comes in Czech crowns and hellers. There are 100 hellers to the crown. It is legal to bring Czech currency into and out of the Czech Republic. Traveller's cheques are by far the safest alternative to carrying cash. It is recommended that you take well-known brands – American Express, Thomas Cook, for example – although it is unlikely that the major banks will refuse any. However, traveller's cheques are not accepted as currency by any shops or restaurants and must be changed at exchanges or banks. The American Express office sells and cashes traveller's cheques. They don't charge commission for cashing their own cheques.

Banknotes

Czech banknotes are now in circulation in the denominations Kč20, Kč50, Kč100, Kč200, Kč500, Kč1,000, Kč2,000 and Kč5,000.

Coins

Coins come in the following denominations: 50 hellers; Kč1, Kč2, Kč5, Kč10, Kč20 and Kč50. All the coins have the Czech emblem, a lion rampant, on one side.

Kč5,000 note

Kč2,000 note

Kč1,000 note

Kč500 note

Kč200 note

Kč100 note

Kč50 note

Kč20 note

50 hellers

1 crown (Kč1)

2 crowns (Kč2)

5 crowns (Kč5)

10 crowns (Kč10)

20 crowns (Kč20)

50 crowns (Kč50)

Communications

The Czech telephone and postal service, Telecom, has undergone a major modernization programme. Digital phones have replaced the older coin-operated ones, and the postal service has become much more efficient. There were some problems in the transition, but the upgrading and improvements have been completed and few problems should be experienced.

USING PUBLIC TELEPHONES

Although there are plenty of public phones on street corners, you can also find them in post offices, where you have to leave a deposit, make the call, and then pay what you owe to the attendant. In hotels, you can usually get a direct line but commission charges on the calls are often exorbitant. Remember also that international calls are extremely expensive, no matter what time of day you phone. But they are at least somewhat cheaper after 7pm, and also on Saturdays and Sundays. The cheapest way to call abroad is after 5pm and on weekends via Telecom's Xcall service (ring 970 00).

There is an increasing number of modern phonecard telephones in Prague. You can buy the cards *(Telefonní karta)* for these phones from most tabáks and newsstands, and from post offices, supermarkets and petrol stations. Two very popular cards are Karta X, a pre-paid calling card which allows you to make national and international calls from any phone, and TRICK, a multifunctional card which can be used to pay for telephone calls and internet services. On all phones in the country the dialling tone is a short note followed by a long one; the ringing tone consists of long regular notes, and the engaged signal has short and rapid notes.

PROBLEM NUMBERS

If you have problems getting through to a number in Prague, it is very likely that the number has changed due to the modernization of the phone system. To check, ring the directory enquiries number and ask for an English speaker.

INTERNET CAFES

There are several internet cafés in Prague. On the whole, prices are modest, and the lines are reasonably fast for email access. One of the best is **Káva**, in the New Town. There is also one at the Trades Fair Palace *(see pp164–65)*.

USING A COIN-OPERATED TELEPHONE

1 Lift the receiver and wait for the dialling tone.

2 Insert a 1, 2 or 5 crown coin in the slot.

3 The digital display shows how much credit is left. If you need to insert more money, the message *Vložte mince* appears.

4 When the words *Volte číslo* come up, dial the number then wait to be connected.

5 When you have finished speaking replace the receiver. Any coins that were unused are returned here. These phones do not give change.

Kč1

Kč2

Kč5

Coins that can be inserted into coin-operated phones

USING A PHONECARD TELEPHONE

1 Lift the receiver and wait for the dialling tone.

2 The message *Vložte telefonní kartu*, asks you to insert your card. The display also shows you how much credit you have left on your phonecard.

3 When the words *Volte číslo* appear, dial the number and wait to be connected.

4 The card is ejected automatically when it runs out of credit.

By pressing this small button on the phone at any time during your call, you can have an English translation of the instructions.

Emergency numbers

The multi-purpose TRICK phonecard

POST OFFICES

There is a number of post offices in Prague *(see Street Finder on pp246–57)*. The best and largest one is the **Main Post Office** in Jindřišská, just off Wenceslas Square. It has a huge variety of services, including a large phone room where you can make international calls. This service operates from 7am to 11pm.

This post office has recently undergone a complete refurbishment, and is now astonishingly modern and straightforward to use, with easy-access information in English. Take a ticket when you enter the building and then follow the number on it to the correct booth, which will be indicated by an electronic display. Much to the delight of locals, the former long queues have at last been replaced by swift and efficient service.

Post Office sign

The main post office on Jindřišská is open from 2am to midnight.

SENDING A LETTER

The postal service is now fast, but prices for all the post office services are expected to increase slightly in the future.

REACHING THE RIGHT NUMBER

	Dial
• Internal (Czech) directory enquiries	1180
• Prague directory enquiries and the operator	1180
• International exchange and to make a collect call *(ask for an English-speaker)*	1181
• International call followed by the country code	00
• International directory enquiries	1181
• In case of emergencies (Police)	**158**
• Emergency operator (English)	**112**

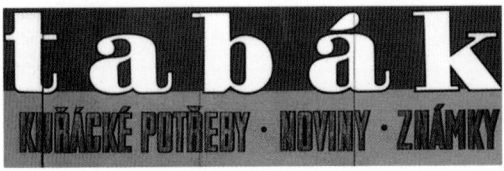

Tobacconist's, where you can also buy stamps and phonecards

There is no first or second class mail in the Czech Republic, but the majority of letters usually arrive at their destination within a few days.

If you want to send something more valuable through the post, use the registered mail service, which is reliable and efficient. Aerogrammes abroad do not exist.

Postcards or letters can be posted in the many orange post boxes scattered around Prague. Both take around five working days to arrive in England and about a week to get to America.

Stamps can be bought from post offices, newsagents or tabáks – who will also tell you what stamps you need. All parcels and registered letters need to be handed in at a post office.

For emergency parcels and packages, you can use an international courier service, such as **DHL**.

One of the new-style post boxes

POSTE RESTANTE

Post restante letters are delivered to the Main Post Office in Jindřišská Street. Go to window 28 (open Monday to Friday 6:30am to 8pm and Saturday 6:30am to 1pm) with your passport or other official identification. The **American Express** office will also hold mail and parcels for up to a month for anyone who is a registered card holder.

USEFUL ADDRESSES

Main Post Office
Jindřišská 14. **Map** 4 D5.
Tel *22 11 31 111.* ***Tel*** *800 10 44 10* (general information).
Open *2am–midnight daily.*
www.cpost.cz

American Express
Václavské náměstí 56.
Map 4 D5.
Tel *22 28 00 237.*
Fax *22 22 11 131.*
www.aexp.com

DHL
Václavské náměstí 47.
Map 4 D5. ***Tel*** *800 103 000.*
Fax *22 15 12 424.*
www.dhl.cz

Káva
Národní 37. **Map** 3 B5.
Open *7am–10pm daily (from 9am Sat & Sun).*
www.kava-coffee.cz

Additional Information

Visitors enjoying tax-free shopping on Na Příkopě

DISABLED TRAVELLERS

Facilities for the disabled are few and far between. Occasionally you will come across a ramp at the entrance to a building to allow the disabled easier access, but this is the exception rather than the rule. There are few organizations that campaign for the disabled and, unfortunately, those that do are currently hampered by both public inertia and a lack of funding.

Despite, this, these attitudes are slowly changing and, although transport around the city is a major problem, groups do now exist who can help you with advice, sightseeing tours, accommodation and getting around the city. Two of the best organizations to contact in advance of your trip are: the **Czech Association of Persons with Disabilities** and the **Prague Wheelchair Association**.

Czech Association of Persons with Disabilities
Karlínské náměstí 12.
Map 5 B2. ***Tel*** *22 48 15 914.*
www.czechia.com/szdp

Prague Wheelchair Association
Beneditská 6.
Map 4 D3.
Tel *22 48 27 210/22 48 26 078.*
Fax *22 48 26 079.*

CUSTOMS REGULATIONS AND IMMIGRATION

A valid passport or, where applicable, an ID card is needed when entering the Czech Republic. Visitors are advised to contact the Czech embassy or consulate, or check details with their travel agent to confirm visa requirements before travelling. British and EU nationals must have a valid passport or identity card, but visas are not required (www.czechembassy.org.uk/consular.htm). Visitors from the United States, Canada, Australia and New Zealand need a valid passport with a minimum of 90 days remaining on it, and can stay for up to three months without a visa. Anyone wishing to stay longer than 30 days will need to register with the border police. Your hotel can usually arrange this for you. If you require a visa you can obtain one from your nearest Czech embassy or consulate.

For non-EU visitors, customs allowances per person are 2 litres (3.6 pints) of wine, 1 litre (1.8 pints) of spirits, 200 cigarettes or equivalent tobacco products. Goods under 175 euros in value can be imported duty-free.

You can take in as much foreign currency as you like, however, it is illegal to take more than Kč350,000 out of the Czech Republic. To export authentic antiques you need to obtain a special licence *(see Shopping p214)*. VAT (value added tax) can be claimed back on items totalling Kč1,000 or more which are carried out of the country within 30 days of purchase.

STUDENT INFORMATION

If you are entitled to an International Student Identity Card (ISIC), it is worth getting one before travelling to Prague. Admission charges into most of Prague's major tourist sights are cheaper on production of a valid ISIC card. Students can also get cheaper coach travel, and while in the country, train travel. There are a couple of youth hostels in the centre of the city *(see Where to Stay, pp186–7)*. For further information about what is available contact the tour operator **Koleje a Menzy**.

Koleje a Menzy
Jednota Youth Hostel, Opletalova 38. **Map** 4 D5. ***Tel*** *22 49 30 010.*
Fax *22 49 30 361.*

EMBASSIES AND CONSULATES

Australian Consulate
Klimentská 10. **Map** 4 D2.
Tel *29 65 78 350.* ***Open*** *8:30am–1pm, 2–5pm Mon–Fri.*

Canadian Embassy
Mickiewiczova 6. **Map** 2 F1.
Tel *27 21 01 800.* ***Open*** *8.30am–12.30pm Mon–Fri.*
www.canada.cz

New Zealand Consulate
Tel *22 25 14 672.* ***Fax*** *22 42 54 640. (Can be unattended. Lost passport: contact UK Embassy; in emergency: call Consulate in Berlin: 00 49 30 20 62 10 or 00 49 17 27 20 69 92 out of hours).*

United Kingdom Embassy
Thunovská 14. **Map** 2 E3.
Tel *25 74 02 111.*
Open *9–11:30am Mon–Fri.*
www.britain.cz

United States Embassy
Tržiště 15. **Map** 2 E3. ***Tel*** *25 75 30 663.* ***Open*** *9am–4:30pm Mon–Fri.* **www**.usembassy.cz

NEWSPAPERS, TV, RADIO

Prague has a number of newspapers including two weekly English-language ones, *The Prague Post and Prague Business Post*. They are both well produced and provide useful tips for visitors

The two English-language newspapers published in Prague

to the city as well as up-to-date and informative pieces on Prague, its people and politics. The former includes a good leisure supplement, *Night and Day*.

Most of the newsstands that are around Wenceslas Square and other popular tourist spots sell the main European papers and the *International Herald Tribune*. A wide selection of international papers is also available at the news-agent's in Jungmannova 5.

These days there is a larger choice of television in Prague than ever before. Western films are interspersed with well-made nature programmes and classic Czech films. The stations also show many soap operas, like *Dallas*. Various satellite channels are also available, plus numerous programmes in English, including the daily news. Foreign films are often shown with optional Czech dubbing.

You can listen to the BBC World Service on 101.1FM, but one of the most popular radio stations is Europe II on 88.2MHz playing a blend of mainstream pop. Other stations include Radio I on 91.9MHz, Radio Golem on 90.3MHz and Radio Bonton on 99.7MHz. Reception can be very bad outside the city. You can also listen to the BBC on the Internet (www.bbc.co.uk/).

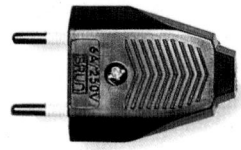

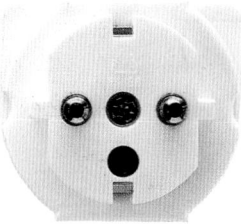

A two-prong and a three-prong plug adaptor for use in Prague

CONVERSION CHART

Imperial to Metric

1 inch = 2.54 centimetres
1 foot = 30 centimetres
1 mile = 1.6 kilometres
1 ounce = 28 grams
1 pound = 454 grams
1 pint = 0.6 litre
1 gallon = 4.6 litres

Metric to Imperial

1 millimetre = 0.04 inch
1 centimetre = 0.4 inch
1 metre = 3 feet 3 inches
1 kilometre = 0.6 mile
1 gram = 0.04 ounce
1 kilogram = 2.2 pounds
1 litre = 1.8 pints

ELECTRICAL ADAPTORS

The electricity supply in Prague is 220V AC and two-pin plugs are used. For British or US plugs, an adaptor is needed. Adaptors may not be easily found in Prague and it is wise to buy one before leaving home.

PRAGUE TIME

Prague is on Central European time, which is Greenwich Mean Time (GMT) plus 1 hour. Summer time runs effectively from the end of March up until the end of October – this is GMT plus 2 hours.

RELIGIOUS SERVICES

Anglican
St. Clement's; Klimentská 5. **Map** 4 D2. ✝ *11am Sun.*

Baptist
Baptist Church of Prague; Vinohradská 68. **Map** 6 F1. ***Tel*** *22 27 11 047.* ✝ *11am Sun.*

Hussite Church
Church of St. Nicholas; Staroměstské náměstí. **Map** 3 C3. ***Tel*** *22 42 15 402.* ✝ *10:30am Sun.* **www**.husiti.cz

Interdenominational
International Church; Peroutkova 57. ***Tel*** *29 63 92 231.* **www**.volny.cz/jx-studio ✝ *(in English) 10:30am Sun.*

Jewish
Old-New Synagogue *(see pp88–9).* Jerusalem Synagogue; Jeruzalémská 7. **Map** 4 E4. **www**.kehilaprag.cz ✡ *(in Hebrew) Sundown Fri; 9am Sat.*

Methodist-Evangelical
Ječná 19. **Map** 5 C2. ***Tel*** *22 43 15 613, 25 75 30 020.* **www**.praguefellowship.cz ✝ *4:30pm Sun.*

Roman Catholic
Services are held in many churches. Some are:
Church of the Infant Jesus of Prague, Karmelitská 9. **Map** 2 E4. ***Tel*** *25 75 33 646.* **www**.apha.cz ✝ *(in English) noon Sun.*
Church of St. Thomas, Josefská 8. **Map** 2 E3. ***Tel*** *25 75 32 675.* ✝ *(in English) 11am Sun.*

A Roman Catholic service

GETTING TO PRAGUE

Prague is located at the heart of Europe and – apart from the Czech Republic's lack of motorways – has good transport connections with the rest of the continent. There are direct flights every day from most of Europe's major cities and, via ČSA, from Newark, in the USA. However, there are no direct flights from Australia. International coach transport is efficient and cheap. But the journey is about 20 hours from London compared to an hour and a half by air. International rail transport is a popular method of travelling to Prague, but trains tend to get booked up early, especially in the summer. The main train station (Hlavní nádraží) is close to Wenceslas Square and the city centre and, except for the airport, other major points of arrival are also fairly central.

ČSA aircraft

AIR TRAVEL

There are 40 international airlines which now fly to Prague airport. If you are flying from the United States, **Delta Air** operate scheduled flights from the east coast of America. But these are not direct flights – there is a stopover in Frankfurt. There are no Australian or New Zealand carriers flying to Prague, although you can fly **British Airways** with a stop in London. Other airlines include **Air France, KLM, Air Canada** and **Czech Airlines (ČSA)**. It takes about one and a half hours to fly from London to Prague and about nine hours from the east coast of America – not including the stopover.

DISCOUNT FARES

Because of the increasing popularity of Prague as a tourist destination, many new airlines are starting to fly to the city. Increased competition has led to a significant drop in the price of flights.

Charter flights have been introduced by a few agents. They are set to become more popular and it is well worth investigating their availability. Remember that these can be subject to last-minute changes and cancellations. Check the ads in the travel sections of major papers for special fares.

APEX (advanced purchase) tickets can be good buys, but they have stringent conditions attached to them. These include having to book your ticket at least a month in advance and severe penalties if you cancel your flight.

If you ring well in advance, airlines will quote you the standard fare, but the price may be lowered nearer the time if seats remain unsold – this is rarely the case in the summer months. Students, senior citizens and regular business travellers may all be able to get discounts. Children under two (who do not occupy a separate seat) pay 10% of the adult fare. Remember fares are more expensive in July and August. If you do manage to get a cheaper deal, ensure that you will get a refund if your agent goes out of business.

Porters at Ruzyně

The recently modernized interior of Ruzyně Airport

AIRLINE OFFICES

Air Canada
Ruzyně Airport. ***Tel*** *22 48 10 181.*
www.aircanada.ca

Air France
Václavské náměstí 57. **Map** 3 D5.
Tel *22 16 62 662.* **www**.airfrance.com

British Airways
Ruzyně Airport. ***Tel*** *22 21 44 444.*
www.britishairways.com

Czech Airlines (ČSA)
V Celnici 5. **Map** 4 D3.
Tel *23 90 07 007.* **www**.csa.cz

Delta Air Lines
Národní 32. **Map** 3 B5.
Tel *22 49 46 733.* **www**.delta-air.cz

KLM
Na Příkopě 21. **Map** 3 C4.
Tel *23 30 90 933.* **www**.klm.com

Lufthansa
Ruzyně Airport. ***Tel*** *22 01 14 456.*
www.lufthansa.cz

RUZYNĚ AIRPORT

Prague's only international airport, Ruzyně, is 15 km (9 miles) northwest of the city centre. The 1936 airport is small, but modern, clean, efficient and functional. It was modernized during the 1960s and now offers all that you would expect from an international airport: 24-hour exchange facilities; car rental offices; a duty-free shop; post office and a left-luggage office.

The airport was bought by Air France in 1992 and has undergone further modernization, including the addition of a business class lounge. Other changes include a newly open catering facility. The quality of the food at the airport's restaurants and on ČSA flights has improved dramatically – a trained French chef has been employed to oversee all the preparation of both the traditional Czech and international dishes.

Sign for passport control

TRANSPORT FROM THE AIRPORT TO THE CITY

The airport is linked to the city centre by a regular minibus service run by **CEDAZ**. For the return trip to the airport, these can be picked up at Náměstí Republiky and Dejvická metro stations. For a group of one to four people, the trip into town costs Kč370; for five to eight people it is Kč720. The buses can also take you to addresses outside the city, and can even be used to tour the Czech Republic. Whatever your destination, make sure to book the bus a couple of hours in advance. The buses can be ordered from 8am to 10pm daily. There is also a regular service to the airport from Dejvická metro (bus 119) and from Zličín metro (bus 100).

Alternatively, there is always a rank of taxis waiting in front of the terminal. Ask at the information booth about the price you should expect to pay for a taxi into town, and use it as a guide for the future.

The airport forecourt, from which buses and taxis can be taken into town

Sign for the CEDAZ airport bus at Náměstí Republiky metro station

CEDAZ

Tel *22 01 14 296 or 22 42 81 005.*
Fax *22 01 14 286.*
www.aas.cz/cedaz

PRAGUE'S EUROPEAN AIR CONNECTIONS

Prague, situated at the centre of Europe, has good flight connections to most major European cities. It can be reached in less than two and a half hours on direct flights from all the airports marked on the map.

The spacious interior of the railway station, Masarykovo Nádraží

TRAVELLING BY TRAIN

Prague is connected by rail to all the major capitals of Europe. Rail travel can be an enjoyable, if rather slow, way to travel to and from Prague. International trains have dining cars and couchettes, and tickets are cheaper than air fares. The railways in the Czech Republic are run by the State (České Dráhy – ČD).

The façade of Hlavní nádraží

There are information offices at stations, and these usually have English speakers, so you shouldn't have any trouble booking a ticket. PIS and Čedok *(see p227)* will help you with timetables and prices. There are four types of train run by ČD. These are the *rychlík* (express) trains; the *osobní* (passenger) trains, which form a local service and stop at all stations, often travelling as slowly as 30 km/h (20 mph); the EX, or national express; and the EC (Eurocity) or international express. International trains are the fastest, but get delayed at borders. Tickets can be bought in advance or on the day at stations or at the **Travel Agency of České Dráhy** *(see p186)*, however, trains tend to get booked up quickly. If you do want to buy a ticket just before your train leaves, be warned that queues at ticket booths can be long. When you buy your ticket, specify exactly where and when you want to go, whether you want a single or return and what class of ticket you want. First class carriages exist on most trains and guarantee you a seat. In the timetable, an 'R' in a box by a train number means you must have a seat reserved on that train. An 'R' without a box means a reservation is recommended. If you are caught in the wrong carriage, you have to pay an on-the-spot fine.

A uniformed ČSD railway porter

TRAIN STATIONS

The biggest and busiest railway station in Prague is Hlavní nádraží which is only a five-minute walk from the city centre. In the 1970s, the original Art Nouveau structure was enlarged and a modern departure hall now dominates the whole terminal. The station is large, efficient and clean with a good-sized, inexpensive, 24-hr left-luggage office in the basement. The nearby luggage lockers are convenient and very cheap. There are also food stalls, bureaux de change and a number of booking and information services in the departure hall.

The other rail stations in the city are Masarykovo nádraží – Prague's oldest terminal, the newly-built and modern Holešovice Station and the smallest, Smíchov Station.

TRAVELLING BY COACH

Coach connections from Prague to many of the major European cities can be infrequent and are often very booked up. However, many of these coach routes are much cheaper, and often faster, than the slower trains. The city's main bus terminal is Florenc, situated on the eastern edge of the New Town. During the summer months there are hundreds of coach trips to all the major coastal resorts in southern Europe. These get booked up quickly by Czechs, so buy your ticket in advance and be sure to reserve yourself a seat. International bus timetables are confusing; check with PIS *(see p227)* for more detailed information. Coach travel is cheap, but long-haul journeys can be uncomfortable and are slower than air.

Passengers boarding a long-haul coach

PRAGUE'S MAJOR RAIL AND COACH STATIONS

The major points of arrival by train and coach are all fairly central and easily accessible by metro – the nearest metro to each terminal is shown in the boxes along with more detailed travel information.

KEY

- Railway station
- Metro station
- Coach station

Holešovice station
Nádraží Holešovice
Express trains from north and west Europe, Berlin, Hamburg and Scandinavia stop here on their way to southern Europe.

Nádraží Holešovice

Florenc coach station
Florenc
The main coach station serves all international and long-distance domestic routes.

Autobus nádraží Florenc

Prague Castle and Hradčany

Jewish Quarter

Masarykovo nádraží

Little Quarter

Old Town

VLTAVA

Masarykovo station
Náměstí Republiky
Serves mainly domestic routes, such as Brno and Liberec.

Smíchov coach station
Anděl
Serves domestic coach routes.

Hlavní nádraží

New Town

Autobus zastávka Smíchovské nádraží

Main station
Hlavní nádraží
The main station serves international trains from all countries, and domestic routes to the south of the country and Slovakia.

Smíchov station
Smíchovské nádraží
Serves domestic rail routes.

Smíchovské nádraží

A Czech motorway sign

TRAVELLING BY CAR

To drive a car in the Czech Republic you must be at least 18. Most foreign driving licences, including Canadian, US and EC ones, are honoured – New Zealand and Australian drivers should get an International Driving Licence. If you bring your own car to Prague, by law you must carry the following with you at all times: a valid driver's licence, vehicle registration card, a hire certificate or, if you are borrowing the car, a letter signed by the owner and authorized by a recognized body, such as the AA or RAC, giving you permission to drive it and a Green Card (an international motoring certificate for insurance). If you drive on the motorway, you will also need to display a special card available at the border, petrol stations and post offices. Other items you have to carry at all times are a set of replacement bulbs, red warning triangles and a first-aid kit. You also have to display a national identification sticker. Headlights must be used even during daylight hours between November and April, and whenever visibility is poor. It is compulsory to wear seatbelts if fitted, and children under 12 are not allowed in the front seat. When you are driving it is strictly forbidden to have any alcohol in your blood and to use a mobile phone.

There are now good connections to all the major cities in the Czech Republic, including Bratislava and Brno, and many more are currently under construction.

Road signs are clear and easy to follow. The speed limit on motorways is 130 km/h (81 mph); on dual and single carriageways 90 km/h (56 mph) and in urban areas 50 km/h (31 mph). The traffic police patrolling the roads are very vigilant, and any infringements are dealt with harshly. There are also occasional road blocks to catch drunken drivers.

The popular, Czech-made Skoda car

GETTING AROUND PRAGUE

The centre of Prague is conveniently small and most of the sights can be reached comfortably on foot. But to cross the city quickly or visit a more remote sight, the public transport is efficient, clean and cheap. It is based on trams, buses and the underground (metro) system, all of which are run by the Prague Transport Corporation (Dopravní podnik). Throughout this guide, the best method of transport is given for each sight. The metro and trams serve the city centre, while buses are used to reach the suburbs. The entire system is simple to use – only one ticket is needed for all three forms of transport. Bus, tram and metro routes are found on city maps, available at most city centre tabáks, bookshops and newsagents; or refer to the map on the inside back cover of this guide.

Walking around the city

DRIVING A CAR

Most visitors are better off not driving around the centre of Prague. The city's complex web of one-way streets, the large number of pedestrianized areas around the historic core of the city and a very severe shortage of parking spaces make driving very difficult. Prague's public transport system is a much more efficient way of travelling around the city centre.

If you do decide to use a car, remember that on-the-spot fines for traffic violations are common, especially if you are caught driving in one of the city's restricted areas, such as Wenceslas Square. Prague's motorists have become less disciplined and caution is often needed, You must drive on the right and the law states that both driver and front- and back-seat passengers should wear seat belts, if they are fitted. The speed limit in the city is 50 km/h (31 mph) unless a sign indicates otherwise. Traffic signs are similar to those in Western Europe. Cars can be useful for seeing sights outside the city. Car rental is inexpensive, but public transport is almost as efficient getting out of the city as in it *(see pp236–9)*.

One-way traffic and No stopping except for supply lorries

PARKING

Car parking spaces in the city centre are scarce and the penalties for illegal parking, harsh. Many parking areas are restricted and the only places to park legally on the street

Pedestrian zone

Pedestrian crossing

PRAGUE ON FOOT

Walking around Prague is the most enjoyable way to see the city. Some pedestrian crossings are controlled by traffic lights, but be sure to cross only when the green man is flashing, and even then, check the road carefully. It is now illegal for drivers to ignore pedestrian crossings, but for years they were allowed to do so, and old habits die hard. Those crossings without lights are still ignored by drivers. Remember that trams run in the centre of the road and go in both directions, which can be confusing. They also travel at high speeds, occasionally coming upon you with little warning. With the uneven cobbled streets, steep hills and a mass of tram lines, flat comfortable shoes are strongly recommended.

Street or square name and Prague district

Street number

City registration number

Brown street signs with tourist information

are in front of the New Town Hall in Karlovo náměstí, in Na Florenci and at Hlavní station. Unfortunately, car theft is rife, and expensive Western cars are a favourite target. It is safer to park in an official – preferably underground – car park *(see the Street Finder pp246–57)*. But these are expensive and tend to get full early on in the morning. Many parking spaces are reserved for office workers and disabled drivers. Parking at central hotels is limited, with only a few spaces allocated. It is better to park at one of the guarded car parks at the edge of the city and use public transport. Parking meters are rare in Prague but traffic wardens are not.

Parking sign

TOWING AND CLAMPING

Many Prague locals park on the pavement. But ignoring *No Parking* signs may well mean that you find your car has been towed away or clamped. Both the municipal and the private firms that patrol the city are vigilant and ruthless with illegally parked cars, especially with foreign cars. If your car has disappeared, ring 158 to find out if it has been towed away or stolen. To reclaim your towed-away car, you have to go to one of the parking lots (the police will tell you which one) and pay a hefty fine before the car is released. Wheel clamping is becoming very popular. You must pay a fine of several hundred crowns at a police station (the ticket on your windscreen will tell you the address) and return to your car to wait for the clamp to be removed.

Prague's colourful clamp, also known as the Denver Boot

THE TRANSPORT SYSTEM

The best way to get around the city centre is by metro or tram. Prague's rush hours are between 6am and 8am and 3pm and 5pm, Monday to Friday. But more trains, trams and buses run at these times, so crowding is not a problem. Some bus routes to the suburbs only run during peak hours. From 1 July to 31 August a summer timetable operates and the entire transport system is reduced. There are information offices at Muzeum and Můstek metro stations (7am–9pm daily) and at Ruzyně Airport (7am–10pm daily); English is spoken.

One of the many newsstands in Wenceslas Square

TICKETS

Paying on the transport system relies on the honour system, with periodic checks by plain-clothes ticket inspectors who levy an on-the-spot and large fine if you don't have a valid ticket. There is one ticket for use on the entire system – bus, tram and metro. Buy the ticket before you travel and stamp or punch it yourself in the machines provided, or you will be travelling illegally. You can buy single ride tickets, from tabák stores and metro stations, or from the driver on buses, with exact change. There are automatic ticket machines in the metros *(see p242)*. Charges vary according to type of journey: up to 15 minutes with no changes (or 30 minutes and four stops on the metro), or up to 60 minutes with the possibility of changing your route. Children under six travel free and 6- to 15-year-olds travel half price.

You can also buy network tickets *(síťová jízdenka)*. These offer unlimited rides on buses, trams and metro for periods ranging from 24 hours to 30 days.

One-day pass

15-day pass

Travelling by Metro

The underground railway, known as the metro, is the quickest and most comfortable form of transport in Prague. Managed by the Prague Transport Corporation *(see p240)*, its construction began in 1967. It has three lines, A, B and C, and 55 stations. The straightforward layout and clear signs make finding your way around the system very easy. Trains run between 5am and midnight.

FINDING YOUR WAY AROUND THE METRO

Metro entrances are not always easy to spot. Look for a sign displaying the 'M' within an upside-down triangle *(see right)*. The street entrance will normally lead you down a flight of steps. A high-pitched bleep (for the blind) at some entrances can also help to guide you.

Once you have purchased your ticket and passed through the unmanned ticket barriers, continue down the fast-moving escalators to the trains. At the bottom of each escalator is a long central corridor with a platform on either side for trains travelling in either direction. Signs suspended from the ceiling indicate the direction of the trains *(see opposite page)*. The edges of the platforms are marked with a white, broken line which should not be crossed until the train stops. Most of the metro doors open and close automatically (you may have to push a button on some trains), giving a recorded message when they are about to close. During the journey the name of the next station is announced in Czech.

The metro sign for Můstek metro station

The spacious interior of Můstek metro station

Maps of the underground system can be found above each metro door.

Line A is the most useful for tourists, because it covers all the main areas of the city centre – Prague Castle, the Little Quarter, the Old Town and the New Town – as well as the main shopping area around Wenceslas Square.

Displayed above some seats are disabled signs. These seats should be given up for the elderly, disabled, and those with small children.

AUTOMATIC TICKET MACHINES

You can buy transport tickets at designated ticket sellers *(see p241)* or at the automatic ticket machines in the metro station. The ticket machines, and tickets themselves, may vary in design and colour, but they are still applicable to all forms of transport. The machine offers a choice of tickets at varying prices, for adults, children, bicycles and other bulky items. Once it has been validated, a single-journey ticket is valid for an hour.

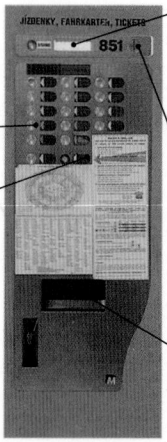

1 Check which price band is the right one to meet your requirements, then press the appropriately labelled button.

2 The visual display unit confirms which type of ticket you are in the process of selecting.

3 If you are happy that you have selected the right type of ticket, then press the *výdej* button to confirm your choice. (If you are unsure, press the button labelled *storno* and start the process again.)

4 When you have confirmed your choice of ticket, insert coins into this slot. Most machines give change.

5 Collect your ticket, and any change that may be due to you, from the large slot at the base of the machine.

MAKING A JOURNEY BY METRO

1 The letters, each in a different colour, indicate the three metro lines. The number above the letter is the time it takes to get from one end of the line to the other.

TRASA 20 min. A
TRASA 23 min. B
TRASA 26 min. C
Platnost jízdenky 60 min. v podzemí
Validate of the ticket 60 min. in the underground
Im U-bahnraum ist die Fahrkarte 60 min. gültig
Validite du ticket est fixée à 60 min. à partir du compostage

Orientační plán

This metro map can be bought from most metro stations, tabáks and news-agents. A metro map has also been included at the end of this book.

2 To decide which line to take, find your destination on the *Street Finder (see pp252–7)*, its nearest metro station and then plot your route on a metro map.

The central corridor with platforms either side and signs indicating the direction of trains

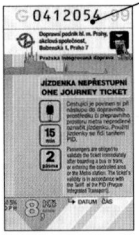

3 You can use single-journey tickets *(left)*, or a network ticket *(below)* which give you unlimited travel for a set period of time, and are also valid for buses and trams *(see p241)*. Generally, a child's ticket costs half that of an adult's.

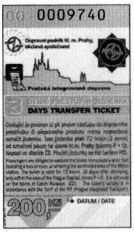

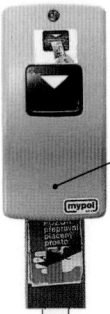

4 Before going down the escalators, you must stamp a single-journey ticket in one of these machines. If the ticket has not been stamped, it is not valid and you will have to pay a fine if caught. Do not stamp tourist tickets.

5 This sign, hanging from the ceiling, is visible when you come down the escalator. It shows the direction of the trains on each platform. This one says that the train's final station *(Stanice)* on the left is Háje, so from the metro map you know the train is travelling south.

"Stanice" means station

"Směr" means direction

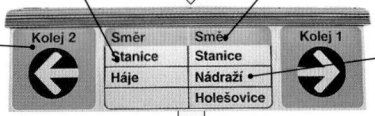

Name of station

The white circle indicates which station you are in

6 This sign along the central platform indicates the station on line C where you are (white circle) and those stations where you can transfer to the other lines (A and B). For stations to the left of the white circle follow the arrow to the left, and vice-versa for stations to the right.

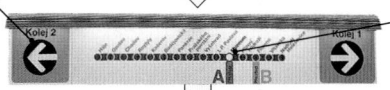

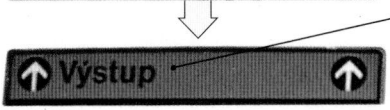

7 Once you are at your stop, follow the exit signs *(Výstup)* leading out of the metro system.

Travelling by Tram

Trams are Prague's oldest method of public transport. Horse-drawn trams appeared on the streets in 1879, but by 1891 the first electric tram was in operation. After the metro, the tram system is the fastest and most efficient way of getting around the city. Some lines only operate in the rush hour and there are a number of night trams, all of which pass by Lazarská in the New Town.

TRAM TICKETS

The tram system is run by the Prague Transport Corporation *(see p240)*. Tram tickets are also valid for the metro and buses *(see p242)*.

You have to buy your ticket before you board a tram. Once you have entered, you will see two or three small punching machines on metal poles just inside the door. Insert your ticket and it will be stamped automatically.

If you do not punch your ticket it is not valid and, if you are caught by a ticket inspector, you will have to pay an on-the-spot fine *(see p241)*. A single-journey ticket is valid for one journey only *(see p241)*, however long.

Each tram stop has a timetable – the stop underlined is where you are standing. The stops below that line indicate where that tram is heading.

Trams run every 10 to 20 minutes. Doors either open and close automatically or by pushing a button and each stop is announced in Czech. After the metro closes, a small number of night trams run every 30 minutes or so. These trams (numbers 51 to 58) are marked by blue numbers at the tram stop. For more information see www.dp-praha.cz.

One of the new trams on the streets of Prague

Tram Signs

These are found at every tram stop and tell you which trams stop there, and in what direction each tram is going.

USEFUL TRAM ROUTES

These three tram routes are the most useful for getting around the centre of Prague. They pass many of the major sights on both sides of the Vltava, so are also a cheap, pleasant way of sightseeing.

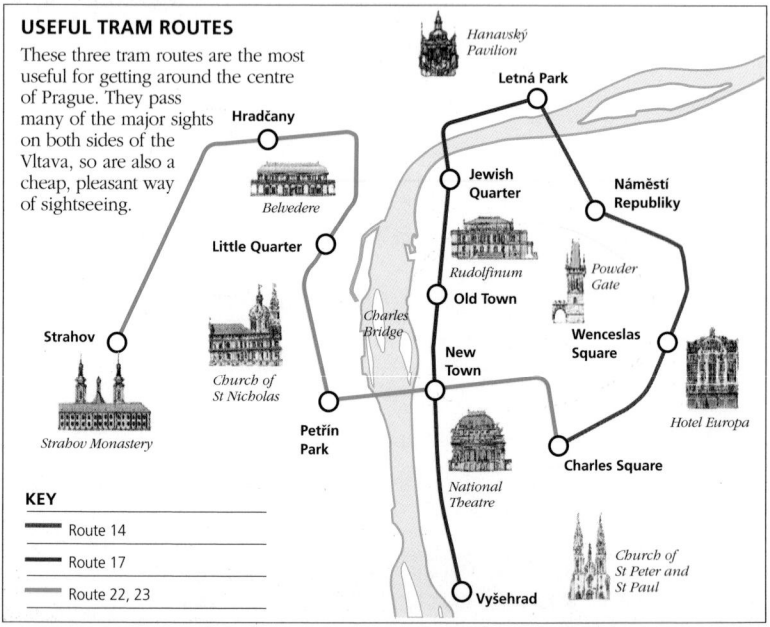

Travelling by Bus

You are unlikely to use a bus unless you want to visit the outer suburbs. By law, buses are not allowed in the city centre (they produce noxious fumes and the streets are too narrow), so they transport people from the suburbs to tram and metro stops outside the centre.

Bus stop logo

BUS TICKETS

A typical public bus in Prague

Unless you have small change, you must buy a ticket before you board a bus. Tickets are available from all the usual agents *(see p241)*.

Again, you must validate your ticket in the punching machine on the bus. If you buy a single-journey ticket, it is only valid for one journey. Each time you change bus, you will have to buy a new ticket, unless you have a tourist ticket *(see p241)*. The doors open and close automatically and the end of the boarding period is signalled by a high-pitched signal. You are expected to give up your seat for the elderly and disabled.

Bus timetables are located at every stop. They have the numbers of all the buses that stop there and the timetable for each route. The frequency of buses varies considerably. In the rush hour there may be 12 to 15 buses an hour, at other times as few as three.

Throughout the night there are 12 buses which go to the outer areas not served by the tram and metro system. For more information see www.dp-praha.cz.

Travelling by Taxi

For visitors to Prague taxis are a useful but often frustrating form of transport. After decades of public ownership, all taxis are now privately owned, but there are many unscrupulous drivers who are out to charge as much as they can get away with. For this reason it's worth taking a few simple precautions. For a start, find out how much a fare should cost.

An illuminated taxi sign

TAXI FARES

One of the many taxi ranks in the centre of the town

As soon as you enter a taxi there is a minimum charge. After that, by law the fare should increase at a set rate per kilometre. However, this set charge is rarely, if ever, adhered to and taxis can be a very expensive way of getting around the city. Taxi meters can be set at four different rates but for journeys in the city it should be set at one (the cheapest). However, rather than depend on the meters – they are often rigged – it is a wise move to negotiate a fare you think is reasonable before you enter the cab. Vigorous bargaining can often bring the price down. Few taxi drivers speak more than the most rudimentary English, so communication can be difficult. Unless your Czech pronunciation is good, write down your destination for them in Czech. At night, charges will increase, sometimes by 200 or even 300 per cent. Be sure surcharges are included in the figure you negotiate beforehand. If problems do arise at the end of the journey, ask for a receipt before you pay. This will normally deter drivers from trying to overcharge you. Avoid taxis around the main tourist sights, these can often be the worst offenders. Despite occasional problems, taxis are a safe form of transport and women should feel comfortable alone in them.

Taxi receipts, if requested, are required to be given by law.

The meter displays your fare and surcharges.

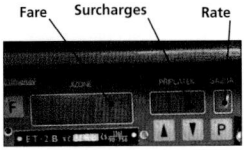

STREET FINDER

The map references given for all the sights, hotels, restaurants, bars, shops and entertainment venues described in this book refer to the maps in this section. A complete index of street names and all the places of interest marked, can be found on the following pages. The key map (right) shows the area of Prague covered by the *Street Finder*. This map includes sightseeing areas, as well as districts for hotels, restaurants, pubs and entertainment venues.

In keeping with Czech maps, none of the street names in the index or on the Street Finder have the Czech word for street, *ulice*, included (though you may see it on the city's street signs). For instance, Celetná ulice appears as Celetná in both the index and the Street Finder. The numbers preceding some street names are dates. In our index we ignore the numbers, so that 17. listopadu (17 November), is listed under 'L'.

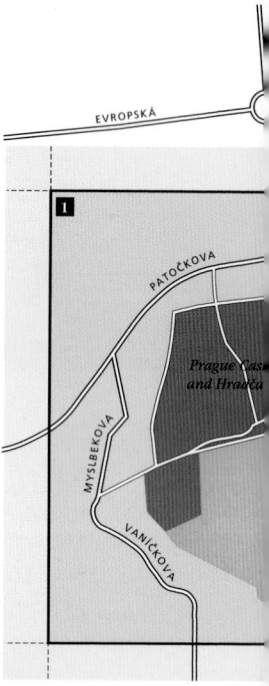

KEY TO STREET FINDER

- Major sight
- Places of interest
- Other building
- Metro station
- Train station
- Coach station
- Tram stop
- Funicular railway
- River boat boarding point
- Taxi rank
- Car park
- Tourist information office
- Hospital with casualty unit
- Police station
- Church
- Synagogue
- Post office
- Railway line
- City wall
- Pedestrian street

SCALE OF MAP PAGES

0 metres 200
0 yards 200
1:8,400

View of the Little Quarter, Hradčany and Prague Castle from the Old Town Bridge Tower

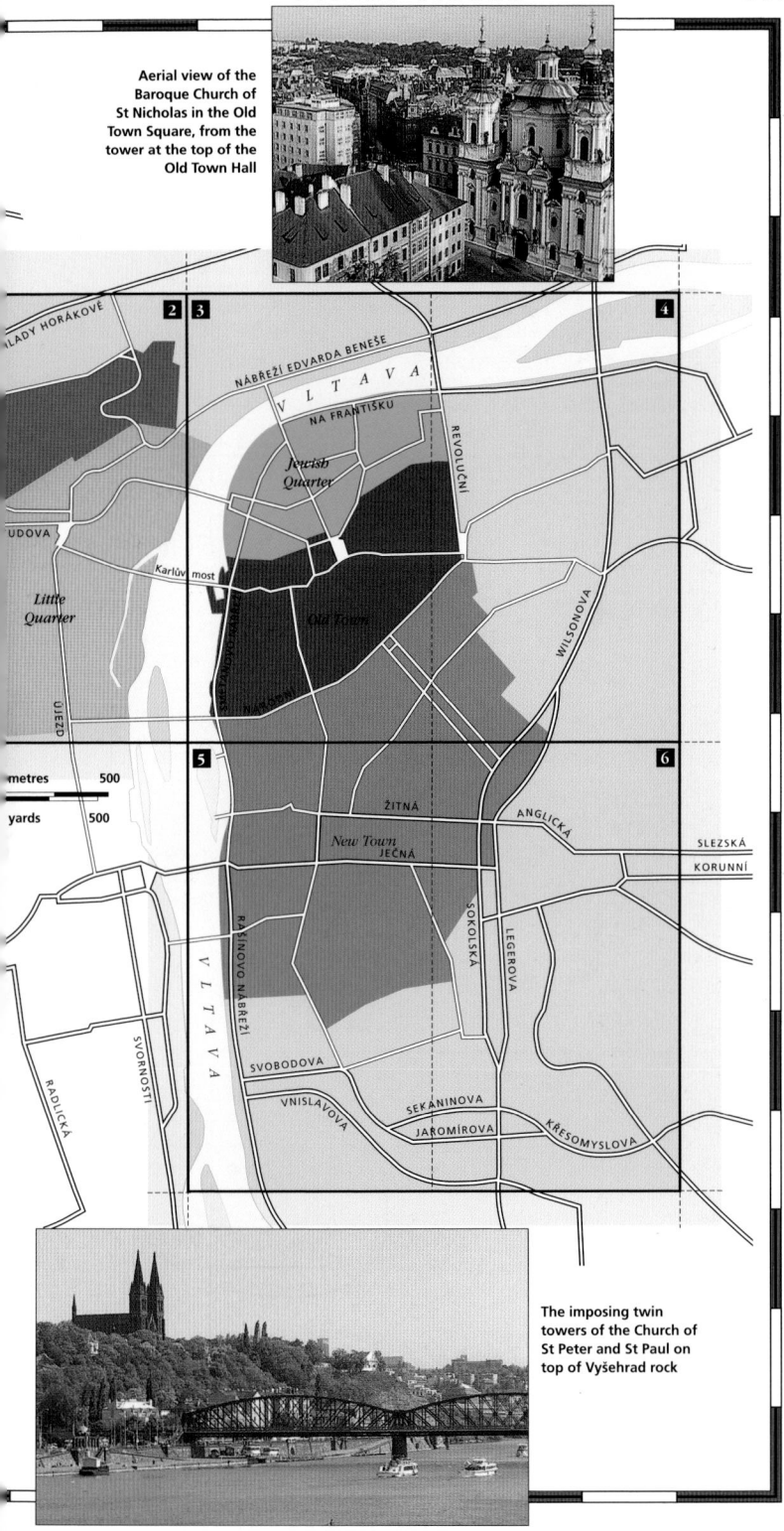
Aerial view of the Baroque Church of St Nicholas in the Old Town Square, from the tower at the top of the Old Town Hall
2
3
4
5
6
NÁBŘEŽÍ EDVARDA BENEŠE
VLTAVA
NA FRANTIŠKU
REVOLUČNÍ
Jewish Quarter
Karlův most
Little Quarter
Old Town
WILSONOVA
NÁRODNÍ
ÚJEZD
metres 500
yards 500
ŽITNÁ
ANGLICKÁ
New Town
JEČNÁ
SLEZSKÁ
KORUNNÍ
SOKOLSKÁ
LEGEROVA
RAŠÍNOVO NÁBŘEŽÍ
VLTAVA
SVOBODOVA
SVORNOSTI
RADLICKÁ
VNISLAVOVA
SEKÁNINOVA
JAROMÍROVA
KŘESOMYSLOVA
The imposing twin towers of the Church of St Peter and St Paul on top of Vyšehrad rock

Street Finder Index

The order of the names in the index is affected by the *háček*, the accent like an inverted circumflex (*háček* means "little hook"). In the Czech alphabet, **č**, **ř**, **š** and **ž** are treated as separate letters. Street names beginning with **ř**, for example, are listed after those beginning with **r** without an accent.

Churches, buildings, museums and monuments are marked on the Street Finder maps with their English and Czech names. In the index, both forms are listed. However, English names for streets and squares, such as Wenceslas Square, do not appear on the maps. Where they are listed in the index, the Czech name is given in brackets in the form that appears on the map.

USEFUL WORDS

dům	house
hrad	castle
kostel	church
klášter	convent, monastery
most	bridge
nábřeží	embankment
nádraží	station
náměstí	square
sady	park
schody	steps
třída	avenue
ulice	street
ulička	lane
zahrada	garden

A

Albertov **5 C4**
Alšovo nábřeží **3 A3**
Americká **6 F3**
Anenská **3 A4**
Anenské náměstí **3 A4**
Anežská **3 C2**
Anglická **6 E2**
Anny Letenské **6 F1**
Apolinářská **5 C4**
Archbishop's Palace **2 D3**
Arcibiskupský palác **2 D3**
At St Thomas's **2 E3**
At the Three Ostriches **2 F3**
autobusové nádraží Praha, Florenc **4 F3**
autobusová zast. Hradčanská **2 D1**

B

Badeniho **2 F1**
Balbínova **6 E2**
Bartolomějská **3 B5**
Barvířská **4 E2**
Bazilika sv. Jiří **2 E2**
Bělehradská **6 E2**
Belgická **6 F3**
Bělohorská **1 A4**
Belvedér **2 E1**
Belvedere **2 E1**
Benátská **5 B3**
Benediktská **4 D3**
Besední **2 E5**
Bethlehem Chapel **3 B4**
Betlémská **3 A5**
Betlémská kaple **3 B4**
Betlémské náměstí **3 B4**
Bílkova **3 B2**
Biskupská **4 E2**
Biskupský dvůr **4 E2**
Blanická **6 F2**
Bolzanova **4 E4**
Boršov **3 A4**
Botanical Gardens **5 B3**
Botanická zahrada **5 B3**
Botič **6 D5**
Botičská **5 B4**
Boženy Němcové **6 D4**
Bridge Street (Mostecká) **2 E3**
Bruselská **6 E3**
Brusnice **1 C2**
Břehová **3 A2**
Břetislavova **2 D3**

C

Capuchin Monastery **1 B2**
Carolinum **3 C4**
Celetná **3 C3**
Chaloupeckého **1 B5**
Chalice Restaurant **6 D3**
Charles Bridge (Karlův most) **2 F4**
continues **3 A4**
Charles Square (Karlovo náměstí) **5 B2**
Charles Street (Karlova) **2 A4**
continues **3 B4**
Charvátova **3 B5**
Chodecká **1 A5**
Chotkova **2 E1**
Chotkovy sady **2 F1**
Chrám sv. Víta **2 D2**
Church of Our Lady before Týn **3 C3**
Church of Our Lady beneath the Chain **2 E4**
Church of Our Lady of the Snows **3 C5**
Church of Our Lady Victorious **2 D4**
Church of St Castullus **3 C2**
Church of St Catherine **5 C3**
Church of St Cyril and St Methodius **5 B2**
Church of St Gall **3 C4**
Church of St Giles **3 B4**
Church of St Ignatius **5 C2**
Church of St James **3 C3**
Church of St John on the Rock **5 B3**
Church of St Lawrence **1 C5**
Church of St Martin in the Wall **3 B5**
Church of St Nicholas (Little Quarter) **2 D3**
Church of St Nicholas (Old Town) **3 B3**
Church of St Simon and St Jude **3 B2**
Church of St Stephen **5 C2**
Church of St Thomas **2 E3**
Church of St Ursula **3 A5**
Church of the Holy Ghost **3 B3**
Cihelná **2 F3**
Clam-Gallas Palace **3 B4**
Clam-Gallasův palác **3 B4**
Clementinum **3 A4**
Cubist Houses **3 B2**
Cukrovarnická **1 A1**

Č

Čechův most **3 B2**
Čelakovského sady **6 E1**
continues **6 D1**
Černá **5 B1**
Černín Palace **1 B3**
Černínská **1 B2**
Černínský palác **1 B3**
Čertovka **2 F4**
Červená **3 B3**

D

Dalibor Tower **2 E2**
Daliborka **2 E2**
Dělostřelecká **1 A1**
Diskařská **1 A5**
Dittrichova **5 A2**
Divadelní **3 A5**
Dlabačov **1 A4**
Dlážděná **4 E4**
Dlouhá **3 C3**
Dražického **2 F3**
Dražického náměstí **2 E3**
Dřevná **5 A3**
Dům pánů z Kunštátu **3 B4**
Dům U Dvou zlatých medvědů **3 B4**
Dušní **3 B2**
Dvořák Museum **6 D2**
Dvořákovo nábřeží **3 A2**

E

Elišky Krásnohorské **3 B2**
Estates Theatre **3 C4**

F

Faust House **5 B3**
Faustův dům **5 B3**
Florenc (metro) **4 F3**
Franciscan Garden **3 C5**
Francouzská **6 F2**
Františkánská zahrada **3 C5**
Fügnerovo náměstí **6 D3**
Funicular Railway **2 D5**

G

Gogolova **2 F1**
Golden Lane (Zlatá ulička **2 E2**
Golz-Kinský Palace **3 C3**

Gorazdova 5 A3
Grand Priory Square (Velkopřevorské náměstí) 2 E4

H

Hálkova 6 D2
Harantova 2 E4
Haštalská 3 C2
Haštalské náměstí 3 C2
Havelská 3 B4
Havelská ulička 3 C4
Havířská 3 C4
Havlíčkova 4 E3
Helénská 4 F5
Hellichova 2 E4
Helmova 4 E2
High Synagogue 3 B3
Hládkov 1 A3
Hladová zeď 1 B4
Hlávkův most 4 F1
Hlavní nádraží 4 E5
Hlavní nádraží (metro) 4 E4
Hlavova 5 C4
Hlavsova 3 B4
Horská 5 C5
Hotel Europa 4 D5
Hotel Evropa 4 D5
House at the Two Golden Bears 3 B4
Hradčanská (metro) 2 E1
Hradčanské náměstí 1 C3
Hradební 4 D2
Hroznová 2 F4
Hunger Wall 1 B4
Husitská 4 F4
Husova 3 B4
Hvězdárna 2 D5
Hybernská 4 D3

I

Ibsenova 6 F2
Italian Street (Vlašská) 2 D3
Italská 4 F5
continues 6 E2

J

Jáchymova 3 B3
Jakubská 3 C3
Jalovcová 3 B4
Jan Hus Monument 3 B3
Jana Masaryka 6 F4
Jánská 2 D3
Jánský vršek 2 D3
Jaromírova 6 D5
Ječná 5 C2
Jelení 1 B2
Jenštejnská 5 A2
Jeruzalémská 4 E4
Jesuit College 5 B2
Jewish Town Hall 3 B3
Jezuitská kolej 5 B2
Jilská 3 B4
Jindřišská 4 D5
Jiráskovo náměstí 5 A2
Jiráskův most 5 A2
Jiřská 2 E2
Jižní zahrady 2 D3
Josefská 2 E3
Jugoslávská 6 E2
Jungmannova 3 C5
continues 5 C1
Jungmannovo náměstí 3 C5

K

K Brusce 2 E1
K Haštalu 4 D2
K Rotundě 5 B5
Kampa 2 F4
Kamzíková 3 C4
Kanovnická 1 C2
Kaprova 3 B3
Kapucínská 1 C3
Kapucínský klášter 1 B2
Karlova 3 A4
Karlovo náměstí 5 B2
Karlovo náměstí (metro) 5 A3
Karlův most 2 F4
continues 3 A4
Karmelitská 2 E4
Karolinum 3 C4
Karoliny Světlé 3 A4
Katedrála Sv. Víta 2 D2
Kateřinská 5 C3
Ke Hradu 2 D3
Ke Karlovu 6 D2
Ke Štvanici 4 F2
Keplerova 1 B2
continues 1 B3
Klárov 2 F2
Klášter sv. Anežky 3 C2
Klášter sv. Jiří 2 E2
Klášterská 3 C2
Klausen Synagogue 3 B2
Klausová synagóga 3 B2
Klementinum 3 A4
Klimentská 4 D2
Knights of the Cross Square (Křižovnické náměstí) 3 A4
Konviktská 3 A5
Koperníkova 6 F4
Korunní 6 F2
Kosárkovo nábřeží 3 A2
Kostečná 3 B3
Kostel Panny Marie pod řetězem 2 E4
Kostel Panny Marie před Týnem 3 C3
Kostel Panny Marie Sněžné 3 C5
Kostel Panny Marie Vítězné 2 E4
Kostel sv. Cyrila a Metoděje 5 B2
Kostel sv. Ducha 3 B3
Kostel sv. Havla 3 C4
Kostel sv. Haštala 3 C2
Kostel sv. Ignáce 5 C2
Kostel sv. Jakuba 3 C3
Kostel sv. Jana na Skalce 5 B3
Kostel sv. Jiljí 3 B4
Kostel sv. Kateřiny 5 C3
Kostel sv. Martina ve zdi 3 B5
Kostel sv. Mikuláše 2 D3
Kostel sv. Mikuláše 3 B3
Kostel sv. Tomáše 2 E3
Kostel sv. Vavřince 1 C5
Kostel sv. Voršily 3 A5
Kostel sv. Šimona a Judy 3 B2
Kostel sv. Štěpána 5 C2
Koubkova 6 E3
Kozí 3 C2
Kožná 3 C4
Krakovská 6 D1
Královdvorská 4 D3
Královská zahrada 2 D2
Královský palác 2 D2
Krocínova 3 A5
Křemencova 5 B1
Křesomyslova 6 E5
Křižíkova 4 F3
Křižovnická 3 A4
Křižovnické náměstí 3 A4
Kubistické domy 3 B2
Kunětická 4 F5

L

Ladova 5 A4
Lanová dráha 2 D5
Lazarská 5 B1
Lázeňská 2 E4
Ledebour Garden 2 E2
Ledeburská zahrada 2 E2
Legerova 6 D2
Letenská 2 F3
Letenské sady 3 A1
Letenský tunel 3 C1
Libušina 5 A5
Lichnická 4 F5
Liliová 3 B4
Linhartská 3 B4
Lípová 5 C2
listopadu, 17. 3 B2
Little Quarter Square (Malostranské náměstí) 2 E3
Lobkovická zahrada 1 C4
Lobkovický palác 2 E2
Lobkowicz Palace 2 E2
Lodecká 4 E2
Lodní mlýny 4 E2
Londýnská 6 E2
Loreta 1 C3
Loretánská 1 B3
Loretánské náměstí 1 B3
Loreto, the 1 C3
Lublaňská 6 E2

M

Magdalény Rettigové 5 B1
Macharovo náměstí 1 A1
Máchova 6 F3
Maisel Synagogue 3 B3
Maiselova 3 B3
Maiselova synagóga 3 B3
Malá Klášterská 3 C2
Malá Štěpánská 5 C2
Malá Štupartská 3 C3
Malé náměstí 3 B4
Malostranská (metro) 2 F2
Malostranské nábřeží 2 F5
Malostranské náměstí 2 E3
Maltese Square (Maltézské náměstí) 2 E4
Maltézské náměstí 2 E4
Mánesova 6 E1
Mánesův most 3 A3
Mariánské hradby 2 D2
Mariánské náměstí 3 B3
Martinic Palace 1 C2
Martinický palác 1 C2
Martinská 3 B5
Masarykovo nábřeží 5 A2
Masarykovo nádraží 4 E3
Masná 3 C3
Melantrichova 3 B4
Melounová 6 D2
Mezibranská 6 D1
Mickiewiczova 2 F1
Michalská 3 B4
Michna Palace 2 E4
Michnův palác 2 E4

Mikovcova **6 D2**
Mikulandská **3 B5**
Milady Horákové **1 C1**
Mirror Maze **1 C4**
Míšeňská **2 F3**
Mlynářská **4 E2**
Morstadtova **1 A3**
most Legií **2 F5**
continues **3 A5**
most M. R. Štefánika **4 D1**
Mostecká **2 E3**
Municipal House **4 D3**
Museum of Decorative Arts **3 A3**
Můstek (metro) **3 C4** **4 D5**
Muzeum (metro) **6 D1**
Muzeum Antonína Dvořáka **6 D2**
Muzeum Bedřicha Smetany **3 A4**
Myslbekova **1 A3**
Myslíkova **5 A1**

N

Na baště sv. Jiří **2 E1**
Na baště sv. Ludmily **2 F1**
Na baště sv. Tomáše **2 F1**
Na bojišti **6 D3**
Na Děkance **5 B4**
Na Fidlovačce **6 F5**
Na Florenci **4 E3**
Na Folimance **6 E5**
Na Františku **3 B2**
Na Hrádku **5 B3**
Na Hrobci **5 A4**
Na Hubálce **1 A2**
Na Kampě **2 F4**
Na Kleovce **6 F4**
Na Libušince **5 A5**
Na Moráni **5 A3**
Na Můstku **3 C4**
Na náspu **1 B2**
Na Opyši **2 E2**
Na Ořechovce **1 A1**
Na ostrůvku **6 F5**
Na Panenské **1 A3**
Na Perštýně **3 B5**
Na poříčí **4 D3**
Na poříčním právu **5 A3**
Na Příkopě **3 C4**
Na rejdišti **3 A2**
Na Rybníčku **5 C2**
Na Salvátorská **3B3**
Na Slovanech **5 B3**
Na slupi **5 B4**
Na Smetance **6 F1**
Na struze **5 A1**
Na valech **2 D1**
Na výtoni **5 B4**
Na zábradlí **3 A4**
Na zbořenci **5 B2**
Na Zderaze **5 B2**
Nábřeží Edvarda Beneše **3 A2**
Nábřeží kpt. Jaroše **4 D1**
Nábřeží Ludvíka Svobody **4 D2**
Nad Octárnou **1 A2**
Nad Panenskou **1 A4**
Nad Petruskou **6 F4**
Nad Vojenským hřbitovem **1 A3**
Náměstí Bratří Synků **6 F5**
Náměstí Curieových **3 B2**
Náměstí I. P. Pavlova **6 D2**
Náměstí Jana Palacha **3 A3**
Náměstí Míru **6 F2**
Náměstí Míru (metro) **6 F2**
Náměstí Pod Emauzy **5 B3**
Náměstí Republiky **4 D3**
Náměstí Republiky (metro) **4 D3** **4 E3**
Náplavní **5 A2**
Náprstek museum **3 B4**
Náprstkova **3 A4**
Náprstkovo Muzeum **3 B4**
Národní **3 A5**
Národní divadlo **3 A5**
continues **5 A1**
Národní muzeum **6 E1**
Národní třída (metro) **3 B5**
National Museum **6 E1**
National Theatre **3 A5**
continues **5 A1**
Navrátilova **5 C1**
Nebovidská **2 E4**
Nekázanka **4 D4**
Neklanova **5 B5**
Nerudova **2 D3**
New Town Hall **5 B1**
New World (Nový Svět) **1 B2**
Nezamyslova **6 D5**
Nosticova **2 E4**
Nové mlýny **4 D2**
Novoměstská radnice **5 B1**
Novomlýnská **4 D2**
Novotného lávka **3 A4**
Nový Svět **1 B2**
Nuselská **6 F5**
Nuselský most **6 D5**

O

Odborů **5 B1**
Obecní dům **4 D3**
Obrazárna Pražského hradu **2 D2**
Observation Tower **1 C4**
Observatory **2 D5**
Old Jewish Cemetery **3 A2**
Old Town Hall **3 C3**
Old Town Square (Staroměstské náměstí) **3 B3**
Old-New Synagogue **3 B2**
Oldřichova **6 D5**
Olivova **4 D5**
Olympijská **1 B5**
Omladinářů **5 B1**
Opatovická **5 B1**
Opletalova **4 D5**
Ostrčilovo náměstí **5 C5**
Ostrov Štvanice **4 F1**
Ostrovní **3 B5**
continues **5 A1**
Otakarova **6 F5**
Otevřená **1 A2**
Ovocný trh **3 C3**

P

Palác Golz-Kinských **3 C3**
Palace of the Lords of Kunštát **3 A4**
Palackého **3 C5**
Palackého most **5 A3**
Palackého náměstí **5 A3**
Panská **4 D4**
Parléřova **1 A3**
Pařížská **3 B2**
Patočkova **1 A3**
Pavlova, I. P. (metro) **6 D2**
Pelclova **2 E4**
Perlová **3 B4**
Perucká **6 F4**
Petrská **4 E2**
Petrské náměstí **4 E2**
Petřín Park **2 D5**
Petřínské sady **2 D5**
Pevnostní **1 B1**
Picture Gallery of Prague Castle **2 D2**
Pinkas Synagogue **3 A3**
Pinkasova synagóga **3 A3**
Plaská **2 E5**
Platnéřská **3 B3**
Plavecká **5 A4**
Pobřežní **4 F2**
Pod baštami **2 E1**
Pod Bruskou **2 F2**
Pod hradbami **1 B1**
Pod Karlovem **6 E4**
Pod Nuselskými schody **6 E4**
Pod Slovany **5 B4**
Pod Větrovem **5 C3**
Pod Zvonařkou **6 E4**
Podskalská **5 A3**
Pohořelec **1 B3**
Politických vězňů **4 D5**
Polská **6 F1**
Pomník Jana Husa **3 B3**
Powder Gate **4 D3**
Powder Tower **2 D2**
Prašná brána **4 D3**
Prašná věž **2 D2**
Prokopská **2 E4**
Provaznická **3 C4**
Průchodní **3 B5**
Přemyslova **5 B5**
Příběnická **4 F4**
Příčná **5 C1**
Pštrossova **5 A1**
Purkyňova **3 B5**
Pútova **4 E2**

R

Radnické schody **1 C3**
Rámová **3 C2**
Rašínovo nábřeží **5 A2**
Rejskova **6 E5**
Resslova **5 B2**
Restaurace U Kalicha **6 D3**
Revoluční **4 D2**
Riegrovy sady **6 F1**
Rohanské nábřeží **4 F1**
Royal Garden **2 D2**
Royal Palace **2 D2**
Rozhledna **1 C4**
Rubešova **6 E1**
Rudolfinum **3 A3**
Rumunská **6 E2**
Růžová **4 D4**
Růžový sad **1 C5**
Rybná **3 C2**
Rytířská **3 B4**

Ř

Řásnovka **3 C2**
Řetězová **3 B4**
Řeznická **5 C1**
Říční **2 E5**
října, 28. **3 C5**
Římská **6 E1**

S

St Agnes's Convent **3 C2**
St George's Basilica **2 E2**
St George's Convent **2 E2**
St Vitus's Cathedral (Katedrála Sv. Víta) **2 D2**
Salmovská **5 C2**
Samcova **4 E2**

Sarajevská 6 E5
Saská 2 E4
Sázavská 6 F3
Schönbornská zahrada 2 D4
Schwarzenberg Palace 2 D3
Schwarzenberský palác 2 D3
Seifertova 4 F4
Sekaninova 6 D5
Seminářská 3 B4
Seminářská zahrada 2 D4
Senovážná 4 D4
Senovážné náměstí 4 E4
Sezimova 6 F5
Sibeliova 1 A2
Skořepka 3 B4
Slavojova 5 C5
Slavonic House 4 D4
Slavonic Monastery 5 B3
Slezská 6 F2
Slovanský dům 4 D4
Slovanský ostrov 5 A1
Slunná 1 A1
Smetana Museum 3 A4
Smetanovo nábřeží 3 A5
Sněmovní 2 E3
Sokolovská 4 F2
Sokolská 6 D2
Soukenická 4 D2
South Gardens 2 D3
Spálená 3 B5
continues 5 B1
Spanish Synagogue 3 C2
Spartakiadní Stadion 1 B5
Spytihněvova 6 E5
Staré zámecké schody 2 E2
Stárkova 4 E2
Staroměstská (metro) 3 B3
Staroměstská radnice 3 C3
Staroměstské náměstí 3 B3
Staronová synagóga 3 B2
Starý židovský hřbitov 3 A2
State Opera 4 E5
continues 6 E1
Státní opera 4 E5
continues 6 E1
Stavovské divadlo 3 C4
Sternberg Palace 1 C2
Strahov Monastery 1 B4
Strahovská 1 B4
Strahovská zahrada 1 B4
Strahovský klášter 1 B4
Strmá 1 B1
Střelecký ostrov 2 F5
Střešovická 1 A2
Stříbrná 3 A4
Studničkova 5 C4
Svatoplukova 6 D5
Svatovítská 1 C1
Svobodova 5 A4

Š

Šafaříkova 6 E3
Šeříková 2 E5
Široká 3 B3
Šítkova 5 A1
Školská 5 C1
Škrétova 6 E1
Špálova 1 A1
Španělská 4 F5
continues 6 E1
Španělská synagóga 3 C2
Šporkova 2 D3
Štěpánská 5 C1
Šternberský palác 1 C2
Štupartská 3 C3
Šubertova 6 F2

T

Templová 3 C3
Těšnov 4 F2
Těšnovský tunel 4 E1
Thunovská 2 E3
Tomášská 2 E3
Trojanova 5 A2
Trojická 5 B3
Truhlářská 4 D3
Tržiště 2 E3
Tychonova 2 E1
Tylovo náměstí 6 E2
Týnská 3 C3
Týnská ulička 3 C3
Tyršova 6 D3

U

U Bruských kasáren 2 F2
U Brusnice 1 B2
U Bulhara 4 F4
U divadla 4 E5
U Dobřenských 3 A4
U Fleků 5 B1
U kasáren 1 C3
U laboratoře 1 A1
U lanové dráhy 2 E5
U letohrádku královny Anny 2 E1
U lužického semináře 2 F3
U milosrdných 3 B2
U nemocenské pojišťovny 4 D2
U nemocnice 5 B3
U Obecního domu 4 D3
U obecního dvora 3 C2
U Písecké brány 2 E1
U plovárny 3 A2
U Prašné brány 4 D3
U Prašného mostu 2 D1
U půjčovny 4 D4
U radnice 3 B3
U Sovových mlýnů 2 F5
U staré školy 3 B2
U starého hřbitova 3 B2
U Sv. Tomáše 2 E3
U Tří pštrosů 2 F3
U Zlaté studně 2 E2
U Zvonařky 6 E4
U železné lávky 2 F2
Uhelný trh 3 B5
Újezd 2 E4
Uměleckoprůmyslové muzeum 3 A2
Uruguayská 6 F3
Úvoz 1 B3

V

V celnici 4 D3
V cípu 4 D4
V jámě 5 C1
V jirchářích 5 B1
V kotcích 3 B4
V pevnosti 5 B5
V tůních 6 D2
Václavská 5 B2
Václavské náměstí 3 C5
continues 6 D1
Valdštejnská 2 E2
Valdštejnská zahrada 2 E3
Valdštejnské náměstí 2 E3
Valdštejnský palác 2 E3
Valentinská 3 B3
Vaníčkova 1 A4
Varšavská 6 F3
Ve Smečkách 6 D1
Vejvodova 3 B4
Veleslavínova 3 A3
Velkopřevorské náměstí 2 E4
Vězeňská 3 C2
Vikářská 2 D2
Vinařického 5 B4
Viničná 5 C3
Vinohradská 6 E1
Vítězná 2 E5
Vladislavova 3 C5
continues 5 C1
Vlašská 1 C4
Vltava 3 A2
continues 5 A3
Vnislavova 5 A5
Vocelova 6 E2
Vodičkova 3 C5
continues 5 C1
Vojan Park 2 F3
Vojanovy sady 2 F3
Vojtěšská 5 A1
Voršilská 3 B5
Votočkova 5 C4
Vozová 4 F5
Vratislavova 5 B5
Vrchlického sady 4 E4
Vrtba Garden 2 D4
Vrtbovská zahrada 2 D4
Všehrdova 2 E5
Východní 1 A1
Vysoká synagóga 3 B3
Vyšehradský hřbitov 5 B5

W

Wallenstein Palace 2 E3
Washingtonova 4 E5
continues 6 D1
Wenceslas Square (Václavské náměstí) 3 C5
continues 6 D1
Wenzigova 6 D4
Wilsonova 4 E5
continues 6 E1

Z

Za Haštalem 3 C2
Za Hládkovem 1 A3
Za Pohořelcem 1 A4
Za Poříčskou bránou 4 F2
Záhořanského 5 A2
Záhřebská 6 F3
Zámecká 2 E3
Zámecké schody 2 D3
Závišova 6 E5
Zborovská 2 F5
Zbrojnická 1 A1
Zítkovy sady 5 A3
Zlatá 3 B4
Zlatá ulička 2 E2
Zlatnická 4 E2
Zrcadlové bludiště 1 C4

Ž

Žatecká 3 B3
Železná 3 C4
Železnični most 5 A5
Židovská radnice 3 B3
Žitná 5 C1

DĚLOSTŘELECKÁ
ZBROJNICKÁ
ŠPÁLOVA
U LABORATOŘE
SLUNNÁ
PEVNOSTNÍ
POD HRADBAMI
SVATOVÍTSKÁ
NA OŘECHOVCE
MILADY
STRMÁ
CUKROVARNICKÁ
PATOČKOVA
U BRUSNICE
VÝCHODNÍ
JELENÍ
STŘEŠOVICKÁ
PRAŽSKÝ HRA
A HRADČANY
PRAGUE CASTL
AND HRADČAN
SIBELIOVA
NA HUBALCE
NAD OCTÁRNOU
OTEVŘENÁ
Brusnice
NOVÝ SVĚT
Šternberský palác
Sternberg Palace
Martinický palác
Martinic Palace
KEPLEROVA
ČERNÍNSKÁ
Kapucínský klášter
Capuchin Monastery
KAPUCÍNSKÁ
KANOVNICKÁ
NA NÁSPU
U KASÁREN
NAD VOJEN. HŘBITOVEM
NA HUBALCE
HRADČA NÁME
Loreta
The Loreto
RADNICK SCHODY
HLÁDKOVEM
HLÁDKOV
Černínský palác
Černín Palace
LORETÁNSKÉ NÁMĚSTÍ
MYSLBEKOVA
MORSTADTOVA
LORETÁNSKÁ
ÚVO
NA PANENSKÉ
PARLÉŘOVA
ÚVOZ
POHOŘELEC
NAD PANENSKOU
Strahovský klášter
Strahov Monastery
ZA POHOŘELCEM
DLABAČOV
VLAŠSKÁ
BĚLOHORSKÁ
DISKAŘSKÁ
STRAHOVSKÁ
LOBKOVICKÁ ZAHRADA
STRAHOVSKÁ ZAHRADA
VANÍČKOVA
Hladová zeď
Hunger Wall
Rozhledna
Observation Tower
Zrcadlové bludi
Mirror Maze
CHODECKÁ
STRAHOVSKÁ
Kostel sv. Vavřince
Church of St Lawrence
RŮŽOVÝ SAD
VANÍČKOVA
OLYMPIJSKÁ
SPARTAKIÁDNÍ STADIÓN
CHALOUPECKÉHO
1
2
3
4
5
A
B
C

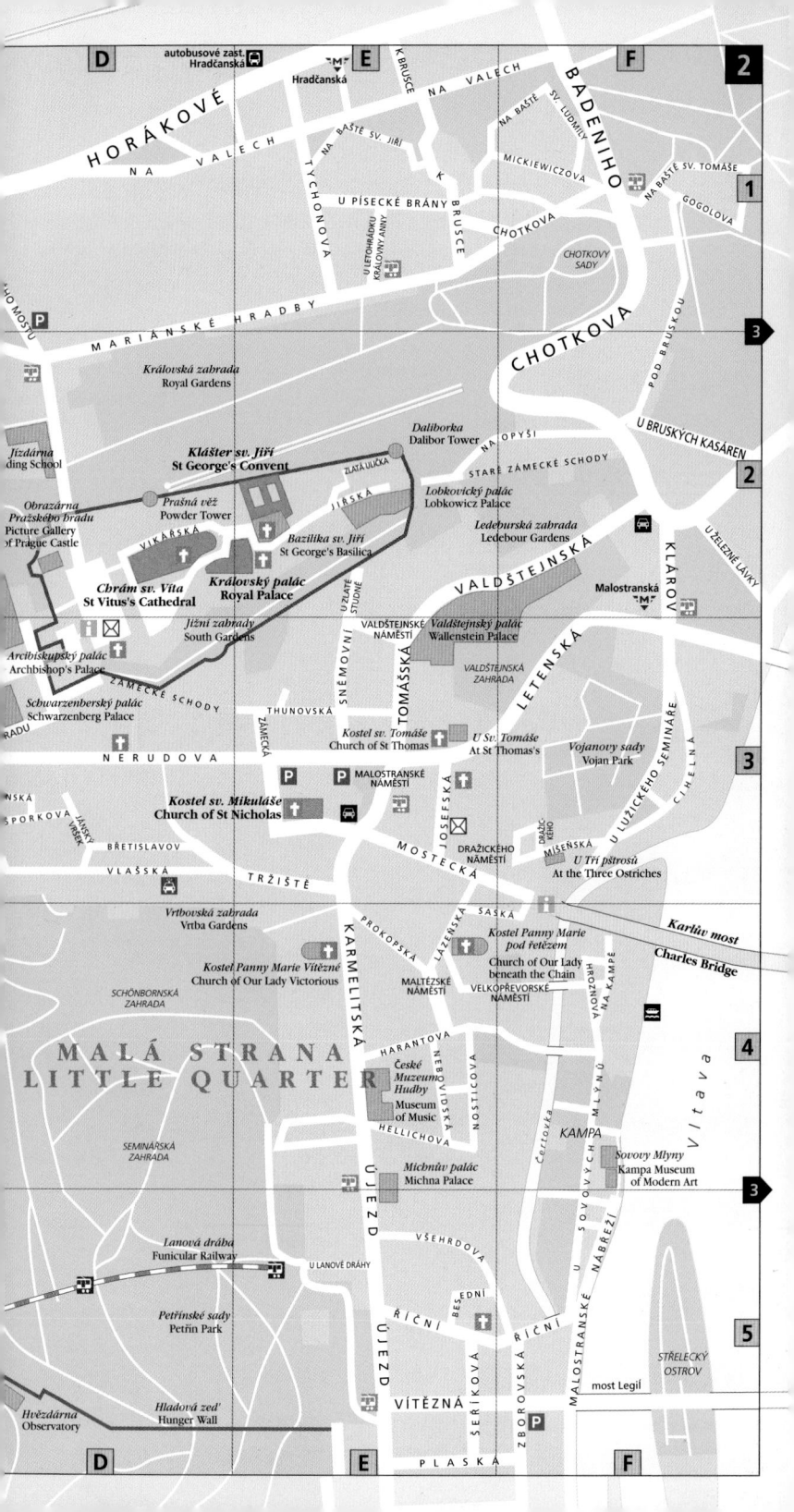
D
E
F
2
1
3
4
5
autobusové zast. Hradčanská
Hradčanská
HORÁKOVÉ
NA VALECH
K BRUSCE
NA VALECH
BADENIHO
NA BAŠTĚ SV. JIŘÍ
NA BAŠTĚ SV. LUDMILY
MICKIEWICZOVA
NA BAŠTĚ SV. TOMÁŠE
GOGOLOVA
TYCHONOVA
U PÍSECKÉ BRÁNY
BRUSCE
CHOTKOVA
U LETOHRADKU KRÁLOVNY ANNY
CHOTKOVY SADY
MARIÁNSKÉ HRADBY
CHOTKOVA
POD BRUSKOU
Královská zahrada
Royal Gardens
Jízdárna
ding School
Klášter sv. Jiří
St George's Convent
Daliborka
Dalibor Tower
NA OPYŠI
U BRUSKÝCH KASÁREN
STARÉ ZÁMECKÉ SCHODY
ZLATÁ ULIČKA
JIŘSKÁ
Obrazárna
Pražského hradu
Picture Gallery
of Prague Castle
Prašná věž
Powder Tower
Lobkovický palác
Lobkowicz Palace
Ledebourská zahrada
Ledebour Gardens
VIKÁŘSKÁ
Bazilika sv. Jiří
St George's Basilica
VALDŠTEJNSKÁ
KLÁROV
U ŽELEZNÉ LÁVKY
Chrám sv. Víta
St Vitus's Cathedral
Královský palác
Royal Palace
U ZLATÉ STUDNĚ
Malostranská
Jižní zahrady
South Gardens
VALDŠTEJNSKÉ NÁMĚSTÍ
Valdštejnský palác
Wallenstein Palace
Archibiskupský palác
Archbishop's Palace
SNĚMOVNÍ
TOMÁŠSKÁ
LETENSKÁ
VALDŠTEJNSKÁ ZAHRADA
ZÁMECKÉ SCHODY
Schwarzenberský palác
Schwarzenberg Palace
THUNOVSKÁ
ZÁMECKÁ
Kostel sv. Tomáše
Church of St Thomas
U Sv. Tomáše
At St Thomas's
Vojanovy sady
Vojan Park
NERUDOVA
MALOSTRANSKÉ NÁMĚSTÍ
Kostel sv. Mikuláše
Church of St Nicholas
JOSEFSKÁ
U LUŽICKÉHO SEMINÁŘE
CIHELNÁ
ŠPORKOVA
JÁNSKÝ VRŠEK
BŘETISLAVOV
DRAŽICKÉHO NÁMĚSTÍ
MÍŠENSKÁ
U Tří pštrosů
At the three Ostriches
VLAŠSKÁ
TRŽIŠTĚ
MOSTECKÁ
Vrtbovská zahrada
Vrtba Gardens
SASKÁ
Karlův most
Charles Bridge
PROKOPSKÁ
LAZEŘSKÁ
Kostel Panny Marie pod řetězem
Church of Our Lady beneath the Chain
Kostel Panny Marie Vítězné
Church of Our Lady Victorious
KARMELITSKÁ
MALTÉZSKÉ NÁMĚSTÍ
VELKOPŘEVORSKÉ NÁMĚSTÍ
HRONOVY
NA KAMPĚ
SCHÖNBORNSKÁ ZAHRADA
MALÁ STRANA
LITTLE QUARTER
HARANTOVA
České Muzeum Hudby
Museum of Music
NEBOVIDSKÁ
NOSTICOVA
HELLICHOVA
Vltava
KAMPA
SEMINÁŘSKÁ ZAHRADA
Čertovka
Sovovy Mlýny
Kampa Museum of Modern Art
Michnův palác
Michna Palace
ÚJEZD
U SOVOVÝCH MLÝNŮ
VŠEHRDOVA
Lanová dráha
Funicular Railway
U LANOVÉ DRÁHY
BĚŠEDNÍ
ŘÍČNÍ
ŘÍČNÍ
Petřínské sady
Petřín Park
MALOSTRANSKÉ NÁBŘEŽÍ
STŘELECKÝ OSTROV
most Legií
ŠERÍKOVA
ZBOROVSKÁ
VÍTĚZNÁ
Hvězdárna
Observatory
Hladová zeď
Hunger Wall
PLASKÁ

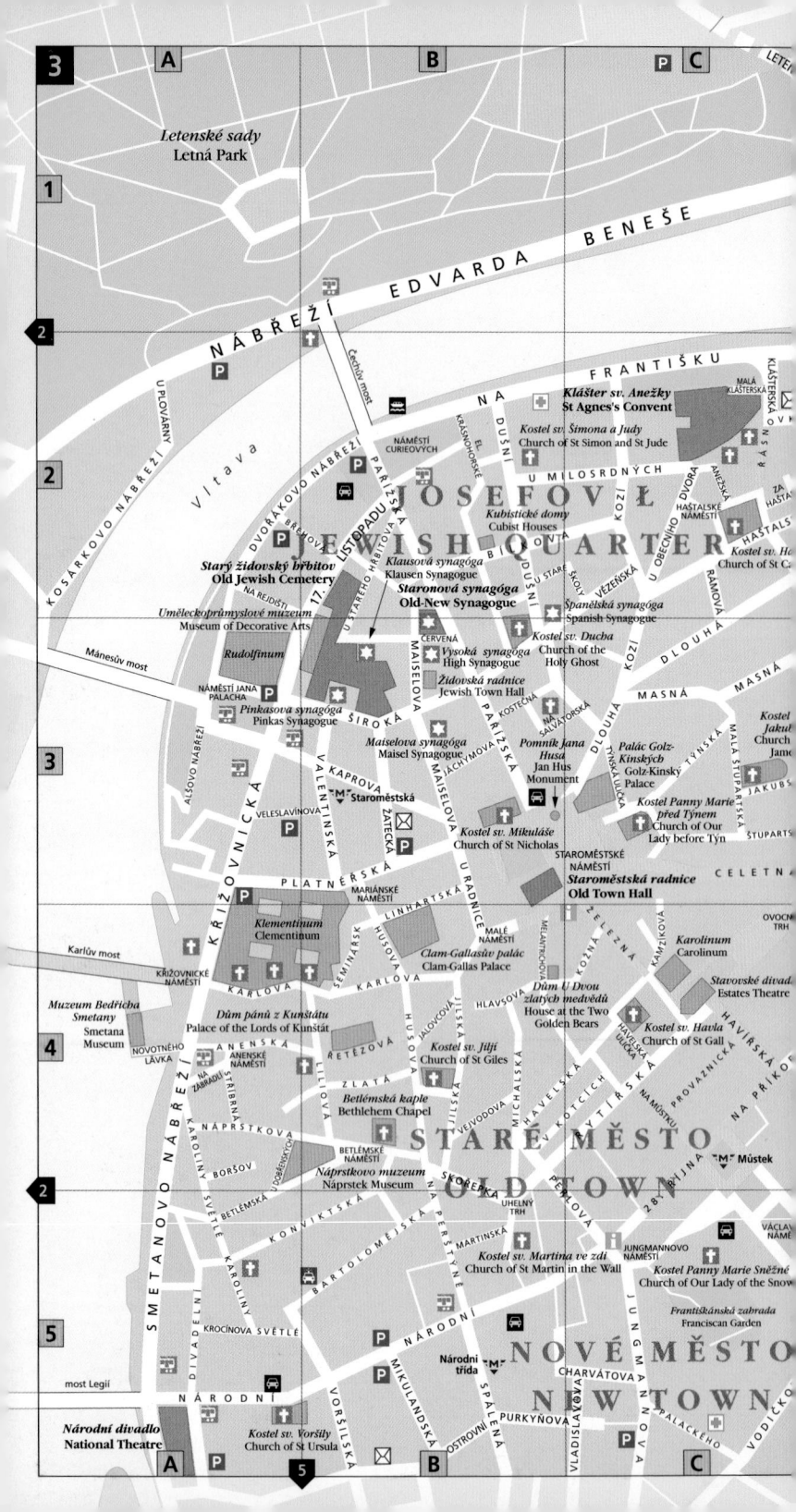
Letenské sady
Letná Park
NÁBŘEŽÍ EDVARDA BENEŠE
Čechův most
Vltava
KOŠÁRKOVO NÁBŘEŽÍ
U PLOVÁRNY
DVOŘÁKOVO NÁBŘEŽÍ
NA REJDIŠTI
Mánesův most
ALŠOVO NÁBŘEŽÍ
FRANTIŠKU
Klášter sv. Anežky
St Agnes's Convent
MALÁ KLÁŠTERSKÁ
Kostel sv. Šimona a Judy
Church of St Simon and St Jude
NÁMĚSTÍ CURIEOVÝCH
U MILOSRDNÝCH
JOSEFOV
JEWISH QUARTER
Kubistické domy
Cubist Houses
Staré židovský hřbitov
Old Jewish Cemetery
Klausová synagóga
Klausen Synagogue
Staronová synagóga
Old-New Synagogue
Španělská synagóga
Spanish Synagogue
Uměleckoprůmyslové muzeum
Museum of Decorative Arts
Rudolfinum
Vysoká synagóga
High Synagogue
Kostel sv. Ducha
Church of the Holy Ghost
Židovská radnice
Jewish Town Hall
NÁMĚSTÍ JANA PALACHA
Pinkasova synagóga
Pinkas Synagogue
Maiselova synagóga
Maisel Synagogue
Pomník Jana Husa
Jan Hus Monument
Palác Golz-Kinských
Golz-Kinský Palace
Kostel Panny Marie před Týnem
Church of Our Lady before Týn
Kostel sv. Mikuláše
Church of St Nicholas
Staroměstská
STAROMĚSTSKÉ NÁMĚSTÍ
Staroměstská radnice
Old Town Hall
PLATNÉŘSKÁ
MARIÁNSKÉ NÁMĚSTÍ
Klementinum
Clementinum
MALÉ NÁMĚSTÍ
Clam-Gallasův palác
Clam-Gallas Palace
Karolinum
Carolinum
Stavovské divadlo
Estates Theatre
Karlův most
KŘÍŽOVNICKÉ NÁMĚSTÍ
Muzeum Bedřicha Smetany
Smetana Museum
Dům pánů z Kunštátu
Palace of the Lords of Kunštát
Dům U Dvou zlatých medvědů
House at the Two Golden Bears
Kostel sv. Havla
Church of St Gall
Kostel sv. Jiljí
Church of St Giles
Betlémská kaple
Bethlehem Chapel
Náprstkovo muzeum
Náprstek Museum
STARÉ MĚSTO
OLD TOWN
Můstek
NOVÉ MĚSTO
NEW TOWN
Kostel sv. Martina ve zdi
Church of St Martin in the Wall
Kostel Panny Marie Sněžné
Church of Our Lady of the Snow
Františkánská zahrada
Franciscan Garden
Národní třída
most Legií
Národní divadlo
National Theatre
Kostel sv. Voršily
Church of St Ursula
KŘÍŽOVNICKÁ
SMETANOVO NÁBŘEŽÍ
NÁRODNÍ
MIKULANDSKÁ
VORŠILSKÁ
PURKYŇOVA
VLADISLAVOVA
JUNGMANNOVA
PALACKÉHO
VODIČKOVA
CHARVÁTOVA
JUNGMANNOVO NÁMĚSTÍ
KONVIKTSKÁ
BARTOLOMĚJSKÁ
MARTINSKÁ
KROCÍNOVA
SVĚTLE
DIVADELNÍ
KAROLINY
BETLÉMSKÉ NÁMĚSTÍ
NÁPRSTKOVA
BORŠOV
ZLATÁ
LILIOVÁ
ANENSKÁ
ANENSKÉ NÁMĚSTÍ
NOVOTNÉHO LÁVKA
RETĚZOVÁ
HUSOVA
JILSKÁ
MICHALSKÁ
HAVELSKÁ
KOTCÍCH
VYTÍŘSKÁ
NA MŮSTKU
PROVAZNICKÁ
HAVÍŘSKÁ
NA PŘÍKOPĚ
ŽELEZNÁ
KOZNÁ
KAMZÍKOVÁ
HLAVSOVA
JALOVCOVÁ
SEMINÁRSKÁ
KARLOVA
LINHARTSKÁ
U RADNICE
MELANTRICHOVA
VELESLAVÍNOVA
VALENTINSKÁ
KAPROVA
ŽATECKÁ
MAISELOVA
PARÍŽSKÁ
JÁCHIMOVA
KOSTEČNÁ
NA SALVATORSKÁ
TYNSKÁ ULIČKA
TYNSKÁ
MALÁ STUPARTSKÁ
STUPARTSKÁ
JAKUBSKÁ
MASNÁ
DLOUHÁ
KOZÍ
RAMOVA
U OBECNÍHO DVORA
HAŠTALSKÉ NÁMĚSTÍ
ANEŽSKÁ
U STARÉ ŠKOLY
VĚŽEŇSKÁ
U TAŘEHO HABITOVA
17. LISTOPADU
PAŘÍZSKÁ
KRÁSNOHORSKÉ
ŠIROKÁ
BŘEHOVÁ
ZÁMECKÁ
ÚHELNÝ TRH
SKOŘEPKA
28. ŘÍJNA
MALÉ NÁMĚSTÍ
OVOCNÝ TRH
CELETNÁ
VÁCLAVSKÉ NÁMĚSTÍ
Letenské sady
Letná Park
Čechův most
Mánesův most
Karlův most
most Legií
Staroměstská
Můstek
Národní třída

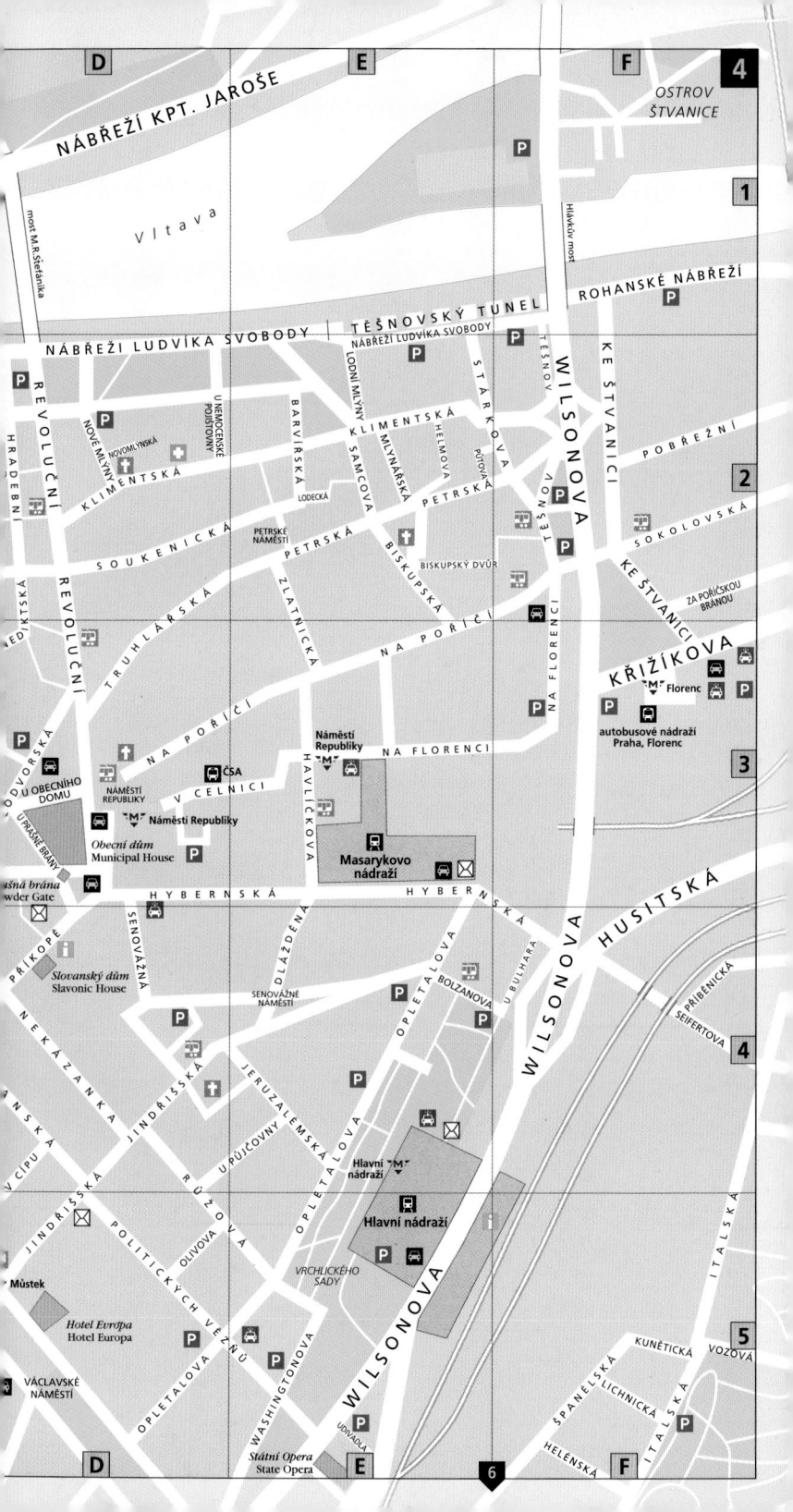
D
E
F
4
1
2
3
5
6
NÁBŘEŽÍ KPT. JAROŠE
OSTROV ŠTVANICE
Vltava
most M.R.Štefánika
Hlávkův most
ROHANSKÉ NÁBŘEŽÍ
TĚŠNOVSKÝ TUNEL
NÁBŘEŽÍ LUDVÍKA SVOBODY
NÁBŘEŽÍ LUDVÍKA SVOBODY
LODNÍ MLÝNY
STÁRKOVA
TĚŠNOV
KE ŠTVANICI
WILSONOVA
REVOLUČNÍ
NOVÉ MLÝNY
NOVOMLÝNSKÁ
U NĚMECKÉHO POJIŠŤOVNY
BARVÍŘSKÁ
KLIMENTSKÁ
SAMCOVA
MLÝNÁŘSKÁ
HELMOVA
PŘÍTOVÁ
PETRSKÁ
POBŘEŽNÍ
HRADEBNÍ
LODECKÁ
SOUKENICKÁ
PETRSKÉ NÁMĚSTÍ
BISKUPSKÁ
BISKUPSKÝ DVŮR
SOKOLOVSKÁ
KEŠTVANICI
ZA POŘÍČSKOU BRÁNOU
TRUHLÁŘSKÁ
ZLATNICKÁ
NA POŘÍČÍ
NA FLORENCI
KŘIŽÍKOVA
Florenc
autobusové nádraží Praha, Florenc
U OBECNÍHO DOMU
NÁMĚSTÍ REPUBLIKY
ČSA
V CELNICI
Náměstí Republiky
Náměstí Republiky
HAVLÍČKOVA
Masarykovo nádraží
Obecní dům
Municipal House
U PRAŠNÉ BRÁNY
HYBERNSKÁ
HYBERNSKÁ
HUSITSKÁ
PŘÍKOPY
Slovanský dům
Slavonic House
SENOVÁŽNÁ
SENOVÁŽNÉ NÁMĚSTÍ
DLÁŽDĚNÁ
OPLETALOVA
BOLZANOVA
U BULHARA
PŘÍBĚNICKÁ
SEIFERTOVA
NEKÁZANKA
JINDŘIŠSKÁ
JERUZALÉMSKÁ
U PŮJČOVNY
Hlavní nádraží
Hlavní nádraží
RŮŽOVÁ
OLIVOVÁ
POLITICKÝCH VĚŽŇŮ
VRCHLICKÉHO SADY
ITALSKÁ
Můstek
Hotel Evropa
Hotel Europa
OPLETALOVA
WASHINGTONOVA
KUNĚTICKÁ
VOZOVÁ
ŠPANELSKÁ
LIBNICKÁ
VÁCLAVSKÉ NÁMĚSTÍ
UDVARA
Státní Opera
State Opera
HELENSKÁ

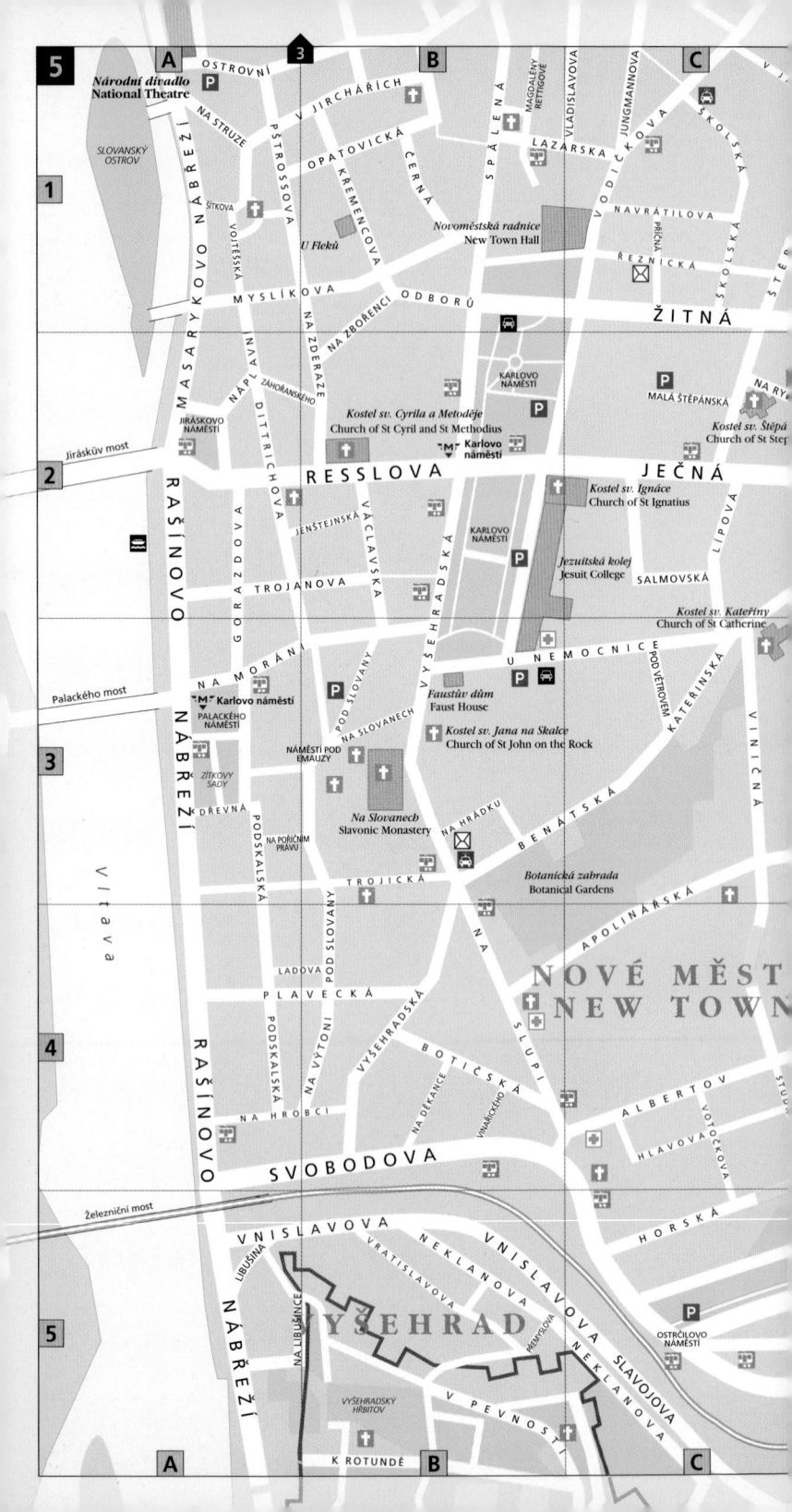
Národní divadlo
National Theatre
SLOVANSKÝ OSTROV
OSTROVNÍ
NA STRUZE
PŠTROSSOVA
VJIRCHÁŘICH
OPATOVICKÁ
KŘEMENCOVA
ČERNÁ
SPÁLENÁ
MAGDALÉNY RETTIGOVÉ
VLADISLAVOVA
JUNGMANNOVA
LAZARSKÁ
VODIČKOVA
ŠKOLSKÁ
NAVRÁTILOVA
PŘÍČNÁ
ŘEZNICKÁ
ŠITKOVA
VOJTĚŠSKÁ
U Fleků
Novoměstská radnice
New Town Hall
MYSLÍKOVA
NA ZÁBORENCI
ODBORŮ
ŽITNÁ
MASARYKOVO NÁBŘEŽÍ
NAPLAVKA
NA ZDERAZE
ZÁHOŘANSKÉHO
DITTRICHOVA
KARLOVO NÁMĚSTÍ
MALÁ ŠTĚPÁNSKÁ
Kostel sv. Cyrila a Metoděje
Church of St Cyril and St Methodius
Kostel sv. Štěpá
Church of St Step
JIRÁSKOVO NÁMĚSTÍ
Jiráskův most
RESSLOVA
JEČNÁ
Kostel sv. Ignáce
Church of St Ignatius
RAŠÍNOVO NÁBŘEŽÍ
GORAZDOVA
JENŠTEJNSKÁ
VÁCLAVSKÁ
VYŠEHRADSKÁ
KARLOVO NÁMĚSTÍ
Jezuitská kolej
Jesuit College
LIPOVÁ
SALMOVSKÁ
TROJANOVA
Kostel sv. Kateřiny
Church of St Catherine
NA MORÁNI
U NEMOCNICE
PODVĚTROVEM
KATEŘINSKÁ
Palackého most
Karlovo náměstí
PALACKÉHO NÁMĚSTÍ
POD SLOVANY
NA SLOVANECH
Faustův dům
Faust House
Kostel sv. Jana na Skalce
Church of St John on the Rock
NÁMĚSTÍ POD EMAUZY
ZÍTKOVY SADY
DŘEVNÁ
PODSKALSKÁ
NA POŘÍČNÍM PRÁVU
Na Slovanech
Slavonic Monastery
NA HRADKU
BENÁTSKÁ
VINIČNÁ
Botanická zahrada
Botanical Gardens
TROJICKÁ
APOLINÁŘSKÁ
Vltava
LADOVA
PLAVECKÁ
NOVÉ MĚST
NEW TOWN
NA VÝTONI
VYŠEHRADSKÁ
BOTIČSKÁ
NA SLUPI
NA HROBCI
NA DĚKANCE
VINAŘICKÉHO
ALBERTOV
HLAVOVA
VOTOČKOVA
SVOBODOVA
Železniční most
VNISLAVOVA
LIBUŠINA
VRATISLAVOVA
NEKLANOVA
HORSKÁ
VYŠEHRAD
NA LIBUŠINCE
PŘEMYSLOVA
OSTRČILOVO NÁMĚSTÍ
SLAVOJOVA
VYŠEHRADSKÝ HŘBITOV
V PEVNOSTI
K ROTUNDĚ

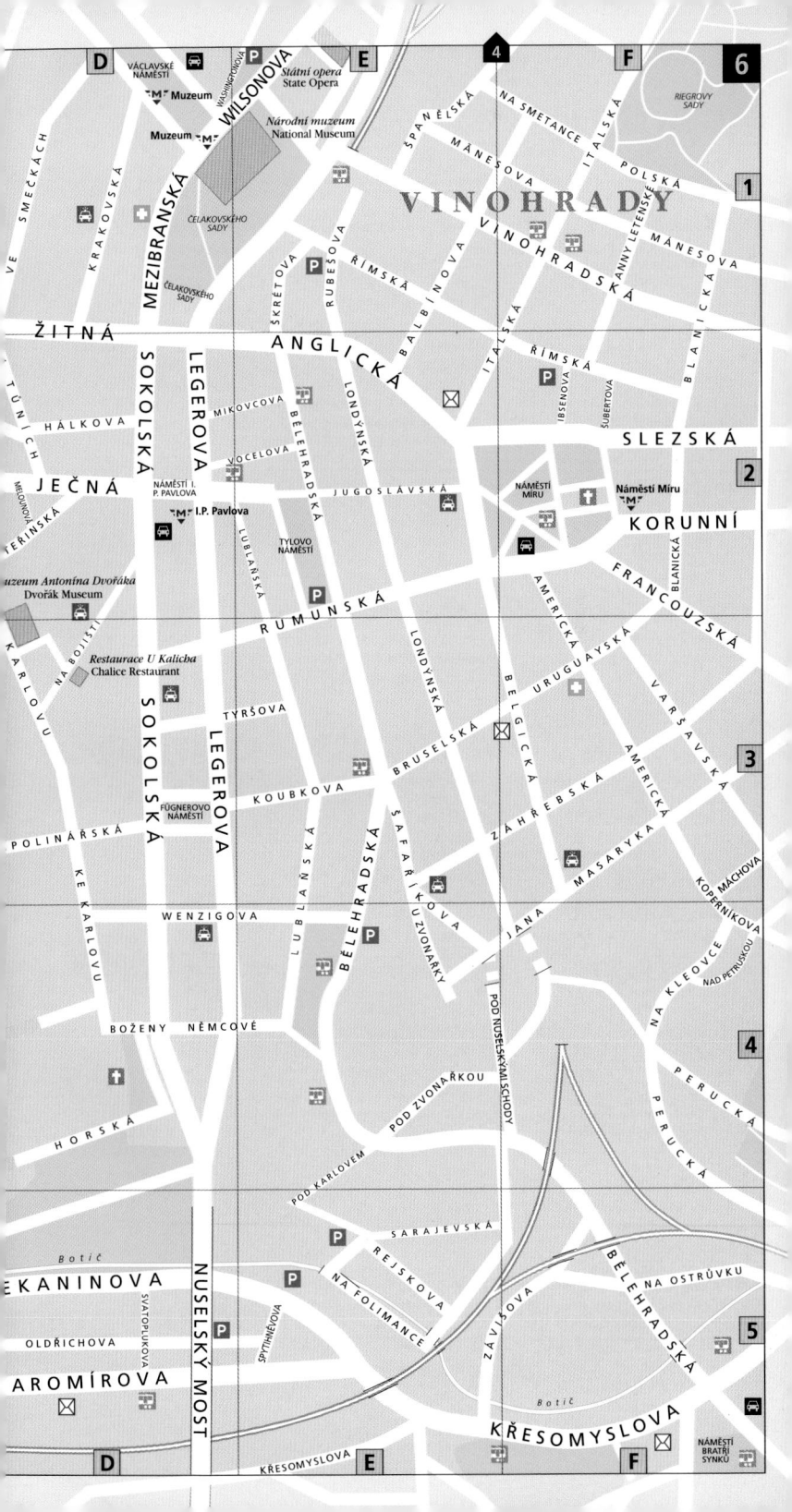
D
E
F
4
6
1
2
3
4
5
VÁCLAVSKÉ NÁMĚSTÍ
Muzeum
Muzeum
WILSONOVA
Státní opera
State Opera
Národní muzeum
National Museum
ČELAKOVSKÉHO SADY
ČELAKOVSKÉHO SADY
RIEGROVY SADY
ŠPANĚLSKÁ
NA SMETANCE
ITALSKÁ
MÁNESOVA
POLSKÁ
VINOHRADY
VINOHRADSKÁ
ANNY LEFENŠE
MÁNESOVA
BLANICKÁ
VE SMEČKÁCH
KRAKOVSKÁ
MEZIBRANSKÁ
ŠKRÉTOVA
RUBEŠOVA
ŘÍMSKÁ
BALBÍNOVA
ITALSKÁ
ŘÍMSKÁ
IBŠENOVA
ŠUBERTOVA
ŽITNÁ
ANGLICKÁ
SOKOLSKÁ
LEGEROVA
MIKOVCOVA
LONDÝNSKÁ
BĚLEHRADSKÁ
TŮNICH
HÁLKOVA
SLEZSKÁ
JEČNÁ
NÁMĚSTÍ I. P. PAVLOVA
I.P. Pavlova
VOCELOVA
JUGOSLÁVSKÁ
NÁMĚSTÍ MÍRU
Náměstí Míru
KORUNNÍ
MELOUNOVA
TEŘINSKÁ
LUBLAŇSKÁ
TYLOVO NÁMĚSTÍ
Muzeum Antonína Dvořáka
Dvořák Museum
RUMUNSKÁ
AMERICKÁ
FRANCOUZSKÁ
BLANICKÁ
NA BOJIŠTI
Restaurace U Kalicha
Chalice Restaurant
KARLOVU
LONDÝNSKÁ
URUGUAYSKÁ
BELGICKÁ
VARSAVSKÁ
TYRŠOVA
SOKOLSKÁ
LEGEROVA
BRUSELSKÁ
KOUBKOVA
AMERICKÁ
FÜGNEROVO NÁMĚSTÍ
POLINÁŘSKÁ
ZÁHŘEBSKÁ
SAFÁŘÍKOVA
BĚLEHRADSKÁ
LUBLAŇSKÁ
MASARYKA
KOPERNÍKOVA
KE KARLOVU
WENZIGOVA
JANA
UŽVONAŘKY
NA KLEOVCE
NAD PETRUSKOU
POD NUSELSKÝMI SCHODY
BOŽENY NĚMCOVÉ
POD ZVONAŘKOU
PERUCKÁ
PERUCKÁ
HORSKÁ
POD KARLOVEM
SARAJEVSKÁ
ŘEJSKOVÁ
NA FOLIMANCE
NA OSTRŮVKU
BĚLEHRADSKÁ
ZÁVIŠOVA
Botič
EKANINOVA
SVATOPLUKOVA
OLDŘICHOVA
AROMÍROVA
SPYTIHNĚVOVA
NUSELSKÝ MOST
Botič
KŘESOMYSLOVA
KŘESOMYSLOVA
NÁMĚSTÍ BRATŘÍ SYNKŮ

General Index

Page numbers in **bold** type refer to main entries.

A

Adalbert, St 21, 22, 136, 140, 163
Adam and Eve (Cranach) 114
Adria Palace 144
Agencies (accommodation) 186
Agnes, St 23, 35, 44, 92
Air pollution 229
Air travel 236–7
Airport (Ruzyně) 236, 237
Aleš, Mikuláš
  George of Poděbrady and Matthias Corvinus 164
  National Theatre murals 33
  Old Town Hall decorations 73
  Star Hunting Lodge museum 163
  Štorch house 62, 68
  U Rotta decorations 62
  Wiehl House 144
All Saints' Chapel (Royal Palace) 104, 105
Allegory of Night (Braun) 111
Alliprandi, Giovanni Battista 110, 135
Altarpiece of the Holy Trinity (Master of the Litoměřice Altar) 108, 109
American Centre 229
American Express 227, 230, 231, 233
Angermayer, Johann-Adalbert 109
  Still Life with Watch 107
Anglican Church 235
Ann, St 138
Anne, Empress 110
Anthony of Padua, St 69, 137
Antiques
  customs regulations 234
Aostalli, Ottavio 127, 141
Apartments (self-catering) 187
Archbishop's Palace 48, **111**
Arcibiskupský Palác 111
Arcimboldo, Giuseppe, *Rudolph II* 28
Art Nouveau 40, 148–9
Asam, Kosmas Damian 71
Assicurazioni Generali Building 145
At the Black Eagle 135
At the Black Madonna 63, 172
At the Black Sun 63
At the Fleks 155
At the Golden Grape (Marienbad) 169
At the Golden Horseshoe 123
At the Golden Snake 78
At the Golden Unicorn (Little Quarter) 132
At the Golden Unicorn (Old Town) 68
At the Golden Scales 124
At the Golden Well 78, 172, 173
At the Haláneks 75
At the Minute 172, 173
At the Ox 69
At the Poor Wretch's 68
At the Red Fox 69
At St Thomas's 125, **127**
At the Spider 172
At the Stone Bell 66
At the Stone Madonna 68
At the Stone Ram 68
At the Three Golden Bells 134
At the Three Little Fiddles 124
At the Three Ostriches 133, **134**
At the Three Red Roses 130
At the Two Golden Bears 29, **71**
  Street-by-Street map 62
At the Two Suns 130
At the Unicorn 172
At the Vulture 172
Atrium 184
Augusta, Bishop Jan 167
Augusta Prison (Křivoklát Castle) 167
Augustine, St 137
Augustinians 115, 127, 154
Austerlitz, Battle of (1805) 32
Australian High Commission 234

B

BBC World Service 235
Ball Game Hall 29, 111
Balšánek, Antonín 64
Bambino di Praga 131
Banknotes 231
Banks 230
Baptist Church of Prague 235
Barbara, St 139
Baroque architecture 30-1, 44, 45, 48–9
Baroque art 109
Bars 208–9, 227
Basle, Council of 152
Bassano, Jacopo 115
Bassevi, Hendela 87
Bayer, Paul Ignaz
  Church of St Ignatius 152
  Jesuit College 152
Bazilika sv. Jiří 98–9
Becherovka 201
Běchovice 52
Beck, Moses 86
Beer 200–201
Beer halls 127, 155, 196, 201, 208–9
Beethoven, Ludwig van 50, 78, 132
Belvedér 110–11
Belvedere 28, 29, **110–11**
  Prague's Best 46, 48
Bendelmayer, Bedřich 148
Bendl, Jan 79
Benedictines 70, 90, 153, 163
Beneš, Edvard 19, 34
Benzi, St Philip 136
Bernard, St 139
Bernini, Gian Lorenzo 138, 163
Bertramka 31
  concerts 51
  Mozart Museum 160
Bethlehem Chapel 75
  history 25, 26, 27
  Prague's Best 44
  Street-by-Street map 77
Betlémská kaple 75
Bílá Hora a Hvězda 163
Bílek, František *The Blind* 164
"Black sheriffs" 228, 229
Blaeu, William 121
Blanche de Valois 167
Boats, Vltava river trips 50
Bohemian Brethren 91
Bohemian Chancellery 105
Bohemian Diet 104
Boleslav I, Prince 17, 18, 20
Boleslav II, Prince 18, 20
  Břevnov Monastery 163
  Church of St Lawrence 140
  St George's Convent 106
  tomb of 99
Borgia, St Francis 138
Bořiat, Jaroslav 118
Bořivoj, Prince 20, 95, 98, 104
Bořívoj II, Prince 22
Borovička 201
Borromeo, St Charles 152
Borromini, Francesco 128
Bossi, CG 66
Botanical Gardens 153
  Prague's Best 49
  Street-by-Street map 149
Botanická zahrada 153
Botels (floating hotels) 184
Bourdon, Sébastien 115
Brahe, Tycho 29, 41, 118, 119
  tomb of 67, 70
Brandl, Petr 40, 65, 98, 109
  Bust of a Talking Apostle 106
  The Holy Family 132
Braník brewery 127
Braque, Georges 115
Braun, Antonín 47, 110
  Allegory of Night 111
  St Nicholas (Old Town) 70
Braun, Matthias 109
  Dvořák Museum 154
  Grand Priory 131
  Hercules statues 47, 78
  Konopiště Castle gate 167
  portrait 138
  St Judas Thaddeus 108
  St Luitgard 137
  Schönborn Palace caryatids 125
  Thun-Hohenstein Palace 124
  tomb of 154
  Vrtba Garden statues 130
Břetislav I, Prince 18
Břetislav II, Prince 22
Břevnov Monastery 21, **163**
Břevnovský Klášter 163
Brick Gate 181

Bridge Street 134–5
Street-by-Street map 132
British Cultural Centre 229
Brokof, Ferdinand 109
Calvary 91
Charles Bridge statues 136
Church of St Gall statues 71
St Francis Borgia 31
St John the Baptist 131
St John Nepomuk 83, 90, 153
Statue of moor 107, 173
statue of 138
tomb of Count Vratislav of Mitrovice 65
Bronzino, Agnolo
Eleanor of Toledo 115
Brothers of Mercy 91
Brožík, Václav 147, 157
Defenestration (of 1618) 105
Bruckner, Anton 169
Brüderle, Jan 117
Brueghel, Jan 29
Brueghel, Pieter the Elder 40
Budweiser Budvar 200, 201
Bufets (snack bars) 196
Buquoy Palace 131
Bureaux de change 230
Buses 241, 245
Bys, Johann Rudolf 109

C

Café Continental 147
Cafés 196–7
opening hours 227
Cajetan, St 137
Calvary Chapel 175
Calvinists 100
Camping 186, 187
Canadian High Commission 234
Canaletto 115
Canon's House 180
Capuchin Monastery 44, 45, **118–19**
Cardinal Cesi's Garden (van Cleve) 112
Carlone, Carlo 78
Carmelites 49, 130–31, 135, 146
Carolinum 65
history 24, 25
Street-by-Street map 63
Cars 228–229
driving in Prague 239–40
Caruso, Enrico 127
Castles
Karlstein Castle 24, 166–7
Konopiště Castle 167
Křivoklát Castle 167
Nelahozeves Castle 168
Veltrusy Château 166
see also Prague Castle
Cathedral *see* St Vitus's
Cathedral Čechův Bridge 54
Čedok 186, 226, 227
Celebration of the Holy Trinity (Palko) 129
Celetná Street 65
Street-by-Street map 63
Cemeteries
Old Jewish 41, 81, 82, 86–7
Olšany 160
Vyšehrad 181
Černín Palace 49, **119**, 135
Černínský Palác 119
Černý, František 148
Čertovka 56, 131, 133
České Budějovice 200
Česko-slovenská stání automobilová doprava (ČSAD) 238
České Dráhy (ČD) 238
Chalice Restaurant 154
Chapel of Elijah 135
Chapel of Holy Cross (Karlstein) 106
Chapel of Mirrors, 79
Chapel of St Theresa 135
Chapel of St Wenceslas, St Vitus's Cathedral 24, 42
Charles I, Emperor 19
Charles IV, Emperor 17, 18, 153, 154
art collection 40, 108
Carolinum 63, 65
Charles Square 152
Church of Our Lady of the Snows 46
churches 44
Hunger Wall 140–41
Karlsbad 168
Karlstein Castle 166–7
Křivoklát Castle 167
Na Slovanech Monastery 57
New Town 143
Prague Castle 95
Royal Palace 104, 105
St Vitus's Cathedral 100
statue of 79, 139
tomb of 103
Vyšehrad Park 181
Charles VI, Emperor 19
Charles Bridge 123
history 25, 85
Little Quarter Side 136–7
Old Town Side 138–9
statues 31, 40, 136–9
Street-by-Street map 133
Visitors' Checklist 139
Charles Bridge and Hradčany (Kokoschka) 164
Charles Square 152
Street-by-Street map 148–9
Charnel House 83
Charter 77 35
Charter flights 236
Chemists *see* Pharmacies
Children 184, 236
Chrám sv. Víta 100–3
Christ on Clouds (Czech Master) 83
Christ's Entry into Jerusalem 114
Christopher, St 138
Churches (in general)
Baroque architecture 30–31
Prague's Best 42–5
services 235
Churches (individual)
Holy Ghost 83, **90**
Holy Rood 96
Holy Rood Rotunda 44
Holy Saviour (St Agnes's Convent) 93
Holy Saviour (Clementinum) 45, 76, **79**
Holy Trinity 130
Loreto, the 42, 45, **116–17**
Nativity, the 117
Our Lady (Capuchin) 118
Our Lady (Karlstein) 167
Our Lady (Prague Castle) 98
Our Lady (Strahov) 120
Our Lady before Týn 5, 43, 44, 63, 67, 69, **70**, 172
Our Lady beneath the Chain 132, **134**
Our Lady of the Snows 44, 108, 144, **146**
Our Lady of Unceasing Succour 130
Our Lady Victorious 45, **130–31**, 132, 163
St Barbara (Kutná Hora) 159, 168
St Castullus 83, **91**
St Catherine 154
St Clement 31, 235
St Cosmas and St Damian 150
St Cyril and St Methodius 51, 148, **152**
St Francis 79
St Gall 71
St George's Basilica 42, 44, 97, **98–9**
St Giles **75**, 77
St Ignatius 149, **152**
St James 43, 63, **65**
St John on the Rock 45, 148, **153**
St Joseph 132, 235
St Lawrence (Petřín) 12, 14, **140**, 171, 174, 175
St Lawrence (Vyšehrad) 180
St Longinus's Rotunda 44
St Ludmilla 45, 161
St Margaret (Břevnov Monastery) 163
St Martin in the Wall 75
St Martin's Rotunda 44, 180, 181
St Michael 174
St Nicholas (Little Quarter) 127, **128–9**
Street-by-Street map 125
St Nicholas (Old Town) 66, 69, **70–71**, 235, 239

Churches (cont.)
Street-by-Street map 62
St Peter and St Paul 43, 45, 57, 181, 239
St Roch (Olšany Cemeteries) 160
St Roch (Strahov Monastery) 45
St Simon and St Jude 83, 91
St Stephen 154–5
St Thomas 42, 45, 115, 125, **127**
St Ursula 155
St Vladimír (Marienbad) 169
St Wenceslas 150
Cihelná Gate 181
Civic Forum 35, 144
Clam-Gallas Palace 78
Prague's Best 47, 49
Street-by-Street map 77
Clementinum 79
architectural features 31
Prague's Best 45
Street-by-Street map 76
Closely Observed Trains (film) 35
Coach travel 238
Codex of Jena 26
Commerce (Gutfreund) 40
Committee for the Defence of the Unjustly Persecuted 35
Communism 17, 34
Concerning Eden (Savery) 113
Concerts *see* Music
Congress Centre Prague
Vyšehrad Walk 180
Constance, Council of (1415) 27, 70
Consulates 234
Convents
of the Barefooted Carmelites 135
St Agnes's 23, 39, 40, 44, 83, **92–3**
St Anne's 76
St George's 40, 97, 106–9
Conversion chart 235
Cook, Thomas 55
Corot, Jean Baptiste Camille 115
Cosmas, St 136
Counter-Reformation 30, 45, 72
Courbet, Gustave 115
Court of the Bishop of Prague 134
Cranach, Lucas the Elder 114
Adam and Eve 114
St Christine 92
Credit cards 230
Croatian Benedictines 153
Crown jewels 24, 99
Crowns (currency) 231
Crucifixion (Stevens) 42
Cubism 40
Cubist Houses **91**, 172
Street-by-Street map 82
Currency exchange 230
Customs and immigration 234
Cyril, St 20, 21, 51, 138
Czech Association of Persons with Disabilities 183, 234
Czech Astronomical Society 175
Czech Industrial Museum 75
Czech Master (*Christ on Clouds*) 83
Czech Technical University 148
Czechoslovak Airlines (ČSA) 236, 237
Czechoslovak Orthodox Church 152
Czechoslovak Republic 18, 34
Czechoslovak Socialist Republic (ČSSR) 35

D

Dalibor of Kozojedy 110
Dalibor Tower 110
Street-by-Street map 97
Daliborka 110
Damajan, Deodatus 78
Damian, St 136
Danube school 109
Day of Liberation from Fascism 50
Day of the Republic 52
Decorative Arts, Museum of 84
Art Nouveau 149
Prague's Best 39, 40, 41
Street-by-Street map 82
Defenestrations of Prague 26, 29, 105, 155
Degas, Edgar 115
Delacroix, Eugène 115
Della Stella, Paolo 29, 111
Dentists 228, 229
D'Este collection 114
Destinn, Emmy 127
Deštná 106, 108
Devětsil movement 34
Devil's Column 181
Devil's Stream 131, 133
Dientzenhofer, Christoph 45, 129
Břevnov Monastery 163
The Loreto 45, 116
St Nicholas (Little Quarter) 45, 128
Dientzenhofer, Kilian Ignaz 45, 129
Břevnov Monastery 163
Church of Mary Magdalene 169
Church of St John on the Rock 148, 153
Church of St Thomas 127
Dvořák Museum 154
Golz-Kinský Palace 47, 49, 70
The Loreto 45, 116
Michna Summer Palace 47
St Nicholas (Little Quarter) 45, 128–9
St Nicholas (Old Town) 70
Dionysius Miseroni and Family (Škréta) 38
Diplomatic Health Centre 229
Disabled travellers 183, 234
hotels 184
restaurants 197
Discounts (hotels) 184
Dominic, St 139
Dominican Priory 235
Dominicans 75, 139
Don Miguel de Lardizábal (Goya) 115
Dopravní podnik 240
Drahomíra 99
Drinks 200–201
Dryák, Alois 148
Dubček, Alexander 35
Dům u Dvou Zlatých Medvědů 71
Dům Pánů z Kunštátu 78–9
Dům umělců 84
Dürer, Albrecht 40, 109
The Feast of the Rosary 38,114
Dušek, František 160
Dušek, Josefina 160
Duty-free allowances 234
Dvořák, Antonín 39, 41, 154
memorial 181
Dvořák, Karel 138, 163
Dvořák Hall (Rudolfinum) 84
Dvořák Museum 154
Prague's Best 39, 41

E

Elbe (river) 54
Eleanor of Toledo (Bronzino) 115
Electrical adaptors 235
Elizabeth, St 139
Elizabeth of Pomerania 42
Emauzy (Slavonic Monastery) 153
Embassies 234
Embassy of the Czech Republic 186
Emergency telephone numbers 229
Emergency First Aid Centre 229
Entertainment 218–223
Epitaph of Goldsmith Mikuláš Müller (Spranger) 106
Equestrienne (Chagall) 115
Ernst, Max 115
Eros (de Vries) 126
Estates Theatre **65**
Street-by-Street map 63
Ethnographical Museum 174
Europa Hotel *see* Hotel Europa
Evening in Hradčany (Schikaneder) 164
Events (seasonal) 50–53
Exhibition Ground **162**
Prague's Best 40

F

Fabricius, Philipp 105
Fakultní poliklinika 229
Fanta, Josef 148

Faust House 153
Street-by-Street map 149
Faustův dům 153
Fauves 40
Feast of the Rosary (Dürer) 114
Federation of Persons with Disabilities 234
Felix de Valois, St 136
Fénix Palace 145
Ferdinand I, Emperor 19, 28, 79
Archbishop's Palace 111
Belvedere 110
Loreto 116
Mausoleum 103
Prague Castle 95
Royal Garden 111
Ferdinand II, Emperor 19, 30, 126
Church of St Giles, 75
defenestration (of 1618) 105, 110
Ferdinand III, Emperor 19
Ferdinand V, Emperor 19, 172
Ferrer, St Vincent 137
Festivals 50–53
Fiala, Zdeněk 56
Fighting Giants (Platzer) 96
Filippi, Giovanni Maria 130
Films *see* Cinemas
Fire services 229
Fischer, Jiří 177
Fischer von Erlach, Johann Bernhard 65, 78
Five Songs (Tulka) 156
Flats (agencies) 186
Flekovský, Jakub 155
Food and drink 198–201
see also Restaurants
Forman, Miloš 63
Fountains
Křížík 51, 176
Singing 46, 48, 111
Venus 46
Four Great Days Out 10–11
Francis of Assisi, St 137
Francis Xavier, St 138
Franciscan Garden 146
Street-by-Street map 144
Franciscans 65, 146
Frankovka 201
Františkánská zahrada 146
Franz II, Emperor 19, 121
Franz Ferdinand, Archduke 167
Franz Josef, Emperor 19, 32, 33
Franz Kafka Gallery 69
Frederick of the Palatinate 30, 72, 103
Funicular railway 11, 141
Fux, Jan 134

G

Galerie Rudolphinum 84
Gall's Town 71
Gallas de Campo, Jan 78
Gallery Křižovníků 79
Galli, Agostino 118
Gambrinus, King of Beer 200
Gans, David 86
Garden on the Ramparts 110
Gardens
Prague's Best 46–9
see also Parks and gardens
Gauguin, Paul 40, 115
George, St 96
George of Poděbrady 19, 26, 27
Church of Our Lady before Týn 70
Palace of the Lords of Kunštát 77
George of Poděbrady and Matthias Corvinus (Aleš) 164
Ghetto *see* Jewish Quarter
"Ginger and Fred" building 57
Glass
Bohemian 41
Museum of Decorative Arts 84
Godyn, Abraham
Personification of Justice 164
Troja Palace frescoes 165
Goethe, Johann Wolfgang von 169
Gogol, Maxim 169
Golden Age of Czech Art (Ženíšek) 156
Golden Horseshoe 130
Golden Lane 99
Street-by-Street map 97
Golem 88
Good Soldier Švejk, The (Hašek) 33, 154, 196
Gossaert, Jan 114
Gothic architecture 44
Gottwald, Klement 19, 34, 160
proclaims Communist state 69, 70
Goya, Francisco de, *Don Miguel de Lardizábal* 115
Grand Priory of the Knights of Malta 131, 133
Grand Priory Mill 56
Grand Priory Square 131
Street-by-Street map 132
El Greco, *Head of Christ* 112, 115
Green Lobster 130
The Guardian 235
Guarini, Guarino 128
Gutfreund, Otto 40, 135, 163

H

Habermel, Erasmus 84
Habsburg dynasty 17, 18, 110
Hanavský Pavilion 56, 161
Hans von Aachen 109
Hanuš (clockmaker) 74
Harovník, Fabian 99
Hartig Garden 110
Hašek, Jaroslav 154
Havel, Václav 19, 96
Civic Forum 144
Velvet Revolution 34, 35
Havelské Město 71
Havlíček, Milan 161
Haydn, Josef 41
Head of Christ (El Greco) 112, 115
Health care 228, 229
Hedvika Francesca Wussin (Kupecký) 109
Heermann, Johann Georg and Paul Troja Palace sculptures 164
Heger, Filip 67
Heger, František 67
Heinsch, Jan Jiří 90, 109, 152, 155
Heinsch, Josef 65
Henlein, Konrad 34
Hercules (Braun) 47, 78
Heydrich, Reinhard 34, 51, 152
High Synagogue 85
Prague's Best 41, 45
Street-by-Street map 82
History of Prague 17–35, 41
Hitler, Adolf 34
Hladová zeď 140–41
Hlahol Choir Building 143, 148
Hlavní nádraží 148, 238
Holbein, Hans the Elder 114
Holešovice Station 238
Holidays, public 53
Holocaust 82, 84
Holy Family (Brandl) 132
Holy Ghost, Church of the 90
Street-by-Street map 83
Holy Infant of Prague 131, 132
Holy Rood, Church of the 96
Holy Rood Chapel (Karlstein Castle) 25
Holy Rood Rotunda 44
Holy Saviour, Church of the (St Agnes's Convent) 93
Holy Saviour, Church of the (Clementinum) 79
Street-by-Street map 76
Holy Trinity, Church of the 130
Homage to Prague (Špillar) 64
Horowitz, Aaron Meshulam 84
Horse-drawn carriages 227
Hospitals 229
Hostels 186, 187
Hotel Central 148
Hotel Europa **146–7**
Street-by-Street map 145
Hotels 184–95
House at the... *see* At the House of Artists 84
House of the Black Madonna 65
House of the Black Mother of God 91
Hradčany 94–121, 227, 238
area map 95
Street Finder maps 1–2
Hunger Wall 140
Hus, Jan 17, 26, 27, 44, 137
anniversary 51
Bethlehem Chapel 75, 77

Hus, Jan (cont.)
Monument 62, 69, 70, 234
Husák, Gustáv 19, 35
Hussite Church 235
Hussites 17, 26–7, 44, 160
Church of Our Lady before Týn 70
Council of Basle 152
Jan Hus Monument 70
occupy St Vitus's Cathedral 100
Utraquists 75
Hvězdárna 140
Hynais, Vojtěch 33, 147, 157

I

Ibsen, Hendrik 169
Ignatius Loyola, St 152
Imperial Sanatorium (Karlsbad) 169
Impressionism 40, 115
Industrial Palace 162
Institute of Gentlewomen 151
Insurance 228, 229, 239
Interdenominational church services 235
International Church 235
International Herald Tribune 235
International Jazz Festival 50, 52
International Student Identity Cards (ISIC) 234
International Union of Students 234
Invention of Destruction, The (film) 34
Iron Man 78
Italian Court (Kutná Hora) 168
Italian Hospital 130
Italian Street 130
Ivan, Blessed 136
IYHF hostels 187

J

Jäger, Joseph 131
Jan Hus Monument 69, 70, 234
Street-by-Street map 62
Jan Vratislav of Mitrovice 43
Jansa, Václav
Melantrichova Passage 69
Old Town Square 62
Jaroš, Tomáš 98, 111
Jazz 50, 52
Jelení skok 169
Jerusalem Synagogue 235
Jesuit College 152
Street-by-Street map 149
Jesuits 28
Baroque architecture 30
Bethlehem Chapel 75
Carolinum 65
Church of St Ignatius 149, 152
Clementinum 31, 45, 57, 76, 79
cult of St John Nepomuk 137
Jewish Burial Society 85
Jewish Quarter 80–93
area map 81
history 32, 33
Jewish Museum 41
sightseeing tours 227
Street-by-Street map 82–3
Street Finder map 3
synagogues 44
Jewish Town Hall 85
Street-by-Street map 82
Jezuitská kolej 152
Jirásek, Alois 163
Jižní Zahrady 110
John the Baptist, St 138
John de Matha, St 136
John of Luxemburg 18, 24, 72
John Nepomuk, St 119, 137
Charles Bridge 137, 138
statues of 83, 90, 135, 153, 155
tomb of 103
Josef I, Emperor 19
Josef II, Emperor 19, 71, 120
Jewish Quarter 81
Josefov 80–93
Joseph, St 138
Jubilee Exhibition (1891) 33, 56, 148
Petřín Park 140, 141
Exhibition Ground 161, 162
Jude Thaddaeus, St 137
Judith Bridge 22–4, 56, 136, 138
Judith Tower 134
Julius II, Pope 114
Jungmann, Josef 144, 160
Jungmannovo Square 144
Just, St 42

K

Kafka, Bohumil, statue of Žižka 160
Kafka, Franz 10, 34, 68, 145
Golden Lane 99
tomb of 160
Kaiserstein Palace 51, 127
Kampa Island 131
Prague's Best 47, 48, 49
Street-by-Street map 133
Kampa Museum of Modern Art 135
Kampa Island (Pinkas) 133
Kaňka, František Maximilián 130, 167
Kapucínský klášter 118–19
Kara, Rabbi Avigdor 86
Karlove ulice 78
Karlovo náměstí 148–9, 152
Karlovy Vary 168–9
Karlsbad 170
Karlstein Castle 24, 25, **168–9**
Karlštejn 166–7
Karlův most 136–9
Kaunic Palace 135
Kelley, Edward 98, 153
Kepler, Johannes 41, 119
Kinský, Štěpán 70
Kinský family 47, 141, 176
Kinský Garden 176
Kinský Palace 66, **70**
Prague's Best 47, 49
Street-by-Street map 62
Kinský Summer Palace 171, 176
Kipling, Rudyard 169
Kisch, Egon Erwin 71
Klášter na Slovanech 153
Klášter sv. Anežky České 92–3
Klášter sv. Jiří 106–9
Klausen Synagogue 85, **86**
Prague's Best 45
Street-by-Street map 82
Klausová synagóga 85
Klementinum 79
Klimt, Gustav 40, 115
Virgin 164
Knights of the Cross Square **79**, 173
Street-by-Street map 76
Knights of Malta 131, 134
Knights of St John 134
Koch, Jindřich 174
Kohl, Hieronymus, *St Augustine* 125
Kohl, John Frederick, *St Paul* 128
Kolar, Jiří, *Egg Object* 165
Kolowrat-Černín Garden 135
Prague's Best 47, 49
Konopiště Castle 114, 169
Koruna Palace 144
Kostel Matky Boží před Týnem 70
Kostel Panny Marie pod řetězem 134
Kostel Panny Marie Sněžné 146
Kostel sv. Cyrila a Metoděje 152
Kostel sv. Ducha 90
Kostel sv. František 79
Kostel sv. Halva 71
Kostel sv. Haštala 91
Kostel sv. Ignáce 152
Kostel sv. Jakuba 65
Kostel sv. Jana Na skalce 153
Kostel sv. Jiljí 75
Kostel sv. Kateřiny 154
Kostel sv. Martina ve zdi 75
Kostel sv. Mikuláše (Old Town) 70–71
Kostel sv. Mikuláše (Little Quarter) 128–9
Kostel sv. Šimona a Judy 91
Kostel sv. Štěpána 154
Kostel sv. Tomáše 127
Kostel sv. Vavřince 140
Kostel sv. Voršily 155
Kracker, Johann Lukas, *St Joseph* 129
Královská zahrada 111
Královský letohrádek 110
Královský palác 104–5
Kramář, Vincenc 40
Krásnohorská, Eliška 149
Křivoklát Castle 169

Křížík, František 176
Křižovnické náměstí 79
Krkonoše (Giant) Mountains 140
Kroměříže, Jan Milíč z 75
Kubistické domy 91
Kučera Palace 119
Kunratice forest 52
Kunštát, Lords of 78–9
Kupecký, František, *Self Portrait* 107
Kupecký, Jan 98, 109
Hedvika Francesca Wussin 109
Self Portrait 107
Kupka, Frantisek 135
Kutná Hora 170
Kysela, František 100

L

Ladislav Posthumus 18
Lamentation of Christ (Lorenzo Monaco) 113, 114
Landscape with Orpheus and Animals (Reiner) 164
Langweil, Antonín 41, 161
Last Judgment (mosaic) 101
Laterna Magika 144
Le Brun, Charles 115
Lebedurská zahrada 135
Ledebour Garden 49, **135**
Ledebour Palace 135
Lennon, John 131, 132
Leopold I, Emperor 164, 165
Leopold II, Emperor 19
coronation 102
Royal Route 69, 172, 173
Leopold Gate 171, 180
Letná Park 161
Prague's Best 49
Library, National 79
Libuše, Princess 18, 21, 180
statues of 76, 181
Libuše (Smetana) 32, 157
Libuše's Baths 180, 181
Lichtenstein Palace 51, 127
Lion Court 111
Lipany, Battle of (1434) 17, 26, 176
Literature, Museum of National 120
Little Quarter 17, 122–41, 175, 238
area map 123
history 22, 23
Street-by-Street map 132–3
Street Finder maps 1–2
Little Quarter Bridge Towers 56, 123, 136, 175
Street-by-Street map 124–5
Little Quarter Town Hall 127
Little Quarter Water Tower 56
Lobkovický palác 99
Lobkowicz, Kateřina of 116
Lobkowicz, Polyxena of 131
Lobkowicz Palace **99**, 130
Lobkowicz Palace (cont.)
Prague's Best 41, 48
Street-by-Street map 97
Longinus, St 181
Lords of Kunštát, Palace of 77, **78–9**
Lorenzetti, Pietro 114
Loreto, the 116–17
Prague's Best 38, 41, 42, 45
Lost and found 229
Louis XIV (King of France) 65
Löw, Rabbi 28, 78, 85, 89
and the Golem 88
tomb of 87
Lucerna Palace 52, 144
Ludmilla, St 20, 97
statue of 137
tomb of 99
Ludvíc II, King 19
Luitgard, St 137
Lurago, Anselmo 120, 129
Lurago, Carlo
Church of St Ignatius 152
Jesuit College 152
Lobkowicz Palace 99
Our Lady beneath the Chain 134
Luxemburg dynasty 18

M

Mácha, Karel Hynek 141
Madonna Aracoeli 40
Maillol, Aristide, *Pomona* 164
Main Post Office 233
Maisel, Mordechai
High Synagogue 85
Maisel Synagogue 82, 90
tomb of 87
Maisel Synagogue 90
Prague's Best 39, 41
Street-by-Street map 82
Maiselova synagóga 90
Malá Strana 122–41
Malé náměstí 173
Malostranské náměstí 127
Maltese Square 131
Street-by-Street map 132
Maltézské náměstí 131
Mánes, Josef 32
Old Town Hall Clock 74
tomb of 160
Manet, Edouard 114, 115
Mannerism 45, 109
Marchfeld, Battle of (1278) 18
Marcomans 20
Marcu, Jan Marek 61
Margaret, St 139
Markets 216–7
Maria Theresa, Empress 19, 31, 172
Marian pillar 40
Mariánské Lázně 169
Mariánské náměstí 78
Mariánské Square 78
Street-by-Street map 77
Marienbad 171
Martinic, Jaroslav 105
Martinic Palace 48, 118
Martinický palác 118
Martyrdom of St Thomas (Rubens) 113
Mary, Virgin 42, 116, 117, 146
Mary Magdalene, Church of 169
Masaryk, Jan 119
Masaryk, Tomáš Garrigue 19, 34
Masarykovo nádraží 238
Master of the Litoměřice Altar, *Altarpiece of the Holy Trinity* 108–9
Master of the Třeboň Altar *The Resurrection of Christ* 39
Master of the Vyšší Brod Altarpiece *The Annunciation of Our Lady* 92
Mathey, Jean-Baptiste 49, 164–5
Matisse, Henri 114
Matthew of Arras 100, 167
Matthias, Emperor 19, 28, 110
Matthias Corvinus 164
Matthias Gate 29, 95, 173
Maulbertsch, Franz, *Struggle of Mankind to Know Real History* 121
Maximilian I, Emperor 114
Maximilian II, Emperor 19, 103
Medek, Mikuláš, *Grand Meal* 164
Medical centres 229
Medici, Cosimo de' 115
Medieval architecture 22–3, 44, 48
Melantrichova Passage 69
Mělník 201
Memorial to František Palacký 57
Menzel, Jiří 35
Merciful Brethren 83
Methodist-Evangelical church services 235
Methodius, St 20, 21, 51, 138
Metro 241, 242–3
Metronome (Letná Park) 34, 161
Michelangelo 109
Michna, Pavel 141
Michna Summer Palace 141
Dvořák Museum 39, 154
Prague's Best 47, 49
Michnův palác 141
Míčovna 111
Mikeš, František 57
Military History, Museum of 118
Prague's Best 38, 41
Mill Colonnade (Karlsbad) 169
Ministerstvo pro místní rozvoj 149
Minorite Order 65
Mint 172
Mirror Maze 140, 175
Mirrors, Chapel of, 79
Mlada, Abbess 106
Mladota, Count Ferdinand 151, 153

Mlýnská kolonáda 169
Mocker, Josef 45, 167
  Church of St Stephen 154
  St Ludmilla 161
  St Vitus's Cathedral 100
Modern and Contemporary Art, Centre for *see* Trades Fair Palace
Monaco, Lorenzo *Lamentation of Christ* 113, 114
Monasteries
  Břevnov 21, 163
  Capuchin 44, 45, 118–19
  Na Slovanech 57
  Slavonic 43, 44, 45, 148, 153
  Strahov 22–3, 30, 44–5, 120–21, 175
  Zbraslav 40, **163**
Monet, Claude 115
Money 230–31
  customs regulations 234
Monuments
  Jan Hus 62, 69, 70, 234
  Letná Park metronome 34, 161
  National Monument 160
  St John Nepomuk 119
  St Wenceslas 145, 146
  to Victims of Communism 145
  to Victims of Communism (2002) 141
  see also Statues
Monuments of the Nation's Past 99
Morzin Palace 49, 130, 173
  Street-by-Street map 124
Mostecká ulice 134–5
Mozart, Constanze 160
Mozart, Wolfgang Amadeus 120
  La Clemenza di Tito 102
  Don Giovanni 31, 65, 160
  plays organ in St Nicholas's 128
Mozart Museum 41, 160
Mucha, Alfons 33, 149
  Allegory of Vigilance 37
  Municipal House 64
  Museum 147
  St Cyril and St Methodius 102
Munch, Edvard 40, 41, 115
Munich Agreement (1938) 34
Municipal House 33, 50, **64–5**, 174
  Mayor's Room 37
  Street-by-Street map 63
Museums
  Prague's Best 38–41
  Czech Glass 69
  Czech Industrial Museum 75
  Decorative Arts 40–41, **82–4**, 149
  Dvořák Museum 39, 41, **154**
  Ethnographical Museum 174
  Kampa Museum of Modern Art 135
  The Loreto 38, 41
Museums (cont.)
  Military History 38, 41, 118
  Mozart Museum 41, **160**
  Mucha Museum 147
  Municipal Mass Transport 227
  Museum of Music 132, 141
  Musical Instruments 41
  Náprstek Museum 41, **75**
  National Literature 120
  National Museum 39, 41, 145, **147**, 176, 226
  National Technical Museum 41, **162**
  Physical Culture and Sport 141
  Prague Museum 41, **161**
  Schwarzenberg Palace 38, 41
  Smetana Museum 38, 41, 57, 76, **79**
  Star Hunting Lodge 163
  State Jewish Museum 39, 41, 226
  Toy Museum 99
  Vyšehrad Museum 180
Music 41, 222–3
Musical Instruments, Museum of 41
Muzeum Antonína Dvořáka 154
Muzeum Bedřicha Smetany 79
Muzeum Hlavního Města Prahy 161
Myslbek, Josef 163
  Přemysl and Libuše 181
  St Ludmilla portal 161
  St Wenceslas 146
  St Agnes 92
  Záboj and Slavoj 149

N

Na Františku Hospital 83, 91
Na Slovanech Monastery 57
Náměstí Míru 161
Náměstí Republiky 184
Napoleon I, Emperor 32
Náprstek, Vojta 75
Náprstek Museum 41, 75
Náprstkovo Muzeum 75
Národní divadlo 156–7
Národní muzeum 147
Národní technické muzeum 162
National anthem 65
National Gallery
  Golz-Kinský Palace 47, 70
  Prague's Best 40
  St Agnes's Convent 92–3
  St George's Convent 106–9
  Sternberg Palace 112–15
  Trades Fair Palace 164–5
  Wallenstein Palace 126
  Zbraslav Monastery 163
National Library 79
National Monument 160
National Museum 147
  history 17, 32, 33
  Hunting Château 177
  Lapidarium 176
National Museum (cont.)
  Lobkowicz Palace 97
  Náprstek Museum 75
  Prague's Best 39, 41
  Street-by-Street map 145
National Revival 32–3
National Technical Museum 41, 162
National Theatre 57, **156–7**, history 17, 32, 33
National Union of Students 234
Nativity, Church of the 117
Nazis 34, 41, 72, 85, 90
Nebozízek 175
Nebozízek station 141
Nelahozeves Castle 168
Neo-Gothic architecture 45
Nephele Mound 86
Neruda, Jan 130, 173
Nerudova Street 31, **130**
  Royal Route Walk 173
  Street-by-Street map 124
Nerudova ulice 31, 130, 173, 124
Neunhertz, Jiří 120
New Deanery 180
New Land Rolls (Royal Palace) 105
New Town 142–57, 171
  area map 143
  history 24, 25, 32
  sightseeing tours 227
  Street-by-Street maps 144–5, 150–51
  Street Finder maps 3–6
New Town Hall 26, **155**
New World 118
New Zealand High Commission 234
Newspapers 235
Nicholas Tolentino, St 137
Night buses 245
Nightlife 210–11
Norbert, St 120, 138
Nostitz, Count 65
Nostitz Palace 131, 132
Novák, Emanuel 149
Nové Město 142–57
Novoměstská radnice 155
Novotný, Antonín 19, 35
Nový Svět 118

O

Obrazárna Pražkého Hradu 98
Observation Path (Kinský Garden) 174
Observation Tower **140**, 177
  Street-by-Street map 77
Observatory **140**, 177
Očko, Jan, Archbishop 24, 92
Old Jewish Cemetery 81, **86–7**
  Prague's Best 41
  Street-by-Street map 82
Old-New Synagogue **88–9**, 235
  history 24
  Prague's Best 43, 44

Old-New Synagogue (cont.)
Street-by-Street map 82
Old School 90
Old Town 22, 60–79
area map 61
Royal Enclosure Walk 178–9
Royal Route Walk 174
sightseeing tours 227
Street-by-Street maps 62–3, 76–7
Street Finder maps 3–4
Old Town Bridge Tower 25, 139, 238
Street-by-Street map 76
Old Town Hall 72–4
Clock 26, 32, 73, 74
Street-by-Street map 62
Tower 73
Old Town Square 5, 50, 61, **66–9**
East and North sides 66–7
hotels 184
South side 68–9
Street-by-Street map 62
Old Town Square (Jans) 62
Olšanské hřbitovy 160
Olšany cemeteries 50, 160
Ondříček, František 118
Opening hours 226–7
Opera 145, 147
Oppenheim, Rabbi David 86
Order of the Golden Fleece 126
Oriel Chapel 73
Orloj 74
Orthodox Church 152
Our Lady before Týn, Church of 5, 67, **70**
history 27, 69
Prague's Best 43, 44
Street-by-Street map 63
Our Lady beneath the Chain, Church of 134
Street-by-Street map 132
Our Lady of the Snows, Church of 108, **146**
Prague's Best 44
Street-by-Street map 144
Our Lady of Unceasing Succour, Church of 130
Our Lady Victorious, Church of **130–31**, 163
Prague's Best 45
Street-by-Street map 132
Ovocný trh 63

P

Palác Kinských 70
Palace Hotel 184
Palaces
Prague's Best 46–9
Palach, Jan 35, 146
Palacký, František (Memorial to) 57
Palacký Bridge 149, 177, 181
Pálffy Garden 135
Pálffy Palace 135
Palko, Franz, *The Celebration of the Holy Trinity* 129
Palliardi, Ignaz 135
Panorama, Marold's 176
Pantheon 181
Paradise Garden 110
Paříž (hotel) 82
Parking 240–41
Parks and gardens
Prague's Best 46–9
Botanical Gardens 49, 151, **153**
Charles Square 148, **152**
Franciscan Garden 144, **146**
Garden on the Ramparts 110
Hartig Garden 110
Kampa Island 47, 48, 49, **131**, 133
Kinský Garden 174
Kolowrat-Černín Garden 47, 49, 135
Ledebour Garden 49, **135**
Letná Park 34, 35, 49, **161**
Pálffy Garden 135
Paradise Garden 110
Petřín Park 49, 140, **141**, 176–7
Rose Garden, (Petřín Park) 175
Royal Garden 46, 49, **111**
South Gardens 46, 49, 96, **110**
Stromovka 49, **162**
Troja Palace 166–177
Veltrusy Château 166
Vojan Park 49, 133, **135**
Vrtba Garden 49, **130**
Vyšehrad Park 51, 181
Wallenstein Garden 46, 49
Parler, Peter
All Saints' Chapel 104, 105
Charles Bridge 138
Karlstein Castle 167
Old Town Bridge Tower 25, 64, 76, 139
St Barbara (Kutná Hora) 168
St Vitus's Cathedral 100, 101, 103
Wenceslas IV 25
Pension Páv 187
People Against Violence 35
Personification of Justice (Godyn) 164
Pesach Haggadah (manuscript) 39
Pešánek, Zdeněk, *Torso* 165
Petřín Hill 49, 121, 140, **141**, 177
Petřínská Rozhledna 140
Pharmacies 229
Phonecards 232
Physical Culture and Sport, Museum of 141
Picasso, Pablo 40
Picture Gallery of Prague Castle 98
Street-by-Street map 96
Pilsner 200, 201
Pinkas, Rabbi 84
Pinkas, Soběslav, *Kampa Island* 133
Pinkas Synagogue **84–5**, 86
Prague's Best 44, 45
Street-by-Street map 82
Pinkasova synagóga 84–5
Pissarro, Camille 115
Plastic People (rock band) 35
Platzer, Ignaz 109
Fighting Giants 96
Golz-Kinský Palace statues 66, 70
Kaunic Palace 135
St John Nepomuk 135, 155
statues in St Nicholas's 129
Strahov Monastery 121
Plečnik, Josip 46, 110
Plzeň 200
Plzeňské (beer) 201
Plzeňský Prazdroj 201
Pohořelec 119
Police 228–9, 239
Polívka, Osvald 64, 67
Pollution 53, 229
Poor Clares 23, 92
Post-Impressionism 40, 115
Post offices 233
Poste restante 233
Powder Gate 64
Street-by-Street map 63
Powder Tower 98
Street-by-Street map 96
Prachner, Peter 128
Prachner, Richard 128
Prager, Karel 156
Prague Burial Society 87
Prague Business Post 235
Prague Castle 17, 48, 94–121, 238
area map 95
Dalibor Tower 110
history 21, 22, 23, 24, 27, 28–9, 30
Lobkowicz Palace 41, 48
Matthias Gate 29, 95, 173
Picture Gallery 40, 41, 96, 98
Powder Tower 98
Royal Garden 46, 49
Royal Palace 97, 104–5
Royal Route 78
South Gardens 46, 49, 96, 110
Street-by-Street map 96–7
Street Finder map 2
Prague City Insurance Company 67
Prague Gallery 40
Prague Information Service (PIS) 186, 226, 227
Prague Insurance Company 148
Prague Museum 41, 161
Prague Post, The 227, 235
"Prague Spring" (1968) 35
Prague Spring Music Festival 50
Prague Transport Corporation 240

Prague Uprising (1945) 34, 50, 72
Prague Wheelchair Association 234
Praha House 148
Praha "Renaissance" 184
Prašná brána 64
Prašná věž 98
Pražská paroplavební společnost 55
Pražský hrad 94–121
Prčice 50
Premonstratensians 120
Přemysl 21, 181
Přemysl Otakar I (King) 18, 23
Přemysl Otakar II (King) 18, 22, 23, 104, 176
Přemyslid dynasty 17, 18, 20–21, 24, 160, 167
Příchovský, Archbishop Antonín 111
Private rooms 187
Procopius, St 137
První pomoc zubní 229
Public holidays 53
Pubs 196, 201, 208–9
Purkyně, Jan (statue) 151

Q

Quitainer, Johann Anton 119
  Strahov Monastery statues 120
Quitainer, Ondřej, 116

R

Radio 235
Rail travel 238–9
Rajská zahrada 110
Red Army 34
Red Eagle 130
Reiner, Václav Vavřinec 109
  Church of the Nativity frescoes 117
  Church of Our Lady Victorious 163
  Church of St Giles frescoes 65, 75
  Church of St Thomas frescoes 127
  Landscape with Orpheus and Animals 106
  Vrtba Garden 130
Rejsek, Matthias 73
Rembrandt 40, 114, 115
  Scholar in his Study 112
Renaissance 17, 28–9
  architecture 44–5, 48
Reni, Guido 98
Restaurace u Kalicha 154
Restaurants 202–7
Resurrection of Christ (Master of the Třeboň Altar) 39
Resurrection of Christ (Spranger) 97
Riding School 111
Ried, Benedikt
  Powder Tower 98
  St Barbara (Kutná Hora) 168
Ried, Benedikt (cont.)
  Vladislav Hall 104
Rodin, Auguste 40, 115
  St John the Baptist 114
Romanesque architecture 22–3, 44
Romanticism 40
Rose Garden (Petřín Park) 175
Rotunda of St Vitus 20, 21
Rotundas, Romanesque 44
Rousseau, Henri "le Douanier" 40
  Self-Portrait 164
Royal Court 64, 172
  Prague's Best 46, 49
Royal Enclosure Walk 178–9
Royal Palace 104–5
  Prague's Best 48
  Street-by-Street map 97
Royal Route Walk 174–5
Rubens, Peter Paul 40, 41, 98, 113, 114–15, 127
  Martyrdom of St Thomas 113
Rudolfinum 32, 57, **84**
  concerts 50, 52
  Galerie 84
  history 17
Rudolph (Crown Prince) 84
Rudolph I, Emperor 165
Rudolph II, Emperor 4, 17, 19, 84, 90
  art collection 40, 98, 108, 114
  history 28–9, 44
  miraculous statue of Madonna and Child 118–19
  Prague Castle 95, 96
Rulandské 201
Ruzyně Airport 236, 237

S

Sadeler, Aegidius, *Vladislav Hall* 104
Safety 228
St Agnes of Bohemia Convent 23, **92–3**
  Prague's Best 39, 40, 44
  Street-by-Street map 83
St Anne's Convent 76
St Augustine (Kohl) 125
St Barbara, Church of (Kutná Hora) 159, 168
St Castullus, Church of 91
  Street-by-Street map 83
St Catherine, Church of 154
  St Christine (Cranach) 93
St Clement, Church of 31, 235
St Cosmas and St Damian 150
St Cyril and St Methodius, Church of 148, 152
St Cyril and St Methodius (Mucha) 102
St Francis, Church of 76, 79
St Francis Borgia (Brokof) 31
St Gall, Church of 71
St George's Basilica 21, 23, 97, **98–9**
  Prague's Best 42, 44
St George's Convent 97, 106–9
  Prague's Best 38, 40
St Giles, Church of 75
  Street-by-Street map 77
St Ignatius, Church of 152
  Street-by-Street map 149
St James, Church of 65
  Prague's Best 43
  Street-by-Street map 63
St John the Baptist (Brokof) 131
St John the Baptist (Rodin) 114
St John Nepomuk (Brokof) 83, 90,
  Charles Bridge 153
St John Nepomuk (Platzer) 135
St John on the Rock, Church of 45, **153**
  Street-by-Street map 148
St Joseph, Church of 235
  Street-by-Street map 132
St Joseph (Kracker) 129
St Lawrence, Church of 12, 14, **140**
  Petřín Park Walk 171, 174, 175
St Lawrence, Basilica of 180
St Longinus's Rotunda 44
St Ludmilla, Church of 45, 161
St Margaret, Church of 163
St Martin in the Wall, Church of 75
St Martin's Rotunda 23
  Prague's Best 44
  Vyšehrad Walk 180, 181
St Michael, Church of 174
St Michael (Solimena) 128
St Nicholas, Church of (Little Quarter) 30, 127, **128–9**
  Prague's Best 42, 44, 45
  Street-by-Street map 125
St Nicholas, Church of (Old Town) 66, **70–71**, 235, 239
  history 69
  Prague's Best 45
  Street-by-Street map 62
St Nicholas (Platzer) 129
St Paul (Kohl) 128
St Peter and St Paul, Church of 57, 239
  Prague's Best 43, 45
  Vyšehrad Walk 181
St Roch, Church of (Olšany Cemeteries) 160
St Roch, Church of (Strahov Monastery) 45
St Simon and St Jude, Church of 91
  Street-by-Street map 83
St Stephen, Church of 154–5
St Thomas, Church of 115, **127**
  Prague's Best 42, 45
  Street-by-Street map 125
St Ursula, Church of 155

St Vitus (Master Theodoric) 25
St Vitus Treasure 40
St Vitus's Cathedral 52, **100–103**
Chapel of St Wenceslas 42
coronations 173
Prague's Best 42, 44, 45
St Wenceslas Chapel 24, stained glass 95,
Street-by-Street map 96
St Vladimír, Church of (Marienbad) 169
St Wenceslas (Feast of) 52
St Wenceslas, Church of 150
St Wenceslas and St Vitus (Spränger) 17
St Wenceslas Chapel (St Vitus's Cathedral) 101, 102, 103
St Wenceslas Crown 24
Šaloun, Ladislav
Jan Hus Monument 70
Zbraslav Monastery 163
Samaritans 229
Samo 20
Santa Casa 116, 117
Santini-Aichel, Giovanni 71
Sausages 196, 194
Savery, Roelant
Concerning Eden 113
Stag Hunt 109
Saxons 30
Schikaneder, Jakub *Evening in Hradčany* 164
Schiele, Egon 40, 115
Schnirch, Bohuslav 156
Scholar in his Study (Rembrandt) 112
Schönborn Palace 125
Schor, Jan Ferdinand 154
Schulz, Josef 84, 147, 156
Schwarzenberg Palace 118
Prague's Best 38, 41, 48
Schwarzenberský palác 118
Science museums 41
Seifert, Jaroslav 35, 99
Self-catering apartments 187
Self-portrait (Rousseau) 112, 115
Seurat, Georges 115
Sgraffito
Ball Game Hall 111
Calvary Chapel 175
House at the Minute 172, 173
Lobkowicz Palace 99
Martinic Palace 118
Royal Palace 104
Schwarzenberg Palace 48, 118
Smetana Museum 79
Štorch House 62
Wiehl House 144
Shopping 212–7
Sicilian Golden Bull 23
Sightseeing tours 227
Sigismund, King 18
Sigismund, Emperor 160
Sigismund, St 138
Singing Fountain 46, 48, 111
Sisley, Alfred 115
Šitka Tower 57
Škréta, Karel 40, 71, 109
The Baptism of Christ 155
Church of Our Lady beneath the Chain paintings 134
Church of St Gall paintings 71
Crucifixion 128
Dionysius Miseroni and Family 38
Slánský Trial 34
Slavata, Vilém 105
Slavic tribes 20
Slavín 181
Slavkov, Battle of (1805) 32
Slavkov Forest 169
Slavonic House 147
Slavonic Monastery Emauzy 153
Prague's Best 43, 44, 45
Street-by-Street map 148
Slovanský dům 147
Smetana, Bedřich 50, 149, 172
Dalibor 110
Libuše 32, 157
tomb of 181
Smetana Museum 79
Prague's Best 38, 41
Street-by-Street map 76
Smíchov Station 238
Smiřický Palace 127
Snack bars 196
Sněžka (mountain) 140
Soběslav I, King 104
Soběslav II, King 18
Sokol 141, 149
Soldati, Tomasso, St Ignatius sculptures 152
Solimena, Francesco, *St Michael* 128
South Gardens 110
Prague's Best 46, 49
Street-by-Street map 96
Špála, Václav 40
Španělská synagóga 90–91
Spanish Synagogue 90–91
Street-by-Street map 83
Spas 168, 169
Spezza, Andrea 126
Špička Gate 140, 180
Špillar, Karel, *Homage to Prague* 64
Spires 44–5
Spirits 201, 234
Sports 222–23
Spränger, Bartholomeus 108
Epitaph of Goldsmith Mikuláš Müller 107
Resurrection of Christ 97
St Wenceslas and St Vitus 17
Spytihněv, Prince 100
Stag Hunt (Savery) 109
Stag Moat 111
Stag's Leap 169
Stalin, Joseph, statue of 34, 35, 161
Stamps, postage 233
Star Hunting Lodge 163
Stará Škola 90
Staré Město 60–79
Staroměstská radnice 72–3
Staroměstské náměstí 66–9
Staronová synagoga 88–9
Starý židovský hřbitov 86–7
State Jewish Museum
Prague's Best 39, 41, 91
see also Spanish Synagogue, Maisel Synagogue, High Synagogue, Old Jewish Cemetery
State Opera 147
Street-by-Street map 145
Státní opera Praha 147
Statues
on Charles Bridge 136–9
Charles IV 79
Hercules 47
Jan Hus 69, 70
Kvapilová, Hana 174
Přemysl and Princess Libuše 181
Princess Libuše 76
Purkyně, Jan 151
on Rudolfinum 57
St John the Baptist 131
St John Nepomuk 83, 90, 135
St Joseph and St John 116
St Wenceslas 145, 146
Vltava 56
Žižka, Jan 160
Stavovské divadlo 65
Sternberg, Count 164
Sternberg, Franz Josef 112
Sternberg Palace **112–15**,
Prague's Best 38, 40–41, 49
Visitors' Checklist 113
Šternberský palác 112–15
Stevens, Antonín, *Crucifixion* 42
Still Life with Watch (Angermayer) 107
Štorch House 68
Street-by-Street map 62
Štork, Lorenc 71
Strahov Gospel (book) 121
Strahov Monastery 120–21
history 22, 23
Philosophical Hall 30, 120
Prague's Best 44, 45
Strahov stadium 34
Strahovský klášter 120–21
Street signs 240
Střelecký Island 51
Stromovka 49, 162, 176–7
Struggle of Mankind to Know Real History (Maulbertsch) 121
Students 234
Stužba prbní pomoci 229
Štvanice Island 54,
Sucharda, Stanislav
New Town Hall sculpture 77
Sucharda, Vojtěch, *Apostles* 74
Suckling Madonna 108

Sudeten German Party 34
Svoboda, Ludvík 19
Synagogues
Prague's Best 42–5
High 41, 45, 82, **85**
Jerusalem 235
Klausen 45, 82, **85**, 86
Maisel 39, 41, 82, **90**
Old-New 24, 43, 44, 82, **88–9**, 235
Pinkas 44, 45, 82, **84–5**, 86
Spanish 83, **90–91**

T

Tábor Gate 180
Taborites 17, 26
Táborský, Jan 74
Tauc, Gustav Makarius 35
Tax
hotels 184
restaurants 197
Taxis 245
Technology museums 41
Telegrams 233
Telephones 232–3
Television 235
Temperature chart 53
Terezín 41, 85, 227
Theatines 130
Theatre Island 51
Theodoric, Master 98
Karlstein Castle panels 108, 167
St Vitus 25
Theresian Way (Royal Palace) 105
Thirty Years' War 17, 28, 30, 105, 138
Thomas, Edward 32
Thomas, St 139
Thun-Hohenstein Palace 130
Street-by-Street map 124
Thurn, Count 105
Tickets,
travel 236–7
entertainment 218–219
Tintoretto 41, 98, 115
Tipping 184, 197
Titian 41
Toilet of a Young Lady 98
Tobacconists 233
Toilet of a Young Lady (Titian) 98
Torah 85, 90
Toulouse-Lautrec, Henri de 115
Tourist information offices 69, 226
Town Halls
Jewish 82, 85
Little Quarter 127
New Town 155
Old Town 26, 32, 62, 72–3, 74, 173
Toy Museum 99
Trades Fair Palace 40, **164–5**
Trains 238–9
Trams 241, 244
Transport
air 236–7
arriving in Prague 239
buses 241, 245
cars 239, 240–41
coaches 238
metro 241, 242–3
trains 238–9
trams 241, 244
Traveller's cheques 230, 231
Trinitarian Order 136
Troja Palace 166–7
Prague's Best 40, 48, 49
Trojský zámek 164–5
Tulka, Josef, *Five Songs* 156
Turba Palace 131
Twain, Mark 169
The Two Suns 175
Týn School 67
Tyrš House 141

U

U Fleků 155
U Fleloh 201
U Halánků 75
U Kalicha 154, 197
U Lazara 68
U Pinkasů
Street-by-Street map 144
U Rotta 62
U sv. Tomáše 127
U Tří pštrosů 134
Street-by-Street map 133
U Zlatého hroznu 169
Uměleckoprůmyslové muzeum 84
Ungelt 184
Union Café 34
United Kingdom Embassy 234
United States Embassy 234
Universities
Carolinum 17, 24, 25, 63, 65
Clementinum 31, 45, 57, 76, 79, 173
Czech Technical University 148
Urban V, Pope 24
Ursuline Order 155
Utraquists 26, 70, 75

V

Václav, Prince of Opava 153
Václava A Vojtécha 100
Václavské náměstí 146
Valdštejnský palác 126
Van Cleve, *Cardinal Cesi's Garden* 112
Van Gogh, Vincent 115
Variant of the Krumlov Madonna 93
Vegetarians 197
Veletržní Palác *see* Trades Fair Palace
Velká Kunratická 52
Velkopřevorské náměstí 131
Veltrusy Château 168
Velvet Revolution (1989) 17, 34, 35
celebration of 52
Civic Forum 144
Letná Park 161
Monument to the Victims of Communism 145
Wenceslas Square rally 146
Veronese, Paolo 98
Villa Amerika 154
Vinohrady Theatre 161
Virgin (Klimt) 164
Visas 234
Vítkov Hill 160
Vitus, St 25, 136, 139
Vladislav Hall (Royal Palace) 105
history 27, 28, 104
Prague's Best 48
Vladislav Hall (Sadeler) 104
Vladislav I, King 18
Vladislav II Jagiello, King 19, 22
Church of Our Lady beneath the Chain 134
Dalibor Tower 110
Powder Gate 64
Prague Castle 95
Royal Palace 27, 104
Strahov Monastery 44
Vlašská ulice 130
Vltava River 38, 51–2, 54–7
Vltava Statue 56
Vojan Park 135
Prague's Best 49
Street-by-Street map 133
Vojanovy sady 135
Volflin of Kamen 73
Votive panel of Archbishop Jan Očko of Vlašim 92
Vouet, Simon 115
Vratislav, Count of Mitrovice 65
Vratislav I, Prince 22, 44, 98, 99
Vratislav II, Prince 18, 23, 180, 181
Vries, Adriaen de 98, 109, 111
statue of Eros 126
tomb of 127
Vrtba Garden 49, **130**
Vrtbovská zahrada 130
Vyletěl, Josef 169
Vyšehrad 160
history 20, 30
Špička Gate 140
Walk 180–81
Vyšehrad Cemetery 181
Vyšehrad Codex 22, 23
Vyšehrad Museum 180
Vyšehrad Park 51, 181
Vysoká synagóga 85
Výstaviště 162, 176–7
Výtoň 41
Výtoň Excise House 57

W

Wagner, Antonín 57, 157
Wagner, Richard 169

Walks 172–9, 240
Petřín Park 176–7
Royal Enclosure 178–9
Royal Route 174–5
Vyšehrad 180–81
Wallenstein, Count Albrecht von 30, 46, 125, 126, 141
Wallenstein Garden 46, 49
Wallenstein Palace 5, 125 **126**
Prague's Best 46, 49
Warsaw Pact 35
Weather in Prague 50–53
Weber, Carl Maria von 169
Weiss, František 77
Wenceslas I, King 18, 65, 167
Wenceslas II, King 18, 127, 163
Wenceslas III, King 18
Wenceslas IV, King 18, 25, 27, 137
statue of 139
Zbraslav Monastery 163
Wenceslas, St 17, 18
Monument 145, 146
murder 20–21, 101, 102
paintings of 68
St Vitus's Cathedral 100
shrine 24
statues of 136, 138
Wenceslas (cont.)
Štorch House decorations 62
tomb of 101
Wenceslas Square 146
Street-by-Street map 144–5
Street Finder maps 3–6
Westphalia, Treaty of (1648) 30
Wheelchair access *see* Disabled travellers
White Mountain, Battle of the (1620) 65, 72, 75, 91, 103
history 29, 30–31
site of 163
White Swan 130
Wiehl, Antonín 144
Wiehl House,
Street-by-Street map 144
Wilsonova Station 238
Wine 200, 201
duty-free allowances 234
Wirch, Johann Georg 152
Wirch, Johann Joseph 111
Wittmann Tours 227
Wohlmut, Bonifaz 71, 104, 111
Women, safety 228
World War I 33
World War II 17, 34
Wycliffe, John 75

Z

Záboj and Slavoj (Myslbek) 149
Zahrada Na valech 110
Zápotocký, Antonín 19
Zbraslav Monastery 40, **163**
Zbraslavský klášter 163
Želivský, Jan 146, 155
Zemach, Bezalel 86
Zemach, Mordechai 86
Zeman, Karel 34
Ženíšek, František 147
Golden Age of Czech Art 156
Židovská radnice 85
Zítek, Josef 84, 156, 169
Žižka, Jan 26, 27
statue of 160
Žižkov 52, 160–61
Zlatá ulička 99
Zoo 162
Zoologická zahrada 162
Zrcadlová kaple 79
Zrcadlové bludiště 140
Zrzavý, Jan 40
Cleopatra 164

Acknowledgments

Dorling Kindersley wishes to thank the following people who contributed to the preparation of this book.

Main Contributor

Vladimír Soukup was born in Prague in 1949. He worked for the daily newpaper, *Evening Prague,* for 20 years, eventually becoming Deputy Chief Editor. He has written a wide range of popular guides to Prague.

Additional Contributors

Ben Sullivan, Lynn Reich.

Editorial and Design

MANAGING EDITOR Carolyn Ryden; MANAGING ART EDITOR Steve Knowlden; SENIOR EDITOR Georgina Matthews; SENIOR ART EDITOR Vanessa Courtier; EDITORIAL DIRECTOR David Lamb; ART DIRECTOR Anne-Marie Bulat; PRODUCTION CONTROLLER Hilary Stephens; PICTURE RESEARCH Ellen Root; DTP DESIGNER Salim Qurashi; CONSULTANT Helena Svojsikova; MAPS Caroline Bowie, Simon Farbrother, James Mills-Hicks, David Pugh (DKCartography).

Russell Davies, Stephanie Driver, Fay Franklin, Alistair Gunn, Elaine Harries, Charlie Hawkings, Jan Kaplan, Dr Tomáš Kleisner, Susannah Marriott, Sam Merrell, Robert Purnell, Marian Sucha, Daphne Trotter, Christopher Vinz.

Additional Photography

DK Studio/Steve Gorton, Ian O'Leary, Otto Palan, M Soskova, Clive Streeter, Alan Williams, Peter Wilson.

t = top; tl = top left; tc = top centre; tr = top right; cla = centre left above; ca = centre above; cra = centre right above; cl = centre left; c = centre; cr = centre right; clb = centre left below; cb = centre below; crb = centre right below; bl = bottom left; b = bottom; bc = bottom centre; br = bottom right; d = detail.

Works of art on the pages detailed have been reproduced with the permission of the following copyright holders:
Aristide Maillol *Pomona* 1910 © ADAG, Paris, and DACS, London, 1998: 164cr. Gustav Makarius Tauc (An der Aulenkaut 31, Wiesbaden, Germany) under commission of the Minorite Order in Rome: 35br.

The publishers are grateful to the following individuals, companies and picture libraries for permission to reproduce photographs or to photograph at their establishments:
ALAMY IMAGES: Chris Fredriksson 199c; Robert Harding Picture Library 10bl; ARCHEOLOGICKÝ ÚSTAV ČESKÉ AKADEMIE VĚD: 20t; ARCHIV FÜR KUNST UND GESCHICHTE, BERLIN: 17b, 18tl (d), 18tr, 18bc(d), 18br(d), 19tl(d), 19tc(d), 19tr(d), 19c(d), 19bc(d), 20clr, 20bl, 23cb(d), 29cla(d), 32t(d), 32bl, 34ca(d), 35ca(d), 35bl, 43tl, 50b(d), 105cr, 118t, Erich Lessing 28ca(d), 31bl(d), 88c, 89cb; ARCHÍV HLAVNIHO MESTA. PRAHY (CLAM-GALLASÚV PALÁC): 23cl, 24bl, 28bl, 28br, 30b, 33clb, 33bc, 72t, 136br, 137br(d), 138ca, 168c. BILDARCHIV PREUSSISCHER KULTURBESITZ: 4t(d), 19bl(d), 29br, 34bc, 68tr, 104bl(d); BRIDGEMAN ART LIBRARY, London: Prado, Madrid 29t; Rosegarten Museum, Constance 26ca. ČESKÁ TISKOVÁ KANCELÁR: 19br, 35cbr, 203cr; ČSA: 244t; JEAN-LOUP CHARMET: 18bl(d), 21c, 31br, 33t, 33bl, 33br(d), 34tr(d), 34bl, 62c, 69tc; ZDENEK CHRAPPEK: 50c; CORBIS: Gail Mooney 192; JOE CORNISH: 58–9, 60, 148br; CZECH NATIONAL BANK: 239. MARY EVANS PICTURE LIBRARY: 9, 59, 138cb, 185, 233. GRAFOPRINT NEUBERT: 31clb, 38clb, 116c. ROBERT HARDING PICTURE LIBRARY: Michael Jenner 128tl; Christopher Rennie 24ca, 103tr; Peter Scholey 30t, 129tl; HIDDEN PLACES RESIDENCES & BOUTIQUE HOTELS: 187bl; HUTCHISON LIBRARY: Libuše Taylor 51b, 52t, 175tl, 205c. THE IMAGE BANK: Andrea Pistolesi 14b; Courtesy of ISIC, UK: 242c. KANCELÁŘ PREZIDENTA REPUBLIKY: 20–1, 21tr, 21bl, 21br, 22c; KAPLAN PRODUCTIONS: 117t; OLDRICH KARASEK: 11tr 56cb, 62tr, 101crb, 134t, 176t, 205c, 227t, 241cl, 249bc; KARLŠTEJN: 25tl; Vladimír Hyhlík 24–5, Oldrich Karasek 135b; KAREL KESTNER: 35cbl; KLEMENTINUM: 23tl; Prokop Paul 22t; THE KOBAL COLLECTION: 35tl; DALIBOR KUSÁK: 164bl, 166–7 all, 16–9 all. IVAN MALÝ: 226t, 226c; MUZEUM HLAVNÍHO MĚSTA PRAHY 32–3; MUZEUM POŠTOVNÍ ZNÁMKY: 149cl. NÁRODNÍ FILMOVÝ ARCHIV: 34br; NÁRODNÍ GALERIE V PRAZE: 24br, 40b; Grafická sbírka 26t, 27bl, 31t, 67b, 69c, 100t, 102b, 121t, 125cb, 129br, 138b, 157cb, 175b, 182b; Klášter sv. Anežky 39tr, 83t, 92–3 all, 133b; Klášter sv. Jiří 16, 37br, 38t, 39tr, 97clb, 106–7 all, 108–9 all, Šternberský palác 38ca, 112–3 all, 114–5 all, Veletržni Palac 164–5 all; Zbraslav 40b; NÁRODNÍ MUZEUM, PRAHA: 147b; NÁRODNÍ MUZEUM V PRAZE: Vlasta Dvořáková 20clb, 26–7, 26bl, 26bc, 26br, 27t, 27cl, 27cr, 27br, 29bl, 39cb, 75b, 72b, Jarmila Kutová 20c, 22bl, Dagmar Landová 28bc, 126c, Muzeum Antonína Dvořáka 39b, Muzeum Bedřicha Smetany 32ca, Prokop Paul 75b, Tyršovo Muzeum; 34cb, 149bl; NÁRODNÍ TECHNICKÉ MUZEUM: Gabriel Urbánek 41t. OBRAZÁRNA PRAŽSKEHO HRADU: 98b; ÖSTERREICHISCHE NATIONALBIBLIOTHEK, WIEN: 25clb, 26cb. PHOTOGRAPHERS DIRECT: Chris Barton 10cra, Eddie Gerald 11bl; PIVOVARSKÉ MUZEUM: 204tr, 204c; BOHUMÍR PROKŮPEK: 25bl, 30t, 120c, 121c, 121bl, 163b. REX FEATURES LTD: Alfred 35tr, Richard Gardener 248t. SCIENCE PHOTO LIBRARY: Geospace 11, 38crb; SOTHEBY'S/ THAMES AND HUDSON: 104c; STÁTNÍ ÚSTREDNI ARCHIV: 23b; STÁTNÍ ÚSTAV PAMÁTKOVÉ PÉČE: 23tc; STÁTNÍ ŽIDOVSKÉ MUZEUM: 39ca, 85t, 85c, 90t; LUBOMÍR STIBUREK, www.czfoto.cz: 55b, 145ca, 163t, 176c, 250c, 251cl, 251cba, 251bca, 252cr; MARIAN SUCHA: front endpaper Lbl, 55t, 56cb, 94, 127b, 174t, 205bl, 205t, 241b, 245tr, 245c; SVATOVÍTSKÝ POKLAD, PRAŽSKÝ HRAD: 14t, 21tl, 24t, 24cb, 28t, 40tr. MARTIN TOUR, PRAHA: 226tr; UMĚLECKOPRŮMYSLOVÉ MUZEUM V PRAZE: 39tl, 40tl, 149c, 149br, Gabriel Urbánek 28clb, 41b; UNIVERZITA KARLOVA: 25tr. U PINKASU RESTAURANT: 198cla; PETER WILSON: 4b, 201t, 232–3, 246. ZEFA: 33cra. Front endpaper: all special or additional photography except (centre) JOE CORNISH. JACKET: Front - CORBIS: Dallas and John Heaton main image; DK IMAGES: Jiri Kopriva bl. Back – JOE CORNISH: bl, tl; DK IMAGES: Jiri Dolezal cla; Jiri Kopriva clb. Spine – CORBIS: Dallas and John Heaton t; DK IMAGES: Peter Wilson b. All other images © Dorling Kindersley. For further information, see: www.dkimages.com

SPECIAL EDITIONS OF DK TRAVEL GUIDES

DK Travel Guides can be purchased in bulk quantities at discounted prices for use in promotions or as premiums. We are also able to offer special editions and personalized jackets, corporate imprints, and excerpts from all of our books, tailored specifically to meet your own needs.

To find out more, please contact:

(in the United States) **SpecialSales@dk.com**

(in the UK) **Sarah.Burgess@dk.com**

(in Canada) DK Special Sales at **general@tourmaline.ca**

(in Australia) **business.development@pearson.com.au**

Phrase Book

In Emergency

Help!	**Pomoc!**	***po**-mots*
Stop!	**Zastavte!**	***za**-stav-te*
Call a doctor!	**Zavolejte doktora!**	***za**-vo-ley-te **dok**-to-ra!*
Call an ambulance!	**Zavolejte sanitku!**	***za**-vo-ley-te **sa**-nit-ku!*
Call the police!	**Zavolejte policii!**	***za**-vo-ley-te **poli**-tsi-yi!*
Call the fire brigade!	**Zavolejte hasiče**	***za**-vol-ey-te **ha**-si-che*
Where is the telephone?	**Kde je telefón?**	***gde** ye **tele**-fóhn?*
the nearest hospital?	**nejbližší nemocnice?**	***ney**-blish-ee **ne**-mots-nyitse?*

Communication Essentials

Yes/No	**Ano/Ne**	***ano**/ne*
Please	**Prosím**	***pro**-seem*
Thank you	**Děkuji vám**	***dye**-ku-ji **vahm***
Excuse me	**Prosím vás**	***pro**-seem **vahs***
Hello	**Dobrý den**	***do**-bree **den***
Goodbye	**Na shledanou**	***na** s-hle-da-no*
Good evening	**Dobrý večer**	***dob**-ree **vech**-er*
morning	**ráno**	***rah**-no*
afternoon	**odpoledne**	***od**-po-led-ne*
evening	**večer**	***ve**-cher*
yesterday	**včera**	***vche**-ra*
today	**dnes**	***dnes***
tomorrow	**zítra**	***zeet**-ra*
here	**tady**	***ta**-di*
there	**tam**	***tam***
What?	**Co?**	***tso?***
When?	**Kdy?**	***gdi?***
Why?	**Proč?**	***proch?***
Where?	**Kde?**	***gde?***

Useful Phrases

How are you?	**Jak se máte?**	***yak**-se **mah**-te?*
Very well, thank you.	**Velmi dobře děkuji.**	***vel**-mi **dob**-rzhe **dye** kuyi*
Pleased to meet you.	**Těší mě.**	***tyesh**-ee mye*
See you soon.	**Uvidíme se brzy.**	***u**-vi-dyee-me-se-**br**-zi*
That's fine.	**To je v pořádku.**	***to** ye **vpo**-rzhahdku*
Where is/are...?	**Kde je/jsou ...?**	***gde** ye/yso ...?*
How long does it take to get to..?	**Jak dlouho to trvá se dostat do..?**	***yak dlo** ho to tr-va se **do**-stat do...?*
How do I get to...?	**Jak se dostanu k ..?**	***yak** se **do**-sta-nu k ...?*
Do you speak English?	**Mluvíte anglicky?**	***mlu**-vee-te **an**-glits-ki?*
I don't understand.	**Nerozumím.**	***ne**-ro-zu-meem*
Could you speak more slowly?	**Mohl(a)* byste mluvit trochu pomaleji?**	***mohl**- (a) **bis**-te **mlu**-vit **tro**-khu **po**-maley?*
Pardon?	**Prosím?**	***pro**-seem?*
I'm lost.	**Ztratil(a)* jsem se.**	***stra**-tyil (a) ysem se.*

Useful Words

big	**velký**	***vel**-kee*
small	**malý**	***mal**-ee*
hot	**horký**	***hor**-kee*
cold	**studený**	***stu**-den-ee*
good	**dobrý**	***dob**-ree*
bad	**špatný**	***shpat**-nee*
well	**dobře**	***dob**-rzhe*
open	**otevřeno**	***ot**-ev-rzhe-no*
closed	**zavřeno**	***zav**-rzhe-no*
left	**do leva**	***do** le-va*
right	**do prava**	***do** pra-va*
straight on	**rovně**	*rov-nye*
near	**blízko**	***blee**-sko*
far	**daleko**	***da**-le-ko*
up	**nahoru**	***na**-ho-ru*
down	**dolů**	***do**-loo*
early	**brzy**	***br**-zi*
late	**pozdě**	***poz**-dye*
entrance	**vchod**	***vkhod***
exit	**východ**	***vee**-khod*
toilets	**toalety**	***toa**-leti*
free, unoccupied	**volný**	***vol**-nee*
free, no charge	**zdarma**	***zdar**-ma*

Making a Telephone Call

I'd like to place a call.	**Chtěl(a)* bych volat**	***khtyel**(a) bikh **vo**-lat*
I'd like to make a reverse-charge call.	**Chtěl(a)* bych volat na účet volaného.**	***khtyel**(a) bikh **volat** na **oo**-chet **volan**-eh-ho*
I'll try again later.	**Zkusím to později.**	***skus**-eem to **poz**-dyey*
Can I leave a message?	**Mohu nechat zprávu?**	***mo**-hu ne-khat **sprah**-vu?*
Hold on.	**Počkejte.**	***poch**-key-te*
Could you speak up a little, please?	**Mohl(a)* byste mluvit hlasitěji?**	***mo**-hl (a) bis-te **mluvit hla**-si-tyey?*
local call	**místní hovor**	***meest**-nyee **hov**-or*

Sightseeing

art gallery	**galerie**	***ga**-ler-riye*
bus stop	**autobusová zastávka**	***au**-to-bus-o-vah za-stab-vka*
church	**kostel**	***kos**-tel*
garden	**zahrada**	***za** bra-da*
library	**knihovna**	***knyi**-hov-na*
museum	**muzeum**	***muz**-e-um*
railway station	**nádraží**	*nab-dra-zhee*
tourist information	**turistické informace**	***toor**ísti-tske **in**-for-ma-tse*
closed for the public holiday	**státní svátek**	***staht**-nyee **svah**-tek*

Shopping

How much does this cost?	**Co to stojí?**	***tso** to **sto**-yee?*
I would like ...	**Chtěl(a)* bych ...**	***khtyel**(a) bikh...*
Do you have ...?	**Máte ...?**	***maa**-te ...?*
I'm just looking.	**Jenom se dívám.**	***ye**-nom se **dyee**-vahm*
Do you take credit cards?	**Berete kreditní karty?**	***be**-re-te **kred**-it nyee **karti?***
What time do you open/close?	**V kolik otevíráte/zavíráte?**	***v ko**-lik **o**-te-vee-rah-te/za vee rah-te?*
this one	**tento**	***ten**-to*
that one	**tamten**	***tam**-ten*
expensive	**drahý**	***dra**-hee*
cheap	**levný**	***lev**-nee*
size	**velikost**	***vel**-ik-ost*
white	**bílý**	***bee**-lee*
black	**černý**	***cher**-nee*
red	**červený**	***cher**-ven-ee*
yellow	**žlutý**	***zhlu**-tee*
green	**zelený**	***zel**-en-ee*
blue	**modrý**	***mod**-ree*
brown	**hnědý**	***hnyed**-ee*

Types of Shop

antique shop	**starožitnictví**	***sta**-ro zhit--nyits-twee*
bank	**banka**	***bank**a*
bakery	**pekárna**	***pe**-kahr-na*
bookstore	**knihkupectví**	***knib**-kupets-twee*
butcher	**řeznictví**	***rzhez**-nyits-twee*
camera shop	**obchod s fotoaparáty**	***op**-khot **sfoto**-aparahti*
chemist (prescriptions etc)	**lékárna**	***leh**-kah-rna*
chemist (cosmetics, toiletries etc)	**drogerie**	***drog**-erye*
delicatessen	**lahůdky**	***la**-hoo-dki*
department store	**obchodní dům**	***op**-khod-nyee doom*
grocery	**potraviny**	***pot**-ra-vini*
glass	**sklo**	***sklo***
hairdresser (ladies)	**kadeřnictví**	***ka**-derzh-nyits-twee*
(mens)	**holič**	***ho**-lich*
market	**trh**	*trkh*
newsstand	**novinový stánek**	***no**-vi-novee **stab**-nek*
post office	**pošta**	***posh**-ta*
supermarket	**samoobsluha**	***sa**-mo-ob-slu-ha*
tobacconist	**tabák**	***ta**-bahk*
travel agency	**cestovní kancelář**	***tses**-tov-nyi **kantse**-laarzh*

**Alternatives for a female speaker are shown in brackets.*

Staying in a Hotel

Do you have a vacant room?	**Máte volný pokoj?**	***mah**-te vol-nee **po**-koy?*
double room	**dvoulůžkový pokoj**	***dvo**-loozh-kovee **po**-koy*
with double bed	**s dvojitou postelí**	***sdvoy**-to **pos**-telee*
twin room	**pokoj s dvěma postelemi**	***po**-koy **sdvye**-ma **pos**-tel-emi*
room with a bath	**pokoj s koupelnou**	***po**-koy s **ko**-pel-no*
porter	**vrátný**	***vraht**-nee*
hall porter	**nosič**	***nos**-ich*
key	**klíč**	***kleech***
I have a reservation.	**Mám reservaci.**	***mahm rez**-ervatsi*

Eating Out

Have you got a table for ...?	**Máte stůl pro ...?**	***mah**-te **stool** pro ...?*
I'd like to reserve a table.	**Chtěl(a)* bych rezervovat stůl.**	***kbtyel(a)** bikh **rez**-er-vov-at stool*
breakfast	**snídaně**	***snyee**-danye*
lunch	**oběd**	***ob**-yed*
dinner	**večeře**	***vech** e-rzhe*
The bill, please.	**Prosím, účet.**	***pro**-seem **oo**-chet*
I am a vegetarian.	**Jsem vegetarián(ka)*.**	***ysem vegbe**-tariabn(ka)*
waitress!	**slečno**	***slech**-no*
waiter!	**pane vrchní!**	*pane **vrkh**-nyee!*
fixed price menu	**standardní menu**	***stan**-dard-nyee **men**-u*
dish of the day	**nabídka dne**	***nab**-eed-ka dne*
starter	**předkrm**	***przhed**-krm*
main course	**hlavní jídlo**	***hlav**-nyee **yeed**-lo*
vegetables	**zelenina**	***zel**-en-yin-a*
dessert	**zákusek**	***zab**-kusek*
cover charge	**poplatek**	***pop**-la-tek*
wine list	**nápojový lístek**	***nab**-po-yo-vee **lee**-stek*
rare (steak)	**krvavý**	*kr-va-vee*
medium	**středně udělaný**	***strzbed**-nye **ud**-yel-an-ee*
well done	**dobře udělaný**	***dobrzbe**-**ud**-yel-an-ee*
glass	**sklenice**	***sklen**-yitse*
bottle	**láhev**	***lab**-bev*
knife	**nůž**	***noozb***
fork	**vidlička**	***vid**-lich-ka*
spoon	**lžíce**	***lzbee**-tse*

Menu Decoder

biftek	***bif**-tek*	steak
bílé víno	***bee**-leh vee-no*	white wine
bramborové knedlíky	***bram**-bo-ro-veh **kne**-dleeki*	potato dumplings
brambory	***bram**-bo-ri*	potatoes
chléb	***kblebb***	bread
cibule	***tsi**-bu-le*	onion
citrónový džus	***tsi**-tron-o-vee dzbuus*	lemon juice
cukr	***tsukr***	sugar
čaj	***chay***	tea
čerstvé ovoce	***cher**-stveh-o-vo-ce*	fresh fruit
červené víno	***cher**-ven-eh vee-no*	red wine
česnek	***ches**-nek*	garlic
dort	***dort***	cake
fazole	***fa**-zo-le*	beans
grilované	***gril**-ov-a-neh*	grilled
houby	***bo**-bi*	mushrooms
houska	***bous**-ka*	roll
houskové knedlíky	***bo**-sko-veh **kne**-dleeki*	bread dumplings
hovězí	***bov**-ye-zee*	beef
hranolky	***bran**-ol-ki*	chips
husa	***bu**-sa*	goose
jablko	***ya**-bl-ko*	apple
jahody	***ya**-bo-di*	strawberries
jehněčí	***ye**-bnye-chee*	lamb
kachna	***kakb**-na*	duck
kapr	***ka**-pr*	carp
káva	***kab**-va*	coffee
krevety	***krev**-et-i*	prawns
kuře	***ku**-rzhe*	chicken
kyselé zelí	***kis**-el-eh **zel**-ee*	sauerkraut
maso	***ma**-so*	meat
máslo	***mab**-slo*	butter
minerálka šumivá/nešumivá	***min**-er-abl-ka **shum**-i-vab/ **ne**-shum i-vab*	mineral water fizzy/still
mléko	***mleb**-ko*	milk
mořská jídla	***morzb**-skab-**yeed**-la-*	seafood
ocet	***ots**-et*	vinegar
okurka	***o**-ku-rka*	cucumber
olej	***oley***	oil
párek	***paa**-rek*	sausage/frankfurter
pečené	***petsb**-en-eb*	baked
pečené	***pech**-en-eb*	roast
pepř	***peprzb***	pepper
polévka	***pol**-eb-vka*	soup
pomeranč	***po**-me-ranch*	orange
pomerančový džus	***po**-me-ran-ch--o-vee dzbuus*	orange juice
pivo	***pi**-vo*	beer
rajské	***rayskeb***	tomato
ryba	***rib**-a*	fish
rýže	***ree**-zhe*	rice
salát	***sal**-at*	salad
sůl	***sool***	salt
sýr	***seer***	cheese
šunka vařená/uzená	***shun**-ka **varzb**-enab **u**-zenab*	ham cooked smoked
telecí	***te**-le-tsee*	veal
tuna	***tu**-na*	tuna
vajíčko	***va**-yee-chko*	egg
vařené	***varzb**-en-eb*	boiled
vepřové	***vep**-rzbo-veb*	pork
voda	***vo**-da*	water
vývar	***vee**-var*	broth
zelí	***zel**-ee*	cabbage
zelenina	***zel**-enyina*	vegetables
zmrzlina	***zmrz**-lin-a*	ice cream

Numbers

1	**jedna**	***yed**-na*
2	**dvě**	***dvye***
3	**tři**	***trzbi***
4	**čtyři**	***cbti**-rzbi*
5	**pět**	***pyet***
6	**šest**	***sbest***
7	**sedm**	***sedm***
8	**osm**	***osm***
9	**devět**	***dev**-yet*
10	**deset**	***des**-et*
11	**jedenáct**	***ye**-de-nabtst*
12	**dvanáct**	***dva**-nabtst*
13	**třináct**	***trzbi**-nabtst*
14	**čtrnáct**	***cbtr**-nabtst*
15	**patnáct**	***pat**-nabtst*
16	**šestnáct**	***sbest**-nabtst*
17	**sedmnáct**	***sedm**-nabtst*
18	**osmnáct**	***osm**-nabtst*
19	**devatenáct**	***de**-va-te-nabtst*
20	**dvacet**	***dva**-tset*
21	**dvacet jedna**	***dva**-tset yed-na*
22	**dvacet dva**	***dva**-tset dva*
23	**dvacet tři**	***dva**-tset-trzbi*
24	**dvacet čtyři**	***dva**-tset cbti-rzbi*
25	**dvacet pět**	***dva**-tset pyet*
30	**třicet**	***trzbi**-tset*
40	**čtyřicet**	***cbti**-rzbi-tset*
50	**padesát**	***pa**-de-sabt*
60	**šedesát**	***sbe**-de-sabt*
70	**sedmdesát**	***sedm**-de-sabt*
80	**osmdesát**	***osm**-de-sabt*
90	**devadesát**	***de**-va-de-sabt*
100	**sto**	***sto***
1,000	**tisíc**	***tyi**-seets*
2,000	**dva tisíce**	***dva** tyi-see-tse*
5,000	**pět tisíc**	***pyet** tyi-seets*
1,000,000	**milión**	***mi**-li-obn*

Time

one minute	**jedna minuta**	***yed**-na **min**-uta*
one hour	**jedna hodina**	***yed**-na **bod**-yin-a*
half an hour	**půl hodiny**	***pool bod**-yin-i*
day	**den**	***den***
week	**týden**	***tee**-den*
Monday	**pondělí**	***pon**-dye-lee*
Tuesday	**úterý**	***oo**-ter-ee*
Wednesday	**středa**	***strzbe**-da*
Thursday	**čtvrtek**	***cbtvr**-tek*
Friday	**pátek**	***pab**-tek*
Saturday	**sobota**	***so**-bo-ta*
Sunday	**neděle**	***ned**-yel-e*

**Alternatives for a female speaker are shown in brackets.*

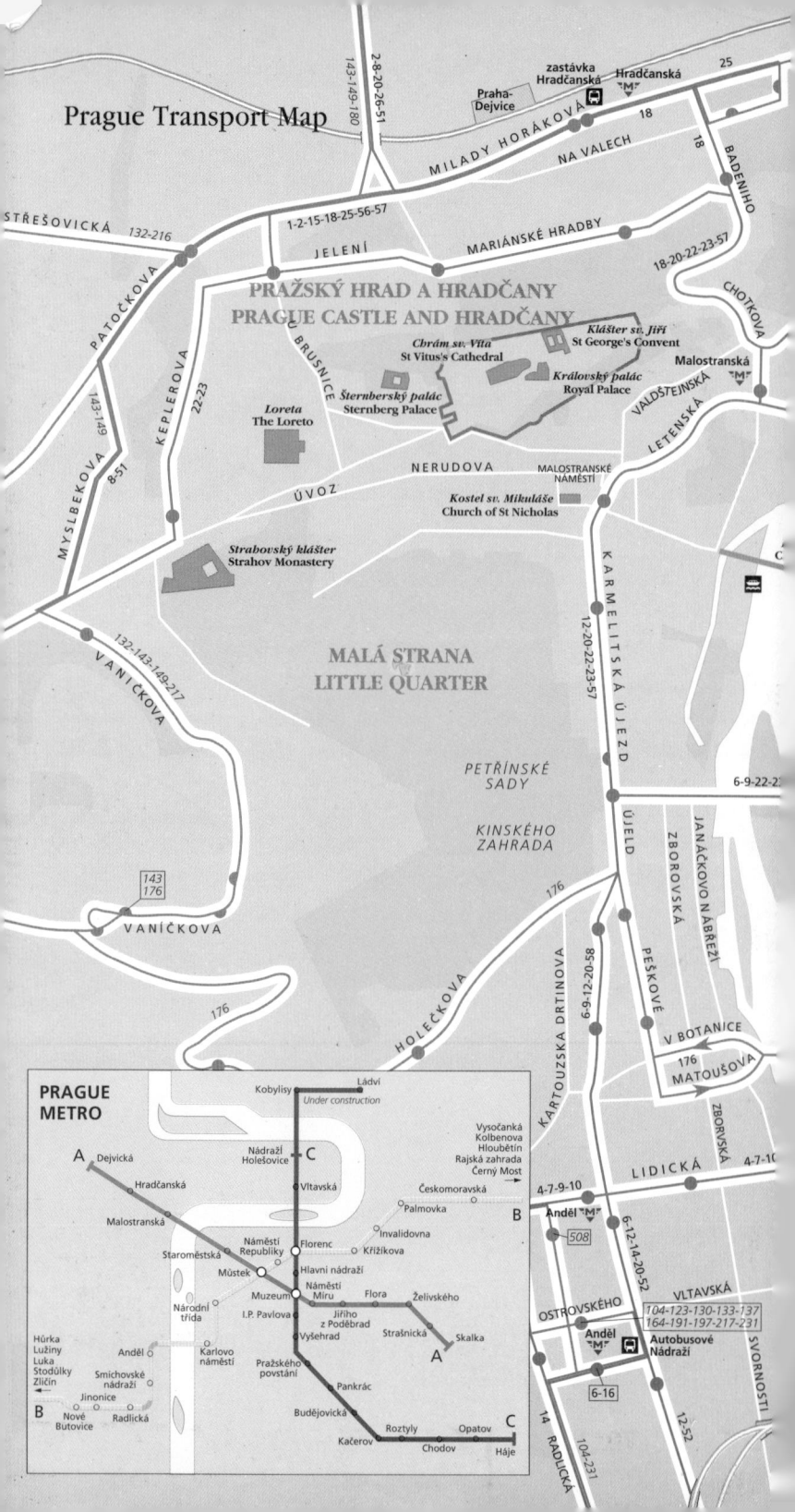
Prague Transport Map
PRAŽSKÝ HRAD A HRADČANY
PRAGUE CASTLE AND HRADČANY
Chrám sv. Víta
St Vitus's Cathedral
Klášter sv. Jiří
St George's Convent
Královský palác
Royal Palace
Šternberský palác
Sternberg Palace
Loreta
The Loreto
Strahovský klášter
Strahov Monastery
Kostel sv. Mikuláše
Church of St Nicholas
MALÁ STRANA
LITTLE QUARTER
PETŘÍNSKÉ SADY
KINSKÉHO ZAHRADA
zastávka Hradčanská
Hradčanská
Praha-Dejvice
MILADY HORÁKOVÁ
NA VÁLECH
BADENIHO
STŘEŠOVICKÁ
PATOČKOVA
JELENÍ
MARIÁNSKÉ HRADBY
CHOTKOVA
KEPLEROVA
U BRUSNICE
VALDŠTEJNSKÁ
LETENSKÁ
Malostranská
NERUDOVA
MALOSTRANSKÉ NÁMĚSTÍ
ÚVOZ
MYSLBEKOVA
VANÍČKOVA
KARMELITSKÁ ÚJEZD
ÚJEZD
ZBOROVSKÁ
JANÁČKOVO NÁBŘEŽÍ
PEŠKOVÉ
V BOTANICE
MATOUŠOVA
HOLEČKOVA
KARTOUZSKÁ DRTINOVA
LIDICKÁ
Anděl
OSTROVSKÉHO
VLTAVSKÁ
Autobusové Nádraží
SVORNOSTI
RADLICKÁ
PRAGUE METRO
Kobylisy
Ládví
Under construction
Dejvická
Hradčanská
Malostranská
Staroměstská
Můstek
Náměstí Republiky
Florenc
Hlavní nádraží
Náměstí Míru
Muzeum
Flora
Želivského
Jiřího z Poděbrad
Výšehrad
Strašnická
Skalka
Národní třída
I.P. Pavlova
Karlovo náměstí
Pražského povstání
Pankrác
Budějovická
Roztyly
Opatov
Kačerov
Chodov
Háje
Nádraží Holešovice
Vltavská
Invalidovna
Křižíkova
Palmovka
Českomoravská
Vysočanká
Kolbenova
Hloubětín
Rajská zahrada
Černý Most
Hůrka
Lužiny
Luka
Stodůlky
Zličín
Anděl
Smíchovské nádraží
Jinonice
Nové Butovice
Radlická